The Arcadian Mystique

The Arcadian Mystique

The Best of
Dagobert's Revenge Magazine

Edited by Tracy R. Twyman

Dragon Key Press
Portland, Oregon - USA

Copyright 2005
Dragon Key Press LLC
All Rights Reserved

No part of this publication may be reproduced in any form or by any means, electronic or mechanical, including photocopying, recording, or by any information storage or retrieval system, without permission in writing from the publisher.

ISBN: 0-9761704-2-6

Layout and Design
Brian Albert

Cover Design by Brian Albert
Painting *"The Shepherds of Arcadia"* by Nicholas Poussin

Acknowledgements

In my work for *Dagobert's Revenge* I was assisted by a number of people, foremost among them Brian Albert. Contributions to the *Dagobert's Revenge* magazine and website were made by people like Boyd Rice (a number of whose contributions are reproduced in this volume), Michael Moynihan (author of *Lords of Chaos*, Adam Gorightly (author of *The Prankster and the Conspiracy*), Vadge Moore (of former Dwarves fame), Danny Carey (of the band Tool) and Blair Mackensie Blake, Templar expert Stephen Dafoe, theoretical physicist Michio Kaku, William H. Kennedy (author of *Lucifer's Lodge: Satanic Ritual Abuse in the Catholic Church*), David Livingstone (author of *The Dying God: The Hidden History of Western Civilization*), Jason Kesselring of the band Skyeklad, Tyler Ferguson, Dan Winter, Ken Ichigawa, Joseph A. Nicholson, Zostrianos Tammuz, S. Michael Adkins, Rayvn Navarro, Todd C. Ruzicka, Micki Pellerano, Jack Cary, John Armstrong, Nicholas Reiter, Phillip Madden, Aaron Garland, Keith Dennis, Anthony D'Ascoli, Amy-Marie Keller, John Lucian (who contributed some great artwork, including a comic strip called *Young Dagobert*), John Gonzalez (another great artist), James Bergman of Circus of the Scars, who edited our music section and conducted some of our best interviews with bands, and Nicholas de Vere (author of *The Dragon Legacy: The Secret History of an Ancient Bloodline*) . For these contributions we are very grateful. We are further thankful for the support extended by people like Stephen Maddux, Ben Ireland, Lisa Fong, Timothy Renner, Jason Kesselring, Dave Onnen, and many others. It goes without saying that we couldn't have done this without our fans, family and friends, whom we treasure. Nor could we have without the stores and distributors who dealt fairly with us and worked hard to promote the magazine, including Seven Stars Books in Cambridge, Massachusetts, See Hear Magazines in New York, Quimby's in Chicago, Reading Frenzy in Portland, Oregon, and Tower Records, especially Clint Johns and Mike Brown. We should also thank Martin Lunn (author of *The Da Vinci Code Decoded*) and Richard Metzger of the Disinformation Company.

The articles in this book reflect the viewpoint of each author at the time of writing, and do not necessarily reflect the viewpoint of the publisher, nor do they necessarily reflect each author's current viewpoint.

- Tracy R. Twyman, Editor

Table of Contents

Introduction: Underground Streams, by Richard Metzger	1
Who is This Man We Call Dagobert?, by Tracy Twyman	2
The Prieure de Sion: A Star-Studded Cast of Grand Masters, by Tracy Twyman	3
Nicholas Poussin and the Incontrovertible Proof, by Tracy Twyman	7
What the Hell is the Holy Grail?, by Tracy Twyman	11
Baphomet: The Severed Head that Wouldn't Die, by Tracy Twyman	14
Anthony Blunt and the Cambridge Spies, by Tracy Twyman	17
Rendezvous at Rennes-le-Chateau, by Tracy Twyman and Boyd Rice	21
The Merovingian Mythos: Its Symbolic Significance, and its Roots in the Ancient Kingdom of Atlantis, by Tracy Twyman	31
The Cross of Lorraine: Emblem of the Royal Secret, by Boyd Rice	39
Lucifer's Children: The Grail Bloodline and the Descendants of Cain, by Boyd Rice	41
The Real Tomb of God: The Grail, the Ark, the Emerald Tablet, and the Forgotten Father of Mankind, by Tracy Twyman	43
The Real Meaning of "Et in Arcadia Ego", by Tracy Twyman	54
The Celestial Sea and the Ark of Heaven, by Tracy Twyman	60
Hiram, King of Tyre, by Boyd Rice	73
Monarchy: The Primordial Form of Government, and its Roots in the "Lord of the Earth" Concept, by Tracy Twyman	76
Dead But Dreaming: The Great Old Ones of Lovecraftian Legend Reinterpreted as Atlantean Kings, by Tracy Twyman	84
Jean Cocteau: Man of the Twentieth Century, by Tracy Twyman	102
The Prophet: Jean Cocteau, by Boyd Rice	120
Sleeping Beauty and the Sacred Mountain: House of God, Gateway to Heaven, by Tracy Twyman	122
Omega and Genesis: Underground Cities, the Deluge, and the Holy Mountain Hypothesesis, by Boyd Rice	130

The Cutting of the Orm: The Golden Age Calendar and the New Cabala, by Tracy Twyman	143
The Tower of Babel: Vessel of God and Ark of His Preservation (and the Secret of the Original Language Which It Contained), by Tracy Twyman	159
The Occult Roots of Christianity, by Boyd Rice	163
The Divine Couple, by Boyd Rice	170
Giants on the Earth, by Boyd Rice	177
Chaldean Genesis: The Secret Legacy of the Architect-Priests, by Boyd Rice	183
The Daughter of God: The Real Story of Joan of Arc, by Boyd Rice	188
Vaincre: The United States of Europe and the Merovingian Master Plan, by Tracy Twyman	191
Call Me Ishmael: The Biblical Roots of the Persian Gulf Conflict, by Tracy Twyman	202
The Choice Vine: Mary Magdalene, the Sacred Whore, and the Benjamite Hypothesis, by Tracy Twyman	209
The Judas Goat: The "Substitution" Theory of the Crucifixion, by Tracy Twyman	238

Introduction:
Underground Streams

By Richard Metzger

It was in 1998 that I first became aware of *Dagobert's Revenge*. I asked Ted Gottfried, owner of the legendary underground "zine" store *See Hear* in New York's East Village if he'd gotten anything in lately that was "really weird", and he immediately pointed me in the direction of a sinister looking magazine called *Dagobert's Revenge* that he was enthusiastic about. A few weeks later I was there again and I told him how much I liked the zine he'd recommended to me. I inquired of its creator, Tracy Twyman.

"Oh, she's totally insane,' he said, shaking his head vigorously to indicate that she was really way out.

"But in a good way," he quickly added.

It was thus that I was introduced to the unusual erudition of Tracy Twyman.

Intrigued, I decided to invite her on to my *Infinity Factory* talk show. I was surprised that she was so young when she turned up, especially having noticed her intellectual command of the minutia of Aleister Crowley's work, something that I know a lot about myself. You can study this stuff for decades and not know half of what she knew. She wrote about these topics in a very original way, as well. She clearly knew what she was talking about, and at such a young age!

Dagobert's Revenge had the kind of editorial philosophy that I myself always try to adhere to: You have to like and be fascinated in every respect by what you write about, or your writing won't be worth reading. In the case of *Dagobert's Revenge,* this meant the editorial policy followed the whims of Twyman's occult interests wherever they took her. It was a fascinating and startling vision she had, a mélange of *Holy Blood, Holy Grail*, Thelema, ancient origins, monarchism, and Goth subculture. But all of the proceedings had the same quirky stamp on it that made *Dagobert's Revenge* what it was: one of the most singular zines out there.

Some of the original articles I read at that time are included in this volume. Reading over these essays and articles again, I remembered what Ted Gottfried had said: "Oh, she's totally insane, But in a good way."

In a very good way.

Richard Metzger, Los Angeles, Fall 2004

Who Is this Man We Call Dagobert?

By Tracy R. Twyman

In the year 469, the Roman Catholic Church made a pact with Clovis I, King of the Franks, bestowing upon him the title "New Constantine", in exchange for his conversion to the faith. Thus began the formation of Holy Roman Empire, with the promise that the title "New Constantine" would be passed down to his descendants from that moment on. In the year 800, that promise was broken.

Dagobert II was a French king from the sacred Merovingian bloodline, the last Merovingian to hold the title "New Constantine." The Merovingians were a dynasty of Frankish priest-kings who were believed by their subjects to have magical powers derived from their long hair. There were rumors of witchcraft, fortune telling and crystal-ball gazing being practiced among them. In fact, portraits of Merovingian kings customarily depict them holding one of these crystal balls in the left hand. Since the time of Clovis I, the Merovingians had presided over the Holy Roman Empire, but by the time Dagobert II was born, the power of the throne had already been weakened, with authority increasingly being usurped by court chancellors known as "Mayors of the Palace." On the death of his father, the 5-year-old Dagobert was kidnapped by then Palace Mayor Grimoald, who tried to put his own son on the throne. Human compassion saved young Dagobert from death, and he was exiled to Ireland, only to return years later and reclaim the throne in 679. But the problems of the Mayors of the Palace continued. Three years later, apparently displeased with Dagobert's lack of allegiance, the Roman Church entered into a conspiracy with Mayor Pepin the Fat. On December 23, while on a hunting trip, Dagobert was lanced through the eye by his own godson, supposedly on Pepin's orders. With Roman Catholic endorsement, Pepin passed political power onto his son, Charles Martel, thus starting the Carolingian dynasty that would later become so famous. After that, the Merovingian bloodline faded into obscurity. All subsequent Merovingian kings were essentially powerless, and they were officially thought to have died out with Dagobert's grandson, Childeric III. 49 years later, Charles Martel's grandson, Charlemagne was anointed Holy Roman Emperor. The Church had finally washed its hands of the Merovingian problem, or so they thought.

And what was the problem, exactly? Well, rumor has it that the Merovingian bloodline was descended from Jesus, or one of his brothers (and thus the Royal House of David), who fled Roman persecution at the time of the crucifixion and escaped to France, where they intermarried with Frankish royalty. This claim is made by certain members of modern European nobility, who trace their own ancestry back to Dagobert's son Sigisbert. According to this claim, the Merovingians knew the truth about Jesus and his actual significance as King of the Jews. They knew the Roman Church had stolen their birthright - Jerusalem, co-opted the idea of Jesus, and created a fictionalized version of the Messiah to further their own agenda - world domination, both secular and spiritual. The Merovingians knew that the fantasy of Christ as a virgin-born deity who suffered willingly for our sins and ascended to heaven was just that - an "opiate of the masses" used by the Roman Church as an excuse to set their priests up as the arbiters of God, and thus perpetuate their faltering empire. This might have been the whole reason for the pact with Clovis I, to effectively shut him and his family up. And with the death of Dagobert II, they thought they had eradicated this threat for good. They were sorely mistaken.

The Prieuré de Sion: A Star-Studded Cast of Grand Masters

By Tracy R. Twyman

The Candidate must renounce his personality in order to devote himself to a higher moral apostolate."
-Article 7, Prieuré Statutes

The Prieuré de Sion (Priory of Sion) was a secret society created in medieval France with the purpose of preserving the Merovingian bloodline and returning them to the throne of France. They were officially founded as the Order de Sion (Order of Sion) by Godfroi de Bouillon, in either 1090 or 1099. This was just prior to the First Crusade, which was also headed by de Bouillon. Their official headquarters was the Abbey of Notre Dame du Mont de Sion in Jerusalem. In March 1117 they had Baldwin I, King of Jerusalem (who, it is said, owed his throne to them due to their efforts on his behalf) negotiate the constitution of the Order of the Temple (a.k.a. the Knights Templar), as the military and administrative arm of the Order de Sion. The Templar order, which had already been around for more than a decade, was headed by Hughes de Payen, who was also a founding member of the Order de Sion. They are not mentioned again in history until 1152, when King Louis VII of France brought them 95 new members and gave them the Priory of Saint-Samson at Orléans.

In 1188 there was a rift between the Order of Sion and the Order of the Temple. The Templars' current Grand Master, Gerard de Ridefort, had recently been responsible for Europe losing the Holy Land to the Saracens, and had also committed some kind of unspecified "treason." So in that year, during a ceremony called "the Cutting of the Elm", the Order of Sion officially disavowed the Templars and cut themselves off from them. The Templars went on to become more closely allied with the House of Stuart, and the Scottish branch of the Grail bloodline. The Order of Sion selected a new Grand Master, Jean de Gisors, changed their name to "Prieuré de Sion", and adopted an odd nickname, "Ormus." This was written with the "M" written as the sign for Virgo (Q) and the other four letters inside of the symbol. "Ormus" is also the name of an Egyptian sage from Alexandria, who in A.D. 46 created an initiative order with the rose cross as its insignia. It is significant, then, that in that same year of 1188, the Priory of Sion also adopted the subtitle "Order de la Rose-Croix Veritas" ("Order of the True Rose-Cross"). They kept that bizarre nickname, "Ormus", until 1306, the year before the downfall of the Knights Templar in France. In that year, 1307, Sion's Grand Master, Guillaume de Gisors, received the golden head called Caput LVIIIQ from the Order of the Temple. Apparently then, there was still some degree of cooperation between the two orders.

In 1619, the Priory of de Sion was evicted from their house at Saint-Samsom. They had incurred the wrath of the Pope and the King of France for spending extravagantly, boycotting Catholic services and being generally irreverent towards all authority. From that point on, they disappear from the pages of history, not to reappear until 1956 - or so it seemed, when someone claiming to be the Priory of Sion began to release a flood of apparent propaganda, the best of which was deposited in Paris' Bibliotheque Nationale. Often it would be released under obvious pseudonyms of symbolic significance, such as "Marie-Madeleine" ("Mary Magdalene') and "Antoine l'Ermite" ("St. Anthony the Hermit"). Other times it was published under the names of actual people, (some of whom died mysteriously shortly after publication). For instance, *Dossiers Secrets* (*Secret Dossiers*), was a strange collection of purported data pertaining to the Merovingians and the Priory of Sion. It contained genealogies, letters, newspaper clippings, and other scraps all thrown together, along with commentary from the author, "Henri Lobineau", and some other unnamed commentator. However, within the *Dossiers* themselves it is revealed that "Lobineau" is a pseudonym, and it is claimed that the real author was one Leo Schidlof, who died in 1966. The authors of *Holy Blood, Holy Grail* talked to his daughter, who denied that he had written the *Dossiers*, but said that during his life and especially on the day of his death a number of people had tried to contact him on the subject, which he claimed to no nothing about. Yet *Secret Dossiers* asserts that he had not only written or compiled most of the material in the book, but had also possessed a leather briefcase filled with secret documents pertaining to the Rennes-le-Chateau between 1600 and 1800. The *Dossiers* claim that shortly before his death M. Schidlof passed the briefcase onto a courier named Fakhar ul Islam, who was supposed to meet in East Germany with an "agent delegated by Geneva" in February 1967 in order to transfer the briefcase to him. However, it is claimed that Fakhar ul Islam was expelled from East Germany before this could occur, and went back to Paris to "await further orders." His body was found on February 20 on the railway tracks at Melan, France, having been thrown from an express train. The details of Mr. Fakhar ul Islam's death turned out to be true, as the discovery of his decapitated were reported in the papers the following day. The briefcase, of course, was gone.

Secret Dossiers makes a number of controversial claims, some of which one would expect: that the Merovingians were descended from Jesus, that the Merovingian bloodline did not fade away with the death of Dagobert II, and that the Priory of Sion has continued its activities on behalf of the bloodline up until the present day. The most outrageous claim, however, was the list of supposed Grand Masters, or "Nautonniers" (Navigators) as they were called, who supposedly headed the order from 1188 until 1918. While a number of them were members of the Merovingian bloodline or well-known friends of the family, others were quite unexpected, names you might have heard before in another context.

Nicholas Flamel (G.M. 1398 - 1418) - A hermetic alchemist and book copyist in Paris during the 1300s, Flamel came across an interesting book during his work that was titled: *The Sacred Book of Abraham the Jew, Prince, Priest, Levite, Astrologer, and Philosopher to that Tribe of Jews who by the Wrath of God were Dispersed Amongst the Gauls*. In 1382 he met a Jew in Léon who told him the secret of the text. He then returned to Paris, and at noon on January 17 of the following year is said to have conducted "the first" alchemical transmutation. After that, he became extremely wealthy, bought thirty houses, and founded a number of churches and hospitals.

Leonardo da Vinci (G.M. 1510 - 1519) - Painter, sculptor, architect, engineer and scientist, Leonardo is well-known as one of the most profound intellects of the Renaissance, and history as we know it, for that matter. It is known that he possessed a mystical point of view and a number of heretical beliefs. Indeed, many list him as one of the first Rosicrucians. He was certainly a member of the Order of the Crescent, created by René d'Anjou, a former Priory Grand Master and one of his closest friends. He is suspected of believing that Jesus had a twin brother, Thomas, and included a second identical Christ-like figure in his famous painting, *The Last Supper*.

Johann Valentin Andrea (G.M. 1637-1654) - Born in Württenberg, Germany in 1586, Andrae is widely thought to have started the first Rosicrucian order. He originally tried to publish his famous "manifesto", *The Chymical Wedding of Christian Rosenkreutz*, anonymously, but later confessed to having written it "as a joke." This is unlikely, however, as it reads less like a comedy and more like a complex web of Hermetic, alchemical and astrological symbolism. After its publication, Andrae created a network of secret societies that he called "Christian Unions", for the purpose of preserving esoteric knowledge threatened by the Church. These unions also served as a refuge for heretics fleeing the Inquisition.

Robert Boyle (G.M. 1654 - 1691) - Recognized as the founder of modern chemistry and the scientific method, Boyle was the first to isolate a gas, and came up with the first atomic theory. He was educated in Geneva, where he became interested in occult subjects like alchemy and demonology. In 1619 he helped found the famous Philosophical College, which later became the Royal Society of London for Improving Natural Knowledge. This was a court-patronized board of influential scientists and philosophers - Jacobite Freemasons all of them - who met to discuss both scientific and esoteric matters. He was also one of the first to publicly welcome back the restored Stuart monarchy in 1660. He conducted voluminous alchemical experiments during his lifetime, which he was very secretive about, and published two treatises on the subject: *Incalescence of Quicksilver with Gold* and *A Historical Account of a Degradation of Gold*. His best friends were Isaac Newton and John Locke, and when he died he left them all of his alchemical papers, as well as a mysterious red powder which he used in his experiments.

Isaac Newton (G.M. 1691 - 1727) - The father of modern science, Newton invented the calculus, discovered the laws of motion and gravity, and established the basic properties of light. Born in 1642, he claimed to be descended from "ancient Scottish nobility", although this claim was severely doubted at the time. He became a member of the Royal Society in 1672, and in 1703 was elected their president. Although not a Freemason as far as we know, he was a member of a quasi-Masonic organization called the Gentlemen's Club of Spalding. He was a practicing alchemist who worked in conjunction with Boyle and Locke, and was also very interested in other esoteric subjects, such as sacred geometry, numerology and Gnosticism. He believed that the ancient Jews, especially Noah and Moses, possessed special divine knowledge, and that the architecture of Solomon's Temple concealed secret alchemical formulas. (He even believed that the ceremonies Solomon conducted there were alchemical experiments.) He was also interested in the origins of monarchy, particularly the ancient Judaic kind, and wrote about it in his book *The Chronology of Ancient Kingdoms Amended*. He considered Pythagoras' "Music of the Spheres" to be an allegory for the laws of gravitation, and thought that there were musical "correspondences" contained in certain architecture. He doubted the divinity of Jesus, the concept of the Trinity, and the reliability of the New Testament. Shortly before his death, during which he refused Last Rites, he and a few friends of his burned a large volume of his personal papers.

Victor Hugo (G.M. 1844 - 1885) - A tremendously influential poet, playwright and novelist, he is said to have provided the "single greatest impetus" to the Romantic movement. His most well-known works are the historical novel *The Hunchback of Notre Dame* and of course the play *Les Miserables*. By the age of 17 he was friends with Charles Nodier (another Priory of Sion Grand Master), and established a publishing house with him in that same year. It was from Nodier that he learned all about Gnosticism, Hermeticism, and Gothic architecture, all of which feature prominently in his work.

Claude Debussy (G.M. 1885 - 1918) - A famous nineteenth century pianist and composer, his most well-known works were *Prélude à l'après-midi d'un faune* ("Prelude to the afternoon of a faun") and *Claire de Lune*. Born into a poor family in 1862, by the time he was in his early teens he was performing for French nobility, and in his eighteenth year was adopted by a Russian noblewoman who took him traveling with her. As he became older, he fell in with influential political and aristocratic circles, as well as prominent members of the developing "French occult revival." These circles included Victor Hugo (whose work he set to music), Emile Hoffet, opera singer Emma Calvé, Rosicrucian playwright the Comte de Philippe Auguste Villiers de l'Isle-Adam, Oscar Wilde, W.B. Yeats, Marcel Proust, Paul Valérey, and Berénger Sauniére, that infamous curé of the Rennes-le-Château.

Jean Cocteau (G.M. 1918 - ?) - A leading member of the proto-surrealist movement, this famous French poet, playwright, novelist, sculptor, painter and designer is probably best known for his films *Orpheé* (*Orpheus*) and *Les Sang d'un Poète* (*Blood of a Poet*), both made while he was recovering from an opium addiction. Born into a politically influential family, Cocteau maintained friends in political and aristocratic circles for most of his life, and at one point was asked by Charles de Gaulle's brother to give a speech on the state of the nation. (De Gaulle, by the way, has also been alleged to be a member of the Priory of Sion.) Cocteau's signature has been found on the Priory of Sion's published statutes, quoted at the beginning of this article. previously-quoted "Prieuré statutes." This is questionable, however, considering what Article 7 of the statutes demands. Given his reputation, one can hardly imagine Jean Cocteau actually "renouncing" his personality.

Whether these people actually served in the office of Grand Master is very uncertain, for many have questioned the veracity of both the *Secret Dossiers* and the modern-day Priory, whose claims include, among other things, possession of the Ark of the Covenant. Especially under suspicion is M. Pierre Plantard de Sainte Clair, who was the modern Priory's Grand Master up until the mid-eighties, and who claimed to be the most direct descendent of the Merovingian kings currently alive. He was extensively interviewed in the works of well-known Priory propagandist Gerard de Sede, as well as for the books *Holy Blood, Holy Grail* and *The Messianic Legacy* by Michael Baigent, Richard Leigh, and Henry Lincoln. However, while conducting their research, these authors came across indications that the Priory had been heavily infiltrated by both the Knights of Malta and the "Propaganda Due" Mason lodge, two secret societies notorious for their involvement with mobsters and fascists. They also discovered that the C.I.A. had smuggled some Priory documents relating to the genealogy of the Merovingians out of France with the help of British Intelligence. They began to doubt the motives behind the Priory of Sion and Pierre Plantard. And they are not alone. Rumors circulate on the internet that M. Plantard is a hoaxster with a criminal record and Nazi affiliations. The truth about Plantard remains to be seen. Perhaps he would like to respond to the charges, in the next issue of *Dagobert's Revenge*.

Nicholas Poussin and the Incontrovertible Proof

By Tracy R. Twyman

Painter Nicholas Poussin's name was mentioned in the mysterious coded parchments found buried in the parish at Rennes-le-Chateau - parchments that have been instrumental in opening up the mystery of the Holy Grail. That area of the Languedoc in Southern France where they were found has long been associated with the Merovingian dynasty, the Knights Templar and the Ark of the Covenant. In fact, Rennes-le-Château itself had been the home of a number of Merovingian princes, including Dagobert the II's son Sigisbert. The parish and other religious monuments in the surrounding area have been dedicated to Mary Magdalene, most likely the wife of Jesus and the sacred "vessel" that carried the royal blood of his offspring into France after the crucifixion. In 1891 the parish's cure, Berenger Sauniere, began a restoration project for the church, during which he found the said parchments, sealed in wooden tubes and hidden inside two Visigothic columns that held up the altar stone. Besides two pages of genealogies detailing the lineage of Dagobert II, two parchments consisted of passages from the New Testament, written with deliberate spelling errors, misplaced truncated letters and spacing anomalies which revealed a clever coding system. Sauniere was sent by Monsignor Felix Billard, the Bishop of Carcassonne to have the parchments interpreted by Father Bieil, Director of St. Sulpice in Paris. However, once deciphered, the parchments still didn't make much sense. One stated:

"To Dagobert II, King, and to Sion belong this treasure and he is there dead."

The second was much more cryptic. It read:

"Shepherdess - No temptation that Poussin and Teniers hold the key; Peace 681 by the cross and this horse of God I destroy this dæmon of the guardian at noon blue apples."

Both of these bizarre quotations have been picked apart by scholars for many years, and much has been revealed. For instance, we know that Dagobert II was the last significant Merovingian king, supposedly descended through Jesus from the House of David, and therefore "of the blood of Sion." We can then determine that "blue apples" - a term for grapes sometimes used by the French, was probably a veiled reference to this royal blood (grapes signifying wine, which symbolizes royal blood), and to the continuation of the royal family genes. Also, other code words have been found in the documents. Certain misplaced letters spell out the word "Sion" twice, and also "Rex Mundi", which means "King of the World." [1] At the bottom of second message we find the initials P.S, for "Priory of Sion", perhaps, which could be a clue as to who put the parchments there in the first place. In addition, we have considerable information on the meaning of the words, "Poussin and Teniers hold the key." For after Father Bieil (and his friend Emile Hoffet) deciphered the parchments, he gave Berenger Sauniere copies of two paintings: *St. Anthony's Temptation*, by David Teniers, and a work by Nicholas Poussin, *The Shepherds of Arcadia*.

Poussin's painting, although once thought to have depicted a figment of his imagination, is now known to have depicted an actual tomb that existed near the village of Arques at the time, six miles from the Rennes-le-Chateau. The inscription on the tomb in the painting reads: "Et in Arcadia Ego", which is the title of an earlier work from 1618 by the painter Guercino, as well as another Poussin painting on the same theme made ten years previously. Often translated "Even in Arcadia I

7

The Shepherds of Arcadia by Nicholas Poussin.

am", and taken to be a reference to the pervasiveness of death, it means, more literally: "And in Arcadia I..." - an unfinished sentence. The phrase also appeared on another tombstone, found in the churchyard at Sauniere's parish, for the grave of Marie, Marquise de Blanchefort. The stone had been designed by the parish's former cure, Abbe Antoine Bigou, and inscribed with a strange mixture of Greek and Latin letters which spelled the words "Et in Arcadia Ego." The inscription was removed by Sauniere, who by this time had learned the "terrible" secrets of the parchments, but he did not realize that somebody had already made an engraving of the stone.

Over the years, much has been made of all of this. Some have suggested that the "he" referred to in the second parchment ("and he is there dead") might have actually been Jesus Christ, who survived the crucifixion only to die years later in Southern France. Thus the painting *The Shepherds of Arcadia* could actually be a map to buried treasure: the remains of the most popular man in history and the link between the Merovingian kings and the House of David. Indeed, Sauniere is said by one witness to have come across "incontrovertible proof" that the crucifixion was a hoax. We know that he learned of some secret, and afterwards exhibited strange behavior after learning this, continuing to renovate his parish in a most bizarre fashion.

For instance, Sauniere arranged the Stations of the Cross inside the church to make it appear that Jesus' body was actually being removed from the tomb, suggesting a resurrection in which instead of ascending to Heaven, Jesus just went on with his merry life. Then he erected a large, Satanic-looking statue above the doorway, which has been said to represent Asmodeus, the keeper of secrets and hidden treasures (and, according to Judaic tradition, the true builder of Solomon's Temple). Above the door Sauniere placed a sign that read "Terribilis est locus ist", meaning "This place is terrible." He erected a Gothic-looking tower called "Tour Magdala" to house his library in, and a villa named "Bethania." [2]

Sauniere could often be found up late at night, walking the grounds, digging in the graveyard and making excavations underneath the parish foundation. One interesting excavation involved lifting what was called "the Knight's Flagstone", which stood before the altar. No one knows exactly what he found under there, but he immediately told his workmen to put everything back, and had the stone (which bore a depiction of two knights riding the same horse, the seal of the Knights Templar) paved over. At about this time he received a large cash deposit from Archduke Johann von Habsburg, a cousin of Franz Josef, emperor of Austria. Sauniere then began to spend extravagantly. He was then hired by Jean-Stephane Habsburg specifically to search for secret documents within the church. He also started hanging out it esoteric circles that included opera singer Emma Calve, his suspected lover, and composer Claude Debussy, Grand Master of the Priory of Sion. Sauniere is believed too have joined a secret society, but we can not be sure if that was the one.

Also known to have traveled in esoteric circles was Poussin himself, and he is thought to have embodied a number of mystical secrets in his work. (On the surface, he is quite obviously obsessed with Venus, Mary Magdalene, and Bacchus, the Greek god of wine.) A booklet has recently been written on this subject called *Poussin's Secret*, by David Wood and Ian Campbell, which explores mathematical coding and sacred geometry in Poussin's work. These two authors, especially David Wood, are known for two earlier books, *Genisis: The First Book of Revelations* and *Geneset: Target Earth*, both focusing on a geometric study of the Rennes-le-Château. Wood, who was joined by co-author Campbell on the second book, has spent years connecting the dots on maps of Southern France to reveal patterns in the placement of the parish at Rennes-le-Château and other significant monuments in the area. The shapes formed were then analyzed for numerological significance in the degrees of the angles and in other measurements. Specifically he was looking for multiples of 9 and 15, which he believed to represent Isis and Osiris His favorite shape that he found was a lop-sided pentagram in a circle (which he called "the Extended Pentagram"), where the top point is elongated and sticks out of the circle. This was especially significant because the angles of the points are 36° (4 x 9, indicating Isis), just like the regular pentagram, yet you can form the Extended Pentagram by "dividing a circle into 15 (Osiris) parts and joining the division."

The pentagram is generally taken to represent the human body, but David Wood says the extended pentagram represents a female body specifically, and a goddess at that. He also finds significance in the fact that this pentagram "generates" the phi ratio, which is the nth term of the Fibonacci sequence, an algorithm mimicked in the growth rate of all living organisms. (Phi and its geometric equivalent, the golden mean section, are essential foundations of mathematics.) From the geometry of Rennes-le-Chateau that he and Ian Campbell found, they somehow "decoded" a message that they believe had been placed there originally by an extraterrestrial civilization the - one that created us, warning us of impending doom. This civilization, they believed, was headed by a being named Satan, which they equated with occultist Eliphas Levi's figure of Baphomet. They also concluded that the prolific worship of Mary Magdalene in that area of France was actually a form of Isis-worship, and that the extraterrestrials had included some sort of mystical sexual imagery in their message. They then attempted to decipher the words "Et in Arcadia Ego", which they did by "translating the letters of the inscription into trigonometric Sine values." When deciphered, the message appeared to be an account of a destructive cataclysm caused by a comet - either one that occurred in the past or one that will occur in the future.

Finally, in *Poussin's Secret*, Wood and Campbell assert that the painting *The Shepherds of Arcadia* contains a scaled down (5/6) version of the Extended Pentagram, except that this one is created from a ten-division circle instead of fifteen, and represents, they say, a mortal woman instead of a goddess, probably the historical Magdalene. The authors believe that the painting tells an allegorical resurrection tale, certainly of Jesus, who lived on to perpetuate his royal blood through Magdalene, and perhaps deeper still the story of Osiris' resurrection by Isis, "which has been plagiarized by Christianity but with the characters changed to Jesus and Magdalene, and so does the theme echo..." Yet at the same time they believe that the painting is a geometric replica of the landscape at Rennes-le-Château, and therefore carries the same apocalyptic warning. Could Poussin have known all this, enough to encode such a message into his picture? We must be reminded that in 1656, Poussin was visited in Rome by Abbe Louis Fouquet, brother of Nicholas Fouquet, Louis XIV's superintendent of finances. After the meeting, while still in Rome, the Abbe sent a letter to his brother saying:

"He and I discussed certain things, which I shall with ease be able to explain to you in detail - things which will give you, through Monsieur Poussin, advantages which even kings would have great pains to draw from him, and which, according to him, it is possible that nobody else will ever discover in the centuries to come. And what is more, these are things so difficult to discover that nothing now on this earth can prove of better fortune nor be their equal."

Shortly after receiving this, Nicholas Fouquet was arrested, imprisoned, and held "incommunicado" for the rest of his life. The letter was confiscated by Louis XIV, who later went to great efforts to obtain *The Shepherds of Arcadia*, which he hung at his private apartments in Versailles. But what was it that Poussin and the Abbe discussed? What had he discovered "which even kings would have great pain to draw from him"? Was it, perhaps, "incontrovertible proof"?

Endnotes:

[1] Rex Mundi was considered by the heretical Cathars who had once occupied the area to be the evil demiurge that had created existence.

[2] Some have claimed that the landscape resembles "Mary Magdalene's walk from Magdala to Bethania", but that may be a stretch.

What the Hell is the Holy Grail?

By Tracy R. Twyman

It is the editorial position of *Dagobert's Revenge* that the "Sangreal", or "Holy Grail", as described in the stories that emerged from the courts of Europe in the early part of this millennium, is actually a veiled reference to the bloodline of David, a play on the words "Sang real", meaning "royal blood." In the stories, the custodians of the Grail are the "Grail family", headed by the Fisher King. They trace their lineage back to Joseph of Arimathea, who, along with Mary Magdalene, was supposed to have brought the Grail (often a cup filled with the "blood" of Jesus) from Jerusalem after the crucifixion. The Grail family is romanticized as being chosen directly by God, just as King David was chosen for Israel, and one of its members, Sir Galahad, is described as "a scion of the House of David." Galahad was also considered by tradition to be the grandfather of a real-life character, Godfroi de Bouillon, who led the First Crusade for the Holy Land, and in 1118 founded the Order of Sion, an organization dedicated to bringing back the lost Merovingian dynasty. The Grail guardians are described in the romances as "Templars", and the Knights Templar were, when first chartered, the military wing of the Order of Sion. The Templars were also at that time very influential in the French royal courts that commissioned most of the Grail romances, so it is possible that the Templars might have had an indirect effect on the contents of the stories. As if that weren't enough, Wolfram von Eschenbach states explicitly in the story *Parzival* that the Grail is the source of kingship. He writes: "And if anywhere a land loses its lord, if the people there acknowledge the Hand of God, and seek a new lord, they are granted one from the company of the Grail." However, the subtle political inferences about "royal blood" in these romances were merely grafted onto a much older tradition, and one cannot ignore the alternate interpretations of just what the Holy Grail might have been.

A Stone

In Eschenbach's *Parzival*, the Grail is a magic stone that can create stuff out of nothing, bring the dead back to life and cause those who looked upon it to never age another day. It also communicates. Written messages appear on its surface detailing the names and lineages of those chosen to seek the Grail, and Parzival actually talked to it. It is called "*lapsit exillis*", which some scholars consider to be a corruption of "*lapis excaelis*", meaning "stone from the heavens." Indeed, in the story it states that angels had "left it on earth and then rose high above the stars, as if their innocence drew them back."
There are those who identify the Grail as a "stone of light" knocked from Lucifer's crown during the war in Heaven. It supposedly made its way into human hands at some point, and some have suggested that it might be analogous to the capstone (perhaps a crystal) which used to top off the Great Pyramid. Certainly it makes sense to think of the Grail stone as a crystal, since crystals have been associated throughout history with a number of fantastic phenomena, believed to possess electromagnetic properties capable of healing and facilitating psychic communication. Others have claimed that the stone from Lucifer's crown was actually a meteorite, perhaps the "Kaaba" revered by the Muslims at the Dome of the Rock in Jerusalem, a sacred black stone which they believe "fell from Heaven" as well. (In fact, the Koran says that Muhammad stood upon this stone when he was taken to Heaven on a "ladder of light" by the angel Gabriel.) Of course, meteorites also have strong magnetic properties. One cannot help but be reminded of the "monolith" in Arthur C. Clarke's *2001*, which was a black rock with amazing magnetic powers anonymously donated by a superior race to bring humanity into the next phase of evolutionary development.

A Cup

As previously mentioned, the Grail is

traditionally thought of as the cup that caught Jesus Christ's blood as it dribbled out of the stab wound that the Roman soldier Longinus had given him while he hung on the cross. This legend was started by Chretien de Troyes' *Perceval*, written in 1182. It is also said to be the cup used by Christ at the Last Supper. One popular candidate for this artifact is a crumbling hunk of olive wood which rests at the Nanteos Mansion in Glastonbury, supposedly brought there by Joseph of Arimathea. (Richard Wagner visited the mansion once and there conceived the idea for his opera *Parsifal*.) But there are many other stories surrounding the Grail. Some versions state that this is the same cup used by the priest Melchizedek to serve Abraham bread and wine on Mount Moriah. From the Grail cup, sometimes described as more of a bowl or a serving dish, one could supposedly obtain whatever kind of food one wished, in limitless abundance, and in this way its legend is obviously based on ancient Celtic myths about Bran the Blessed's "cauldron of rebirth" and the magical "Horn of Plenty." When not filled with blood or food made from thin air, the Grail was empty, and its emptiness was heavily stressed, perhaps because emptiness is the supreme state of being and enlightenment: the annihilation of the ego.

Mystical Union

This brings us to another point of view on the Grail: that it is a spiritual experience. The Grail is described as the most worthy thing that one can seek, and those who embark upon the quest for the Grail must be completely pure of heart. One does not merely "find" the Grail; one "achieves" it, and at that point is initiated into its secrets. Just seeing it causes an overwhelming, trance-like state of awe and reverence, and the experience causes a complete transformation of the soul. "Upon a green achmardi she bore the consummation of heart's desire, its root and its blossoming - a thing called 'The Gral', paradisal, transcending all earthly perfection!", writes Wolfram von Eschenbach. In the story of *Parzival* the Grail has been lost, causing a state of infertility called "the Wasteland." The Fisher King, Parzival's uncle, is wounded in the crotch, and the festering sore, along with The Wasteland, cannot be cured until the Grail is found - an obvious metaphor for redemption. This is the redemption that occurs when one's polarities (male/female, light/dark, etc.) are aligned, equalized, and transcended, creating a feeling of sublime nothingness that leaves one receptive to divine influence. It is union with God, the Great Void, that state of "Samadhi" that is the goal of yogic meditation. It is written that, "In Samadhi the Many and the One are united in a union of Existence with Non-existence", and that is exactly what's being alluded to in the Grail myths. Perhaps that is why the metaphor of the cup was used. The heart chakra is often described as a cup - one that must be emptied of all its mundane contents to make way for the Water of Life. This water, in turn, must be perfectly stilled so as to reflect a gaze downward from the face of the Most High.

Bodily Secretions

Famed magician Aleister Crowley had quite a different take on the meaning of the Grail. Noted for his work in the field of sex magic, he combined Tantric theory learned in India with methodology learned in the German *Ordo Templi Orientis*. He believed that sex performed ritually could result in transcendence of the ego and union with the Godhead. This was possible if one was "in conversation with the Holy Guardian Angel" at the moment of orgasm, and the process for reaching that state is detailed in *The Book of the Unveiling of the Sangraal*. Afterwards, all fluids created during sex must be consumed in full by the participants, so as to retain their potency (in the same way that Tantrics retain their semen so as to prevent a loss of energy). Crowley referred to semen as "red tincture", vaginal secretions as "white tincture", and the mix of the two, the Elixir of Life. He also called it the "Magnum Opus" or "Philosopher's Stone", in reference to the universal solvent long sought by alchemists. The holy vessel (vagina) from which one drinks the Elixir of Life he called "the Sangraal." Interestingly, when Crowley wrote about his own sex magic rituals he referred to himself as "The Great Beast" and his consort as "Babalon the Great." I am reminded of a passage in St. John the Divine's *Revelation* describing her thusly:

"And the woman was arrayed in purple and scarlet colour, and decked with gold and precious stones and pearls, having a golden cup in her hand full of abominations and filthiness of her fornication. And upon her forehead was a name written: MYSTERY, BABYLON THE GREAT, THE MOTHER OF HARLOTS AND ABOMINATIONS OF THE EARTH. (Revelation, 17:4-5.)"

The Ark

In his book *The Sign and the Seal*, Graham Hancock argues that the Grail might have actually been the Ark of the Covenant, the revered Judaic relic designed by Yahweh and built by the Israelites to absolute geometric perfection. This was the 1 cubit x 1 cubit x 2 cubit wooden cedar box into which Moses placed the Tablets of the Testimony: tablets of stone written with the "Finger of God" (*Exodus 31:18*.) The Ark was overlaid with the purest of gold, one of the most electrically conductive element known to man, and crowned with two mysterious winged objects called "cherubim" who each had two faces, of a lion and eagle, a man and an ox, respectively. Between their outstretched wings stood the Mercy Seat, where the priest could literally talk to God. In fact, God was referred to as actually *living in* the Ark. "The Lord reigneth; let the people tremble: he sitteth between the cherubims; let the earth be moved." (*Psalm 99*.) The prophet Samuel was said to have seen and conversed with a "form", which he took to be God, in the vicinity of the Ark. Later, King Solomon had a temple built for the Ark, in which he used it to conjure up not only Yahweh, but a host "false gods" and "demons", "angels" and "archangels." The Ark "smote" those who touched it, move objects at will and produced "manna" for the Israelites to eat while they were starving in the desert - all attributes shared by the Grail. The Ark had to be obscured by a veil at all times, lest those who looked upon be killed, and, only the sons of the High Priest Aaron were allowed to actually see it, protected by a "breastplate of judgment" made from gold and precious stones.

Graham Hancock bases his argument on the fact that the Knights Templar, called "guardians of the Grail", were known to have excavated a treasure from the caverns underneath Solomon's Temple which made them extremely rich and powerful. They were rumored to have taken this treasure to Montsegur in the Languedoc region of the French Pyrenees, which seems to be the same mountain as the setting of most of the Grail romances, "Montsalvat" ("Mount of Salvation"). It is also quite close to the Rennes-le-Chateau, a location tied in local legend to the Holy Grail. If this is correct, then the Grail might really be a combination of all the phenomena listed above: a "sacred vessel" housing a "stone from God" - the tablets - with intense electromagnetic properties, which, when combined with the electro-conductive properties of the Ark, created a device capable of transmitting audio-visual signals, mortally "zapping" people and changing physical reality. Such a device would certainly be able to produce the transcendental experience associated with the Grail, by means of aligning electromagnetic polarities within the brain and body. As the Ark and its contents were basically the foundation upon which the Kingdom of Judah was built, the "sign and the seal" of Yahweh's covenant with His chosen people, it would by right be under the custodianship of the Kings of Judah, the "blood royale" of the House of David, and the Templars would indeed be its guardians. However, at this point such a conclusion is still theoretical, and the keepers of the secret do not intend to clear up the mysteries any time soon.

Baphomet: The Severed Head That Wouldn't Die

By Tracy R. Twyman

Friday the 13th, October, 1307 - a dreadful day. Especially if you happened to be a Templar knight. For on that dreadful day, just as the Sun was rising, King Philip IV's seneschals descended upon all of the order's French holdings, arresting the members and seizing their property. The king had owed the order a lot of money, and he had hoped to get his hands on the rumored Templar treasure that had made them fabulously rich. But they had been forewarned, and had moved the treasure, along, perhaps, with some mystical artifacts, to their preceptories in Scotland, where the atmosphere was much more pleasant for them.

Nevertheless, with the assistance of Pope Clement V, his so-called "puppet", King Philip had the knights tortured and executed by the Inquisition. They were accused, among other things, of heresy, necromancy, homosexual practices, and conducting a bizarre ritual that involved spitting on, defecating on, or in some way desecrating the cross (which, if true, is perhaps evidence that they did not believe in the crucifixion). Under extreme physical duress, most of them confessed. In fact, many of their confessions were remarkably similar in detail. By far the most popular theme of the confessions was the worship of an idol called "Baphomet." Sometimes described as a cat or a goat whose anus was ritually kissed, Baphomet was most often referred to as a severed head. A list of charges drawn up by the Inquisition on August 12th, 1308 reads:

"Item, that in each province they had idols, namely heads.
Item, that they adored these idols.
Item, that they said that the head could save them.
Item, that it could make riches.
Item, that it could make the trees flower.
Item, that it made the land germinate.
Item, that they surrounded or touched each head of the aforesaid idol with small cords, which they wore around themselves next to the shirt or the flesh."

In light of the probability that these charges were true, it would bid us well to examine the possible origins and meanings of the famous dreaded head.

Where did it come from?

The Templar legends regarding the head's origin are numerous and confusing. Some said

Eliphas Levi's depiction of Baphomet.

it was a man's head, and some said that it was a woman's head. Some said that it was bearded, and some said that it was clean-shaven. Some said that it was made of glass or crystal, and some said that it had two faces. A popular tale held that it was the head of the Templars' first Grand Master, Hughes de Payens. Others said that it was made of gold and called "Caput LVIIIQ", meaning Head 58", combined with the symbol for Virgo. One recurrent story that kept popping up in several confessions says that a Templar called "the Lord of Sidon" was in love with a young woman named "Yse" (possibly derived from "Isis") who died suddenly. On the night of her burial, the knight dug up her body and copulated with it. Nine months later a voice "from the Void" told him to go back to the grave, where he would find his son. There he discovered a head resting on a pair of leg bones (perhaps the origin of the Templar's famous "skull and crossbones" symbol). The voice told him that if he was careful to guard the head, it would be "the giver of all things." He took it with him, and for the rest of his days it protected him. Later on the Templar order got a hold of it and incorporated it into their rituals.

Islamic Origins

A common claim by historians is that the name "Baphomet" was derived from "Mahomet" an Old French corruption of the name of the prophet Muhammad. Others have said that it comes from the Arabic word "abufihamet", meaning "Father of Understanding." Whatever the specific derivation, the idea that the Baphomet legend was influenced by Islam is quite logical. The Templars were known to have cavorted with Sufis and other unorthodox Muslims while stationed in the Middle East, as well as in Spain and perhaps even Jerusalem, where they were supposed to be fighting the "infidel" during the Crusades. This would have given them ample opportunity to pass on the legend of Baphomet, if not the actual item. In his book *The Sufis*, Idries Shah argues that Baphomet was really the head of a mystic revered by a number of Sufi sects called "Hallaj", who was executed for testifying about his spiritual experiences. After he got decapitated, the Caliph's Queen Mother had the head embalmed, and it later came into the possession of certain Sufi masters, who revered it for its magical powers. Shah claims that Hallaj, a "son of a widow" was not only the source of the legend of Baphomet, but also the model for the Masonic figure of Hiram Abiff. He, of course, was the architect of Solomon's Temple who, in Masonic legend, was killed by his underlings with three ceremonious blows to the head for not revealing the secret words, grips and signs of a Master Mason.

Wisdom

In *Holy Blood, Holy Grail* the authors point out that when run through a certain cabalistic cipher known as "Atbash", the word "Baphomet" (written in Hebrew) renders "Sophia", the name of the Greek goddess of wisdom. This makes sense, for the Templars were known to be the keepers of an ancient "wisdom tradition", and a logical representation of wisdom is the human head. Interestingly, Aleister Crowley, who adopted the name "Baphomet" upon joining the Ordo Templi Orientis, believed the name to derive from two Greek words joined together which mean "baptism of wisdom" or "absorption into wisdom." Indeed, the experience of "absorption into wisdom" could be considered an ego death, and the skull and crossbones became a well-known symbol for death.

Bran the Blessed

Elements of the Baphomet story are quite obviously Celtic in origin. The Celts believed that the soul resided in the head, and therefore they would sever the heads of their enemies, preserving them as magical talismans. The most well-known severed head among the Celts was that of the legendary giant Bran the Blessed, which is said to be buried outside London, facing France. It was put there to ward off the plague, to ensure fertility and to protect the city from foreign invasion. Similar powers are also attributed to the head of the Green Man, the Celtic fertility God, as well as the head of Merovingian King Dagobert II.

Levi's Baphomet

Baphomet was sometimes described by the tortured Templars as having a human form, with wings, cloven feet, and the head of a goat. From this came the nineteenth century occultist Eliphas Levi's well-known depiction of Baphomet, now incorporated into the Waite tarot deck as "the Devil." This popular image, sometimes referred to as "the Sabbatic Goat", was made to embody symbols of conflicting dualities. Thus the beast bears the breasts of a woman and the organs of a man. He is poised between the waxing and waning moon symbols, with his right and left hands pointing up and down, respectively. Levi, who was obsessed with dualities, was the first occultist to come up with the idea of "good" (upward-pointing) and "evil" (downward pointing) pentagrams, and his version of the "evil" pentagram included Baphomet's goat face superimposed onto it, from whence came the "Sign of Baphomet" used by Satanist Anton LeVey. Levi believed Baphomet to be the symbolic form of the absolute supreme being, and claimed that all occultists, including Templars and Freemasons, actually worshipped the Baphomet. He even believed that the name "Baphomet" was a code for Solomon's Temple, because if you spell it backwards you get the letters: "TEM-OH-AB", which he said stood for: *"Templi omnivm hominum pacis abbas"*, meaning "the Father of the Temple of Peace of All Men." Despite this, Levi's characterization of the Baphomet led to the popular conception of the Devil as we know him today, and gave fodder to the theories that Freemasonry is Satanic.

Anthony Blunt and the Cambridge Spies

By Tracy R. Twyman

During the 1930's, in the years preceding World War II, four young Englishmen known as "the Cambridge Spies" were used by the KGB to infiltrate British intelligence. They had been recruited from the university's Trinity College, chosen for their keen minds and their Marxist sensibilities. Their names: Donald Maclean, Harold Adrian Russell "Kim" Philby, Guy Francis de Moncy Burgess, and Anthony F. Blunt, the man this article is concerned with. All but one of them – Philby - was a homosexual. It was Blunt who was recruited first, and he soon began recruiting other alumni, (although he was not responsible for recruiting the other three Cambridge Spies). He and Burgess had been members of a Marxist secret society called "the Cambridge Apostles." The son of an Anglican Bishop, Blunt has been described as "tall, charming, arrogant, somewhat cold, and a dedicated communist." Of the four, Blunt's espionage career lasted the longest. After establishing himself as a French tutor, art historian, and advisor to Queen Elizabeth (for which he was knighted), he joined MI5, Britain's domestic intelligence service, in 1939. Burgess and Maclean became secretaries to the British Foreign Office, and Philby, who would become the ringleader of the Cambridge Spies, served the Communists as a member of MI6, Britain's CIA.

Between 1940 and 1945, these men did some serious damage to Britain and the United States. Blunt and Burgess provided the KGB with secret Foreign Office and MI5 documents describing Allied military strategy. Maclean reported directly to Stalin, and was his "main source" for information on the communications between Churchill and Roosevelt, then later between Churchill and Truman. This included updates on the development of the atom bomb, and how much uranium the U.S. had stockpiled. Philby informed the Russians when the Nazi code "Enigma" was broken by the Brits, and fingered British agents who were working inside Russia, to be dealt with swiftly by the KGB.

After the war, the Cambridge Spies continued to clandestinely serve the Communist cause. Maclean reported to Stalin about Truman and Churchill's plans to occupy Germany and alter the borders of the Eastern European countries - information he was armed with at the Yalta conference. Philby was sent to Washington to work as a liaison between MI6 and the CIA, and also the FBI. This gave him access to all of the FBI reports shared by the British, and he was able to tell the Russians when the FBI had broken the Soviet code ("Venona"). He also forewarned them that the United States would not use nuclear weapons during the Korean war, and that MacArthur would be prevented from carrying the war beyond the Yalu river. Burgess continues to provide top secret documents to the KGB while working in his capacity as secretary to the British Deputy Foreign Minister. During these years, Blunt mainly acted as a middle man for these transactions.

In 1949, Philby became aware that his partner Maclean had been identified as a Russian spy, and that the British would shortly close in on him. He sent Burgess, who was living with him at the time, back to London to warn Maclean of his impending capture, and to suggest that Maclean defect at once to Mother Russia. Before Burgess left, Philby asked him not to defect along with Maclean, lest suspicion fall on Philby himself, whom he was rooming with. Of course, that is exactly what happened, and Philby, who never forgave the betrayal, became known to British intelligence as "the Third Man", the one suspected of having warned Maclean. He was able to stay on MI6 for several more tumultuous years, but in 1963, while working on assignment in Beirut, an MI6 associate was sent to question him. He confessed, but managed to defect to Russia before he was sent back to London for prosecution.

After Philby's defection, suspicion began to fall quite heavily on our man Anthony Blunt, whom British intelligence called "the Fourth Man." One of his recruits from Cambridge, an American named Michael Straight, pointed him out to MI5. Blunt was offered immunity, and on April 23, 1964, confessed. He was then interrogated by "Spycatcher" Peter Wright, but was careful to provide only information pertaining to agents who were already dead, or who had already been found out. But he was not publicly unmasked until 1979, when Margaret Thatcher revealed his treachery to the world and stripped him of his knighthood. He was also forced to resign his post as Adviser to the Queen's Pictures. But that was the worst punishment he ever received, and he continued to live in England with his lover, John Gaskin, until he died of a heart attack in 1983.

The reason why we here have an interest in Anthony Blunt is because of his unusual expertise in the field of art history, for he was actually acknowledged as the world's foremost expert on the works of Nicholas Poussin. This was the famous French artist who's painting *The Shepherds of Arcadia* is so central to the thesis of this magazine and the whole issue of the Holy Grail. Poussin was one of the names mentioned in the parchments found at the parish in Rennes-le-Chateau, France, which stated:

"To Dagobert II, King, and to Sion belong this treasure and he is there dead. Shepherdess no temptation that Poussin and Teniers hold the key; Peace 681 by the cross and this horse of God I destroy this daemon guardian at noon blue apples."

After these parchments were found by the parish's cure, Berenger Sauniere, he purchased a copy of *The Shepherds of Arcadia*, and began performing excavations on the parish grounds in the middle of the night. He soon became fabulously rich, with the help of mysterious contributions from the aristocratic Blanchefort family. It is believed by many, as speculated in the book *Holy Blood, Holy Grail*, that Sauniere found the "treasure" that was referred to in the parchments. This treasure was purportedly something which may have proved that Jesus had survived the crucifixion, and that his descendants were none other than France's original royal family, the Merovingians, of whom King Dagobert II was one. Thus the treasure really would belong to "Sion", meaning the royal House of David, and to "Dagobert II, King." It would have also been of interest to the Blanchefort family, which was related by blood to the Merovingians. And such a treasure would most certainly be of interest to the Catholic Church because of the potentially disastrous theological implications, and certainly they would have wished to silence Father Sauniere, with cash contributions perhaps.

Sauniere's own bizarre behavior following these events - renovating the parish to include a statue of the demon Asmodeus, installing Stations of the Cross that made it look like Jesus was removed from the tomb before the Resurrection, and placing a plaque outside which said "This place is terrible" - are enough to indicate that his own religious beliefs had been shaken to the core. He also began hanging out with known occultists, including opera singer Emma Calve and composer Claude Debussy, who is supposed to have at one time led the infamous Priory of Sion. The Priory was dedicated to the restoration of the Merovingian dynasty, and it was they who chartered the Knights Templar back in 1118, drafted originally as their own military arm. The Templars later became the official guardians of Scotland's House of Stuart, which is also related to the Merovingians, and interestingly, the Templars are referred to in the Arthurian legends as the "guardians of the Grail." This is significant, for it is believed by many, including the authors of *Holy Blood, Holy Grail*, that the "Sangreal", which is the word originally used in these romances and has been translated as "Holy Grail" is actually a play on the French words "sang real", or "royal blood." It is therefore a veiled reference to the bloodline of Christ - the Merovingian dynasty and its various offshoots. Thus the "treasure" that Sauniere found, if he did indeed, might have actually been the Holy Grail itself, proof of the continuation of the Royal House of David through the royal house of France.

It was speculated by the authors of *Holy Blood, Holy Grail*, especially co-author Henry Lincoln in his subsequent book *The Holy Place*, that Poussin's painting *The Shepherds of Arcadia*, which depicts three shepherds and a pregnant shepherdess looking at a tomb, upon which are etched the words "Et in Arcadia Ego" ("And in Arcadia I...") is actually a depiction of a tomb that really existed in the area surrounding Rennes-le-Chateau. Lincoln found, with the help of his informant Gerard de Sede, a tomb which resembles precisely the one featured in the painting, including the surrounding landscape, although it is missing the etched words and has since been destroyed due to all the attention it has gotten. It was Henry Lincoln's belief that this tomb may have at one time held the bones of Jesus Christ himself, and that the pregnant woman shown in the painting represents Mary Magdalen, Jesus' wife according to this theory, who was heavy with a child of his royal Davidic blood. While writing his book on the subject, Lincoln consulted with the world's Poussin expert, Anthony Blunt, about the possibility that Poussin's painting was a depiction of this tomb. Surprisingly, to Lincoln, at least, Blunt would not even hear if it. "This is a mere coincidence", he is quoted as saying. "An extraordinary coincidence, but a coincidence nonetheless!" Blunt maintained that the tomb in *The Shepherds of Arcadia* was a purely made-up tomb, and that was all there was to it, because Poussin had never been to that part of France where the tomb was. Indeed, Poussin did spend almost every moment of his life in Rome, and only left for a two-year period to work in Paris as Painter to the Court of King Louis XIII between 1640 and 1642. When asked which route Poussin had taken from Rome to Paris, and if he might have passed by the tomb, Blunt replied, "He took the usual route."

Blunt was then asked about a significant letter from 1656 sent by Abbe Louis Fouquet to his brother Nicolas Fouquet, Superintendent of Finances at the Court of Louis XIV, which said: "Poussin and I discussed certain things which I shall be at ease to explain to you in detail. Things which will give you, through M. Poussin, advantages which even kings would have great pains to draw from him..." Blunt merely admitted that the letter "had never been properly understood by art historians", but that he thought it might be about "a commission for ornaments for Fouquet's garden." This of course does not explain the great caution that was taken when discussing the matter, nor what occurred subsequently. Nicolas Fouquet became extremely rich while managing the Royal Exchequer, and in 1661 he was, for reasons unknown, removed from office and thrown into prison, where he stayed until his death 20 years later. Upon his death his two servants were locked up as well, so that, as their jailer was told, "they will have no communication with anyone either by speech or by writing", because they might have knowledge of "the majority of important matters of which M. Fouquet was cognizant."

Why would Anthony Blunt, the world's expert on Poussin, have found no interest in these extraordinary facts and their earth-shattering implications? Did he just not want to admit that there might have been something about Poussin of which he did not already know? Or did he already know, in fact, all of these "matters of which M. Fouquet was cognizant"? Is it possible that he had been told to keep quiet about such subjects, and to dismiss any such notions as nonsense? We must remember the interest the Catholic Church has in keeping this secret, and the involvement the Church has had historically with both the Mafia and with government intelligence agencies, including MI5 and MI6, especially via their "military arm", the Knights of Malta. It should also be recalled by those who have read the literature that the Priory of Sion in its current incarnation has also proved itself to have influence in intelligence circles, aristocratic circles, and with leading figures in government and finance. In addition, their most recently-known Grand Master, Pierre Plantard has confessed that they have been "heavily infiltrated" by the Knights of Malta.

So it is possible that the influence of these groups could have touched Anthony Blunt, and they would have had every reason to try, for anyone investigating the mysteries of Poussin would naturally go to Blunt for help. Also let us not forget that Blunt was an employee of the House of Windsor, who would very well have wanted to keep unknown the sacred Davidic/Messianic origins of their rivals, the exiled Stuarts. And it is quite possible, if not probable that Blunt already had knowledge of the Poussin-Holy Grail connection, either through his own researches, or from information given to him by other intelligence agents. He had a history of belonging to secret societies, such as the Cambridge Apostles, and might have been a member of some rouge group within MI5 or the KGB that had an interest in this particular issue. Maybe that is how he got interested in Poussin in the first place. We may never know, for Blunt died not long after this visit from Henry Lincoln, and never spilled the beans. But instead, he left us wondering: What arcane mysteries was he privy to, this learned scholar, Communist revolutionary and traitor to his country? And was it worth the national disgrace he suffered just for the thrill of being a secret agent? We shall continue to wonder.

Rendezvous at Rennes-le-Chateau

By Tracy Twyman and Boyd Rice

The Languedoc region of France is a strange part of the world. It has been centuries since the Albigensian Crusade, but signs on the freeway constantly remind you that you are in "Cathar Country." A sign with a picture of a pig superimposed upon a family having a barbecue reads, "Demand pork in Cathar country – It's part of a tradition of good taste" - never mind the fact that the Cathars were strict vegetarians. Pull into a roadside shop and you can get Cathar soap, Cathar letter openers, and even Cathar. There is even a museum called "the Catharama." The Cathars may have been wiped out by the Inquisition in the thirteenth century, but they live on as a powerful source of tourism in this part of the world where seemingly nothing else of consequence has taken place in the intervening 700 years.

We had come here on behalf of Fox TV to do a segment for their updated version of "In Search Of…", the show dealing with unsolved mysteries and unexplained phenomena. Our episode of the show was about secret societies, and we had come to comment on the mystery of Rennes-le-Chateau and the Priory of Sion. It was in this village that a poor parish priest named Berenger Sauniere discovered four parchments that were to change his life, and the surrounding village, forever. Two of these parchments were genealogies of Dagobert II, the last of the Frankish dynasty of priest-kings known as the Merovingians. The other two contained ciphered messages which, when decoded, displayed the following:

The statue of Asmodeus at Sauniere's church.

"To Dagobert II, King, and to Sion belong this treasure and he is there dead."

and:

"Shepherdess - No temptation that Poussin and Teniers hold the key; Peace 681 by the cross and this horse of God I destroy this dæmon of the guardian at midday blue apples."

After finding these parchments, this once-poor parish priest became suddenly and inexplicably wealthy, perhaps because of having found some buried treasure. He started associating with members of the Parisian upper-crust occult demimonde, such as composer Claude Debussy and opera singer Emma Calve. He began redecorating his church and surrounding property in a most strange fashion, leaving behind odd clues in an effort to communicate to future generations the secret that he had learned from the parchments. These clues, many involving the use of occult, cabalistic, alchemical, Masonic, and Templar-oriented symbolism, seem to indicate the involvement of a secret society known as the Priory of Sion, who were and are dedicated to the service of the Merovingian bloodline, which they claim, contrary to popular belief, has survived until the present day. Sauniere's clues lead to the unshakable conclusion that Jesus did not die on the cross, that he fled to France with his pregnant wife, Mary Magdalene, and that his descendants intermarried with local Frankish royalty to eventually become the Merovingian dynasty. They also indicate that an artifact commonly known as the "Holy Grail" may be found there as well. These clues led us and a five-man Fox television crew out to Rennes le Chateau in October of 2000.

After a lengthy overseas flight and an unpleasant encounter with local hospitality at Charles de Gaulle airport (named after a former President of France and suspected puppet of the Priory of Sion), we were driven to a nice little hotel right next to the village of Rennes-le-Chateau, an intimate "family-style" environment heavily saturated with motifs of seashells, mermaids, busts of horses, and bad taxidermy. We got the feeling that our hosts knew a lot more about the mystery of the nearby village then they let on, a feeling that was confirmed later when we found an empty bottle of *Berenger Sauniere* brand wine - with a picture of the priest on the label - in the hotel dining room. On the very first evening, the Fox crew took us to the church grounds to scout the location. Having both studied the subject of Rennes-le-Chateau with enthusiasm for a number of years, it would be an understatement to say that our first glimpse at this mysterious property was absolutely overwhelming. We had heard Henry Lincoln talk about the "stunningly beautiful landscape" in his documentaries before, but the natural grandeur of the scenery is minusculed by the drab medium of videotape.

We pulled up next to the Tour Magdala and clamored out of the car. Immediately we noticed something that previous authors had not commented upon - a long, slender window with the bricks around it shaped like the double-barred Cross of Lorraine. Around the corner was another tiny window, and Tracy had the pleasure of climbing up the side of the tower in high-healed plastic boots in order to get a peek inside, but all she could see were some dusty old tables. On the opposite side, protected by a thick

The four elements are represented by Asmodeus (earth); the holy water stoop (water); the salamanders (fire); and the angels (air).

fortress of bramble bushes was a crude Templar-like cross patee etched into the brick, probably by some modern graffiti artist.

After that, we walked over to the Church, and for the first time laid eyes upon the "house of God" that hid so many terrible secrets. We searched for the curse that Sauniere had placed over the door, "This Place is Terrible", but unfortunately it was covered with scaffolding. No one was there, though, so Tracy took the opportunity to climb all over the grotto, which held a tiny little statue of Mary Magdalene, and which, Boyd noted, was made of coral.

The following morning, we were treated to a complete tour of the Sauniere domain by the current curator of the Church, an English lady named Jane. She was very knowledgeable about the layout and past history of the grounds, but not terribly interested in the theoretical implications of it. She delighted in telling us about all of the details that Henry Lincoln and other researchers had gotten wrong. This was not discouraging to us in the least. For every fascinating, mysterious fact that turned out to be either made up or misinterpreted, we learned or discovered half a dozen true mysterious facts that have never been noted before in the genre literature. We had read about the statement "This place is terrible" above the church door, which is a quote from *The Book of Genesis*, specifically the story in which the patriarch Jacob falls asleep on a stone and has a vision of a ladder leading up to Heaven, with angels ascending and descending upon it. This stone is the same as the Stone of Destiny brought to Scotland by the prophet Jeremiah, and it became the stone upon which British monarchs are coronated to this very today. What is noteworthy is that beneath the words "This place is terrible" on the doorway, we have the rest of the quote from *Genesis*: "This is the house of God and the gateway to Heaven." It is thus not a curse but a statement upon the dual nature of divinity. This is actually how the quote from We also found quite a bit of iconography etched over the doorway that has not been previously noted, including two Templar crosses, two Crosses of Lorraine, and the Masonic image of the "Blazing Star" which purportedly fell from the heavens to enlighten mankind.

As soon as the door was opened, we were smacked in the face with the image of a horrible, grimacing demon, which we recognized to be Asmodeus, the diabolic statue that Sauniere had placed inside the door to hold up the holy water stoop. This was the demon who, according to cabalistic tradition, was the builder of Solomon's Temple, the keeper of buried treasure, and "the destroyer", as well as "Rex Mundi", the "Lord of the Earth." Above the fountain are two fire-breathing salamanders, and above them, four ceramic statues of angels making the sign of the cross, marked with the caption "Par Ce Signe tu Vaincras" ("In this sign you will conquer"). The entire display, then, can be taken to represent a "marriage" or "crossing" of the four elements. Each element of this configuration represents one of the four primary elements of magic or alchemy. Asmodeus represents Earth; the holy water represents (of course) Water; the salamanders indicate Fire; and the angels signify

The Sun-host Grail cup depicted on the altar of Sauniere's church.

Air. Across the hall from the demon stand statues of Christ kneeling before John the Baptist, a sorrowful look on his face, waiting to be blessed. As has been previously stated, all of these statues are looking at the floor, tiled in the black and white chequerboard style used by Templars and Freemasons to symbolize the co-equal powers of light and darkness.

One noticeable variation from popular myth is that in the Station of the Cross featuring the black child wearing what has been called a "Scottish kilt" by other researchers, it appears that he is actually wearing some kind of yellow and orange grass skirt. The Station with Christ being placed inside the tomb - or perhaps, as many have claimed, being removed from the tomb - is indeed as peculiar-looking as people have said. Across from this, there are two figures of Christ, seemingly identical in representation, and placed in such close proximity to one another that one could not help but notice the seeming redundancy. Both Christs are pointing skyward with their right forefinger, and are separated by a few feet, with one situated just above the other. Closer inspection reveals that they aren't identical, despite initial appearances. The one on the bottom holds a symbol of papal authority in his left hand, and is surrounded by his chief disciples. The one above, whom the lower one points up towards, stands alone. His left hand is at his side pointing down, *ala* the Eliphas Levi etching of Baphomet. This Christ, placed as he is above the other, seems to indicate that he stands above the Christ of orthodox Christianity. And if one follows the path of his pointing finger, he seems to be pointing to a cupola affixed to the wall far above him. At the top of the cupola is the sign of the rose cross.

The "Tour Magdala", or "Tower of Magdalene."

The dual Christ-children, one held by Joseph, the other by Mary, which flank the altar, seem equally redundant. Joseph is not generally shown holding the baby Jesus. Is this a reference to Joseph's patrimony, or to Christ's reputed twin brother, Thomas? Or could it be something altogether different? Except for the inscriptions reading "St. Joseph" and "St. Virgin Mary", one could easily mistake this couple for Christ and Mary Magdalene. Is this meant to tell us that Christ and Mary had two sons, perhaps even twins? Wherever one encounters these dual sets of two, a coded story is told. Most often, the story echoes the thesis of *Holy Blood, Holy Grail*, but sometimes it hints at something more as well.

The statues of the five saints, whose initials spell out "G.R.A.A.L." (St. Germaine, St. Roch, St. Anthony d'Padoue, St. Anthony the Hermit, and St. Luke) were certainly there, in the "M" shape that has been previously described by author Gerard de Sede. This letter "M" stands for "Mary Magdalene", he says. Upon the altar we see another image of the Magdalene, kneeling in prayer before her trademark skull, and a cross made from two wooden branches, out of which is growing a live branch. This, some say, represents the bloodline of Christ living on after his death. Above this scene is a depiction of a holy chalice with a sun descending into it. The Sun is often used to represent the alchemical Philosopher's Stone, and the Grail is often depicted as a stone inside of a cup, so that is, logically, what this symbol on the altar represents. But the predominant symbol found in the church is not Christ, nor Mary Magdalene, but the rose cross. It is everywhere – above Christ, above John the Baptist, even above Asmodeus, and it is above every Station of the Cross. It is depicted both as a red Christian cross, and as an equilateral Templar-type cross with a rose at the center. The only symbol which is more prevalent than the rose cross is one not commonly found in most Catholic churches – the fleur-de-lys. The confessional is covered with stylized fleur-de-lys. Christ is crucified on a cross whose ends blossom out into fleur-de-lys. The ends of the rose crosses turn into fleur-de-lys. A series of intersecting circles on the wall are decorated with the letters "S.M." (Saint Mary), and gold fleur-de-lys. This monarchist symbol is more prevalent here than any Christian symbol, and surprisingly, no previous researchers have seen fit to comment on it. This is odd, because surely this recurring motif is intended to indicate a connection between the Grail family and French royalty, and as such would represent a strong piece of circumstantial evidence in favor of the *"Holy Blood, Holy Grail* theory." Yet it seems to have gone unnoticed.

The "calvaire" or calvary outside of the church.

We were also surprised to learn something that no one has ever before commented on, which is the fact that the church wall features the telltale marking - a yellow stripe embedded into the foundation - which was used when it was placed there in the eighth century to indicate that someone of royal blood was interred inside the church. No one knows who, but this is a rather out-of-the-way spot for the final resting place of royalty. It is strange that someone of importance was brought all the way to this obscure location, and stranger still that their name has been forgotten by history. It is yet another indication that this place was viewed to be important even in the distant past, centuries before the whole Sauniere affair.

The pews are all numbered, for the most part consecutively, except for a few anomalies. As we were ushered into the "Sauniere museum" next door, where certain relevant artifacts have been housed, we learned from our guide a little bit about this numbering system. It seems that only members of certain noble families in the area were allowed to attend this church, with the peasants being assigned to another across the way, and each attendant had an assigned seat number. These seat assignments would be changed every season, with a different section of the pews left clear each time. Our tour guide believed that these sections were being left unused because Sauniere was digging under those particular areas at the time.

We also learned that there seems to be a disagreement about which pillar Sauniere found the parchments in. One candidate, which she showed us, is a wooden pillar that is hollow with a removable piece on top. Then there is the famous "Visigothic pillar", which bears the words "MISSION 1891." In this year, the "Children of St. Vincent", a subsection of the Priory of Sion, was created. This pillar had been holding up the altar, but Sauniere had it turned upside down so that it read "1681", which is significant, since the words "Peace 681" were mysteriously mentioned in the parchments he found. Interestingly, 1891 is the same date that can be found etched next to an inscription on a rock at nearby "Lover's Fountain" that reads "E. Calve", illustrated by a heart with an arrow through it. Author Henry Lincoln believes that this is an artifact of Sauniere's love relationship with Emma Calve, but our tour guild assured us that "there is absolutely no evidence that Calve and Sauniere

The statue of Joseph, holding the Christ child.

ever knew each other!" Yet she also told us that there was no evidence for a connection between Rennes-le-Chateau and the Knights Templar, and considering the Templar imagery we had already seen, it was hard to take her dogged assertions too seriously.

Outside in the courtyard we got to see the very Visigothic pillar itself, now holding up a statue of Mary with the face painted blue, although which "Mary" is depicted (Virgin or Magdalene) may be open for debate. On top of her head is a crown made of towers. Because the name "Magdala" means "tower", we suggest that this is a statue of the Magdalene, not the Virgin. Directly across from her is placed the Calvary, on top of which is a crucified Christ, with a Sun shape behind Christ's head. It just so happens that at sundown every night, the real Sun shines directly onto the sun shape behind Christ's head and reflects onto the mirror behind the statue of Mary Magdalene. Because the Sun metaphorically represents the seed of God inseminating the Earth, we speculate that this represents the seed of Christ inseminating the Magdalene. It is on this same Calvary that we find the words (in Latin) "Christ Defend - AOMPS", which Henry Lincoln says stands for "Ancient Mystical Order of the Priory of Sion."

The statue of Mary on the opposite side of the altar, shown holding yet another Christ child.

Next, we visited the inside of the Tour Magdala (the Magdalene Tower), and walked up the twenty-two steps through the narrow stairway to the roof above with its twenty-two turrets. In the hallway, we were shown how one of the tiny square tiles on the floor was a different color from the rest, indicating that some of the treasure might be buried there. Outside, underneath the "Glass Tower" is another set of twenty-two steps leading down into a dark basement, which we were not allowed to visit, and nearby, two sets of eleven stairs each leading down into the garden. There Jane showed us a huge tunnel which someone had haphazardly dug underneath the foundation of the tower. As we made our way into the graveyard, she pointed out that on the skull and crossbones relief above the gate (a Templar and Masonic symbol, by the way), the skull has twenty-two teeth. Then, embossed onto the gate itself, we noticed another Masonic symbol: the winged hourglass, an emblem of fleeting time, and the temporary nature of our short lives. But unlike the angelic wings we usually see with this symbol, we noted that these wings were distinctly bat-like, emphasizing the demonic and infernal themes at Rennes-le-Chateau. Surrounding this symbol of mortality is an oak wreath, a symbol of eternal life.

After the tour, we broke for lunch at the nearby *Le Pomme Bleu* restaurant, named after the "Blue Apples" reference in the Sauniere parchments. We sat outside and enjoyed some *Marie de Blanchefort* brand wine while looking across the fence at the Castle of Blanchefort which stands right next door. The Blancheforts were related by blood to the Merovingians, and one of the Blancheforts had been a Grand Master of the Knights Templar at one point. Furthermore, it was the gravestone of Marie de Blanchefort, once situated in Sauniere's graveyard, that had at one time been inscribed with a coded cipher which contained the message "Et in Arcadia Ego", a phrase which relates to the Rennes-le-Chateau mystery on many levels.

Following lunch, it was time for our interviews. The actual interviews were rather restricted in scope, the subject matter limited to the details of Sauniere's life, his discovery, and his possible connection to the Priory of Sion. It was a bit frustrating, and yet even within this narrow context we were able to slip in a number of details that have seemingly escaped the notice of most researchers. For instance, many still dismiss the Priory of Sion as a mere hoax, yet it can be demonstrated that as early as the late 1940s the Priory was advocating a United Europe. Today the European Union is a reality. The emblem that the Priory suggested for a United Europe was a circle of stars – the very emblem that adorns the flag of the EU today. Is this a coincidence? The specific bloodline that the Priory was so obsessed with was that of Dagobert II and Godfroi de Bouillon – a bloodline from which numerous US Presidents have claimed descent (including the Bush family).

While it is easily conceivable that any organization could construct for themselves a false pedigree by stringing together bits and pieces of past history, it is impossible to 'fabricate' what hasn't yet happened.

Part of the interviews took place in front of the Tour Magdala, just as the Sun was going down. And guess what drunk old lady decided to pay us a visit just then? Why, none other than the daughter-in-law of Neil Corbu, the man who had bought the Sauniere property from the priest's housekeeper, Marie Deneraud. She stumbled up to us while we were getting ready to tape and slurred:

"Are you the Americans?! Yes, I'm sorry, but Martin will be absolutely unable to do an interview right now. Please understand, we've been tormented enough by reporters, who blow this story all out of proportion. It's all because of that fool Henry Lincoln! I mean, he's just a journalist! The Visigoths had nothing to do with this place! If you lived here you would know! One of you should just do a documentary that demystifies all this rubbish, because that would be really interesting! But you guys are just going to do what you want to do, I know! So I'm sorry but Martin will be absolutely unable to do an interview, and I don't think I can fit one in until tomorrow. You see, I'm very sorry but I'm just bored with the whole thing, and I don't want to talk about it...!"

On and on she continued like this for forty-five minutes without taking a breath. The group listened politely, all the while wondering who on Earth this woman was. And too, who the fuck was Martin?

Following the interviews, Jane showed us to a room that most tourists do not get to see: Sauniere's sacristy. This is where Sauniere donned his robes prior to commencing services. It was a small room that featured a stained glass window depicting Christ on the cross, and was empty but for a table, a box of old candles, and a white robe adorned with blue silk fleur-de-lys patterns. Toward the back wall was a wooden door, nailed permanently shut with an ancient rusted nail. It had been a closet, we were told, but the closet had featured a secret panel in the back that lead to Sauniere's *secret room*. Jane had no idea how long the room had been sealed off, but with a little coaxing, saw no reason why we couldn't pry out the nail and have a peek inside. So we pried out the nail, popped open the secret panel, and stepped inside Berenger Sauniere's legendary treasure room. We could not help wondering who had last come into this place, or whether any of the writers who had referred to this room had ever laid eyes upon it.

The floor of the room was dirt. Whatever floorboards were once here had long since been torn up, and the dirt was soft from digging. A pile of rubble was heaped into one corner. From ground level, one could peer beneath the floor of the sacristy, but there was little to see except cobwebs and mounds of oxidized dirt that looked as though they had not been disturbed for centuries. The room was decaying, squalid, and entirely unimpressive, and yet we could not lose sight of the fact that within this filthy cubicle with its peeling paint, a great treasure of some sort had at one time been secreted away.

Boyd also made another strange discovery while we were walking around in the graveyard. On Berenger Sauniere's gravestone there was a bas relief of him on his tombstone, but it looked like someone had chipped away at his face to make it resemble a skull. We continued walking around, and on the other side of the graveyard, Boyd found, in a pile of rocks, the missing piece of Sauniere's face! He held it up to the tombstone and it matched perfectly. If this is a clue of some sort, who left it? It is clear from the weathering on Sauniere's face, and on the missing piece itself, that this was no recent alteration. Could Sauniere himself have added this embellishment while he was still alive? There was no telling how many years this oddly-shaped piece of rock had laid at the other side of the cemetery until we happened upon it. Looking at old photos or footage of the stone bearing Sauniere's profile was no help in making a determination, because except for a few hours each day when the position of the sun cast a harsh shadow, the alteration was so subtle as to be virtually imperceptible. Any person viewing the stone in the morning or afternoon could easily never have noticed anything out of the ordinary.

Later, we visited the occult bookstore next to the church and got some really nifty stuff: medieval maps, Templar key chains, Rennes-le-Chateau cigarette lighters, a Henry Lincoln video - things of that nature   We also got to meet the mayor of Rennes-le-Chateau, who welcomed us warmly and made the peculiar remark that "This place is the center point of the world." *Center-point of the world* is a very odd choice of words. Every mythology or religious ideology has some specific geographical location they declare to be the "center-point of the world." At one time, Solomon's Temple was claimed to be such a place. Heinrich Himmler maintained that his Grail castle, the Wewelsburg, was such a spot. And of course, for Islam, Mecca is the world's center-point. Clearly, this was no ordinary small town mayor. He obviously viewed Rennes-le-Chateau not as a mere township, but as a holy place.

In our hotel that evening, we met some interesting characters. One was an old Flemish man who was convinced that he had discovered the origin of all Indo-European languages, and that it was Old Flemish. He said that this language was very similar to Old English, and thus the explanation for the global success of the modern English language. He had discovered a book which he claimed was the oldest book ever written in Europe, and the title translated to *History of Atlant*. He said that "Atlant" is the actual name of the ancient lost continent of lore, and that "Atlantis" really means "Atlantish", or somebody from Atlant. He showed us the book in question. There were indeed many recognizable words in there, and they were written in characters that were more than a little bit Runic. We inquired as to the original meaning of the word "Cathari", and he explained that it was a conjunction of "cat" and "ari." "Ari", he told us, was the same as "Aryan", meaning "noble", "lofty one", "shining one." This much we knew. So the Cathars were Aryans and Cats. Who then were the Cats? "Cats", he replied. "You know, *cats.*" One of us made a meowing sound, almost as a joke. "Yes!", he exclaimed. "Cats, as in *Cat*holic or *Cat*alonia – cats!"

We found this intriguing, since one of the most notable aspects of the village of Rennes-le-Chateau is that it is covered almost carpet-like with swarms of stray cats, which the local farm women keep well-fed, and we had wondered if these cats had been allowed to proliferate so much as a deliberate attempt at symbolism by the townspeople - one which we did not, at the time, understand. But only a week or so later, while perusing the works of Sumeriologist L.A. Waddell (a man who believes that the world's first civilization, in Sumer, was built by "Aryans") we discovered that the word "cat" came from "Kad", a title used by the kings of this first civilization. Waddell convincingly argued that this civilization had once colonized the entire globe, and had invented the world's first written language, which he compares both to Sumerian, and to Old English! Later still, we surmised that this original, global civilization was the same as the kingdom of "Atlant" that the old Flemish guy had been talking about. Everything he had said to us had been correct, and has since served as a springboard for some of our most revelatory ideas regarding the mystery of Rennes-le-Chateau. If only we had understood then what he was getting at back then, we could have questioned him in more detail.

At any rate, we had come to Rennes-le-Chateau fully confident that we would discover much that had escaped the scrutiny of previous researchers, and indeed we had. Far too much, in fact, to fit within the confines of this short essay. The bits and pieces we have detailed here represent a small fraction of what we found at Rennes-le-Chateau, the proverbial tip of the iceberg. Not only did Rennes-le-Chateau live up to our expectations, it far exceeded them. And in so doing, the place has become for us (as for the mayor) the center point of the world.

The Merovingian Mythos, Its Symbolic Significance, and its Roots in the Ancient Kingdom of Atlantis

By Tracy R. Twyman

The Frankish King Dagobert II, and the Merovingian dynasty from which he came, have been romantically mythologized in the annals of both local legend and modern mystical pseudo-history, but few have understood the true meaning and origins of their alluring mystery. The mystique that surrounds them includes attributions of saintliness, magical powers (derived from their long hair), and even divine origin, because of their supposed descent from the one and only Jesus Christ. However, the importance of the divine ancestry of the Merovingians, and the antiquity from whence it comes, has never to this author's knowledge been fully explored by any writer or historian. However, I have uncovered mountains of evidence which indicates that the origins of the Merovingian race, and the mystery that surrounds them, lies ultimately with a race of beings, "Nephilim" or fallen angels, who created mankind as we know it today. It also originated with a civilization, far more ancient than recorded history, from which came all of the major arts and sciences that are basic to civilizations everywhere. As I intend to show, all of the myths and symbolism that are associated with this dynasty can, in fact, be traced back to this earlier civilization. It is known, in some cultures, as Atlantis, although there are many names for it, and it is the birthplace of agriculture, astronomy, mathematics, metallurgy, navigation, architecture, language, writing, and religion. It was also the source of the first government on Earth - monarchy. And the first kings on Earth were the gods.

Their race was known by various names. In Assyria, the Annodoti. In Sumeria, The Annunaki. In Druidic lore, the Tuatha de Danaan. In Judeo-Christian scriptures, they are called the Nephilim, "the Sons of God", or the Watchers. They are described as having attachments such as wings, horns, and even fish scales, but from the depictions it is clear that these are costumes worn for their symbolic value, for these symbols indicated divine power and royal blood. The gods themselves had their own monarchy, with laws of succession similar to our own, and they built a global empire upon the Earth, with great cities, temples, monuments, and mighty nations established on several continents. Man was separate from the gods, like a domesticated animal, and there was a great cultural taboo amongst the gods against sharing any of their sacred information with humanity, even things such as writing and mathematics. These gods ruled directly over Egypt, Mesopotamia, and the Indus Valley, and their rule is recorded in the histories of all three civilizations.

This global monarchy was the crowning glory of the ages, and the period of their rule came to be called "the Golden Age", or as the Egyptians called it, "the First Time", when the gods watched over man directly, like a shepherd does his flock. In fact, they were often called "the Shepherd Kings." One of the symbols of this world monarchy was an eye hovering over a throne, and this eye now adorns our American dollar bill, presented as the missing capstone of the Great Pyramid of Giza, underneath which are written the words "New World Order." Clearly this New World Order is the global monarchy that or Founding Fathers (not a Democrat among them) intended for this nation to participate in all along, symbolized by a pyramid as a representation of the ideal and perfectly ordered authoritarian empire. During the Golden Age of the gods, a new king's ascendance to the global throne would be celebrated by the sacrifice of a horse, an animal sacred to Poseidon, one of the Atlantean god-kings and Lord of the Seas. [1]   In fact there is an amusing story about how King Sargon's rebellious son Sagara tried to prevent his father's assumption to the world throne from being solidified by stealing his sacrificial horse. The horse was not recovered until years later, and Sagara, along with the "sons of Sagara", i.e., those members of his family who had assisted him, were forced to dig their own mass grave. This grave was oddly called "the Ocean."

It was a rebellion such as this that led to the downfall of the entire glorious empire. At some point, it is told, some of the gods broke rank. This is again recorded in just about every culture on Earth that has a written history or oral tradition. Some of the gods, finding human females most appealing, intermarried with them, breaking a major taboo within their own culture, and creating a race of human/god hybrids. Some of these offspring are described as taking the form of giants, dragons, and sea monsters, while others are said to have borne a normal human countenance, with the exception of their shimmering white skin and their extremely long life spans. This is the bloodline that brought us Noah, Abraham, Isaac, Jacob, King David, Jesus Christ, and many others - in other words, the "Grail bloodline." Legend has it that these beings taught mankind their secrets, including the above-mentioned arts of civilization, as well as a secret spiritual doctrine that only certain elect humans (their blood descendants) would be allowed to possess. They created ritualistic mystery schools and secret societies to pass this doctrine down through the generations.

However, these actions (the interbreeding with and sharing of secrets with humans) incurred the wrath of the Most High God, and a number of other gods who were disgusted by this interracial breeding. This sparked the massive and devastating battle of the gods that has come down to us in the legend of the "war in Heaven." Then, in order to cleanse the Earth's surface of the curse of humanity, they covered it with a flood.

Interestingly, this flood is mentioned in the legends of almost every ancient culture on Earth, and the cause is always the same. Often the waters are described as having come from *inside* the Earth. "The Fountains of the deep were opened", it is said. "Suddenly enormous volumes of water issued from the Earth." Water was "projected from the mountain like a water spout." The Earth began to rumble, and Atlantis, fair nation of the gods, sunk beneath the salty green waves. As we shall see, this is analogous to part of the "war in Heaven" story when the "rebellious" angels or gods were punished by being cast down "into the bowels of the Earth" - a very significant location.

To be certain, some of the Atlanteans managed to survive, and many books have been written about the Atlantean origin of the Egyptian, Sumerian, Indo-Aryan, and native South American civilizations (bringing into question the validity of the term "Native American"). Little, however, has been written about those who escaped into Western Europe, except for a passing reference in Ignatius Donnelly's *Atlantis: The Antediluvian World*, in which we writes:

"The Gauls [meaning the French] possessed traditions upon the subject of Atlantis which were collected by the Roman historian Timagenes, who lived in the first century before Christ. He represents that three distinct people dwelt in Gaul: 1. The indigenous population, which I suppose to be Mongoloids, who had long dwelt in Europe; 2. the invaders from a distant land, which I understand to be Atlantis; 3. The Aryan Gaul."

That the Merovingian bloodline came from elsewhere is clear because of the legend that surrounds their founder, King Meroveus, who is said to have been the spawn of a "Quinotaur" (a sea monster), who raped his mother when she went out to swim in the ocean. Now it becomes obvious why he is called "Meroveus", because in French, the word "mer" means sea. And in some traditions, Atlantis was called Meru, or Maru. [2] For these gods, navigation above all was important to them, for it was their sea power that maintained their military might and their successful mercantile trade. [3] The Atlanteans were associated with the sea and were often depicted as mermen, or sea monsters, with scales, fins, and horns. They were variously associated with a number of important animals, whose symbolism they held sacred: horses, bulls, goats, rams, lions, fish, serpents, dragons, even cats and dogs. All of these things relate back to the sea imagery with which these gods were associated.

Now lets go back to the Quinotaur, which some have named as being synonymous with Poseidon, the Greek god of the sea and, according to Plato, one of the famous kings of Atlantis. Others have seen it as being emblematic of the fish symbol that Christ is associated with, thus indicating that he was in fact the origin of the Merovingian bloodline. However, the roots of this Quinotaur myth are far more ancient. The word itself can be broken down etymologically to reveal its meaning. The last syllable, "taur", means "bull." The first syllable "Quin", or "Kin", comes from the same root as "king", as well as the Biblical name of Cain, whom many have named as the primordial father of the Grail family. [4] The idea of the "King of the World" taking the form of a sea-bull was a recurring them in many ancient cultures, most notably in ancient Mesopotamia. In fact it originated with that dynasty of kings who reigned over the antediluvian world and who were all associated with the sea, as well as this divine animal imagery. These kings included Sargon, Menes, and Narmar. Their historical reality morphed into the legends we have in many cultures of gods said to have come out of the sea at various times and to teach mankind the basic arts of civilization. They were known by various names, such as Enki, Dagon, Oannes, or Marduk (Merodach). They were depicted as half-man and half-fish, half-goat and half-fish, or half-bull and half-fish, but as I have said, in many of these depictions it is clear that this affect was achieved merely by the wearing of costumes, and that these god-kings were using this archetypal imagery to deify themselves in the minds of their subjects.

Dagon was depicted with a fish on his head, the lips protruding upward, making what were referred to as "horns." This may be the origin for the custom (common in the ancient world) of affixing horns to the crown of a king. It has also been historically acknowledged as the origin of the miter worn by the Catholic Pope. [5] The Christian Church has always been associated with fish. Christ himself took on that imagery, as did John the Baptist, and the early Christians used the fish sign of the "Ichthys" to designate themselves. From the name "Oannes" we get the words "Uranus" and "Ouranos", but also supposedly "Jonah", "Janus", and "John." Perhaps we finally now understand why the Grand Masters of the Priory of Sion assume the symbolic name of "John" upon taking office.

The syllable "dag" merely means "fish", which makes it interesting to note that the Dogon tribe of Africa, who have long baffled astronomers with their advanced knowledge of the faraway star-system from which they say their gods came, claim that these gods were "fish-men." We may wonder if the words "dag" and "dog" are not etymologically related, especially since the star from whence these fish-men supposedly came is named Sirius, "the Dog Star." From Dagon comes our word "dragon", as well as the biblical figure of Leviathan, "the Lord of the Deep", a title also applied to Dagon. In fact, many of these Atlantean god-kings received the titles "the Lord of the Waters", "The Lord of the Deep", or "the Lord of the Abyss", which appear to have been passed down from father to son, along with the throne of the global kingdom. These kings were specifically associated with the Flood of Noah, which, as I have mentioned, destroyed their global kingdom, and was somehow linked to their disastrous breeding experiment with the human race that lead to the "Grail bloodline." For this they were consigned to the "Abyss" or the underworld, which is why these gods were known as the lords of both.

In addition, Enki was known as the "Lord of the Earth", and it is because of this "amphibious" nature of their progenitor, who reigned over both land and sea, that the Merovingians are associated with frogs. But this "Lord of the Earth" title is significant, for this is a title also given to Satan. It has been acknowledged elsewhere that Enki, as the "fish-goat man", is the prototype for the Zodiac sign of Capricorn, which is itself recognized as the prototype for the modern conception of Satan or Lucifer. Furthermore, a well-known and pivotal episode in Enki's career was his fight against his brother Enlil over the succession of the global throne. Enki eventually slew Enlil, something that is recorded in the Egyptian myth of Set murdering Osiris, and perhaps in the Biblical story of Cain murdering Abel. The connection between Enki and Enlil and Cain and Abel can be further proven by the fact that Enki and Enlil were the son of Anu (in some Sumerian legends, the first god-king on Earth), whereas Cain and Abel were the sons of the first man, called "Adamu" in Sumerian legends. "Adamu" and "Anu" appear to be etymologically related.

This family feud erupted into a long and overdrawn battle between the gods, who were split into two factions over the issue. These appear to be the same two factions who were at odds over the mating of gods and men to create the Grail bloodline. Those who supported Enki/Satan and Cain were clearly the ones who were inclined to breed with mankind, perhaps in an attempt to create a hybrid race that could assist them in retaining the throne for Cain. But they were overpowered. After they lost the "war in Heaven", they were cast into the Abyss (according to legend, now the realm of Satan), and the Earth was flooded so as to rid it of their offspring.

Yet according to the legends, those gods who had created the hybrid race contacted one of their most favored descendants (called Uta-Napishtim in the Sumerian legends, or Noah in the Jewish), helping him to rescue himself and his family, preserving the seed of hybrid humanity. [6] We see remnants of this in the Vedic legends of the Flood, in which the Noah figure, here called "Manu", is warned about the Flood by a horned fish (who turns out to be the Hindu god Vishnu in disguise). The fish tells Manu to build a ship, and then tie its tip to his horn. He then proceeds to tow Manu's ship to safety upon a high mountain. So clearly Vishnu is connected to Enki, Dagon, and Oannes, and clearly he is the same one who saved Noah from the Flood. Yet this very deed became attributed, in the Old Testament, to the same god, Jehovah, who had purportedly caused the Flood to begin with. In fact the word Jehovah, or "Jah" is said to have evolved from the name of another Sumerian sea god-king, Ea, "the Lord of the Flood." Likewise, Leviathan is responsible, according to some references, for "vomiting out the waters of the Flood." This occurs at the Apocalypse in the *Revelation of St. John the Divine* as well. Leviathan, like many of these sea gods, was the Lord of the Abyss, and these waters were believed to be holding the Earth up from underneath, in the regions of Hell. Yet "Leviathan" is almost surely etymologically related to the Jewish name "Levi", and therefore to the "tribe of Levi", the priestly caste of the Jews that formed part of Christ's lineage.

This dual current, being associated with both the heavenly and the infernal, with both Jesus and Jehovah, as well as Satan and Lucifer, is something that is consistently found throughout the history of the Merovingian dynasty, as well as all of the other Grail families, and the entire Grail story itself. It is at the heart of the secret spiritual doctrine symbolized by the Grail. This symbolism hits you immediately when you walk through the door of the church at Rennes-le-Chateau, France, and see those opposing statues of the demon Asmodeus and Jesus Christ staring at the same black and white chequered floor, which itself symbolizes the balance of good and evil. This principle is further elucidated by the words placed over the doorway, "This place is terrible, but it is the House of God and the Gateway to Heaven." This phrase turns up in two significant places. One is in the Bible, when Jacob has his vision of the ladder leading to Heaven, with angels ascending and descending. The other is in *The Book of Enoch*, when Enoch is taken for a tour of Hell. The existence of this phrase at the entrance to the church, coupled with the images that meet you immediately therein, render the meaning obvious. For Berenger Sauniere, who arranged these strange decorations, this Church represented some kind of metaphysical gateway between Heaven *and* Hell.

For this reason, the double-barred Cross of Lorraine, symbolizing this duality, has come to be associated with the Merovingians. In a now famous poem by Charles Peguy, is it stated:

"The arms of Jesus are the Cross of Lorraine,
Both the blood in the artery and the blood in the vein,
Both the source of grace and the clear fountaine;

The arms of Satan are the Cross of Lorraine,

*And the same artery and the same vein,
And the same blood and the troubled fountaine."*

The reference to Satan and Jesus sharing the same blood is very important. A tradition exists, one which finds support among *The Book of Enoch* and many others, that Jesus and Satan are brothers, both sons of the Most High God, and they both sat next to his throne in Heaven, on the right and left sides, respectively, prior to Satan's rebellion and the War in Heaven. This may be just another version of the persistent and primordial "Cain and Abel" story. It makes sense that Satan should be a direct son of God, since he is described as God's "most beloved angel" and "the brightest star in Heaven." [7]

However, this symbol is far older than the modern conceptions of Christ and Satan, or Lucifer. This symbol can be traced back to the hieroglyphs of ancient Sumer, where it was pronounced "Khat", "Kad", and sometimes even "Kod." This was another title for the kings who were known as gods of the sea, and the word "Khatti" became associated with this entire race. Their region's capitol was called "Amarru" - "the Land to the West" (like Meru, the alternate term for Atlantis). This land was symbolized by a lion, which may explain the origin of the word "cat", as well as why the lion is now a symbol of royalty. Furthermore, the word "cad" or "cod" has also become associated with fish and sea creatures in the Indo-European language system. [8] I would argue that this was at the root of the word "Cathari" (the heretics associated with the Holy Grail who occupied the Languedoc region of France that the Merovingians ruled over), as well as Adam *Kad*mon, the Primordial Man of alchemy, and "*Cad*uceus", the winged staff of Mercury. It is also the root for the name of the Mesopotamian kingdom of "Akkadia", which itself has morphed into "Arcadia", the Greek concept of Paradise. This further morphs into "acacia", the traditional Masonic "sprig of hope" and symbol of resurrection after death.

Perhaps this sheds further light on the phrase "Et in Arcadia Ego", which pops up more than once in association with the mystery of Rennes-le-Chateau and the Merovingians. This phrase was illustrated by Nicolas Poussin with the scene of a tomb, a human skull, and three shepherds. The tomb and skull clearly represent death, while the Sprig of Acacia implied by the word "Arcadia" translates to "resurrection from death." The shepherds, furthermore, represent the divine kingship of the Atlantean gods and the Grail bloodline, for these god-monarchs were also known as the "Shepherd Kings" (a title, notably, taken up by Jesus as well). This indicates that it is the global monarchy of these Atlantean gods that shall rise again from the tomb, perhaps through the Merovingian bloodline.

This archetype of the fallen king who shall one day return, or the kingdom that disappears, only to rise again in a new, golden age, is a very common one, and one that I have shown in another article to be integral to the Grail legend. It was also one used quite effectively by the last of the Merovingian kings who effectively held the throne of the Austrasian Empire - this magazine's mascot, Dagobert II. Dagobert's entire life, as historically recorded, is mythological and archetypal. His name betrays the divine origins of his bloodline. "Dagobert" comes, of course, from Dagon. Now the word "bert", as the author L.A. Waddell has shown, has its roots in the word "bara", or "para", or Anglicized, "pharaoh", a "priest-king of the temple (or house)." So Dagobert's name literally means "Priest-King of the House of Dagon." Interestingly, a rarely-found but nonetheless authentic variation on Dagobert's name was "Dragobert", emphasizing his lineage from the beast of the deep waters, the dragon Leviathan.

Dagobert made use of the myth of the returning king early on in life. His father had been assassinated when he was five years old, and young Dagobert was kidnapped by then Palace Mayor Grimoald, who tried to put his own son on the throne. He was saved from death, but an elaborate ruse was laid out to make people think otherwise. Even his own mother believed he was dead, and allowed his father's assassins to take over, placing Grimoald's son on the throne. Dagobert was exiled to Ireland, where he lay in wait for the opportunity to reclaim his father's throne. This opportunity showed itself in the year 671, when he married Giselle de Razes, daughter of the count of Razes and niece of the king of the Visigoths, allying the Merovingian house with the

Visigothic royal house. This had the potential for creating a united empire that would have covered most of what is now modern France. This marriage was celebrated at the Church of St. Madeleine in Rhedae, the same spot where Sauniere's Church of St. Madeleine at Rennes-le-Chateau now rests. There is an existing rumor that Dagobert found something there, a clue which lead him to a treasure buried in the nearby Montsegur, and this treasure financed what was about to come. This was the re-conquest of the Aquitaine and the throne of the Frankish kingdom. As Baigent, et. al write in *Holy Blood, Holy Grail*, "At once he set about asserting and consolidating his authority, taming the anarchy that prevailed throughout Austrasia and reestablishing order." The fallen king had risen from his ashes, born anew as Dagobert II, and had come to once more establish firm rule and equilibrium in his country. The similarities to the Parzival/Grail story don't even need to be repeated.

Sadly, Dagobert II would himself play the role of the fallen king just a few years later, in 679, and the circumstances were decidedly strange. You see, since the time of King Clovis I, the Merovingian kings had been under a pact with the Vatican, in which they had pledged their allegiance to the Mother Church in exchange for Papal backing of the their united empire of Austrasia. They would forever hold the title of "New Constantine", a title that would later morph into "Holy Roman Emperor." But that "allegiance" on the part of the Merovingians towards the Church began to wear thin after a while. Obviously, given their infernal and divine origin, their spiritual bent was slightly different from that of organized Christianity. In addition, as direct descendants of the historical Christ himself, they would have possessed access to the secret teachings of Christ, no doubt shockingly different from the ones promoted by the Church, and reflecting more of the "secret doctrine" of the rebellious gods that I have talked about in this article. Any public knowledge of this or the blood relationship between Christ and the Merovingians would have been disastrous for the Church. Christ would therefore be a man, with antecedents and descendants, instead of the "son of God, born of a virgin" concept promoted by the Church. Seeing in Dagobert a potential threat, the Roman church entered into a conspiracy with Palace Mayor Pepin the Fat.

On December 23, while on a hunting trip, Dagobert was lanced through the left eye by his own godson, supposedly on Pepin's orders. There are many aspects to this event that appear to be mythologically significant. For one thing, it took place in the "Forest of Woevres", long held sacred, and host to annual sacrificial bear hunts for the Goddess Diana. Indeed, the murder may have taken place on such a hunt. This was near the royal Merovingian residence at Stenay, a town that used to be called "Satanicum." We must also consider the date itself, which was almost precisely at the beginning of the astrological period of Capricorn. As I have mentioned, Capricorn is based on Enki, and is thus connected to the Quinotaur that spawned the Merovingian bloodline. It is also close to the Winter Solstice, the shortest day in the year, when the Sun was said to "die", mythologically, and turn black, descending into the underworld. This "black" period of the Sun is associated with the god Kronos or Saturn, another horned sea-god, ruler of the underworld, and king of Atlantis who figures repeatedly in this Grail/Rennes-le-Chateau mystery. [9] Secondly, the murder is said to take place at midday, which, as I have mentioned in another article, is an extremely significant moment in time for mystery schools of the secret doctrine, like Freemasonry. The parchments found by Berenger Sauniere and the related poem, *Le Serpent Rouge* makes a special mention of it. This is when the Sun is highest in the sky. The fact that Dagobert's murder was committed by a family member is significant too. This is similar to the "Dolorous Stroke" that wounds the Fisher King in the Grail story, something which also took place at midday and was inflicted by the king's own brother. In this story, the brother who wounds the Fisher King is known as the "Dark Lord", and during the fight he is wounded in the left eye, precisely as Dagobert was wounded. The same thing happened to Horus in Egyptian mythology, fighting his uncle, Set. The "Left Eye of Horus" came to symbolize the hidden knowledge of the gods, just as the "left hand path" does today. Dagobert's death appears to follow the same patterns as many other fallen kings or murdered gods whose death must be avenged. It is meant to symbolize the concept of the lost or fallen kingdom the same way the Dolorous Stroke does in the Grail story.

Clearly, Dagobert's death meant the end for the Merovingian kingdom. All subsequent Merovingian kings were essentially powerless, and they were officially thought to have died out with Dagobert's grandson, Childeric III. 49 years later, Charles Martel's grandson, Charlemagne was anointed Holy Roman Emperor. But in 872, almost 200 years after his death, Dagobert was canonized as a Saint, and the date of his death, December 23, became "St. Dagobert's Day." Write Baigent, et. al.:

"The reason for Dagobert's canonization remains unclear. According to one source it was because his relics were believed to have preserved the vicinity of Stenay against Viking raids - though this explanation begs the question, for it is not clear why the relics should have possessed such powers is the first place. Ecclesiastical authorities seem embarrassingly ignorant on the matter. They admit that Dagobert, for some reason, became the object of a fully fledged cult... But they seem utterly at a loss as to why he should have been so exalted. It is possible, of course that the Church felt guilty about its role in the king's death."

Guilty, or afraid? For surely they knew that this "Priest-King of the House of Dagon", with his divine lineage, so beloved by his people that they worship him like a god 200 years later, would of course be avenged for his treacherous murder. Surely they knew, as most *Dagobert's Revenge* readers know, that the Merovingian bloodline didn't die out, surviving through his son Sigisbert, and continues to jockey for the throne of France to this very day through the actions of various royal bloodlines throughout Europe. Surely they knew that this kingdom would rise again, and that the lost king would return someday. The seeds of his return have already been planted. France is united into the political mass that Dagobert had envisioned it to be when he united Austrasia, and the "Holy Roman Empire", which the Merovingian kings were clearly attempting to form with the help of the Vatican, has now become a reality in the form of the European Union. During WWII and immediately afterwards, the Priory of Sion, that secret order dedicated to the Merovingian agenda, openly campaigned for a United States of Europe. They even proposed a flag, consisting of stars in a circle, which is identical to the flag used by the European Union today. [10] Furthermore, the world empire of the Atlantean kings who spawned the Merovingians is more complete now than it has ever been since the gods left the earth during the Deluge. The United Nations, a feeble example, will surely give way at some point to a united world government strong enough and glorious enough to be called an empire. The fallen kingdom of the gods is clearly returning, and the new Golden Age is upon us. If this author's hunch is correct, this is, indeed, a glorious time to be alive.

Endnotes:

[1] Recall that Merovingian King Clovis was buried with a severed horse's head.

[2] It is also the name of the famous "world mountain" of Eastern tradition.

[3] Note that "mer" is also the origin of the word "mercantile."

[4] Cain's name has been said to be the origin of the word "king"

[5] Now we understand why, in the post-mortem photo of Berenger Sauniere lying on his death bed, this small parish priest is seen next to a bishop's miter.

[6] Uta-Napishtim contains the Sumerian and Egyptian word for fish, "pish", and perhaps we can see why some authors have claimed that the character of Noah is in fact based on Oannes, Dagon, or Enki as well.

[7] *The Book of Enoch* refers to the Watchers, or Nephilim, as "stars", with various "watchtowers" in the houses of the Zodiac. Bear in mind that the ancients saw the sky above as a giant "sea", the waters of which were kept at bay by the "Firmament of Heaven" - that is, until the Flood.

[8] At this writing, a large sea serpent 20 meters long has just been discovered off the coast of Canada named "Cadborosaurus Willsi", nicknamed "Caddy."

[9] Kronos or Saturn is the inspiration for the figures of Capricorn and the Judeo-Christian Satan.

[10] This flag was shown carried by a divine white horse, a symbol of Poseidon and world monarchy.

The Cross of Lorraine: Emblem of the Royal Secret

By Boyd Rice

When various members of the House of Anjou plotted to topple the Valois dynasty of France, the symbol of the conspirators was the Cross of Lorraine, the heraldic emblem of René d'Anjou, said by Charles Peguy to represent the "arms of Christ", "the arms of Satan", and, strangely, the blood of both. René was the Angevin monarch who, at the time of the renaissance, single-handedly spearheaded a Hermetic revival in Europe. It was he who personally convinced Cosimo de Medici to translate many ancient texts such as the *Corpus Hermeticum* into various European tongues for the first time ever. And when *Corpus Hermeticum* was first published in France, the dedication it bore was to Marie de Guise, wife of James Stuart V, mother of Mary Queen of Scots, and a descendant of René who also adopted the Cross of Lorraine as a personal symbol.

That the Cross of Lorraine is a symbol embodying the Hermetic ideal is fairly obvious. The Angevins were primarily advocates of the "Regia", or Royal Art, of Hermeticism; a tradition which according to legend was passed down to man by a race of fallen angels. This isn't at all inconsistent with the perennially Luciferian overtones associated with the entire Angevin saga.

Interestingly, the Cross of Lorraine bears an uncanny resemblance to the sigil of Baphomet employed by British Magus Aleister Crowley, and the meaning of the two symbols would appear to be virtually synonymous.[1] Baphomet is, after all, the penultimate Hermetic symbol, whether depicted by Crowley in the form of a cross, or by Eliphas Levi as a goat-headed hermaphrodite. And the sigil used by Crowley was also employed by ancient alchemists as a device whose meaning was literally "very poisonous." In fact, the symbol was commonly affixed to containers of toxic substances in Europe as recently as the mid-twentieth century. To the alchemists, of course, the symbol and its very meaning had far more esoteric connotations. To them, poison represented an agent of transformation, a vehicle for the reconciliation of opposites. And there is an alchemical myth about a poison which for most men is extremely deadly, while for the elect it confers mastership and absolute power. Echoes of this idea recur as a motif in various aspects of the Grail lore. It would seem that the alchemists accorded this symbol very much the same meaning attributed it by Crowley, which in turn echoes what the Cross of Lorraine embodied for Rene d'Anjou. It is little known, but the Cross of Lorraine was also the official emblem of the Knights Templar.

Though they are more frequently associated with the symbol of the red equilateral cross, their true symbol first and foremost was the Cross of Lorraine, and many Templars awaiting death at the stake pursuant to the Friday the 13th persecutions drew the emblem on the walls of their cells. There is still a degree in certain rites of Freemasonry called the Knights Templar, whose symbol is the Cross of Lorraine.[2] It is interesting to note that even the less esoteric-looking equilateral cross used by the Templars had essentially the same meaning: that of the union of opposites, the intersection of creative force and destructive force, or the union of male and female principles. It was a fundamental occult symbol, and it was in deference to the idea which it embodied that medieval occult rituals were often held at crossroads.

The Cross of Lorraine is far more explicit in its iconography: the bar above mirroring the bar below, both of which are symmetrically affixed to a central pillar that provides balance and equilibrium. As above, so below is, after all, a Hermetic maxim. And the three bars of which the cross is composed echo Eliphas Levi's concept of the true trinity. Levi posited that the world is governed by two primordial forces, one creative, the other destructive. The equilibrium between these two forces constitutes a third force, and the union of the three constitutes what some might refer to as... God.

The central role of the principle of equilibrium in various occult arts cannot be overstressed. For Master Mason Albert Pike, equilibrium represented the Royal Secret, the pivotal principle upon which the universe is ordered. And Pike's specific designation of equilibrium as a royal secret is of particular significance because, as previously mentioned, Hermeticism has traditionally been known as the "Royal Art", and its central tenet is essentially that of equilibrium. And too, when Pike calls it a royal secret, he isn't speaking figuratively, but strictly in literal terms. Hermes, according to legend, was the sole receptacle of the secret doctrine of the antediluvian world, which he revived after the flood and passed down to the kings. As you'll recall, this secret knowledge was thought to have been taught to man by a race of gods or fallen angels. This knowledge was kept secret because it was probably recognized that for all but an elect few, such thought would no doubt bring about their ruin. This brings to mind the concept of the alchemical poison. Kings and aristocrats would understand how to wield and apply the secret doctrine because it was believed that they were in fact flesh and blood descendants of the Forgotten Race which had come down to take the daughters of men.

References to this Forgotten Race occur repeatedly in numerous religions and mythologies throughout the world, and should most likely be known to readers of this magazine. Their doctrines have been enshrined in myth, legend, and many religious symbols, in which they are looked upon by many, and recognized by but a few. They are, and shall remain, the Royal Secret. The Cross of Lorraine is a sigil of that Royal Secret, the doctrine of the Forgotten Ones.

Endnotes

[1] Editor's note: It is uncertain how "uncanny" this resemblance is, as the Cross of Lorraine has two bars, and the Sigil of Baphomet has three. They look as much alike as any two crosses would.

[2] Editor's note: The degree of Freemasonry associated with the Cross of Lorraine is actually the thirty-third degree of the Scottish Rite, while the "Knights Templar" degree is completely separate, a part of the York Rite of Freemasonry.

Lucifer's Children:
The Grail Bloodline and the Descendants of Cain

By Boyd Rice

Conventional wisdom has it that the Grail bloodline is sacred because it came from Christ, a man still considered by much of the world to be the true son of God. And yet the dynasty of kings who descended from this bloodline were known as sorcerer-kings, some of whom hinted or even stated outright that they were in fact descendants of Lucifer. A number of authors claim this thesis is true, but they are predominantly hardcore Christian conspiracy theorists, and stop well short of explaining why they believe this, or of giving any tangible details to substantiate their claims. Says one: "In typical Gnostic fashion, descendants of the Merovingians claim to have the blood of both Christ *and* Satan in their veins." Given the fact that this theme (or a variation of it) recurs with some regularity, and given that it would appear to be consistent with the sort of dual vibe which permeates the saga of this bloodline, I began to wonder if there might not be some traditions from which such a notion could have arisen. At length, several were discovered.

Firstly, let's remember that this bloodline descended from a figure who equates with the Biblical Cain. In certain rabbinic lore, we come across the very interesting notion that Cain was not the son of Adam, but of Samael. It was thought that when Samael appeared to Eve as a serpent, he seduced her. The fruit of that union was Cain. Now Samael was a fallen angel, essentially the Judaic Lucifer. If the Merovingians knew of this version of the story (which they no doubt did), and believed it, it could be the basis of their alleged assertion that they possessed the blood of both Christ and Lucifer.

An alternate version of the Cain saga, equally Luciferian in its connotations, says that he was the son of Adam's first wife, Lilith. She had been the consort of God before coming to Earth as a fallen angel. The full details of her story are probably too well-known to bear repeating here, but it's interesting that of the two alternate traditions concerning Cain's parentage, both involve the Luciferian Nephilim bloodline. Also of interest is the fact that the lily is known to have taken its name from "Lilith", and the heraldic device emblematic of this bloodline is the fleur-de-lys (widely accepted as symbolic of the lily.) Could not this symbol, viewed within this context, in fact be the "Flower of Lilith"?

The Lilith/Samael connection is also pertinent in regard to the Grail saga insofar as the two have a son of their own who seems to play a recurring role in the whole mythos: Asmodeus. Not only is Asmodeus the dominant image (shown mirroring Christ) in Rennes-le-Chateau, he is said to have played the central role in building the Temple of Solomon, the edifice from which the Knights Templar took their name. The recurrence of this strange figure in Grail lore has long perplexed observers, yet it would appear that both he and the descendants of Cain may in fact have shared a kindred ancestry. It is even said in some traditions that it was Asmodeus whom Moses called upon to part the Red Sea, and not God. Though portrayed as a demon or devil figure, his name reveals that he may not always have been viewed as such, for Asmodeus translates simply to the Lord God (Ashma = Lord, and Deus = God).

Another possible genesis of the idea of a Luciferian bloodline may have come from the Elohim, who in the Bible say: "Let *us* make man in *our* image." Elohim is generally thought to be a plural of God, or to be "the gods." But it is also widely believed to denote the Nephilim, the fallen angels known as the Watchers in *The Book of Enoch*. It is believed that the word "Elohim" comes from the much more ancient Babylonian word "Ellu", which means "Shining Ones." This phrase has a distinctively Luciferian connotation, because the name "Lucifer" literally means "light bearer." And the descendants of Cain, who were the deified kings of Sumeria, bore the title of "Ari", a term which also meant "Shining Ones." The Sumerian pictogram for "Ari" is an inverted pentagram, a symbol long associated with Lucifer. And the phrase "Shining Ones" would be a very apt description for the descendants of Enoch's fallen angels, who were said to have hair white as snow, pale eyes, and pale skin which seemed literally to glow and fill the room with light. The Sumerian Ari are almost always depicted as wearing crowns bearing horns, and some of their descendants were said actually to have *had* horns. For instance, the most famous statue of Moses (that of Michelangelo) depicts him with horns atop his forehead, not wholly inappropriate for someone who may be a blood relation of Asmodeus. Theologians protest that they are not horns, merely rays of light. But even rays of light suggest a Luciferian subtext. Alexander the Great declared himself the son of God, and he too was said to have horns. In fact, to this very day, if you talk to people on the streets of Iran (who remember his invasion as though it happened last week), they will tell you in all solemnity that it's a historical fact that Alexander had horns, which he wore his hair long to cover up.

In closing, we note the fact that Cain seems to have engendered his own tradition, as evidenced in a strange Gnostic sect called the Cainites. Like the Carpocrateans, the Cainites believed that no one could be saved except by "making the journey through everything." Epiphanius describes them as a group "consecrating... lustful or illegal acts to various heavenly beings" as a sort of sacrament. Interestingly, many scholars compare them to... *Satanists*.

The extent to which the Merovingians knew of these alternate traditions is uncertain. Whether or not they believed in them is more uncertain still, yet it remains likely that they both knew about these traditions and took them quite seriously. To this very day, the coat of arms of the capital of the Merovingian empire, Stenay, bears an image of the Devil. And the original name of Stenay was "Satanicum."

The Real Tomb of Gods The Grail, the Ark, the Emerald Tablet, and the Forgotten Father of Mankind

By Tracy R. Twyman

The mythology surrounding Christian Rosenkreutz, the legendary namesake of the Rosicrucian Brotherhood, may provide us with clues as to the location of the Emerald Tablet of Hermes, upon which their Hermetic wisdom is based, as well as the famed relic of the Holy Grail which this magazine is largely about. It may also shed some light on the mythological importance of the so-called "Hollow Earth" theory, and tell us the location of the body of a dead god or king. In question: the location of Rosenkreutz's tomb. He is said to have died at the age of 106, in the year 1484, and was buried in a secret vault, deep in a cave inside of a mountain, which was "lit by an inner (or artificial) sun." The location of this tomb was kept secret, until 120 years later, when it was discovered by a group of Rosicrucian brethren. Here they found a cache of sacred mystery writings, which became the core wisdom of their order. And yet, their wisdom is said to be based on the Emerald Tablet of Hermes, begging the question of whether or not it was in fact the Emerald Tablet that they found. They also found the body of their master, "pure and unconsumed", his flesh having not decomposed one bit, but appearing to be made of candle wax. With the discovery of the tomb and the sacred mystery writings, the Rosicrucian brotherhood, having been ostensibly dead since the demise of their leader 120 years previously, was born anew, and the brethren who made the discovery took off to spread the news to all the corners of the Earth.

As Christopher McIntosh points out in his book *The Rosicrucians*, many elements of this story are very familiar. "The idea of a monarch or leader who is not dead, but asleep, and will one day awaken is a familiar one. It was applied not only to King Arthur, but also to such historical figures as Charlemagne and Frederick Barbarossa. In Rosicrucian legend, it is the Brotherhood which reawakens, while its founder, although ostensibly dead, remains undecayed as a symbol of his abiding influence through his followers." Indeed this idea of a "sleeping god" or "lost king" who will one day awaken/return is an extremely prevalent archetype. It has been applied to the Greek Kronos, the Roman Saturn, and Satan/Lucifer of the biblical legends, as well as Jesus Christ of the same, an entire host of Sumerian gods, and the "Fisher King" of the Grail Story, to name but a few.

But are there any other clues to indicate that this Rosenkreutz story may be a part of a much older tradition? A telling example can be found in the Adeptus Minor ritual of the Hermetic Order of the Golden Dawn. In this ritual the aspirant is made to pretend that he is in fact the discoverer of Rosenkreutz's tomb. The Chief Adept plays the role of the dead Rosenkreutz, and at the height of the ceremony, is resurrected again. It is the Golden Dawn's version of the Masonic Hiram Abiff ritual, and that is important, for just as Hiram Abiff has been associated by the Masons with Osiris, and the Egyptian rituals that also involved feigned death and resurrection, so is Rosenkreutz in this ritual likened to Osiris as well. A quote from the ritual reads: "This place was entitled by our still more ancient fratres and sorores 'the Tomb of Osiris Onnophris, the Justified One.'"

Other details of the tomb that are given in the ritual yield parallels even more shocking. The tomb, says the ritual, has seven sides, upon which are written "emblems", etched on colored squares that appear to the naked eye to be "flashing." Behind each of these flashing squares is found a drawer, each one containing a part of the sacred mystery writings which are the "Corpus Rosicianicum" of the Brotherhood. In the midst of the tomb, directly over the body is a circular altar, upon which are inscribed the four figures of the Kerubim - The Lion, the Eagle, the Man, and the

Ox - as well as the following queer phrases:

"Nequaquam Vacuum - Nowhere a Void
Libertas Evangelii - Liberty of the Gospel
Dei Intacta Gloria - Unsullied Glory of God
Legis Jugum - The Yoke of the Law"

Above the altar, shining down on the undecayed corpse of their founder, is the "artificial sun", except that in this ritual, it is not described as a sun at all, but as a rose! To quote from the ritual: "Although in the Tomb, the Sun does not shine, it is lit by the symbolic Rose of our Order in the center of the first heptagonal ceiling."

As many *Dagobert's Revenge* readers are probably aware, this "inner sun" concept closely parallels a similar myth in regards to the so-called "Hollow Earth" theory. According to these legends, some of which are modern, others surprisingly old, the sphere of the Earth is hollow, the Earth's crust being only 300 feet thick, beyond which a new world can be found, called "Agartha", which can be entered at the North and South Pole, populated, according to some, by giants who live unto the ages of the Biblical patriarchs. In fact, according to some, this is the actual location of the Garden of Eden, or the Abode of the Gods, located literally in the center of things, in the womb of the Earth. It also rests atop a magical white mountain that appears over and over again in various mythologies, for this is the "world mountain" that provides the axis of the Earth. This inner world is lit, according to legend, by an "artificial sun", or "the Smoky God", as it has been called, a ball of electro-magnetism that is said to provide warmth and light for the inhabitants of the inner Earth. While this sounds like science fiction, it actually has many parallels in the biblical and apocryphal stories of the fallen angels who, after the war in Heaven, were imprisoned in Hell, the Pit, located in the bowels of the Earth. There they are ruled over by Satan, who is called, according to tradition, "the Lord of the Earth." [1] There are also many parallels in the world of Hermeticism and alchemy.

Alchemy concerns itself with the search for the elusive "Elixir of Life", a sort of cure-all substance that is capable if bringing health, wealth, immortality, and spiritual emancipation to him who possesses it. Literally, it involves the transformation of base metals into gold, while figuratively, it involves the transformation of the dross of the unrefined Soul into the "Lapsit Exillis" - the Stone from Heaven. This stone represents perfection idealized, the amalgamation of opposites into a unified whole. And yet it is also called "the Hidden Stone" because it lies in the midst of all things, and men do not see it, giving rise to the Masonic parable of the "stone that was rejected" in the building of Solomon's Temple, which in the end becomes the cornerstone for the House of God. This stone has also been equated with the Sun, shining in perfect brilliance, ruling the Heavens like a king over his realm.

The alchemical process, both the physical and the figurative, involves a stage called Dissolution, when the elements (or the base emotions and Ego of the aspirant) are dissolved, to be replaced later by purity of spirit, or "gold." This stage is symbolized by... a black sun! And this black sun stage is equated with none other than Saturn, or Kronos, the sleeping god buried in a subterranean tomb who is called "the Hidden One"! And this is precisely why Elixir of Life is called "the Hidden Stone" - because it is hidden in the midst of this dross or base matter, the Black Sun, which, once dissolved, reveals the shining brilliance within. This dross matter is called the Prima Materia, the "original matter" from which all other forms were made. At the same time, the concept of the Black Sun arose, some say, because ancient civilizations believed that the Sun died at night as it set in the West, and descended into the Underworld, where it turned black. The next day it would resurrect again in the East. They imagined the Sun actually traveling underneath the Earth via a secret subterranean passageway, and had hieroglyphs depicting this. Significantly, there is an alchemical motto called "V.I.T.R.I.O.L", an acronym for Latin words which translate to "Visit the Interior Parts of the Earth; by Rectification Thou Shalt Find the Hidden Stone."

Is this Hidden Stone, then, the same as the Black Sun that lights the inner Earth, and the "hidden sun" which lights the tomb of Christian Rosenkreutz? Clearly, from the phrasing of the ritual, the Golden Dawn considers the hidden sun to be synonymous with the mystic rose which is the symbol of their order. This rose has always been equated, not only with the female vagina, but with the Holy Grail, which is also called the "Hidden Stone" and the "stone that fell from Heaven", and is also believed to contain the Elixir of Life. So it would appear that these five symbols - the Black Sun, the Mystic Rose, the Holy Grail, the Stone from Heaven, and the Elixir of Life - all represent essentially the same thing, or at least portions of the same thing, stages in the same process. The fact that the rose is surmounted upon an equilateral cross could be seen as symbolic of its place "in the center of things" - which is, figuratively, to be found in the deepest recesses of one's soul, wherein resides the equilibrium of opposing forces; and literally, in the center of the Earth's axis. But is there any further evidence that ties this in more directly with the inner earth, the Holy Grail and a buried or "hidden" god?

Yes there is. Lots more. Some of this evidence is to be found in the same Adeptus Minor ritual of the Golden Dawn, and the correlations are, in fact, pretty direct. In the beginning of the ritual it is states:

"The Tomb is symbolically situated in the centre of the Earth, Mountain of the Caverns, the Mystic Mountain of Abiegnus. The meaning of this title of Abiegnus - Abi-Agnus, Lamb of the Father. It is by metathesis Abi-Genos, Born of the Father. Bia-Genos, Strength of our Race, and the four words make the sentence: ABIEGNUS ABIAGNUS ABI-GENOS BIA-GENOS. "Mountain of the Lamb of the Father, and the Strength of Our Race."

As I have mentioned, the dead but dreaming god buried in a secret tomb who will one day arise is a recurring theme in many mythologies. There is even a similar story related in *The Chymical Wedding of Christian Rosenkreutz*, when the title character stumbles upon the tomb of the Lady Venus, her body lying undecayed in a death-like slumber, an well-known attribute of Venus which has given rise to the tale of "Sleeping Beauty." More striking parallels, however, are to be found with Hermes, the god-man who is said to have brought the alchemical wisdom of the Gods to mankind. He has thus been equated with the Egyptian Thoth, as well as with Enoch, the patriarch in the Bible who was allowed to go to Heaven and take the Elixir of Life, which caused him to live forever. Enoch also was allowed to write down the secrets of the gods upon a tablet, which was brought down to Earth and given to Noah to enlighten mankind. Hermes had a similar tablet, said to be the color of emerald, and to contain all the secrets of alchemy, known to the gods. Because he revealed this hidden knowledge to man, Hermes therefore has a Luciferian, Titanic and Promethean aspect to him. Hermes is said to never die, but to fall into periods of prolonged sleep, from which he is awakened at regular intervals by the periodic rediscovery of his tomb. The descriptions of these discoveries, said to have been given by both Paracelsus and Alexander the Great, among others, parallel directly that of Christian Rosenkreutz's tomb, even down to the "mystery writings" contained therein, i.e. the Emerald Tablet of Hermes, upon which the Rosicrucian writings are undoubtedly based.

The form which the Emerald Tablet takes has been described in a variety of ways, each with a symbolic meaning which holds a clue as to the overall meaning. A 1609 portrait of the Emerald Tablet by Henry Kunrath portrays it in the form a mountain inscribed with words, fire issuing from its summit. We are reminded of the mountain upon which (or within which) Moses acquired the Tablets of Testimony. In occult lore these tablets are traditionally equated with the Emerald Tablet as well, for there is a secret legend which states that Moses acquired the Tablet from the priests of Egypt prior to the Exodus. One is also reminded of the reference to the "Mountain of Abi-genos" in which Rosenkreutz is buried, and which is inscribed with magical writing. As McIntosh writes in *The Rosicrucians*, "... a mountain covered with symbols is used as an allegory of the alchemical process." He also quotes the author Thomas Vaughn, who wrote about "a mountain situated in the midst of the Earth, or the center of the world, which is both great and small. It is soft, also, above measure, hard and stony. It is far off and near at hand, but by the providence of God invisible. In it are hidden the most ample treasure, which the world is not able to value." [2] This mountain is clearly a representation of the aforementioned "world mountain", which is common to all cultures, and is often described as white, or sitting in the middle of a white island. Thus the word "albi", meaning "white", is used in the Golden Dawn ritual to designate the mountain. This parallels, for instance, the Greek Mt. Olympus, or the abode of the gods which, according to Plato, was the largest mountain on Earth, capped with snow, and with four rivers issuing from its top, residing in midst of the isle of Atlantis. This same mountain is said by some to now sit in the center of the Earth, and the four rivers are the Euphrates, the Pison, the Gihon, and the Hiddekel, the same ones which flowed in the Garden of Eden. This symbolic mountain is undoubtedly the same one, in the center of the Earth, which the Golden Dawn's Mountain of Abigenos represents.

And yet, there is a real, existing mountain in the south of France which is worthy of the title "Mountain of Abi-Genos", and which is also rumored to house the Holy Grail. In fact, local legend says that the Grail has always been there, ever since a dove from Heaven descended upon the mountain, split it open with its beak, and dropped the Grail inside. This is the mountain of Montsegur, which was the last Cathari stronghold defeated by the Albigensian Crusade. (This was the only crusade waged by Christiandom against people who were Christians themselves.) The term "Cathar" was a catch-all term used by the Catholic church for the numerous Gnostic Christian cults that proliferated across the Languedoc region of France during the Middle Ages. As they grew in numbers, they gradually became a threat to orthodox Christianity. Finally, in 1208, the Pope declared war on any Cathar who would not immediately repent and convert to the True Faith. Most of the Cathars held to their convictions and many of the local townspeople protected them from the crusading soldiers, for the Cathars were seen by the general public to be eccentric but essentially good and moral people. Even the famous crusaders, the Knights Templar, refused to fight in this battle, and some say they actually assisted the Cathars secretly. The term "Cathari" means "the Pure Ones", as so they were also called Albigensians, purity being traditionally associated with the color white. Finally, the enemy was cornered, holed up in the mountain fortress of Montsegur, which eventually capitulated on March 1, 1244. The Cathars were immediately put to death. The leader of the Crusades, Simon de Montfort, issued the now famous order, "Kill them all. God will know his own." Thus, the Albigensian Crusade has been called the first genocide in history. But the night before Montsegur fell, a group of Cathar knights disappeared over the walls with the so-called Cathar treasure of Holy Grail, which they deposited, according to rumor, inside one of the many caves in Montsegur.

Now fast forward to WWII, in which France is occupied by the Nazis, and a young German author, researcher and S.S. Lt. named Otto Rahn is sent by the Nazis to Southern France to look for the Holy Grail, which many in the Nazi hierarchy are eager to possess. The Nazis, it will be recalled, also believed whole-heartedly in the theory of the Hollow Earth, and sent expeditions down to Antarctica looking for the entrance. Furthermore, the Nazis had great admiration for the Cathars, especially their disciplined lifestyle, vegetarian diet, and sophisticated Gnostic theology. In fact, there were elements within the Nazi hierarchy who were hoping to resurrect the Cathar religion. So it was only natural that Otto Rahn would go looking for the Holy Grail at the place where the Cathars were said to have left it - Montsegur. He also knew that in the Grail romances of the Middle Ages, the Grail is said to reside in a castle at the top of Mount Salvat, which Rahn believed to be the same as Montsegur. So he stayed for a number of years, off and on between 1928 and 1931, exploring the caves of Montsegur and the tunnels of the surrounding Languedoc, even the village of Rennes-le-Chateau. Interestingly, another group of people were also exploring Montsegur at this same time. This group was known as the Polaires, a secret mystical society (influenced by Rosicrucian and Martinist teachings) that at one time included the author Rene Guenon, another believer in the inner Earth. And what were they looking for at Montsegur? Why, none other than the tomb of Christian Rosenkreutz, which according to a local newspaper, they suspected to be in the nearby ruined castle of Lordat.

If this is not enough to conclude that the so-called Tomb of Christian Rosenkreutz was believed by these occultists to be the location of the Grail, this should tie up the loose ends. The information comes from a remarkable book by Col. Howard Buechner called *Emerald Cup - Ark of Gold: The Quest of S.S. Lt. Otto Rahn of the Third Reich*. According to Buechner, Otto Rahn did discover something in the caves around Montsegur, just as Parzival had discovered the Holy Grail in a cave near Montsalvat. Buechner says that Rahn found that the landscape paralleled exactly that of Mount Salvat in Wolfram von Eschenbach's *Parzival*, and writes that, "The grotto and certain other rock formations in the story bear the same names as those in a massive cave near Montsegur." It was the clues in this book which, according to Buechner, led him to make his first awesome discovery. Writes Buechner:

"He explored the grottoes of an area known as Sabarthez, notably the grottoes of Ornolac and the massive cavern of Lombrives. Here he found a huge chamber which was known to the local mountain people as the 'Cathedral' because it had served as a meeting place for the ancient Cathars. In the main hall was a great stalagmite known as the 'Tomb of Hercules.' In a third grotto, that of Fontenet, was a stalagmite which was white as snow. It was called the 'Altar'... Deep within the grottoes of the Sabarthez he found chambers in which the walls were covered with characteristic symbols of the Knights Templar, side by side with the well-known emblems of the Cathars... One very interesting image which had been carved into the stone wall of a grotto was clearly a drawing of a lance. This depiction immediately suggested the bleeding lance which appears over and over again in Arthurian legends, and which is, of course, the Holy Lance which pierced the side of Christ at the crucifixion."

The reference to the Tomb of Hercules is interesting because of the implication that a god is buried within the mountain, just as Rosenkreutz is buried within the mountain of Albi-genos. Furthermore, Hercules, like Hermes, was another one of those "Luciferian" gods that went about spreading knowledge and civilization to men all over the world. Far from being the dumb jock that modern conceptions depict him to be, with the physique and mentality of a WWF wrestler, Hercules was actually very wise. In fact, according to Ignatius Donnelly, he was one of the kings of Atlantis. Just as Hermes possessed a magic stone which fell from Heaven which had strange electromagnetic properties, and which has been associated with the Holy Grail, Hercules also possessed a heavenly stone, and a special golden cup that he carried it in! [3] As Ignatius Donnelly wrote in his book *Atlantis: The Antediluvian World*:

"The Magnet was called the 'Stone of Hercules.' Hercules was the patron deity of the Phoenicians. He was, as we have shown elsewhere, one of the Gods of Atlantis - probably one of its great kings and navigators... Hercules, it was said, being once overpowered by the heat of the sun, drew his bow against that luminary: whereupon the god Phoebus, admiring his intrepidity, gave him a golden cup, with which he sailed over the ocean. This cup was the compass, which old writers have called Lapis Heracleus. Pisander says Oceanus lent him the cup, but Lucian says it was a seashell. Tradition affirms that the magnet originally was not on a pivot, but set to float on water in a cup. Some even see a compass in the Golden Fleece of Argos, and in the oracular needle which Nero worshipped... Hercules was, as we know, a god of Atlantis, and Oceanos, who lent the magnetic cup to Hercules, was the name by which the Greeks designated the Atlantic Ocean. And this may be the explanation of the recurrence of a cup in many antique paintings and statues. Hercules was also represented with a cup in his hand... So oracular an object as this self-moving needle, always pointing to the north, would doubtless affect vividly the minds of the people, and appear in their works of art. When Hercules left the coast of Europe to sail to the island of Erythea in the Atlantic, in the remote west, we are told, in Greek mythology, that he borrowed 'the cup' of Helios, in with which he was accustomed to sail every night. Here we seem to have a reference to the magnetic cup used in night-sailing; and this is another proof that the use of the magnetic needle in sea voyages was associated with the Atlantean Gods."

In this paragraph, Donnelley has therefore

summed up an explanation for why the Holy Grail is associated with a stone, a cup, the Sun, and the Emerald Tablet. We see also why the Grand Masters of the Priory of Sion, as "guardians of the Grail", would have been called 'Navigators", as well as why the lodestone is sacred to the Freemasons, the inheritors of that tradition. What has not been explained is why the Grail is still associated with a bloodline, and why the Emerald Tablet, if it comes from this solar stone, is green. Well, as I have explained in other articles throughout this issue, these gods of Atlantis were the same as the ancient antediluvian kings in the records of the Sumerian, Egyptian and Indus Valley civilizations. These "gods" intermarried with their subjects, and their divine-human offspring became lords over various kingdoms on Earth, this bloodline becoming known as the "Grail bloodline." It became associated with the symbols of the stone and the cup, which were also used to symbolize the secret knowledge of this race, passed down to their descendants throughout the generations.

Furthermore, the electro-magnetic properties of the stone are associated with giving life to the inanimate. Thus Donelly writes, "We find that Ouranus, the first god of the people of Atlantis, devised Baetulia, contriving stones that moved as having life, which were supposed to fall from Heaven. These stones were probably magnetic loadstones; in other words, Ouranus, the first god of Atlantis, devised the Mariner's compass." Furthermore, earlier in the same chapter Donelley says that the Egyptians referred to the lodestone as the bone of Hareori, and iron as the bone of Typhon. Hareori and Typhon were both descendants of Rhea, the goddess of the Earth. He continues:

"Do we find in this curious designation of iron and loadstone as 'bones of the descendants of the Earth' an explanation of that otherwise inexplicable Greek legend about Deucalion 'Throwing the bones of the Earth behind him, when instantly men rose from the ground, and the world was repeopled [i.e., after the Flood]?"

This may shed further light on certain legends concerning the Black Sun, which also has strange electro-magnetic properties, and is also conceived of by many who believe in it as being the mother (or father) of a particular race of man. There are even references to the "children of the Black Sun" as having unique sanguinary properties, meaning that their blood is literally made from the light of the Black Sun, which according to some is called "the Green Ray." Here we may find a connection to the color of the Emerald Tablet, made out of a hitherto mysterious material also said to possess such electro-magnetic properties. Furthermore, this may explain the origin of Howard Buechner's conception of the Grail as an "Emerald Cup." The fantastic properties of the Black Sun are linked closely with the Holy Grail, being able to entrance those who gaze upon it, and supply limitless sustenance for them. And Hercules's cup was made of gold, just as the Ark of the Covenant - which also had strange electro-magnetic properties, and is also rumored to have contained the Emerald Tablet - was plated with gold. Of course, gold is highly conductive, and the gold plating must have been instrumental in the functioning of the Ark as a machine. The Ark also had another purpose: it was the throne of Jehovah, who was said to be actually living in between the Cherubim. Yet some have said that Jehovah's throne is seated in the midst of the Black Sun. Is it possible to synthesize the prevalent idea that there are two "Grail stones" (one larger than the other), which keep in contact with each other via a magnetic link, with the concept that the Jehovah of the Bible, when using the Ark for communication, was merely talking to his subjects from his real throne inside the Earth, via an electromagnetic hologram communication? Could it be like in *Raiders of the Lost Ark*, where the Ark of the Covenant acted as "a radio for talking to God"? Is it possible that the Black Sun, the seat of Jehovah's throne, is the larger Grail, whereas the Ark, a sacred gold-plated vessel containing the Tablet, is the smaller Grail? Perhaps the ancients, after discovering the lodestone, conceived of the concept of the electromagnetic spectrum, and a ball of energy in the center of the Earth from whence it all issued. They may have even figured out how the compass behaves when sailing over the poles, and perhaps, how it behaves as you go beyond the poles into the world within. Is this what ancient man meant when he talked about sailing to the ends of the Earth, where the gods lived?

Who knows. We do, however, find an interesting example of the "two Grails" theory in Howard Buechner's book, for as the tale of Otto Rahn's discovery continues, all of these disparate elements are tied together quite nicely. Writes Buechner:

"Rahn must have discovered something which caused him to espouse a strange theory. He came to the conclusion that the Emerald Cup was only one Holy Grail, while in fact there was another... The second Grail, according to Rahn, was a Stone, or more specifically, a collection of stone tablets... on which was written the wisdom of the ages or the ultimate truth, but in a language that no one could decipher (the mountain covered with symbols?) ...In ancient times, the word 'Gorr' meant 'Precious Stone', and 'Al' meant 'a splinter' or 'stylus' with which to write. Hence came the contraction to Gorral or Graal, meaning Precious Engraved Stone."

This parallels another ancient Sumerian myth which is written about in *Egyptian Civilization: It's Sumerian Origin and Real Chronology*, by L.A. Waddell, which he equates with the myth of the Holy Grail. Waddell writes: "The earliest known specimen of historical Sumerian writing [is] the votive inscription on the trophy stone-bowl or 'Holy Grail' captured from the Serpent-Dragon worshippers by the first Sumerian King Zass, Ukusi, or Tur (Ar-Thur) and engraved by his great-grandson King Udu of Kish about 3245 B.C." This itself also corresponds nicely with Buechner's description of the first Grail, the Emerald Cup, as having been inscribed with cuneiform (Sumerian writing) and handed down "by God" to Melchizidek - that biblical character who used it to serve wine to Abraham and who was undoubtedly one of the priest-kings of ancient Mesopotamia.

Sadly, according to Buechner, Rahn was not destined to discover his first Grail, the Emerald Cup. He died under mysterious circumstances before he was able to, some say with the complicity of the Nazi hierarchy. To replace him they sent the swashbuckling Otto Skorzensky, "Chief of Germany's Special Troops", who allegedly found the Grail with little difficulty on March 16, a day sacred to the Cathars. Buechner relates the story in which "the local descendants of the Cathars" happened to be on top of the mountain celebrating some mystical rite when the S.S. helicopter came down to scoop up Otto Skorzensky and his treasure. "At exactly high noon on March 16, 1944, a small German aircraft appeared. In flew over Montsegur several times, dipping its wings it salute. Then it used skywriting equipment and formed a huge Celtic cross in the sky. The Celtic Cross was a sacred emblem of the Cathars."

The entirety of the treasure actually consisted of several things, including: "Items which were believed to have come from the Temple of Solomon which included the gold plates and fragments of wood which had once made up the Ark of Moses... Twelve stone tablets bearing pre-Runic inscriptions, which none of the experts were able to read... and a beautiful silvery cup with an emerald-like base made of what appeared to be jasper. Three gold plaques on the Cup were inscribed with cuneiform script in an ancient language." Much of this treasure, he writes, was, "buried deep beneath the castle wall of Heinrich Himmler's Grail fortress, Wewelsburg.... According to persistent rumors, at least part of the treasure was sent to the 'Externsteine', where it was sealed off in one of the many grottoes which pock-mark the great rock formation"

As to what happened to the Grail afterwards, Buechner relates that after a time spent at Wewelsburg in which it "is believed to have been exhibited to Himmler's innermost circle of senior Knights of the Holy Lance on several occasions", the cup was then removed, for safety reasons, and "was then carried by submarine (U-530) to Antarctica where it found repose in a cave of ice in the Muhlig Hoffman mountains." This cave thereafter became known as "the Emerald Cave." And supposedly this cave lead into a secret tunnel that went all the way down into the inner Earth. A stone obelisk about one meter high and "made of polished black basalt" was placed at the entrance to this cave and bore the inscription: "There are truly more things in heaven and 'in' Earth than man has dreamt. (Beyond this point is

Agartha.)" This was prepared by Professor Karl Hauhofer. Inside this obelisk was supposed to be placed the Emerald Cup itself. But instead Hauhofer wrote a note onto a piece of parchment detailing the actual location of the Cup, and put that inside the obelisk instead. Perhaps the Cup itself was actually placed somewhere amongst the kingdoms of the Earth's interior.

That the Grail should find its repose in the center of the earth is only fitting, considering the fact that, as I have previously argued, the Grail, especially in its form as a stone, has always traditionally resided there, and represented the same things that the inner Earth and its "central sun" represent. In Julius Evola's *The Mystery of the Grail*, he argued that the Holy Grail is synonymous with the "Victory Stone" of the monarchs of this inner kingdom. The Grail Castle, with its Grail King or "Fisher King", is located in a supernatural world that is "in the midst of things", yet invisible to all but the elect. According to many traditions, this is located on a "spinning island", the white island of Avalon, which England (also called "Albion", meaning "white") has come to be associated with. However, Evola equated the image of a spinning white island with the polar myth of the island of Thule, or with Atlantis, and the way it spins around on an axis is symbolic of the "central kingdom" of Agartha. The centrality of this kingdom represents equilibrium, and equality of opposing forces, especially male and female, or good and evil. It is the combination of these opposing forces that creates the "Elixir of Life", the stone of the alchemists, which is equivalent to the Grail, and which represents the powers of both good and evil which are the property of the gods and their human offspring, the "Grail Kings." The stone is also a symbol of their rightful rule, like the Stone of Scone upon which English monarchs are coronated, which incidentally is also a stone that fell from Heaven. It is believed to be the same stone that Jacob was resting his head on when he saw a vision of a ladder to Heaven.[4] To Evola, the "Grail kingdom" represented "the invisible regnum and the Supreme Center of the world", the true and rightful rule of the true and rightful King of the World. This also equates with the symbols of Paradise or the Garden of Eden. Knowing what we know about how the "gods" ruled as kings over an international government in the antediluvian age, and thereafter passed true kingship onto their human descendants, this Grail kingdom can be said to represent the Golden Age of their rule, prior to the Flood and the intermarriage of gods with human females. The Grail itself, as the Stone of Heaven, represents the divine foundation upon which this kingdom is founded, the stone from Lucifer's crown, which was given to man by rebellious angels. This stone embodies (a) the principles of royal, solar and divine leadership, (b) the secret spiritual doctrine of equilibrium, or Hermetic alchemy, which was meant to be the exclusive property of the gods and their royal human inheritors, and (C) the actual transmission of royal (and thus divine) genetic material in the form of a bloodline. In this aspect it can be seen as both the Grail cup (or the vessel/womb), and as the Stone (or blood) which is contained in that cup. Incidentally, many representations of the Grail show a stone inside of a cup, which has evolved into the symbol of the Sun or "Holy Host" descending into a cup, a popular Catholic icon. Thus, is it not possible to see the Hollow Earth as such a vessel for the Grail stone in the form of the Black Sun? In one tradition, the stone that fell from Heaven was originally a white stone, but became corrupted and turned black at the moment that Abel's blood hit the ground after being slain by his brother Cain. This is the story surrounds the Muslim Kaaba stone.

It is this corruption of the Stone, symbolized by the Dolorous Stroke that in the Grail legends wounds the Fisher King, usually in the crotch or thighs. At this point the king loses the ability to properly perform his regal function (which is symbolized by his loss of virility, i.e., ability to pass on his royal blood), and the entire kingdom falls into a deathless sleep which is known as "the Wasteland." This is analogous to the fall from the Garden of Eden and the sinking of Atlantis, which may represent an actual historical event, in addition to a symbolic principle. The king thereafter must continue to nurse his festering wound, which will not heal, and can never die until the chosen knight comes to liberate him by learning the secrets of the Grail, and by taking up the mantle of kingship himself. His kingdom exists in a similar state of perpetual malaise, until the coming of a chosen hero, who will liberate the dying king and resume the proper function of kingship, thus bringing stability and *equilibrium* to the land. Again, these are common themes in world mythology. Most notably analogous to the story of the Fisher King is that of Kronos (Saturn), who, writes Evola, "after having been the Lord of this earth, the King of the Golden Age, was dethroned and castrated (that is, deprived of the power to beget, to give life to new stock). He still lived on, though asleep, in a region located in the Far North, closer to the Arctic Sea, which was also called the Cronic Sea." Keeping this in mind, it is interesting to note that in many of the Grail romances, the Fisher King complains that his wounds become more painful when Kronos is dominant in the Heavens. It is also noteworthy that Saturn is called "the Hidden One", thus alluding perhaps to his seclusion inside of the Earth. Many researchers have equated him with the prototype for Satan, given that he was horned, rebellious, and cast down into the Abyss (the Chronian Sea) to become Lord of the Underworld. Also note that, like Satan, he was called "the Lord of the Earth", and that "Saturn" and "Satan" may be etymologically linked, as many have argued. Furthermore, Saturn is also called "the Lord of the Mountain", and so is Satan. And is that not what we are talking about when we speculate about a dead god being buried in Montsegur, or in the center of the Earth?

Interestingly, the phrase "Rex Mundi" appeared in the parchments that were found at Rennes-le-Chateau, and the Cathars accused the Catholic Church of secretly worshipping Rex Mundi in the form of Jehovah, the Earth's creator, whom they regarded as an evil demiurge. And of course, Jehovah, as "El Shaddai", was also the Lord of the Mountain. Moreover, as I have previously noted, the "Black Sun" stage of alchemy is attributed to the powers of Saturn, where his "element" – sulfur - is mixed with the "element" of Hermes - mercury. Hermes, of course, was representative of the light-bearing aspects of Lucifer, whereas Saturn represented more of the "Dark Lord" aspects of what we would now call the Devil, as ruler over the Underworld and the Abyss. While figures such as Hermes, Saturn, Hercules, and the others I have discussed so far were undoubtedly separate people in history, and were at one time god-kings, because they all had similar titles, attributes and teachings, and ruled over the same global empire, they have gotten blurred together in the mythic consciousness of legend. Thus, the sleeping, half-dead gods who inhabit the subterranean tombs of Saturn, Satan, Hermes, Hercules, and even Christian Rosenkreutz (as an embodiment of Osiris, the solar god-king) could all mythically represent the same fallen kingdom, which, having lost the Grail and its mandate to rule, has occulted itself, gone underground, become invisible, or fallen asleep, until such time as the proper individual shall come along to liberate him/it. Then the sunken kingdom shall rise, the dreaming lord shall awake, the phoenix emerge from the ashes, and the proper universal balance shall be restored. In the meantime, the secret royal doctrine is kept alive by the initiates/descendants of that sleeping god (the same doctrine that is written upon the Grail in its form as the Emerald Tablet, or Gorral). It is in this light that Evola examines the myth of Christian Rosenkreutz, writing that, "Having withdrawn into a cave which becomes his tomb, he wanted his tomb to be left alone until the right time came, namely, 120 years after his death. Since Rosenkreutz allegedly died in 1484, the discovery of the cave and of his tomb occurred in 1604; This is more or less the time in which the Rosicrucian movement begins to be known and emerges in history, as if it literally sprang from beneath the ground."

In light of what has been examined in this article, we can now understand all of the many forms that the Grail has taken in various myths, and the various interpretations, none of which are really at odds with the others. Rather they all point to the same symbol of the primordial, perfect kingdom ruled over directly by the gods during a Golden Age, which has since fallen into a state of deathless sleep, and which is waiting to be restored via a chosen avatar who is of the very bloodline of the primordial (antediluvian) kings themselves. The various symbols of the Grail all go together to form a complete whole - as a cup, as a bloodline, as a spiritual experience, as a secret doctrine, as a stone, and even as a tablet upon which secret characters are written. This may even be found inside of a sacred vessel (such as the Ark of the Covenant), which itself becomes synonymous with the Grail. This may even give us an understanding of why the word "Ark" is used to describe both the vessel which carried Noah, and that in which Moses placed the Tablets of Testimony, which many believe to be the Emerald Tablet, not the Ten Commandments. Oddly, it is according to the same tradition that we hear that the Emerald Tablet was given to Noah by Enoch prior to the Flood, and thus Noah's Ark may have carried the Tablet as well. Herein lies the significance which I am about to point out: the Ark, which carries with it the Grail (in the form of the Emerald Tablet) also contained the seed of preserved life.

One will recall that Moses, one of the rumored possessors of the tablet, also had his own life preserved by a floating vessel, namely the basket of bulrushes in which he was placed upon the Nile river by his mother, who wished to save him from slaughter. This is based upon an older, similar story about the Babylonian King Sargon the Great, but it also brings to this author's recollection the story of Osiris, who, after being murdered by his brother Set (an older version of the Cain and Abel story) was chopped up and dumped in that very same river. Later, all of his parts were rediscovered by Isis, except for the penis, which was substituted by an artificial penis (like the substitution of the Lost Word in Freemasonry). She then used his dead body to conceive the child Horus. Evola sees in this post-mortem coitus a hidden reference to the repopulation of the Earth after the Flood. Does this explain why Kronos (another dead-but-not-really god who lost his penis in a fight) is referred to as "the Forgotten Father"? The Fisher King in the Grail story, who, we now see, clearly represents Kronos, was also castrated by his brother (the evil Klingsor), and also turned out to be the ancestor (or "Forgotten Father") of many of the characters in the story, though most of them were not aware of it (having forgotten). One should also look again at the Greek myth of Deucalion. Is this not enough to indicate that the dead or sleeping lord who in so many legends lies beneath the Earth, under the seas, or inside of a mountain, was associated by our ancestors with the repopulation of the flood-drenched Earth -

moreover that they saw him as their very ancestor, or at least, the ancestor of their royal and priestly castes? The Forgotten Father was also in many traditions buried with a magic stone (the stone that fell from Heaven, the Emerald Tablet, the loadstone that repopulated the Earth, etc.), which contained secret wisdom teachings, possessed strange electromagnetic properties, and was itself associated with the re-population, as well as the vessel (the Grail or Ark) that carried it. Thus, all of these things: the stone/tablet, the ark/vessel, and the bloodline of the Forgotten Father - came eventually to be called the Grail, while in certain cultures, the myth of the dead but dreaming lord and his magnetic stone evolved into the Lord of the Earth and the Black Sun ruling over a subterranean kingdom. With this conclusion, it is easy to note that the word "Ark" is contained in "Arktos", the Great Bear constellation that marks the North Pole (as well as, supposedly, the entrance to the inner earth), and also in "Arcadia", the Greek term for paradise that pops up so frequently in the Grail research. With this hypothesis, we can also understand why Rene d'Anjou and others chose to represent the secret doctrine of the Grail wisdom with an *underground* stream, as well as a tomb, and why Poussin chose to mark that tomb with the words "Et In Arcadia Ego." Thus we have found the real Tomb of God, and we need not pinpoint its specific location.

In conclusion, it is this author's finding that the various myths describing the Grail in multiple forms are all part of the same corpus, and that these various forms compliment rather than contradict one another. Moreover, the Grail legend is as old as history itself. It is integrally connected with the universal tale of a race of gods who intermarried with mankind and passed their secret doctrine of hidden knowledge onto certain members of our race, but were thereafter imprisoned inside of the Earth. An equally integral part of the myth is that these sleeping gods shall some day awake and their kingdom rise again, just as the rediscovery of the Grail shall bring an end to the Wasteland and restore rightful kingship, bringing with it a new Golden Age. Then again, their kingdom may already be here, and men do not see it, as Christ said in *The Gospel of Thomas*, being invisible to all but the elect. Thus it remains the responsibility of those who feel worthy to receive these secrets to reach out and grab them, for they remain the divine inheritance of all who are children of the Forgotten Father.

Endnotes:

[1] Interestingly, in the Golden Dawn ritual, it is the "Lord of the Earth" who causes Rosenkreutz to rise again.

[2] Another, similar poem says this land was lit by a "midnight sun."

[3] According to legend, it was written on a jewel out of Lucifer's crown.

[4] This is the biblical passage from whence came the term, "This place is terrible", which is written on the outside of the church at Rennes-le-Chateau.

The Real Meaning of "Et in Arcadia Ego..."

By Tracy R. Twyman

"*Et in Arcadia Ego...*" - These words first appeared, to my knowledge, in a painting by Il Guercino (c.1618) of the same name. Throughout the Renaissance, this phrase was used as a sort of code word for "the underground stream", an invisible college of kindred souls who secretly shared their esoteric knowledge with one another, passing it around Europe via a network of secret societies and mystery schools, often utilizing its arcane symbolism in works of art and literature. Such symbolism shows up, for instance, in the works of René d'Anjou, Giordano Bruno, Leonardo da Vinci, Nicholas Poussin, and many others. The authors of *Holy Blood, Holy Grail* (Michael Baigent, Richard Leigh, and Henry Lincoln) describe thusly the symbolism of the underground stream:

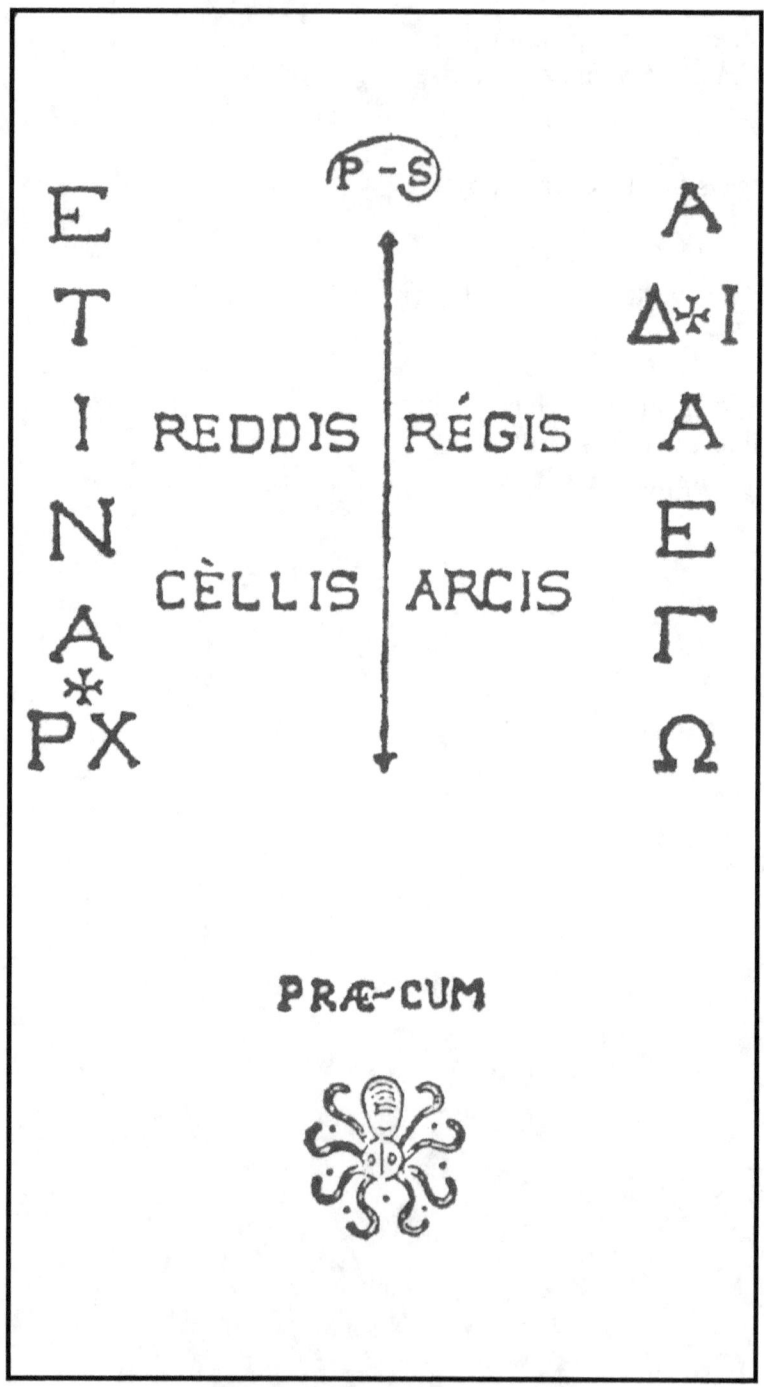

The mysterious plate from Marie de Blanchefort's tomb.

"...the motif of an underground stream seems to have been extremely rich in symbolic and allegorical resonances. Among other things, it would appear to connote the 'underground' esoteric tradition of Pythagorean, Gnostic, Cabalistic, and Hermetic thought. But it might also connote something more than a general corpus of teachings, perhaps some very specific factual information - a 'secret' of some sort transmitted in clandestine fashion from generation to generation. And it might connote an unacknowledged and thus 'subterranean' bloodline."

The phrase "Et in Arcadia Ego" is normally translated from the Latin, "And I am in Arcadia", or "I am even in Arcadia." The "I" is supposed to be death, and since Arcadia is the Greek conception of Paradise, it is presumed to mean that death is everywhere, even in Paradise. The reason for this is that in the art and literature of the period in which the phrase "Et in Arcadia Ego" was used or referenced in some way, it was almost always associated with a tomb of some sort, and usually with a skull as well. For example, a skull can be found in Guercino's *Et in Arcadia Ego* bearing a mysterious hole on its left side. The phrase was inscribed, in code, on the gravestone of Marie de Blanchefort, whose grave at the church at Rennes-le-Chateau Berenger Sauniere is believed to have successfully plundered of some treasure. Nicholas Poussin, who's painting *The Shepherds of Arcadia* is so central to the mystery of Rennes-le-Chateau and, therefore, *Dagobert's Revenge,* depicted in that painting a group of shepherds pointing to a tomb that was inscribed with the phrase "Et in Arcadia Ego." This was believed by Henry Lincoln to depict a tomb that, until recently, still existed in the region of Rennes-le-Chateau. But the authors of *The Tomb of God* (Richard Andrews and Paul Schellenberger) think that the real tomb which Poussin was alluding to is not the one that Henry Lincoln found, but one that they say is buried between the twin peaks of nearby Mt. Cardou, which they believe to be the tomb of the one and only Jesus Christ. Their interpretation of the word "Arcadia" - specifically in the context of that phrase - is reached by breaking the word down phonetically, and then translating, not just the letters, but the sounds from the Latin, thereby arriving at the result, "the tomb of God." They write:

"It is not too difficult to imagine how Arcadia (arcar-deear - the contemporary pronunciation, not the modern one) could be identified with the sound of Arca Dei (arcar-dayee), thus suggesting an anagram. Arca Dei would mean 'Ark of God'... This, combined with the quite excessive emphasis of the idea of 'tomb'... convinces us that were are to interpret 'ARCA' as 'tomb'; this would be another legitimate translation of the word."

Using similar methods, they translate the entire phrase, *"Et in Arcadia Ego"* into an anagram which phonetically means, in Latin, "I touch the Tomb of God." By adding the Latin word "Sum" at the end, which they believe to be implied by the sentence, then creating another anagram, they further render it, "I touch the tomb of God, Jesus."

But is it really the tomb of Jesus, a Jewish priest-king de jure who failed in his bid for the throne, that kings, popes, and other men of renown (most of them religious heretics) have dedicated their lives to, and on occasion, given their lives for? Is this the secret which has been preserved by some of the world's most elite and powerful secret

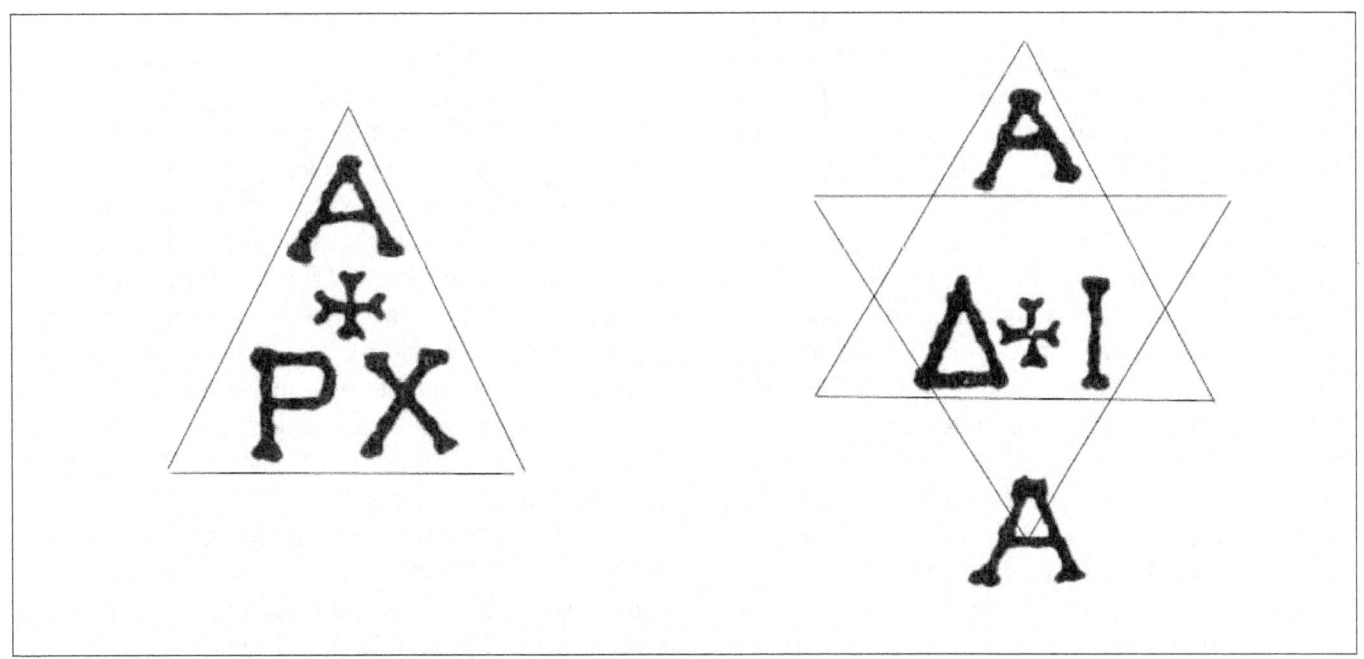

Hidden geometry on the Blanchefort tombstone.

societies for millennia? The mystery of Rennes-le-Chateau, and for that matter, the roots of Southern France's esoteric tradition would appear in fact to be much older than 2000 years. References to Jesus and his presumed wife, Mary Magdalene, are almost always coupled or superimposed over images of another, far more ancient divine couple, known to the Egyptians as Isis and Osiris. Their presence is Rennes-le-Chateau is repeatedly symbolized by the appearances of the pentagram and the hexagram in the landscape of the area, and the decor in Sauniere's church. The most well-known pentagram is formed quite exactly by the perfect formation of five mountains within the area. The odds of this perfect formation occurring naturally are infinitesimal, and indicate that an intelligent being or group of beings must have been involved. As author Colin Wilson has pointed out in a recent radio broadcast, the uppermost point of the pentagram points directly at where the North Pole was 100, 000 years ago. This implies great antiquity for the treasure of Rennes-le-Chateau, dating it back to a period when no human civilization is supposed to have existed, and it is debated whether or not humans existed at all. Certainly there was no historically acknowledged civilization at that time capable of the mathematical formulation necessary to create such a perfect pentagram, or the technology to move five huge mountains into place. However, there is such a civilization acknowledged in legend, and that is the global kingdom of Atlantis, ruled over directly by the gods - Kronos or Saturn, the horned "fish-man-god" being one of them. In Sumeria, the oldest civilization recognized by historians, Kronos was known as "Enki", and according to some experts, another name for Enki in Sumeria was "Ia", the "Lord of the Deep Waters", the father of the Atlantean dynasty of god-kings. These god-kings have been much talked about in recent *Dagobert's Revenge* articles, for I believe this pre-diluvian dynasty to be the real root of the sacred Merovingian bloodline, and therefore, the bloodline of Jesus, the Grail bloodline. Such a decent from the kings of Atlantis is implied in the story of the Quinotaur (a sea-monster, synonymous mythologically with Kronos), who supposedly spawned the Merovingian race.

So this is the true significance of the blood: it comes directly from the god-kings of Atlantis, the beings who, according to legend, created us, then intermarried with us to create a hybrid race of partially human god-kings, passing onto these offspring the secret doctrine of their sacred knowledge. According to those same legends, they were cast down from heaven for this indiscretion, which was against the rules of the divine hierarchy, and were imprisoned in the underworld, in the bowels of the Earth. Such a tradition is preserved in the Greek story of Kronos (obviously the prototype of the Biblical Satan) being cast down from Heaven and landing in the center of the Earth. This legend even exists in the East, where the "Lord of the Earth" (another title shared by Kronos, Ia, and Satan) is believed to be in a death-like sleep in a magical city in the center of the Earth. There is even scientific evidence that this story is rooted in the historical occurrence of a "falling star", or meteorite that plunged into the Earth, cracking its crust and disfiguring its face, then buried itself deep within the center of the Earth where it remains as our planet's inner core. This is, perhaps, the "12th Planet" that Zecharia Sitchin is always referring to. And it must also be the "stone that fell from Heaven", supposedly chipped from Lucifer's crown, which according to legend is called "the Grail." Recall, then, that the Grail is the treasure said to be buried at Rennes-le-Chateau. Also, rumors persist that Rennes-le-Chateau contains an entrance to the underworld. The event of this falling star may itself be commemorated by a symbol that was used at least as far back as ancient Sumeria, where it was known as the "Ar", the Plough Sign. That sign is the pentagram, associated with both Satan and the planet Venus, as well as with Rennes-le-Chateau. In fact, the prefix in the word "Quinotaur" - Quin - means the number five in Latin, and some have suggested that the word is in fact a reference to the pentagram at Rennes-le-Chateau - that perhaps each man-made mountain conceals the "head" of some enormous subterranean sea monster which our ancestors considered to be their God, and in fact, *their* ancestor as well.

The "Ar" sign, in Sumeria, usually just referred to as "the Plough Sign", actually has two very specific definitions. One explains the translation of "plough", and it literally means "to cause dirt to go up", something that would certainly occur during the meteoric impact described above. Yet "Ar" has another meaning in Sumerian - one that is very pertinent to or examination, and that is "to shackle, to imprison", which is exactly what was done to Kronos when he fell to Earth and was imprisoned in the underworld. Esoteric legend states that Kronos was shackled and bound to the underworld by just such a pentagram. This would seem to indicate that the pentagram at Rennes-le-Chateau acts as a prison or shackle as well, perhaps for Kronos himself.

In this context, it is interesting to examine the prefix "arc" in Latin. In the Latin dictionary, the first word we encounter in the "arc" family is "arca", which Andrews & Schellenberger have translated as "tomb." It does indeed mean that, but it also means "A chest box, esp. a money coffer", and "a cell for close imprisonment"! This is amazing! Not only do we have a reference to a prison *and* a tomb, as it would have been for Kronos (which explains how we get the word "arcane", as in buried or concealed, from the Latin "arceo", meaning "to protect, keep safe", or "to hinder, prevent"). It is also possible for an "ark" to hold money, something that the treasure at Rennes-le-Chateau is believed to consist of in part. In fact, it has often been assumed that the treasure at Rennes-le-Chateau is the same treasure that the Templars stole from Solomon's Stables, said to include gold, jewels, and the most precious of Jewish relics, the Ark of the Covenant. But Solomon's Stables were also the burial place for Judah's upper crust, and embalmed corpses are further said to have been part of the treasure of the Templars, especially a head or skull that they worshipped under the name of Baphomet, said to represent a hermaphroditic goat-horned figure from which our modern conception of the Devil comes. Could the "Ark of the Covenant", or the "Ark of God" also have been, literally, the tomb of God? Jehovah, or Jah is often referred to in the scriptures as literally being inside the Ark. Perhaps the Ark contained the remains of someone that they believed to be their god. But the traditionally accepted contents of the Ark, the Tablets of Moses, have long been regarded in esoteric circles as having been made from some radioactive substance, like a meteorite. Likewise the Tablets inside the ark have long been speculated to have actually been the Emerald Tablets of Hermes, which bear instructions on how to create the Philosopher's Stone, or the Holy Grail. And the Ark of the Covenant has long been associated with the Holy Grail also. Could they then have been the remains of this meteorite, which plunged to Earth as a meteorite and was buried in the underworld, later becoming known to occultists as the Grail? And could this meteoric fall have been the inspiration for the legend of Saturn or Kronos, the Atlantean priest-king from which the Grail bloodline sprung, whose life-story included a similar meteoric fall from heavenly grace?

Interestingly the word Jah (the name of the Jewish god inside the Ark of the Covenant) comes from the name Ia, the Lord of the Earth and Lord of the Deep Waters in Sumeria on which the Hebrew god Jehovah's character is partially based. The symbols of the god-king's tomb and throne would appear to be related to certain depictions of Jehovah. As I have already mentioned, Ia is believed by many experts to be the same as Enki, Saturn or Kronos, and therefore, the Quinotaur, as well as, ironically, Satan. Enki, as a king of Atlantis, was often referred to under the title that all Atlantean world-monarchs were given. That title was "Kad", depicted by a hieroglyph of an uplifted hand with the fingers erect. This title was also used by the kings of Sumeria, Egypt and Phoenicia, and it meant literally, "be strong, protect, save", which is noteworthy, considering that the word "arceo" has a similar meaning in Latin. Titularly, this term, when applied to a monarch, meant "King of the Four Corners of the Earth." Ia was sometimes pronounced "A-ha", and written as a pair of hieroglyphs featuring a squiggly line and an upstanding fish. Obviously, just from looking at it, one can tell that this symbol is the basis for the "Ichthys" fish sign that is now used to symbolize Christ.

Knowing what we now know, it becomes possible to write out the word "Arcadia" in cuneiform, or Sumerian hieroglyphs, and to interpret its meaning there from. There are three possible ways of writing out the symbol for "kad", and therefore different ways to write (and interpret) the phrase. (See the chart.) "Arcadia" could mean, for instance, "prison of the Lord of the Earth, Ia",

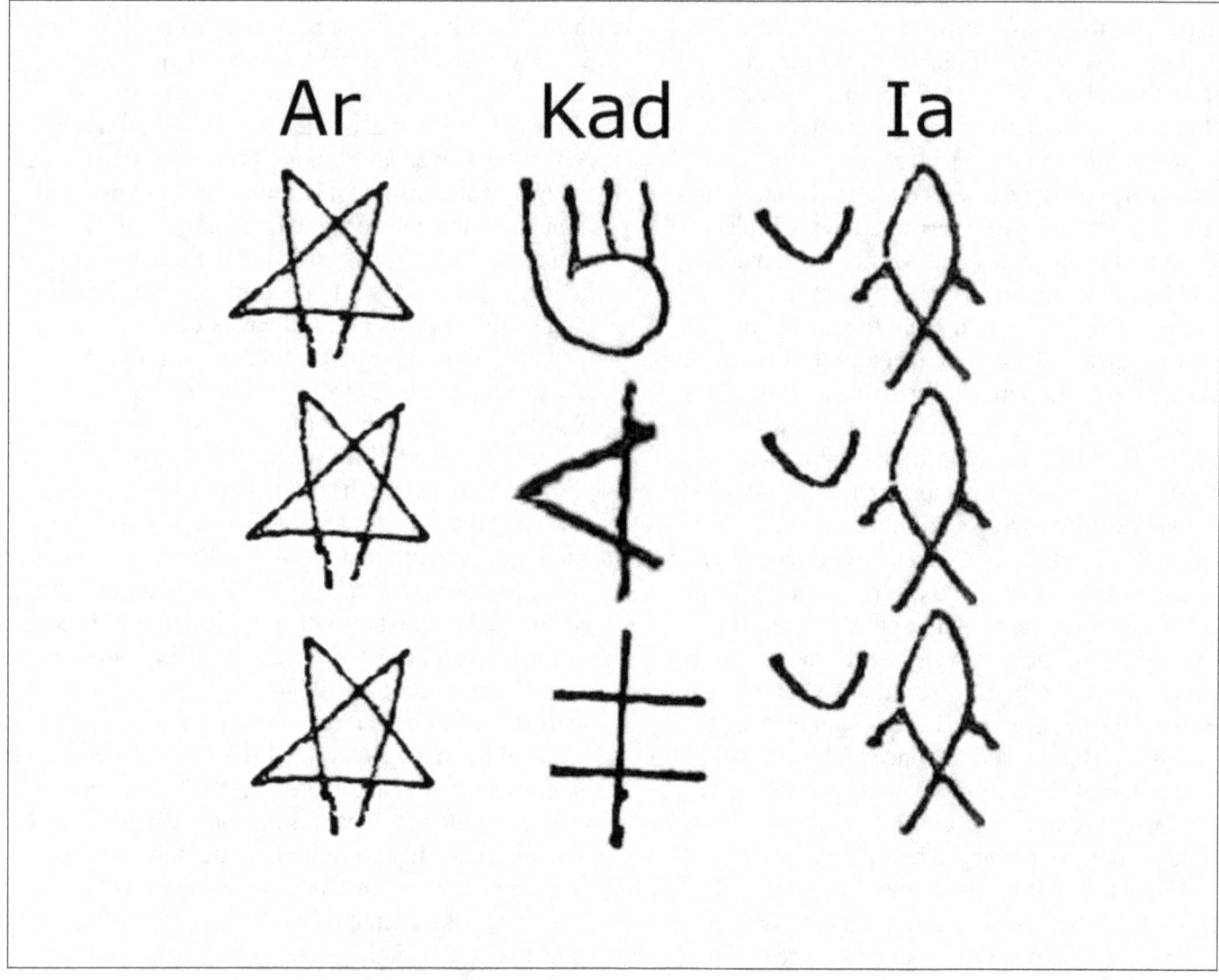

"Arcadia" written with Sumerian characters.

or "tomb of King Ia." The phrase "Et in Arcadia Ego" could then be rendered as a combination of Latin and, oddly, Sumerian, and read as: "I am the Tomb of King Ia." Also, bearing in mind that "arceo" means "to protect, save, or conceal" in Latin, and "kad" means the same thing in Sumerian, it could also be read, "I conceal (or protect) the tomb of Ia." This is remarkable, considering the famous anagram of "Et in Arcadia Ego' that was suggested in *Holy Blood, Holy Grail*: "I Tego Arcana Dei", which means: "Begone, I conceal the secrets of God." That god, it would seem, was Ia, or Kronos, the Atlantean king and "Lord of the Earth" - progenitor, perhaps, of a human line of kings from which the Merovingians, and Jesus Christ as well, believed themselves to come from.

The word "Ia" consists of the letters "I" and "A". The letter "I", phonetically, is the same as the word "eye", and therefore, in occult parlance, implies the same. The letter "A", as I pointed out in the very first issue of *Dagobert's Revenge* in 1996, suggests the shape of the Great Pyramid with its missing capstone returned, and on the dollar bill, this pyramid is shown with an eye inside the capstone. This is the "All-Seeing Eye", associated in the occult underworld with the god of light, Lucifer, (a.k.a. Satan, Kronos), and the Grail stone. The shape of the letter "A" can also be found within the shape of the pentagram, if two lines and two half-lines are removed. Recall also that one of the Sumerian symbols for "Kad" was an "A" turned on its side, a rough-looking "A" much in the likeness of the familiar "Anarchy" symbol.[1] The letter "A", used as a coded reference to both the Great Pyramid and the pentagram, was found in the

Sauniere parchments at Rennes-le-Chateau by the authors of *The Tomb of God*, Andrews & Schellenberger. For instance, at the bottom of the Parchment One, in between the upside-down letters that spell "SION", we see a weird squiggly arrow pointing to a lone, out of place and upside-down "A", seemingly for no reason. I have also found another conspicuous occurrence of the letter "A": on the tombstone of Marie de Blanchefort, where the words "Et in Arcadia Ego" are etched in code. There, the syllables "Arca" and "Dia" (in a mix of Greek and Latin letters) are separated on either side. Look at the illustration. In both instances, the letters are bunched together in the shape of a pyramid, each of which includes a Templar cross, and each of which contains the letter "A" at the top of the pyramid. Surely, some sort of statement is being made here. And in the pyramid on the right, the bottom row of letters is formed by an "I", a Templar cross, and a delta triangle. If we take the triangle as a code for the letter "A", and the Templar cross as a plus sign, then it would be "I" + "A" - in other words, "King Ia." In fact, on the entire gravestone there are five As, in addition to the "delta" triangle. Perhaps, underneath the five mountains that form the pentagram at Rennes-le-Chateau, we shall one day discover five artificially constructed pyramids acting as tombstones for the ancient deified king.

Let us now re-evaluate the painting of Mary Magdalene that Berenger Sauniere himself created and placed on the altar of his church. That Sauniere would show Magdalene inside of a cave, next to a skull, kneeling in front of a cross that seems to be growing out of the ground like a tree indicates that the painting does indeed represent a tomb, perhaps the tomb of Christ, and perhaps Magdalene is there mourning for her companion. Then again, perhaps it indicates that she is buried there with him as well. But maybe Jesus and Mary Magdalene are also being used as symbols to represent another, more ancient divine couple, Kronos and his consort. Let us not forget that Kronos was, according to some, also called "Atargatis", except that Atargatis was a female sea-monster, thought to be synonymous with Kronos as well. Could we be dealing with a god that was perceived as both male and female, like the Baphomet which the Templars worshipped?

The Grail, which is what the treasure of Rennes-le-Chateau is supposed to be, is associated with alchemy, and in the alchemical process, the achievement of the Grail, or the Philosopher's Stone, is symbolized by the Hermaphrodite - the combination of male and female qualities in perfect harmonious balance.

The Hermaphrodite was, of course, in Greek mythology, a combination of Hermes (a.k.a. Mercury) and Aphrodite (a.k.a. Venus.) Hermes was the trickster god who led folks along the alchemical path to enlightenment, and the souls of the dead to the underworld. He is the god of buried treasure, which is why St. Anthony the Hermit, who represents him, is the patron saint of the same. The Tablet of Hermes, believed to be the source of all alchemical knowledge, is said to have been found in Hermes' tomb. And guess where Hermes was born? In a cave inside Mt. Cyllene in Arcadia. Guess where Hermes spent all of his childhood? In Arcadia. Guess where the worship of Hermes began ? In Arcadia. In fact, Hermes was sometimes known by the title 'Lord of Cyllene and Arcadia." Is it so illogical to assume, then, that he might have been buried there as well? In *Myths and Legends*, by Amparo Ponce (which is an anthropological study of world mythology that never once mentions Rennes-le-Chateau or the Merovingian saga) we read:

"Hermes was also honored by <u>the shepherds of Arcadia</u>, whose mission it was to watch over their flocks and huts."

These things always seem to come full circle, don't they?

Endnotes:

[1] The other symbol for "Kad" was identical to the double-barred Cross of Lorraine.

The Celestial Sea and the Ark of Heaven

By Tracy Twyman

"And God said, Let there be a firmament in the midst of the waters, and let it divide the waters from the waters. And God made the firmament, and divided the waters which [were] under the firmament from the waters which [were] above the firmament: and it was so." (Genesis 1: 6-7)

There can be no doubt that the ancients conceived of the sky above as a great cosmic ocean, or as it was called in the Bible, the "firmament of Heaven." In the above quote, God is described as having to literally separate the seas of the firmament from those on the Earth. In the Hittite text, *The Song of Ullikumi*, the gods are said to have "cut apart the celestial realm and the Earth with a cutter." For people who did not realize that they lived on a spherical rock floating in empty space, but instead saw a flat landscape, with a point on the horizon where the sky met the seas, this was an acceptable explanation. It seemed to them that they were surrounded by seas, beyond which was nothing but more water, stretching out to infinity, arching over their heads in what was called "the canopy of Heaven." Surrounded by water, they could only imagine that this is where they and their gods had come from. In fact, in *The Book of Genesis*, the heavenly waters are described as giving birth to creation itself. "And God said, Let the waters bring forth abundantly the moving creature that hath life, and fowl [that] may fly above the Earth in the open firmament of Heaven." God himself first made his appearance by manifesting within these waters. "And the spirit of God moved upon the face of the waters."

Another interesting thing about this heavenly ocean is that it was at one time depicted as literally being frozen, leading many fringe theologians to postulate that a layer of ice did at one point surround the Earth, having been melted by some natural disaster, perhaps causing the Deluge of Noah, when the "floodgates of Heaven were opened." The crystalline structure of Heaven is confirmed in *Exodus 24:10* when it says: "And they saw the God of Israel: and there was under his feet as it were a paved work of a sapphire stone, and as it were the body of Heaven in his clearness." Then later on in *Job 38:30*, we read: "The waters are hid as [with] a stone, and the face of the deep is frozen." Finally in *Revelation 4:6*, St. John the Divine declares: "And before the throne [there was] a sea of glass like unto crystal." This throne is of course the throne of God. A similar description is made by the title character in The Book of Enoch, an apocryphal scripture supposedly written by the only human figure in the Bible (besides Jesus) who was actually transmuted alive into Heaven. As Enoch described it:

"They elevated me aloft into heaven. I proceeded, until I arrived at a wall built with stones of crystal. A tongue of fire surrounded it, which began to strike me with terror. Into this vibrating flame I entered. And drew nigh to a spacious habitation built with stones of crystal. Its wall, too, as well as pavement, were formed with stones of crystal, and crystal likewise was on the ground. Its roof had the appearance of the running of the stars and flashes of lightening...."

In *The Book of Enoch* the angels of Heaven, or "the Watchers', as they are called, are described specifically as "stars." They are called "Watchers" because they look down on Earth from Heaven, and they travel around through the twelve "watchtowers", which are obviously the houses of the zodiac. One should assume that the planets were included among the "stars" in the ancient world. These planets travel in orbits called "oaths", since it was conceived that the planets or "stars" were intelligent beings – gods - who had taken an oath with the Most High God to travel these specific paths at specific intervals of time throughout eternity. Writes Enoch:

"I marked their rich progress; their observance of a mutual fidelity by an oath to which they adhered; their proceeding forth before the sun, and their adherence to their oath, in obedience to the command of the Lord of spirits."

The Egyptians believed that their sun-god Ra, traveling in his daily orbit, was actually the pilot of the "Boat of Heaven" which navigated the Celestial Sea. "Adoration of Ra on the day he saileth in the boat. Homage to thee within his boat, rising, twice, shining with rays", we read in *The Book of the Dead*. With it he sailed to the underworld, and then back up to Heaven again. The Egyptians believed that they too would make this journey upon the Boat of Ra after their death, to be judged by Osiris in the underworld. In fact the priests of Egypt actually built a life-sized replica of this boat, which they would drag around the walls of the city in a daily ritual meant to imitate the revolutions of the Sun. This boat was actually discovered by archeologists in 1954, buried next to the Great Pyramid at Giza.

Many other cultures had similar myths about the Sun. The Greeks had the story of Hercules sailing to the Underworld in the cup of Helios every night. Because of this, many believe, we have the ancient myth of the Black Sun. As the Sun descended into the underworld at night, it died, and turned black. It then traveled via a subterranean passageway to the Western side of the Earth, and re-emerged alive again from the sea the next morning. This has itself evolved into a modern-day belief that the Earth is hollow, and that inside, the "underworld" is lit by a subterranean black sun. This world can be entered at the Earth's poles, and the black sun rests stationary in the center, along the Earth's central Axis. Since the Black Sun is linked to the poles and the axis, many have confused it with Arktos, the Pole Star.

But as I have previously written in earlier articles, the "Black Sun" is also a stage in the alchemical process, and there it is associated with the planet Saturn, which in traditional occult systems has always been linked with the color black. Furthermore, the mythology of Saturn, or Kronos, says that he was the leader of the gods known as "Titans", whom Zeus overthrew and cast into the underworld, where Saturn became their Dark Lord, paralleling very closely the story of the Black Sun. Yet the "Elixir of Life", or the Grail Stone which is the end result of the alchemical process, is most certainly associated with the solar Sun above. How is it, then, that the planet Saturn could come to be associated with the Sun?

Puzzled by this inconsistency, I was at a loss as to how to finish this article, until coming across, through a weird twist of fate, an article written by David Talbott for *Aeon Magazine* called "The Ship of Heaven." I was shocked to discover that yet another author had linked Saturn, not only with the Black Sun, but with the Boat of Ra as well. According to Talbott, the sky once looked much different than it does now. He proposes a pre-diluvian cosmology in which the dominant figure in the night sky was the planet Saturn. As this and other planets moved closer to Earth, a reflection from the light of Saturn created the appearance of a crescent of light revolving around him. [1] This, according to Talbott, became interpreted by the ancients as "the Ship of Heaven", and this, he says, was the real Boat of Ra. He points out that the Egyptian descriptions of the Boat of Ra have it sailing through the sky at night, and journeying through the underworld during the day, as well as setting in the East instead of the West, exactly the opposite behavior of our current Sun. [2] Writes Talbott:

"According to the model, the apparition began to grow bright as the crescent descended to the left of Saturn; reached its point of greatest splendor when the crescent was directly below Saturn; began to diminish when the crescent rose to the right; and was its weakest when the crescent was directly over Saturn."

One will recall that in Judeo-Christianity, Satan's transgression against God was that he wanted to be the brightest light in the heavens. According to this theory, as Saturn, he certainly was. In fact Saturn was, originally, a solar deity, and at the time, the most celebrated figure in the night sky. Talbott writes that:

"Long before the age of Latin Poets and historians, however, the Sumerians and Babylonians celebrated the ship of the planet god Saturn. The priests of Lagash knew Saturn as Ningirsu, owner of the 'the beloved ship', a celestial vehicle that 'rises out of the dam of the deep.'"

This figure, if it actually existed, could have been the source for a number of mythological archetypes. For one thing, it could be the source for the symbol of the crescent itself, which has always been associated with the Moon. Talbott believes that this is a misunderstanding that has caused many Saturnian gods and symbols to be mistranslated as lunar gods and symbols:

"The specific character of the ship as a crescent and the relationship of the crescent to the sun god is well illustrated by the Sumerian and Babylonian God Sin, probably the most familiar crescent-divinity in the ancient world. While Sin is titled 'Udsar', 'the crescent', he is also proclaimed to be 'the shining bark of the Heavens.'...In view of the acknowledged identity of Saturn as the sun god, it is significant that in numerous Mesopotamian illustrations of the Sin-Crescent, the sun is shown resting in the center of its embrace... Of course the usual identification of the crescent-ship with the Moon is due to one fact alone: the new Moon is the only crescent familiar to the modern age." [3]

Talbott further claims that this symbol of Saturn inside the crescent also evolved into the solar symbol of the dot inside a circle, as well as the "Eye of Horus" that we see each day on the back of our dollar bill. Since Saturn's throne is in the midst of this boat, this must be the source of the ancient "Eye of the Throne" symbol for world monarchy. I would add that this is possibly an origin for the familiar Catholic icon of the Holy Grail with the stone inside, or the communion cup receiving the sun-host. As well, the double masts of the boat became, according to Talbot, the two horns of the Bull of Heaven. Thus, the horns which the deities of so many cultures have been said to possess, and which became synonymous with divinity and royalty, are not a lunar symbol, but a solar symbol, much more fitting to be adorning the crown of a king, as they did throughout the ancient world. And since Saturn is Satan, this is why Satan is said to have horns, as well as many other gods of the ancient world. Says Talbott:

"The Sumerian Nannar, Babylonian Sin, esteemed as a celestial bull with glistening horns, is also, 'the shining bark of the heavens.' An identical role of the celestial bull occurs in Egypt, where the Pyramid Texts declare: 'May you ferry over by means of the Great Bull... The Bull of the Sky has bent down his horn that he may pass over thereby. Thus a Coffin Text celebrates the 'long-horn which supports the bark of Anubis.' And if these are not explicit enough, we have from the Coffin Texts: 'O Horn, ferry across Him who is in is shrine." [4]

These two horns also became, in mythology, the two peaks of the world mountain, while the circuit in which the boat traveled around Saturn became the wheel of the world axis. Talbott points out that the world mountain of the Hindus, Mount Meru, was "designated as... 'the mast' of the Argha, the ship the gods."

Interestingly, in Egypt, the ship was likened to a serpent, as was the celestial "stream" in which it traveled. Egyptian depictions show the two masts of the ship as two serpent heads, and others depict the circuit in which the boat travels as a serpent biting its tail - the universal symbol of the Orobouros. The body of the serpent is depicted as a wavy line, emphasizing its association with water. Both the ship and the watery pathway were also identified with the womb of the mother goddess. Writes Talbott:

"Virtually every mythical form of the sun-god's dwelling...was declared to be a 'ship' sailing on the cosmic waters. The ancient mother goddess, conceived as a luminous 'womb' in the sky, was also invoked as the 'ship.' Thus, 'ship' is the name of the womb of the Sumerian Inanna. Correspondingly, 'the ship of the brilliant offspring' was an epithet of the Babylonian goddess Bau. The Egyptians conceived the band of the enclosed sun as the womb of the goddess

Nut, also called a 'ship.' The Pyramid Texts say, 'Row me, O mother of mine; row me O abode of mine. O Boat of the sky... O Boat of Nut.'"

This celestial stream or waterway which was the pathway of the Heavenly Boat was also symbolized as "a lake of hair." Furthermore, a lock of hair was affixed to the mast so that the ship could be towed across the sky. Who did the towing? Why, none other than our old friend, the planet Venus! This is important because Venus and Saturn, or Kronos, had a very special relationship.

According to many versions of the tale, Venus was actually Saturn's daughter. He had been feuding with his father, Ouranus, and was castrated. His penis fell to Earth, plunged into the sea, and inseminated Rhea, the Earth goddess. A cloud of foam rising from the sea gave birth to Venus. This is where we get our picture of Venus rising from the half-shell out of the ocean. Those who have read the other articles in this issue will see the parallels to the "Dolorous Stroke" which castrated the Fisher King, as well as Osiris being murdered, dismembered, and dumped in the Nile river by his father, where his penis was eaten by a fish. There is also an obvious parallel with the story of the "Quinotaur" or the sea monster that spawned the Merovingian kings. One of my sources claimed that Venus was sometimes depicted as the fish-goddess "Atargatis", and another source claimed that Dagon "sometimes incarnated as a female, 'Atargatis.'" (Note that the word is very similar to "Astarte" and "Agartha".) Furthermore, Dagon is connected to the figure of Oannes, who is connected to Janus, the double-headed one. One source also pointed out that the "vesica pisces" is an emblem the female vagina, as well as the Christian "ichthys." As I have said many times previously in my Grail writings, we seem to be running up against something with Hermaphroditic qualities. Incidentally, just as Kronos is symbolized by a six-pointed star, Venus is symbolized by a five-pointed star, and both symbols have shown up repeatedly in the story of Rennes-le-Chateau and the Priory of Sion. [5]

The birth of Venus is believed to have taken place at a specific spot in the ocean, "Petra tou Romiou", or "the Rock of the Romans." This brings to my mind the similarity between the story of Kronos' penis being pitched to Earth and the story of the stone that fell from Heaven, which as I have established in a previous article, symbolizes both the secret doctrine of knowledge that the gods taught to mankind, and also the divine seed which they passed down to their human/hybrid descendants. The fact that the disembodied penis produced progeny implies that this myth is a statement on Kronos' title "the Forgotten Father." And it was Kronos who was the father of the Titans, the race of gods who were cast into the underworld by Zeus after being overthrown by him. H.P. Blavatsky wrote in *The Secret Doctrine*:

"...it is suspected that the name of 'Titan' is derived from Tit-Ain - 'The fountains of the chaotic abyss' (Tit-Theus, or Tityus is 'the divine deluge.); and thus the Titans... are shown to be connected with the Flood..."

Indeed, the Titans would have been connected with the Flood, for they were the kings of Atlantis according to author Ignatius Donnelly, and therefore masters of navigation. Even David Talbott confirms this:

"It is generally agreed that Ovid is correct in saying that this ship of Saturn is that which appears on the reverse of coins stamped with the double face of Janus. The latter god, Saturn's acknowledged alter ego, was remembered as the 'inventor' of ships."

This statement is interesting not only because it implies that Janus and Saturn are the same, and therefore, so are Dagon, Oannes and Poseidon. It also says that the Titans, as literal historical figures, had actual boats, on Earth, upon which they sailed the seven seas. This is how they built their global empire, discussed in other articles in this issue. This is not mere symbolism. This actually happened. It makes sense then, that these gods who were masters of navigation would have been the ones to assist Noah, or whatever he was called depending on the culture, in the survival of the Flood, by teaching him navigation. It is clear that man knew nothing of this prior to the Flood.

This was one of the most vital transmissions of sacred, forbidden knowledge from god to man that ever happened. And navigation is done by means of the stars!

This is perhaps the point at which all of these symbols converge. Wisdom has always been associated with the stars. Wise men are said to be able to "read" the stars. There are even alphabets in which the characters are based on constellations, or the movement of stars. The night sky, therefore, can be likened to a book, or perhaps, better yet, a tablet. Is this what Enoch meant when he wrote that the gods showed him "The Tablet of Heaven", from which he copied and inscribed his own Emerald Tablet of forbidden knowledge? *The Book of Enoch* itself attests that this knowledge consisted largely of the specific mathematics of the revolutions of the heavenly bodies. And this Emerald Tablet which Enoch wrote was then given to Noah, who took it on board the Ark. As noted in another article, this same tablet may have also ended up in the Ark of the Covenant, making one wonder if the word itself does not imply a vessel containing this tablet.

It is worth noting other similarities between the "Ark of Heaven", the Ark of Noah, and the Ark of the Covenant. Just as the celestial boat was sometimes called the "Chariot of the Sun", the Ark of the Covenant was called the "Chariot of God." Also, God's throne in Heaven is described in the Bible as a chariot, and the Ark of the Covenant is referred to as God's throne, while the Ship of Saturn was believed to contain his throne as well. Both the Ark of the Covenant and the Ark of Noah were built according to specific instructions supplied by God, and therefore involve the principles of sacred architecture. This, along with navigation, was another piece of divine knowledge passed down during the Flood, and notably, both are now associated with the use of a compass, although the word signifies a different device depending on the context in which we are speaking. Furthermore, this knowledge was passed down from the "Arch of Heaven", but only to the elite descendants of the gods, and is therefore "*arcane.*" We seem to be witnessing a convergence of symbols that were once thought to be completely separate.

H. P. Blavatsky wrote in *The Secret Doctrine* that: "...like all other legends, that of 'the Deluge' has more than one meaning... some accounts refer to the sidereal and cosmic Flood before the so-called creation, the others treat, one of the Great Flood of Matter on Earth, and the other of a real watery deluge." I would certainly agree that there is more than one meaning. For at some point in the mythic consciousness of our ancestors, the real, literal, and historically existent god-kings of Atlantis, who were masters of navigation, and therefore sea-gods, got merged with the occurrences in the celestial sea, with the pilot of the Boat of Heaven. This is undoubtedly because the real, historical gods purposely associated themselves with the stars.

As I mentioned previously, *The Book of Enoch* describes the gods, angels, or "Watchers" in heaven as literally being stars. According to the text, at some point these stars descended from Heaven to mate with the human females below:

"I looked in my vision and surveyed heaven; when behold I saw many stars which descended... they all protruded their parts of shame like horses, and began to ascend the young cows, all of whom became pregnant, and brought forth elephants, camels, and asses."

The cows represent the human females, and the other animals are the "giants" or "monsters" which were said to have come from this union of god and man. Such breeding was, of course against the rules in Heaven. And so the Lord had the Earth flooded, to rid it of this pestilence, while the rebellious angels were imprisoned in Hell, situated in the center of the Earth.

Likewise, Kronos is said to have fallen from Heaven, and been imprisoned in the underworld as the "Lord of the Earth", a title also given to Satan. Even David Talbott's model of the ship of Saturn had to at one point changed into the night sky that we see today. This is described in *The Book of Enoch* when it says, "The face of Heaven will change." Some change of orbit must have occurred, and a heavenly body must have fallen out of the sky, plunging to Earth. This could certainly have caused a flood, in all of the manners in which it is described by the ancients. If the "firmament of Heaven" had still been in existence at that point, it would have been melted, or busted open. Thus, the "Floodgates of Heaven were opened." The impact would have caused the seas to overflow, and if the Earth is full of water as some have claimed, it would have cracked the crust of the Earth open and brought those waters forth as well, just as the flood accounts describe, when the Earth opens up and "the Fountains of the Deep" are loosed. It may have even caused a changed in polarity of the Earth. All of these things are described very explicitly in *The Book of Enoch*:

"In those days Noah saw that the earth became inclined, and that destruction approached."

In almost every culture, a myth like this exists. Rebellious gods breed with humans, and give forbidden knowledge to mankind. This causes anger with the other gods, who flooded the Earth in retaliation. The rebellious gods decide to save one family, or one person, by teaching him how to build a boat. A long period of time passes. He washes up on a mountain top. He sends out a bird, and when it returns with mud on its feet, or a branch in its beak, or doesn't return at all, he deems it safe to disembark.

Especially interesting is the recurrence of the word "Ark" in reference to the boat, which gets confused mythologically with the divine boat of Heaven. "Argha" was the celestial boat of the Hindus, while the Boat of Ra was called the "Bark." Hercules, who sailed the night in the Cup of Helios, the Sun, was sometimes referred to as "Arkaleus." "Argo" was the name of another mythological ship in which the Greek gods sailed (most notably, Jason and the Argonauts), which itself was said to be made from the "guiding timber" of the "Ark" of Deucalion, the Greek Noah character. Deucalion was also said to have repopulated the Earth by throwing stones behind his back, which then magically transformed into a race of humans. Once again, the stone that fell from Heaven implies the transference of divine seed into humans, who then repopulate the post-diluvian world. And quite notably, in other instances, "Arks" are referred to as containers of divine seed. In the Masonic ritual of the "Prince of the Tabernacle", an "Ark" is proceeded around the room which is said to contain "the organs of generation of Osiris." Likewise, in the Grecian "Mysteries of Samothrace", a similar myth was re-enacted. As Albert Pike describes, "The Diosairi, tutelary Deities of Navigation [emphasis added], with Venus, were invoked." The ceremony involved the mimicked the death of someone "slain by his brothers, who fled into Etruria, carrying with him the chest or Ark that contained his genitals: and there the phallus and the sacred Ark were adored."

In these various myths, the person playing the character of Noah is almost always a literal blood descendant of the rebellious gods. The historian Berosus wrote that Noah himself was married to the goddess Titea, who some say was the mother of the Titans. G.S. Faber tried to identify Noah with the Phoenician god "Agruerus", and H.P. Blavatsky writes of him:

"Agruerus is Kronos, or Saturn, and the prototype of the Israelitish Jehovah. As connected with the Argha, the... Ark of Salvation, Noah is mythologically one with Saturn."

Yet from another source, we have the following account:

"Xisuthrus (the Babylonian Noah) was warned about the flood beforehand by the deity Cronos, and told to build a ship and take with him his friends and relations and all the different animals with all necessary food and trust himself fearlessly to the deep."

Although the accounts are confused, it is clear that Kronos is associated with the Ark of Noah one way or another. Perhaps the most obvious answer is that Noah has been confused with Kronos because he was a blood relation to Kronos, perhaps even his son. We know that Noah had some sort of divine parentage. This is made clear in the Biblical account of his birth, and even more so in *The Book of Enoch*:

"She [Noah's mother] became pregnant by him, and brought forth a child, the flesh of which was white as snow and red as a rose; the hair of whose

head was white like wool, and long; and whose eyes were beautiful. When he opened them, he illuminated all the house, like the sun; the whole house abounded with light. And when he was taken from the hand of the midwife, opening also his mouth, he spoke to the Lord of righteousness. Then Lamech his father was afraid of him, and flying away came to his own father Mathusala, and said: I have begotten a son, a changed son. He is not human; but resembling the offspring of the angels of heaven, is of a different nature from ours, being altogether unlike us. His eyes are bright as the rays of the sun; his countenance glorious and he looks not as if he belonged to me, but to the angels."*

Noah, clearly then, was of divine parentage, as are all the characters who play his role in the various myths throughout the globe. In the Noah myth, this divine father appears to be Kronos, or perhaps, as some sources say, Oannes, who himself appears to be either the same, or at least represents basically the same things as, Kronos. As the father of Noah, therefore, Kronos would have become the ancestor of all humanity, for it was Noah's line alone that would survive the Flood. Now we understand his title of "the Forgotten Father." Indeed, it appears that he was also involved in warning Noah of the Flood and helping him to build the Ark.

This is the point that I wish to get across. The Deluge was a most pivotal time period, in which the divine seed was passed down to mankind, and the forbidden knowledge of the gods was passed down to those offspring. In *The Book of Enoch* we read of the Flood:

"In those days shall punishment go forth from the Lord of Spirits; and the receptables of water which are above the heavens shall be opened, and the fountains likewise, which are under the heavens and under the earth. All the waters which are in the heavens and above them, shall be mixed together. The water which is above heaven shall be the male; And the water which is under the earth shall be female; and all shall be destroyed who dwell upon the earth, and who dwell under the extremities of heaven."

Clearly the Flood itself is being likened to this insemination, when the waters from above meet the waters below. The sky was literally falling. Heaven and Earth were becoming one. The divine wisdom (symbolized by the celestial waters) poured down on their human offspring, and the divine seed poured into the human females. This is at once, symbolically, the cause of the Flood, and the Flood itself. And the Ark of Heaven, piloted by Saturn, became the Ark of Noah, piloted by his son, navigating the Earth, in search of the Mount of Salvation.

The Ark, therefore, is the symbolic vessel that carried both that divine seed and that divine knowledge. This is at one with the symbol of the Earth itself being inseminated, like in the birth of Venus. It is remarkable, then, that in the Egyptian versions of the story, it was Isis herself (the Egyptian equivalent of Venus) who was shut up in the Ark, and who piloted it to safety. Also note that in the Sumerian legends, the celestial Ark was piloted by Enki (whom the Greeks considered to be the same as Saturn), and it was called the "Magur-boat." Magur is reminiscent of "Magdalen", whom I have established in previous articles as being a personification of Venus. I am reminded of the story of the Ship of Solomon, piloted by an unseen force, which brought Mary Magdalen and her divine/royal offspring (the child of Jesus) to France. Note also that I have already drawn a connection between Solomon and Kronos, because of the etymology of Solomon's name, and because they both use the same seal, the six-pointed star. Venus is symbolized by a five-pointed star, which is "Star of David", the head of the royal house from which Magdalen's child came.

It was this the bloodline which, according to the Bible, ultimately came from Noah, and which ultimately resulted in Jesus Christ, the Merovingian Kings of France (including Dagobert II), and finally, most of the royal houses of Europe, as well as all of the Presidents of the United States. This is what I have referred to repeatedly in this magazine as "the bloodline of the Holy Grail." And the Ark, as the sacred vessel, can be likened to the Grail cup which metaphorically received that blood. Like the Grail, the ark is a symbol of the vessel that received the divine transmission of both seed and sacred knowledge. And though the waters of the deluge have subsided, the holy ark of God sails on, ready to alight in fresh ports where the light of this divine knowledge has yet to be disseminated.

Appendix:

From the recently-published *Space Travelers and the Genesis of the Human Form* by Joan d'Arc I have, since writing the above article, gleaned the following, highly relevant information, indicating that the Flood was associated with the planet Saturn not only by ancient man, but by the famous astrophysicist, Emmanuel Velikovsky. It also suggests the theory, proposed in the *Dagobert's Revenge* article "Le Serpent Rouge Reinterpreted", that the Noah's Ark scenario occurred for a number of people on Earth during the Flood, each landing on a different mountain, which was for them the equivalent of Mt. Ararat. I quote from *Space Travelers*:

"[Velikovsky] noted that rabbinical sources refer to the building of many arks before the deluge. Velikovsky suggested that there were perhaps many Noahs, but only one of the arks actually survived. He wrote, however, that ancient stories say that other people survived the flood waters in caves high in the mountains, in far separated regions of the Earth... The continents changed their places, and even the sky was not the same.

The Astrological connection between Saturn and water catastrophes was a very ancient origin, wrote Velikovsky. Many ancient astrologers, including Ptolemy, attributed floods to the planet Saturn. The Hindus assigned the deluge to the end of the Satyu Yuga, and the reign of the Satyavrata, or Saturn. The Saturnian age was the age of the Flood, and Brahma (the planet Saturn) is said to have warned Manu of the deluge. After the waters covered the Earth, Brahma is said to have 'floated over the expanse of the ocean.' An ancient woodcut portrays Brahma seated 'on a rayed disk', which is hovering over the waters of the deluge. The woodcut contains the words: 'Then the Lord floated over the vast ocean, void of the sun and moon.'

In his publication Kronos, Velikovsky noted that the identification of Brahma with Saturn is evidenced by the fact that the god is assigned a celestial sphere. A celestial sphere could be interpreted as an 'orbit.' Velikovsky noted that legends tell that the 'high-souled Brahma is seated in the highest abode', and that the 'highest celestial sphere is that of Brahma.'

... Velikovsky ascribed the universal deluge to a catastrophe, invoking the planet Saturn, which, he believed, exploded like a supernova. The date of the event, he claimed, was possibly about ten thousand years ago. He believed the solar system, and perhaps points beyond, were illuminated by this exploding star, 'and in a matter of a week the Earth was enveloped in waters of a Saturnian origin.'"

This sounds very similar to the Saturnian catastrophe that David Talbott described in his article, which, he believes, also caused the Flood, even implying, as Talbot did, that Saturn was the brightest object in the night's sky at that time. Such a catastrophe would have been huge, and global, wiping out 90% of all life. Any survivors, locked in the many arks that Velikovsky imagined, would have had to remain floating aimlessly until the water began to subside, and then only the mountain tops would be inhabitable, as I have speculated must have occurred in the French Pyrenees mountains, one of the first post-Diluvian settlements. Joan d'Arc makes a similar observation later on:

"Archeologists have always been curious about the peculiar origins husbandry and agriculture in the mountainous regions of Mt. Ararat - a strange place for agricultural beginnings. Even the Table of Nations in Genesis 10 seems to suggest that higher areas were populated first... The first seven nations to be established by the lineage of Noah were situated in the highlands of Asia Minor, the Black Sea, and the Caspian Sea. The lower coastal areas and islands were settled by much later descendants, since these areas were not habitable until much later."

Evidence that a civilization did spring up in the immediate surroundings of the landing-point of

Noah's Ark is presented in the book *The Day Behemoth and Leviathan Died*, by David Allen Deal. Deal writes about the archeological team that discovered what were believed to be the remains of Noah's Ark in Turkey in 1977, and an ancient city near the surrounding area that was presumably built by Noah himself. Deal writes:

"On October 7th, 1998, confirmation and identification of the lost city of Naxuan was made by a team of three... of an ancient culture just at the place of the Ark's landing at 7400' up on Judi Dagi, just east of Dogubayazit, adjacent to the Iranian border. This site is also an ancient necropolis, used for thousands of years, with millions of graves extant... Hood, Sura of the Koran proclaims that the Ark landed on 'Al-Judi' (Cudi Dagi in Turkish is pronounced Judi.) The name Cudi is derived from the ancient Shemitic cognate khud, meaning 'first', or 'the first.' It is not only the name of the mountain - the first settlement after the flood, but it is the source of the name of its perennial occupants as well, the Khurds. The ancient rendering for the region is the mountains of Corduria, the 'mountain of the Khurds.'"

This etymology is particularly interesting given that which I have already examined in other articles. "Cudi" is similar to "Cadi", which, as I have stated, refers to the Akkadians, and the ancient god-kings of Atlantis known as the "Khatti." The word "Cuddy" still implies fish in many languages, thus, for instance, the word "cuttlefish." In fact one of the Atlantean kings wrote his name as the hieroglyph for a cuttlefish. That this would mean the same thing as "Judi" implies that the word "Judah", and thus "Jew", came from this root in addition to the tribal name "Khurd." That it has the word "Dagi" attached to it is also interesting, for it implies the Atlantean King Dagon, who was also known as "El", or "Al", meaning "lord." Deal continues:

"This is the very important mountain that is mentioned by ancient writers such as Berosus and the Koran. It is the very twin-peaked (breasted) 'Mountain of Mashu or Mesha' which was written of in the ancient Sumerian/ Babylonian Epic of Gilgamesh, as well as the Bible. (Genesis 10:30) It is in the 'hairy Urartu' or 'mountains of Urartu', to quote the Bible, seventeen miles across the valley from Mt. Ararat."

Readers may recognize these "Mountains of Mashu" from the article "Dead But Dreaming", about H.P. Lovecraft and *The Necronomicon*, where the "Mountains of Mashu" are named as the place where the evil ancient ones, consigned to the underworld, congregate, and it is suggested that they can travel from the underworld, to Earth and all the way up to Heaven via these mountains. A similar implication is brought forth by David Allen Deal later on. He also elaborated on the meaning of the name:

"This mountain [Dagi] has an adjacent, or descent which is called Masher in Turkish, meaning doomsday - or Mashur, meaning resurrection; both probably deriving from the Shemitic word for rescue from the water (Mashesh.) Moses was similarly named Moshesh - because he was rescued from death out of the Nile waters... Judi-Cudi Dagi is the name of the highest peak on the Ark mountain, a modern city in present-day Armenia, situated 75 miles east of both Mount Ararat and the Ark of Mount Judi (Cudi), near Dogubayazit, Turkey, bears the name 'Nachicevan', which is the same as Noah's city Naxuan (a) noach (= Noah) - tsywn (= Zion, meaning 'capitol city'), or also, possibly Noakh-tswaneh, (meaning 'Noah's sheepfold')."

This paragraph is interesting for several reasons. For one, it states that "Mashu" may come from a word that means "rescue from water", bringing to mind the phrase "deliver me from the mire" from the poem *Le Serpent Rouge*. It also states that the name of Noah's capital was "Noah's Sion", and that the word Sion means capitol. This may shed new light the Priory of Sion's apparent interest in the Flood of Noah, referred to repeatedly in *Le Serpent Rouge*, which they published. Perhaps the "Sion" which they are dedicated to is something more that just a symbol of Jerusalem, and perhaps the "Ark" treasure believed to be buried at Rennes-le-Chateau is more than just the Ark of the Covenant, as has been previously presumed. The phrase "Noah's sheepfold" also implies the kings of Atlantis, who were called shepherds. And the fact that the place of the Ark's landing became a large necropolis, known as "Doomsday", is significant too, for in *Le Serpent Rouge* it is implied that part of the buried treasure of Rennes-le-Chateau involves "embalmed corpses." Deal continues in detail:

"...Nearly two thousand years before our time, Josephus the Jewish historian made mention of the city of Naxuan... Noah had been dead for 2100 years before Josephus took up his writings in the first century A.D. Such a time span is terribly long to keep a monument active. Facts which shall be presented give rise to the following hypothesis; in order for such a monument to remain in service it would have to be a secular necropolis, a city of the dead, totally independent of the empires - a burial ground that everyone could be connected to no matter which family of man, religion, or state, because at this level all men are descendants of Noah... All families of the earth, all nationalities, all religions, all united in death, awaiting doomsday on Masher Dag with Noah and his Ark... 'Mashu-Mesha-Mashur' meaning 'Judgment Day' or 'Doomsday'... In The Epic of Gilgamesh, *the hero comes to the mountain called Mashu, to meet with Utnapishtim, the 'ageless one' who has been saved from the Deluge. David Fasold points out that the name Mashu is virtually the same as the name of the slope where the Ark remains are found, 'Mashur.' This name is the same as the name given in the Bible in Genesis, Mesha."*

Deal goes on to present archeological evidence that while the Ark had originally been parked on Naxuan, which is called locally 'the place of first descent', soil erosion caused it to slide downhill. He writes, "The old Ark had broken away, hull still intact, from just below the escarpment known locally as Yigityatagi, or 'Hero's Bed.'" This is fascinating, because it implies a connection to the other "hero's bed' believes to be located in Montsegur, France, along with the treasure - the Tomb of Hercules. Writes Deal:

"Near the site where the ruined Ark now rests, is a small town of stone an mud-walled Kurdish houses, and most likely is the remains of the latest and final permutation of Seron, known as 'the city of dispersion.' Nearby towns called "sar" and "Na-sar" may have been reflections of the original name Seron... The Ark descended, and impaled itself on a sharp rock, or 'tsar', in the Shemitic Aramaic Hebrew languages, giving name to the city of 'Tsaron.'"

In this paragraph, Deal not only shows that the Biblical name of Sharon (as in "the Rose of Sharon") derives from the name for "sharp rock", but I feel that the words "Tsar" (meaning "king") and "star" may be linked as well. This makes sense, because a king's rule symbolically rests upon a stone - a stone which in many cultures is said to have fallen from Heaven, and which is sometimes referred to as a "star." In Jewish culture, this stone is the "rock of Sion." He comments further:

"The point of impact and penetration of the side of the hull by the great sharp rock (tsar) shows quite well how the forces of impact have both distorted the hull and bent the pulpit by means of its pivotal motion after it became attached to the sharp rock. Anchor stones, huge one, have been discovered both neat the Ark (Kazan) and have been reported hundreds of miles up-course at the original site of Ankara, Turkey. (Ankara means anchor in Greek.) Ton Wyatt of Tennessee reported finding one near the ark ruins and has shown a photo of it on his website... Gilgamesh stated that, 'It is impossible to pass over the waters of death without the stone things."

While the author obviously thinks that this is a reference to the use of anchors, I think it is more likely a reference to the use of lodestone for a compass in navigation, which was then known of, and even worshipped, by ancient man. It is worth noting that both compasses and anchors are important symbols in Freemasonry. Deal next turns his etymological insights to the word "ark":

"An ark, in Shemitic, is a chest or box, even a boat, properly (tubah.) Egyptians made chests in the shape of cats and other zoomorphic and even

anthropomorphic shapes. Sailors still call their boats 'tubs.' Could this be a reflection of the ancient word used for the great ship of Noah, a Tub-ah? The English word 'ark' also is a coffin in Hebrew. It is possible that Noah is still in his Ark, preserved as a lasting monument until doomsday? (Arwn is an ark: as in ark of the covenant. It also means coffin, as in <u>Genesis 50:26</u>.)"

These are important statements. For one thing, the emphasis on "Tubah" is interesting because Noah had a descendant named "Tubal-Cain" who is very important in Masonic lore, his name even being used as password in their order, and he is credited with having invented metallurgy. The notion of Noah being buried in his Ark ties in directly with the notion that Hercules, who also had an Ark, is buried within it, at Montsegur, the French equivalent to Ararat. Noah was supposedly the progenitor of all men, like Kronos, the "Forgotten Father", and his remains were therefore revered inside a sacred "ark." In this context it is worth reviewing Joan d'Arc's own examination of the word "ark" in *Space Travelers and the Genesis of the Human Form*, where she writes:

"The story of the Flood and the ark, which contains the 'archetype of all living creatures in pairs (the word arche in Greek is related to ark) goes back to at least Sumerian times. Robert Temple writes in <u>The Sirius Mystery</u> that the ark stories of the Greeks and of the Hebrews are 'extremely late forms of an exceedingly ancient story, which existed thousands of years before there were such things as Greeks or Hebrews in existence.' He research concludes that both sources are describing magical ships in which sit 'those who come out of the womb' in the sense that they repopulate the world after the deluge.' Specifically, the reference to those who come out of the womb, Temple writes, 'seems to refer to the children of the Earth goddess springing from the womb of the Earth.'"

David Allen Deal seems to come to similar conclusions after examining the Mountains of Mashu, and the legends that surround them, for he felt that the mountains themselves symbolized both the center and the origin of all things. The fact that the mountains of Mashu are twin-peaked ties them in directly with the "world mountain" with "two horns" that David Talbott associates with the ship of Saturn. Deal makes the same connection, and also associates it with the origination of the mother-goddess concept. Deal quotes from *The Epic of Gilgamesh*:

"So at length Gilgamesh came to Mashu, the great mountains about which he had heard many things, which guard the rising and the setting of the sun. Its twin peaks are high as the Wall of Heaven, and its paps reach down into the Underworld... the mountains that guard the rising sun."

There you have it. The "world mountain" of Mashu was considered a gateway to both Heaven and Hell, as well as the place where the Sun rises. You couldn't ask for imagery more closely associated with the Grail. Deal then comments:

"This term, 'its paps', define it as a female place, at least in the view of the author of the Epic of Gilgamesh. This Mashu was the dwelling-place of Noah (Utnapishtim of the Akkadians.) Others have identified this place as Naxuan. It has been spelled variously Naxuan... Naxuana, Nachidsheuan (literally, Noach-tsywn, which means Noah's Zion, or capitol.) ... It is the place that 'first man' and 'first woman' emerged from Mother Earth."

Deal believes that the mountains and the remains of the Ark itself physically suggest the body of the Mother Goddess:

"Looking up to the mountain Cudi Dagi, it is a simple analog to identify the female breasts along the escarpment, the 'twin peaks' and 'paps' of Gilgamesh. But what really ties the thought together is the vaginal shape of the vessel, the remains of the ark laying in a large triangular patch of expansive mud flow soil, a true Mons Venis. And how fitting it is to have humanity emerge again, in rebirth, as it were, from the female-formed vessel that had so recently saved them from the flood of destruction... The Mother Earth concept must surely have sprung from it at

an early date, and this means that Byanu, or Venus of the Celts must have also derived from it as well."

Recalling how Venus' own birth had once been achieved from the severed penis of Kronos, cast into the ocean, and what we know about Egyptian legends that Venus was in fact the pilot of the Ark, this is very important. Deal continues.

"...The Venus connection is a very simple one, although it has, as with most mystery religions, a double-entendre or hidden meaning. Since we see that the Mother Ship of mankind (and the scene about her) had taken on the attributes of a part of the anatomy of a woman - interestingly, boats are female in our culture - a woman who is now embedded in the mud of the earth, who had, in an abstract sense, given birth to a new generation of humanity, or at the very least had been an instrument of that rebirth, we may look to the Shemitic double-meaning in the earth-goddess name 'byanu.' In Hebrew, a Shemitic language (Akkadian Shemitic is the language of the Epic of Gilgamesh), the letter 'b' is a prefix that means by, in or at. Then 'an' is a singular form of 'ani', meaning ships. Nu is a well-known short form of the name of the flood hero, Noah (e.g. AN-NU of the Egyptians, also a Shemitic language.)

Therefore, 'b-an-nu', an early name for the earth-mother goddess of the Gaelic-Keltic peoples of Europe and otherwise known as the goddess Venus, may also simply mean 'by our ship.'"

It would also mean, by implication, that Anu, the forefather of the Sumerian god-kings who gave them the name "Annunaki", has a name that is a compound of "ship" and the Sumerian name for Noah. And Deal makes it clear that these "gods" and "goddesses" were based on real, historical people. He writes of the goddess:

"... She began as a human personage, Queen Semeramis (her name means doves), who along with her husband, Assur, or Nimrod, the mighty hunter who opposed Yahweh (he is claimed to have begun a war against the 'god of heaven' and built a high tower to shoot arrows up at the 'gods.') started a free-love religion and was prosecuted (and executed) by Shem, and a counsel of eighty elders. His body was hacked to pieces and sent to all the city-states of the day as a warning to any future apostates... Of course, by the next cultural generation in Egypt, Shem 'the righteous' became Set, the 'evil', and poor 'Osiris' (Egyptian Nimrod) is seen as having been hacked to pieces."

Deal ties the goddess concept in with the Ark, and shows that the Ark represented the "Cosmic Egg" from which, in mythology, the human race emerged after the Flood (or sometimes, at the beginning of creation). He also shows how it lead to the universal association of eggs and goddess-worship, inherent in the ritual celebration of Easter. Of Ishtar he writes:

"In her myth, she was supposedly born from a huge egg that, according to the legend, had landed somewhere not far from the river Euphrates. After she somehow got out of this great egg, which Hyslop quite accurately equates to Noah's Ark, Ishtar was attended by doves, which have ever since become her symbol, one freely used for her in Christianity to this very day. She is also normally seen as a mother holding a child, a Madonna with doves descending as a major motif.

Meanwhile, back in reality, the Ark of Noah had indeed been 'attended to by doves', the very dove or doves sent out a week apart to determine the level of the water as the flood subsided. The parallel is clear once one is able to equate Ishtar (Great Mother Goddess) with the Ark of Noah. As her religion developed observances of Ishtar's feast day, or more properly, her husband Marduk the Babylonian sun god's day, it came to involve pre-dawn gathering to face the east and the sun rising on vernal equinox morning (surprisingly close to Easter with its pagan sun worship). This idea ultimately became associated with Ishtar/Easter eggs, recalling her 'great egg' that had in reality been 'the Ark of Noah.'"

Then Deal points out something very interesting about Noah which may link him even more closely with Kronos. You will recall that Kronos was castrated, his penis landing in the ocean next to the "Rock of the Romans", miraculously spawning the Lady Venus of the ocean waters. Deal writes:

> "In the biblical story, Noah is 'harmed' in some physical way after the flood by kHam's son Canaan while drunk from wine he had made. Canaan is subsequently cursed. Extra-biblical accounts claim that Shem castrated his grandfather, and that is the reason for the radical curse cast on him. There is much in Greek mythology to support this idea."

The element in Greek mythology that I presume he is talking about is the story of Kronos. Deal continues, linking the castrated Canaan with the fratricidal Cain of <u>Genesis</u> - forefather, some believe, to the divine/infernal Grail family. In this light, it is interesting to examine Deal's contention that a conspiracy existed even before the Flood to marry the line of Cain in with the line of Noah to ensure that the bloodline survived the deluge. Deal states:

> "In Cain's lineage, the ninth generation, a female is mentioned in the Bible. She is Naamah, the sister of Tubal-Cain. It is rare for a female to be listed in the biblical genealogies of any family. If Naamah had married kHam, she would have accomplished three things.
>
> First, she would have brought Cain's bloodlines through the flood. Secondly, she would have become the mother of Canaan (named for Cain?) and therefore all the kHametic peoples of the post-flood world. Lastly, she may have caused Noah's distress that his number-one son, kHam had seen fit to marry a descendant of Cain, the murderer, rather than a female from Seth's good line... Naamah would have been the mother of the cursed Canaan and would have been viewed as the great matriarchal ancestral personage that came through the 'primordial flood waters, opposed to the bad male Shem', who, acting as world-king, later hacked her grandson Nimrod to death. These two opposing forces were in play very early on. KHametic peoples with their prevalent matriarchal beliefs, and Shemitic peoples with their male deity Yahweh. Nimrod, the grandson of kHam and Naamah, was claimed to have instituted a great apostasy against Yahweh, who 'dwelt in the skies.' He built a high tower for the fight. He was possessed with hate against Yahweh, probably brought on by his grandmother Naamah's hate of Adam's king line, and perhaps even for Noah, her father-in-law, who was a lineal descendant in the king line."

Interestingly, Deal points out that Set, or Seth, is portrayed as alternately a godly man, in the Jewish tradition, or the Devil himself, in the Egyptian tradition, proving that good and evil are subjective according to the local politics of a given culture. Such a transformation seems to have occurred with Satan, of whom Set is a prototype, and who was, in earlier times, perceived as a good guy, a bearer of wisdom and good intentions towards mankind. Deal also show that the Tower of Babel story has a historical basis in the true story of the Babylonian king Nimrod. It is worthy of note that the Tower of Babel story shows up closely in proximity to the Flood story, and would seem to be interrelated somehow. Most cultures that have Flood stories also have Tower of Babel stories, also located closely together in chronological time.

Endnotes:

[1] If the Earth really was covered with a "Firmament" of ice this reflection of light would have become even more distorted and pronounced.

[2] This would explain while the Black Sun is sometimes called "the Midnight Sun."

[3] The word Moon is very close to "Mon", an incarnation of Ra who was called "the Hidden God." This is almost exactly like the title "the Hidden One" which is applied to Saturn. Note also that in occultism Saturn is associated with the six-pointed star, sometimes called the "Seal of Solomon." Solomon's name, taken apart, could translate to "Sol-Mon" - "the Hidden Sun."

[4] We are reminded of the Hindi story of the fish who towed the Ark to safety during the Deluge by means of his horn.

[5] Often, the six-pointed star is erroneously referred to as "the Star of David", and has been branded as such in popular culture.

Hiram, King of Tyre

By Boyd Rice

The Phoenician city of Tyre is most well-known from the legendary tale of its siege by Alexander the Great. When Alexander decided to capture Tyre, he had a string of victories under his belt, and seemed an unstoppable force. But even his staunchest supporters questioned the wisdom of trying to take a city as mighty as Tyre. Conventional wisdom deemed Tyre as virtually unconquerable, as it was situated on an island surrounded by a turbulent sea. It had been a powerful city-state for centuries, and was a place viewed by outsiders with a kind of mythic awe. This, of course, made Alexander all the more determined to succeed in his quest. So his soldiers put aside their swords, and spent the next seven months constructing a land bridge out to the island. The Tyrians, who had ruled the seas for nearly a thousand years, were out of their element in a land battle.

Having taken Tyre, Alexander ordered the construction of 2000 crosses upon which the vanquished males would be crucified. The crosses were placed along the shore so as to be visible across the waters. 30,000 men, women and children were sold into slavery. Alexander's measures were generally not so harsh, but the Tyrians had offended him. He had been on his way to Egypt, and merely wanted to visit the Temple of Melqart in Tyre to make a sacrifice. When he was refused access, he became angry. And the rest, as they say, is history.

This is perhaps the most famous episode in the life of Alexander, a man whose life was an endless strong of spectacular dramas. Alexander claimed to be the son of God, and to the Macedonians, who worshipped Hercules, the Herculean task of building a causeway through the sea to Tyre must have seemed like something right out of their myths and legends. The feat still astounds historians to this very day, and to this very day that same land bridge connects Tyre to the coast. Unfortunately, Alexander's spectacular triumph has tended to overshadow a far more astounding aspect of the story of Tyre: that the very island to which Alexander's army built a connecting bridge *was itself* man-made.

The Tyrian Phoenicians were a sea people, and when their most famous king decided to build himself a palace, he chose to build it on the sea. In order to do this, he had first to construct an island on which to build it. Historians speculate that an undertaking of such grand proportions must have kept thousands of people busy for many years. But when the island was completed, it became the center of the ancient world for centuries. Had the Tyrians not snubbed Alexander the Great, its likely that their power would have continued to grow exponentially.

The sea king at whose command Tyre was built was Hiram, most well-known for his role in building the Temple of Solomon. The reason for building a palace on an island seems to be part strategic and part symbolic. From the strategic point of view, a man-made island has far more disadvantages than advantages. Food and water had to be imported since the island was solid rock. But the Phoenicians were legendary traders, and this seems not to have constituted too great a difficulty. And for centuries, their isolation afforded the Tyrians a degree of security unknown to their neighbors. In symbolic terms, the sea seems to have been central to the religious beliefs of these people. Their principle gods were connected to the sea. They worshipped the sea god Melqart (the son of Poseidon), and Baal (son of the fish-god Dagon).

Baal, as son of Dagon, was a patron deity of mariners. He is depicted as having the horns of a bull, symbolism which links him to the notorious Quinotaur that purportedly fathered the race of Merovingians. Jurgen Sparruth, in *Atlantic of the North*, says:

"Schachermeyr has pointed out the importance which the sacrifice of bulls had in the cult of Poseidon. This god was worshipped as 'bull-formed', and in that shape he inhabited rivers and seas. One is reminded of the legend of the Elbstier,

the bull who lives in the mouth of the river Elbe, and in his rage arouses the flood; or of the story that the ancestor of the Merovingian kings was a sea-monster in the shape of a bull."

Worship of Baal was so central to the sea peoples that his name was often attached to the names of their city-states. For instance, Tyre, Sidon and Hazon were once called Baal-Tyre, Baal-Sidon, and Baal-Hazon. His consort Astarte was known as "our lady of the sea." Her cult is thought to have been transposed onto the Mary cult of Southern France. Interestingly, history records seven or eight crucified messiahs, all born of virgin births, and each having a mother named Mary (or some derivation thereof). Christ had both a mother *and* a wife named Mary.

Melqart is also a sea god, and strangely, is also deemed to be a consort of Astarte. In Hebrew tradition, he is Lord of the Underworld. Melqart is depicted on ancient coinage as riding on a sea horse. He is thought to be a derivation of the Akkadian god of the underworld, Nergal, and later became synchronized with the Roman Hercules. At first glance, the addition of Melqart to the Divine Couple of Baal and Astarte may seem to constitute an unlikely trinity; yet some observers speculate that Melqart was perceived as an alternate manifestation of Baal - essentially an evil twin of sorts. This seems consistent with what is known of the two. Baal lives atop a mountain, whereas Melqart dwells in the underworld. Baal is the patron deity of mariners, while Melqart is the god of storms and the sea. The Baal/Melqart hypothesis is certainly logical, and would explain how Astarte was viewed as a consort to both gods. Further evidence in support of this hypothesis is that Melqart is assumed to be synonymous with the Babylonian/Akkadian Marduk or Merodach. Marduk was also known under the name "Bel", which as you might well guess, equates with "Baal." The sea peoples carried the idea of Baal/Bel to the British Isles, where he was known as "Belenus." Celts celebrated his festival, known as "Beltane", on May 1.

King Hiram seems to have made a conscious effort to manipulate the archetype embodied in the Phoenician gods, so that he himself appeared to be a flesh and blood incarnation or extension of them. His throne sat before large windows opening upon the sea and crashing waves. Visitors to his palace may well have thought they'd entered the domain of Poseidon himself. That Hiram's status as a god-king was well-established at the time is evidenced by his inclusion as such in the Bible. In *Ezekiel*, Jehovah himself speaks to King Hiram, saying: *"Thou hast said I am a God, I sit in the seat of God, in the midst of the seas...."* Jehovah, a very jealous and angry God, would ordinarily smite whoever tried to usurp his authority, yet here he doesn't seem the least displeased. Elsewhere in *Ezekiel*, he even says, *"Thou hast been in Eden the garden of God... Thou wast perfect in thy ways..."* Why would the god of the Old Testament say such a thing to a Phoenician king? And why would Jehovah be so well-disposed to a man who erected temples to sea gods and proclaimed himself to *be* a god? The answer is simple: Hiram, like Solomon, was a descendant of King David; a fact that must have been common knowledge at the time *Ezekiel* was written.[1] Most historians present Hiram and Solomon as being from different nations, different cultures, and different races - in fact, they were relatives. What's more, a direct descendant of King Hiram was Joseph of Tyre, better known as St. Joseph, the father of Christ. If Hiram's role as Christ's ancestor has been glossed over by compilers of the Bible, it's probably because he was too legendary a figure, and his religious views too well-known to overlook or explain away. Consequently, his role was marginalized so as not to muddy the theological waters.

Many authors, both occultists and straightforward historians, maintain that Hiram of Tyre is synonymous with Hiram Abiff of Masonic legend. One theory says that Hiram Abiff is a code name and simply means "Hiram *who has vanished.*" Could King Hiram be that Hiram who has vanished? Did Hiram vanish essentially from Christ's genealogy because his strange beliefs might give too much insight into the genuine tradition in which this dynasty was rooted?

We know that Solomon put statues of Astarte in his temple. We are told that Solomon, in doing this, was simply "corrupted" by one of his many wives, who came from a place where such worship was common. And yet, Hiram too erected a temple to Astarte. This is not, as modern historians will tell you, merely indicative of goddess worship. Astarte was worshipped in conjunction with Baal, and was perceived both as his consort, and as an emanation of him. Many early religions were based on the concept of a Divine Couple, the most famous example being Isis and Osiris. Even the Judaic El was once part of a Divine Couple, his consort being Asherat. Asherat, of course, is synonymous with Astarte, and El mutated into Baal. In light of this we can see that even as the patriarchal Jehovah was gaining a stranglehold on the hearts and minds of his emerging cult, Hiram and Solomon remained true to the more ancient tradition of the divine couple. Rather than being heretics or eccentrics, they were purists maintaining a tradition in its original form. Church elders, in order to forever banish the Divine Couple concept, later changed references to "Astarte" to "Ashtoreth", thereby changing the female consort of God into a *male demon*.

Solomon's famous Temple, built by Hiram, is so well-known for its pillars of Jachin and Boaz (representing creative force and destructive force, respectively) that one would assume that it was wholly unique. In fact, it was patterned on three temples that existed on Tyre: one for Baal, one for Astarte, and one for Melqart. All three had the duel pillars of Jachin and Boaz. This lead one author, Gerhard Herm, to conclude that the Jachin/Boaz concept central to the cabala was of purely Phoenician origin, and had no "connection to any part of Jewish liturgy." Similar pillars were found at the Temple of Baal on Cyprus, and in Samaria, Megiddo, and Hazor. The descriptions of such pillars are invariably identical: Jachin is covered with gold and Boaz is covered with some emerald-colored material. Such descriptions also mention that the emerald pillar "shone brightly at night." This bizarre-seeming observation has lead to the speculation that the emerald pillar may have been constructed out of some kind of green glass tube in which there was a flame.

At any rate, it is clear that Hiram and Solomon were followers of the same basic doctrine. They employed the pillars of Jachin and Boaz for the same reason they refused to abandon the principle of the divine couple: both represented the dual nature of God. This is probably the same reason that the royal colors of the Merovingian kings were gold and green, a reminder of the true doctrine of their forebears, and the knowledge that perfect power comes from the equilibrium between mildness and severity.

Addendum: God the Father

The gods of the Tyrians are interesting insofar as they represent a stage in the evolution between what had come before and what eventually came after. On the one hand they were patterned after far more ancient deified kings; on the other hand, they obviously served as the prototypes for the deities of later cultures such as the Greeks and Romans. For instance, Melqart, patterned upon Marduk, was known as the "Tyrian Hercules", and later became synchronized with Hercules. The father of Hercules was Zeus, that of Marduk, Dagon. It follows then that Zeus and Dagon represent different incarnations (or representations) of the same figure. This premise seems to be substantiated by the fact that Zeus was also known as "Dyaus", and Dagon was also known as Daonos, two names so similar as to imply a common origin for the two. Dagon was likewise known as "Daos", from which we probably derive the word "Deus", or "God." Furthermore, Zeus was at times referred to as "Diu-Pater", which served as the basis for the Roman Jupiter. "Diu-Pater" translates simply as "God the Father." Though a title such as God the Father isn't paid too much serious attention in modern times, it could well indicate an important aspect of how the ancients viewed the notion of deity. This is to say, perhaps they viewed God, not as any sort of supernatural being, but rather as an *ancestor*.

Endnotes:

[1] Editor's note: It seems impossible that Hiram could have been a descendant of King David, as they both reigned at the same time. Hiram is recorded in II Samuel 5:11 as having assisted David in the building of the Temple, which was later finished with Hiram's help by David's son Solomon.

Monarchy: The Primordial Form of Government, and its Roots in the "Lord of the Earth" Concept

By Tracy Twyman

When the Stewart King James VI of Scotland ascended the throne of England to become King James I of Great Britain, he made a speech that shocked and appalled the nobles sitting in Parliament, who had been waxing increasingly bold over the last few years, attempting to limit the powers of the crown to strengthen their own. What shocked them was that James used his coronation speech to remind them of the ancient, traditional belief that a monarch is chosen by God to be his emissary and representative on Earth, and ought therefore to be responsible to no one but God. In other words, James was asserting what has become known to history as "the Divine Right of Kings", and the nobles didn't like it one bit. Quotes from the speech show how inflammatory his words actually were:

"The state of monarchy is the most supreme thing upon earth, for kings are not only God's lieutenants upon earth, and sit upon God's throne, but even by God himself are called gods... In the Scriptures kings are called gods, and so their power after a certain relation is compared to divine power. Kings are also compared to fathers of families: for a king is truly Parens patriae, the politique father of his people... Kings are justly called gods, for that they exercise a manner of resemblance of divine power upon earth: for if you will consider the attributes to God, you shall see how they agree in the person of a king."

The nobles were aghast. This fat, bloated pustule telling everyone to worship him as a god! It seemed patently ridiculous. Even more offensive, James finished up his speech by putting Parliament in its place, basically telling them that, since he ruled by the grace of God, any act or word spoken in contradiction of him was an act against God himself. James continued:

"I conclude then this point, touching the power of kings with this axiom of divinity, That as to dispute what God may do is blasphemy... so is it sedition in subjects to dispute what a king may do in the height of his power. I would not have you meddle with such ancient rights of mine as I have received from my predecessors... All novelties are dangerous as well in a politic as in a natural body, and therefore I would loath to be quarreled in my ancient rights and possessions, for that were to judge me unworthy of that which my predecessors had and left me."

Although it was James I that made the concept famous, he certainly did not invent the idea of Divine Right. The concept is, as I shall show, as old as civilization itself.

As harsh and dictatorial as it may seem, such a system actually protected the rights of individual citizens from even larger and more powerful bullies such as the Parliament and the Pope. When power rests ultimately in the hands of a single individual, beholden to nobody except God, who need not appease anyone for either money or votes, injustices are more likely to be righted after a direct appeal to the king. Furthermore, past monarchs who held their claims to power doggedly in the face of increasing opposition from the Catholic Church managed, as long as they held their power, to save their subjects from the forced religious indoctrination and social servitude that comes with a Catholic theocracy. Author Stephen Coston wrote in 1972's *Sources of English Constitutional History* that:

"Without the doctrine of the Divine Right, Roman Catholicism would have dominated history well beyond its current employment in the Dark Ages. Furthermore, Divine Right made it possible for the Protestant Reformation in England to take place, mature and spread to the rest of the world."

The Divine Right practiced by European monarchs was actually based on a more ancient doctrine practiced by the monarchs of Judah and Israel in the Old Testament, whom many European royal families considered to be their ancestors, tracing their royal European lineage back to the Jewish King David, sometimes through the descendants of Jesus Christ. Such as line of descent was (and is) known as the "Grail bloodline." One of Europe's most famous monarchs, Charlemagne the Great, was often called "David" in reference to his famous ancestor, and Habsburg King Otto was called "the son of David." In fact, the European tradition of anointing kings comes from that practiced in the Old Testament. Author George Athas describes how the ceremony symbolized the Lord Yahweh adopting the new king as his own son:

"Firstly, the king was the 'Anointed' of Yahweh - the mesiach, from which we derive the term 'Messiah.' At his anointing (or his coronation), the Spirit of Yahweh entered the king, giving him superhuman qualities and allowing him to carry out the dictates of the deity. The psalmist of Psalm 45 describes the king as 'fairer than the sons of men', and continued to praise his majestic characteristics. This king also had eternal life granted to him by Yahweh. The deity is portrayed as saying to him, 'You are my son - today I have sired you.' The king was Yahweh's Firstborn - the bekhor - who was the heir to his father's estate. He was 'the highest of the kings of the earth.' Thus, the king was adopted by Yahweh at his coronation and, as such, was in closer communion with the deity than the rest of the people. On many occasions, Yahweh is called the king's god. The king was distinguished far above the ordinary mortal, rendering him holy and his person sacred. It was regarded as a grievous offence to lay a hand on him. Thus, to overthrow the king was rebellion of the most heinous sort and an affront to the deity who had appointed the king... We can note that the king of Judah and Israel is described in divine terms. He is, for example, seen as sitting at Yahweh's right hand, and his adopted son. We find similar motifs of Pharaohs seated to the right of a deity of Egypt. Psalm 45:7 calls the king an 'elohim' - a god. Psalm 45:7 also says 'Your throne is like God's throne.'"

Here we see the basis for King James' claim that the scriptures likened human kings to gods. As such, kings were strongly associated with the priesthood as well, and in some cases took on priestly functions. However, traditionally, the Jewish priesthood was dominated by the tribe of Levi, which was biologically related but functionally separate from the royal line of David - that is, until Jesus came along, heir to both the kingly and priestly titles through his lineage back to both tribes. However, in other more ancient cultures, such as the Egyptian, the royal and priestly functions were inseparable. In addition to regarding their pharaohs as the literal offspring of deity, and in fact, deities themselves, the Egyptians believed that the institution of kingship itself had been given to them by the gods. Their first king had been one of their main gods, Osiris, whom all human kings were expected to emulate. Richard Cassaro, in his book, *A Deeper Truth*, elaborates:

"... during the First Time (the Golden Age when the gods ruled directly on Earth) a human yet eternal king named Osiris initiated a monarchial government in Egypt and imparted a wise law and spiritual wisdom to the people. At the end of his ministry, Osiris left his throne to the people. It was, thereafter, the duty of every king to rule over Egypt in the same manner Osiris had ruled."

This concept that kingship began with a single divine ruler who all subsequent human kings are descendants of can be traced back to the oldest civilization acknowledged by history, Sumeria, and the other Mesopotamian cultures that followed, such as the Assyrians and the Babylonians. To quote Henri Frankfort:

"In Mesopotamia, the king was regarded as taking on godhood at his coronation, and at every subsequent New Year festival. However, he was often seen as having been predestined to the divine throne by the gods at his birth, or even at the beginning of time. Through a sacred marriage, he had a metaphysical union with the mother goddess, who filled him with life, fertility, and blessing, which he passed onto his people."

The *Encyclopedia Britannica* has identified three different types of sacred kingship that were recognized in the ancient world. The king was seen as "(1) the receptacle of supernatural or divine power, (2) the divine or semi-divine ruler; and (3) the agent or mediator of the sacred." However, this author believes it is safe to say that all of these concepts stem from the almost universal belief that kingship descended from Heaven with a single divine being who was literally thought of as the ancestor of all those who followed. This king, I believe, was known to the ancients as Kronos, the Forgotten Father, and this is another name for the deity/planet, Saturn. He was the "brightest star in the heavens", who fell to Earth and intermarried with the daughters of men to breed a race of human kings (the Grail Bloodline), but was thereafter imprisoned in the underworld by his father, Zeus. Some might think this contradicts the traditional association of ancient kings with the Sun-god, but in fact, Saturn himself *was* a sun god of a sort. Some believe that in ancient times Saturn was the dominant figure in the night sky, and as such became known as "the midnight sun" (a term later used by occultists to refer to the Grail). From its position in the sky it appeared to stand still, as the rest of the night sky revolved around it. It was therefore also called "the Central Sun."

Interestingly, although this theory of mine has long been in the works, I have recently stumbled across an author named David Talbott who shares my hypothesis on the origin of kingship. From a piece on his website, www.kronia.com, entitled "Saturn as a Stationary Sun and Universal Monarch", we read:

"A global tradition recalls an exemplary king ruling in the sky before kings ever ruled on earth.
This mythical figure appears as the first in the line of kings, the father of kings, the model of the good king. But this same figure is commonly remembered as the central luminary of the sky, often a central sun, unmoving sun, or superior sun ruling before the present sun.
And most curiously, with the rise of astronomy this celestial 'king' was identified as the planet Saturn."

One can see traces of this ancient progenitor of kings just in the word "monarchy" itself. The syllable "mon" means "one" in Indo-European language systems, as in "the one king who rules over all.", but in Egypt, it was one of the names of the sun god (also called "Amun-Re"). It denoted the Sun in its occluded state (when it passes beneath the Earth at night), and the word meant literally for them, "the Hidden One", because the Sun ruled the world (and the underworld) from his secret subterranean prison. The syllable "ark" comes from the Greek "arche", meaning original, or originator. As the first "*monarch*", Kronos was the one originator of kings, the Forgotten Father of all royal bloodlines. Many of our commonly associated symbols of kingship date back to the time when Kronos first introduced it, and are directly derived from him. For instance, the crown symbolizes the (central) Sun, the "godhead" descending upon the brow of the wise king, and the Sumerian kings adorned their crowns with horns, just like Kronos was believed to have on his crown. The throne was Kronos' seat on his celestial boat in heaven, and has been passed down to us as well. Kronos and his descendants were known as "shepherd kings", an appellation used by royalty throughout history, and this is the origin of the king's scepter, which was once a shepherd's staff. The coronation stone and the orb surmounted by a cross are also Saturnian/solar symbols, and the Egyptian word for the Sun, "Re", maybe the source of the French word for king, Roi.

Kronos, and the god-kings who followed him were known by the title "Lord of the Four Corners of the World." This has given birth to the universal, recurring archetype of "le Roi du Monde", a concept that was brilliantly explored in a book by René Guenon of the same name. In a surprising number of cultures throughout the world and throughout history, there is this concept of "the Lord of the Earth", an omnipresent and eternal monarch who reigns from within the very center of the Earth itself, directing events on the surface with his superhuman psyche. In the Judeo-Christian tradition, "the Lord of the Earth" is a term applied to Satan, or Lucifer, who, like Saturn, was the brightest star in Heaven, but was cast down by God and, like Saturn, imprisoned inside the bowels of the Earth, in a realm called Hell. In fact, it is quite clear that the figure of Satan comes from Saturn, the "Fish-Goat-Man", and obviously the two words are etymologically related. Perhaps this is why the "Grail bloodline" a divine lineage from which all European kings have come, is traced by many back to Lucifer. The Medieval Christian heretics known as the Cathars took this concept to its logical conclusion and insisted that, since Satan is the "King of the World" ("Rex Mundi', as they called him), and Jehovah was, in the Bible, the one who created the world, Jehovah and Satan must be one and the same. For preaching this they were massacred unto extinction by the Papacy.

However, in the Eastern tradition, the Lord of the Earth represents the ultimate incarnate manifestation of godhood. They too saw him as ruling his kingdom from the center of the Earth, in a subterranean city called either "Shamballah" or "Agartha." And in this tradition, the Lord of the Earth was also a super-spiritual being capable of incarnating on the surface of the Earth in a series of "avatars", or human kings who have ruled various eras of existence. According to New Age author Alice Bailey:

"Shamballa is the seat of the 'Lord of the World' (who has made the sacrifice (analogous to the Bodhisattva's vow) of remaining to watch over the evolution of men and devas until all have been 'saved' or enlightened."

One of the names that the Hindus used for "the Lord of the Earth" was Manu, who, writes Guenon, is "a cosmic intelligence that reflects pure spiritual light and formulates the law (Dharma) appropriate to the conditions of our world and our cycle of existence." Author Ferdinand Ossendowski adds:

"The Lord of the World is in touch with the thoughts of all those who direct the destiny of mankind... He knows their intentions and their ideas. If they are pleasing to God, the Lord of the world favours them with his invisible aid. But if they are displeasing to God, He puts a check on their activities."

These are obviously activities that human kings, as incarnations of the Lord of the Earth, are expected to replicate in their own kingdoms to the best of their ability. In fact, a number of human kings throughout history have been viewed by their subjects as incarnations of the Lord of the Earth, embodying the concepts that he represents. These include Charlemagne, Alexander the Great (who was believed to have horns on his head), and Melchizedek, a mysterious priest-king mentioned repeatedly in the Old Testament and imbued with an inexplicable importance. He was called the "Prince of Salem" (as in Jerusalem), and is said to have shared bread and wine with Abraham during a ritual. Some believe that the cup which they used is the artifact that later became known as the Holy Grail. Some have also identified Melchizedek with another king of Jerusalem, Adonizedek, and with Shem, Noah's son. Nobody knows what his ancestry is, who his descendants might have been, or why, thousands of years later, Jesus Christ was referred to in the scriptures as "a priest according to the Order of Melchizedek." Of his significance, René Guenon writes:

"Melchizedek, or more precisely, Melki-Tsedeq, is none other than the title used by Judeo-Christian tradition to denote the function of 'The Lord of the World'... Melki-Tsedeq is thus both king and

priest. His name means 'King of Justice', and he is also king of Salem, that is, of 'Peace', so again we find 'Justice' and 'Peace' the fundamental attributes pertaining to the 'Lord of the World.'"

Even more pertinent information is provided by René Guenon's colleague Julius Evola, who in his book *The Mystery of the Grail* wrote:

"In some Syriac texts, mention is made of a stone that is the foundation, or center of the world, hidden in the 'primordial depths, near God's temple.' It is put in relation with the body of the primordial man (Adam) and, interestingly enough, with an inaccessible mountain place, the access to which must not be revealed to other people; here Melchizedek, 'in divine and eternal service', watches over Adam's body. In Melchizedek we find again the representation of the supreme function of the Universal Ruler, which is simultaneously regal and priestly; here this representation is associated with some kind of guardian of Adam's body who originally possessed the Grail and who, after losing it, no longer lives. This is found together with the motifs of a mysterious stone and an inaccessible seat."

Clearly, that foundation stone of the world is the same as the Black Sun in the center of the Earth, or the "Grail Stone" which is said to be hidden in that location. The Grail Romances provide us with much insight into the "King of the World" concept. This figure is represented in the story by one of the supporting characters, Prester John, a king who is mentioned in passing as ruling over a spiritual domain in the faraway East, and who, quite fittingly, is said to come from Davidic descent. Evola continues:

"The Tractatus pulcherrimus referred to him as 'king of kings' rex regnum. He combined spiritual authority with regal power... Yet essentially, 'Prester John' is only a title and a name, which designates not a given individual but rather a function. Thus in Wolfram von Eschenbach and in the Titurel we find 'Prester John' as a title; the Grail, as we will see, indicates from time to time the person who must become Prester John. Moreover, in the legend, 'Prester John' designates one who keeps in check the people of Gog and Magog, who exercises a visible and invisible dominion, figuratively, dominion over both natural and invisible beings, and who defends the access of his kingdom with 'lions' and 'giants.' In this kingdom is also found the 'fountain of youth.'

The dignity of a sacred king is often accompanied by biblical reminiscences, by presenting Prester John as the son or nephew of King David, and sometimes as King David himself... 'David, king of the Hindus, who is called by the people 'Prester John' - the King (Prester John) descends from the son of King David."

The Lord of the Earth, or the figures that represent him, are often symbolized by a victory stone, or foundation stone which is emblematic of their authority. For instance, British kings are coronated on the "Stone of Destiny", believed to have been used as a pillow by Jacob in the Old Testament. Such as stone is often referred to in mythology as having fallen from Heaven, like the Grail Stone, which fell out of Lucifer's crown during his war with God, and became the foundation stone for the Grail kingdom, having the power, as it is written, to "make kings." Because it fell from Heaven, the Grail is also often associated with a falling star, like that which Lucifer is represented by, and of course the Black Sun in the center of the Earth also represents Rex Mundi's victory stone. It is interesting, then, that in the Babylonian tongue, the word "tsar" means "rock", and is not only an anagram of "star", but a word that in the Russian language refers to an imperial monarch. Sometimes the monarchial foundation stone is represented as a mountain, especially the world or primordial mountain that in mythology provides the Earth with its central axis. The Sumerians referred to this as Mount Mashu, and its twin peaks were said to reach up to Heaven, while the tunnels and caves within it reached down to the depths of Hell. Jehovah in the Bible, sometimes called El Shaddai ("the Lord of the Mountain") had Mount Zion for a foundation stone, and some believed he actually lived inside of the mountain. Later, the kingdom of Jesus Christ was said to be "founded upon the

Rock of Sion."

The stone that fell form Heaven, the royal victory stone, is also sometimes depicted under the symbolic form of a castrated phallus, such as that of Kronos, whose disembodied penis was hurled into the ocean, and there spawned the Lady Venus. This story is a recapitulation of the Osiris story, as well as the inspiration for the Grail legends, in which the Fisher King is wounded in the genitals, causing the entire kingdom to fall under a spell of perpetual malaise. The only thing that can heal the king, and therefore the kingdom, is the Grail. This is a recurring theme in world mythology: the king and/or the kingdom that temporarily falls asleep or falls under a magic spell which renders it/him ineffectual for a time, until the stars are right, or the proper conditions are met, causing the king and his kingdom to reawaken, to rise from the ashes, from the tomb, or often, to rise out of the sea. This cycle recurs in the tales of the Lord of the Earth, who alternates between periods of death-like sleep within his tomb in the center of the Earth, and rebirth, in which he once again returns to watch over his kingdom, restore righteousness and justice to the land, and preside over a new, revitalized "Golden Age." Julius Evola writes of the archetype:

"It is a theme that dates back to the most ancient times and that bears a certain relation to the doctrine of the 'cyclical manifestations' or avatars, namely, the manifestation, occurring at special times and in various forms, of a single principle, which during intermediate periods exists in an unmanifested state. Thus every time a king displayed the traits of an incarnation of such a principle, the idea arose in the legend that he has not died but has withdrawn into an inaccessible seat whence once day he will manifest or that he is asleep and will awaken one day... The image of a regality in a state of sleep or apparent death, however, is akin to that of an altered, wounded, paralyzed regality, in regard not to its intangible principle but to its external and historical representatives. Hence the theme of the wounded, mutilated or weakened king who continues to live in an inaccessible center, in which time and death are suspended.... In the Hindu tradition we encounter the theme of Mahaksyapa, who sleeps in a mountain but will awaken at the sound of shells at the time of the new manifestation of the principle that previously manifested itself in the form of Buddha. Such a period is also that of the coming of a Universal Ruler (cakravartin) by the name of Samkha. Since samkha means 'shells', this verbal assimilation expresses the idea of the awakening from sleep of the new manifestation of the King of the World and of the same primordial tradition that the above-mentioned legend conceives to be enclosed (during the intermediate period of crisis) in a shell. When the right time comes, in conformity with the cyclical laws, a new manifestation from above will occur (Kalki-avatara) in the form of a sacred king who will triumph over the Dark Age. Kalki is symbolically thought to be born in Sambhala, one of the names that in the Hindu and Tibetan traditions designated the sacred Hyperborean center.

...many people thought that the Roman world, in its imperial and pagan phase, signified the beginning of a new Golden Age, the king of which, Kronos, was believed to be living in a state of slumber in the Hyperborean region. During Augustus' reign, the Sibylline prophecies announced the advent of a 'solar' king, a rex a coelo, or ex sole missus, to which Horace seems to refer when he invokes the advent of Apollo, the Hyperborean god of the Golden Age. Virgil too seems to refer to this rex when he proclaims the imminent advent of a new Golden Age, of Apollo, and of heroes. Thus Augustus conceived this symbolic 'filiation' from Apollo; the phoenix, which is found in the figurations of Hadrian and of Antonius, is in strict relation to this idea of a resurrection of the primordial age through the Roman Empire... During the Byzantine age, the imperial myth received from Methodius a formulation that revived, in relation to the legend of Alexander the Great, some of the themes already considered. Here again, we find the theme of a king believed to have died, who awakens from his sleep to create a new Rome; after a short reign, the people of Gog and Magog, to whom Alexander had blocked the path, rise up again, and the 'last battle' takes place."

Rene Guenon believed in this concept literally, and believed that the periods of slumber for the Lord of the Earth have been cyclically brought to a close by apocalypses, after which "le Roi du Monde" would return again to clean up the wreckage and once more look after his faithful flock. In *The Revelation of St. John the Divine*, three kings actually return from periods of slumber, death, or prolonged absence: Jesus, Satan, and Jehovah, and naturally, the governmental entity that God chooses for this utopian world is the one which has always been associated with holiness and righteousness: monarchy.

Monarchy was the first form of government observed by man, and it was, according to almost every culture, created by God himself. It is the primordial, archetypal form of government, the most natural - that which all other forms of government vainly try to mimic, while at the same time violating its most basic tenets. Monarchy was, for thousands of years, all mankind knew, and the idea of not having a monarch, a father figure to watch over them, to maintain the community's relationship with the divine, represented to them not freedom, but chaos, uncertainty, and within a short time, death. The common people did not jealously vie for positions of power, nor did they desire to have any say in the decision of who would be king. In fact, most of them preferred that there be no decision to make at all: most monarchies functioned on the principle of primogeniture, passing the scepter and crown down from father to son, or in some cases, through the matrilineal line. The decision was up to nature or God, and therefore just and righteous in itself. Furthermore, the people knew they could count on their monarch to watch over them like he would their own children, to be fair and honest, to protect them from invasion, and to maintain the proper relationship between God and the kingdom. They desired to make their kingdom on Earth reflect the order and perfection that existed in God's kingdom in Heaven. For thousands of years before the modern era, when 90% of the population was not intellectually capable of participating in government or making electoral decisions, monarchy stood as a bulwark against the disintegration of the societal unit, providing a stability that otherwise could not be achieved. If monarchy had not been invented, human history could never have happened. Richard Cassino, in *A Deeper Truth*, said it best:

"Since the obligation of every king... is to maintain law, order, morality, spirituality, and religion within his kingdom, then the very design of a monarchy itself was probably conceived by the superior intelligence called God so as to endow mankind with a sound system of government. In other words, the concept of kingship was designed for, and delivered to, the peoples of earth by God to teach mankind to live in a humanized social environment... Human history, with its past and present kingdoms and kings - Egypt, Assyria, Persia, Babylon, Sumer, Aztec, Inca, Jordan, Saudi Arabia, Great Britain, to name a few - stands as a testimony to the fact that the monarchial form of government has been the basis for almost every civilization."

If monarchy is the most perfect form of government, and if it has been responsible for providing us with at least 600 years of human history, why now does it seem to be only an ancient pretension? Why is the concept of having a monarchy actually function in government considered to be a quaint but laughable thing of the past? Have we really moved beyond monarchy?

Hardly. If you were to graph the entire 6000 years of known human history and isolate the period in which civilized nations have been without monarchs, it would be merely a blip on the spectrum. In fact, of the civilized Western nations, few do not have a monarch reigning either *de jure* or *de facto* (although they continue to elect Presidents from royal European lineage). Most nations that maintain representational government still have a monarch either recognized by the government, or by the people at large, and though essentially powerless, these monarchs maintain a symbolic link between a nation and its heritage - its most sacred, most ancient traditions. They also constitute a government-in-waiting, should the thin veneer of illusory "freedom" and "equality" that maintains democracy break down. The modern system of Republican government is based not so much on the freedom of the individual, but on the free flow of money, on debt, usury, inflation, and on a monetary house of cards known as "Fractional Reserve Lending." It would only take a major and slightly prolonged collapse of the monetary system to eliminate this governmental system. At that point, civilized man will have essentially two choices: anarchy or monarchy, and if people have any sense at all they will choose the latter, rather than subjecting themselves to a chaotic succession of despots interspersed with periods of violence and rioting, and the poverty that comes with the lack of a stable state. It would be the most natural thing in the world for the royal families of Earth, and the monarchial system which they have maintained, to just slide right into place. The kingdom of the gods, who once ruled during man's Golden Age, would then awaken from their slumber and heed the call to duty, like Kronos, their Forgotten Father, and monarch of all, who soundly sleeps within his tomb in the primordial mountain, waiting for his chance to once again hold dominion over the Earth.

Dead But Dreaming: The Great Old Ones of Lovecraftian Legend Reinterpreted as Atlantean Kings

By Tracy Twyman

The Secret Doctrine given to the elite castes of mankind by the "Annunaki" (the gods of ancient Sumeria and Atlantis), has been passed down through the ages, not only to the Masons, Templars, Rosicrucians, and other fraternal orders which perpetuate the tradition, but also to the teenage geeks and "gamers" of today. The Lovecraft/Necronomicon lore has given birth to a cornucopia of role-playing and computer games, in much the same way that Monty Python and the Society for Creative Anachronism have kept the Grail myth alive for these same teenagers. The fact that S.C.A.'s membership correlates strongly with participation in Lovecraftian role-playing games is no coincidence, for the "demons" of the "Cthulhu Mythos" as its called, are the same as the gods of ancient Sumer, and the fallen angels who spawned the Grail family. The "Grail Blood" and the "bloodline of the Great Old Ones" are the same thing. They also represent the same archetypes as legendary sea-monsters such as Leviathan or Dagon, the "Lords of the Deep" and gods of the "underworld", or "Abyss" recorded in the legends of many ancient cultures.

It takes only a cursory examination of H.P. Lovecraft's most quintessential work, *The Call of Cthulhu* to see that his entire system of mythology is based on *The Book of Enoch*, the Nephilim story in *Genesis*, and the universal tale of the fall of Atlantis. In this story, Lovecraft's main character finds a strange carved idol in his late grand-uncle's affects, its appearance described as that of, "an octopus, a dragon, and a human caricature... scaly body, rudimentary wings." The discovery of this idol leads to his investigation and uncovering of a sinister, age-old "cult of Cthulhu" (the name of the idol), who worshipped the creature represented by the idol, and the entire race of demons from which he had come. The description of the idol bears a striking resemblance to the descriptions of the Sumerian god-king Enki, also known as Dagon or Oannes, a half-human, half-fish combination who was known as the "Lord of the Flood", and was said to rise out of the sea every day to teach his secret knowledge to those who followed him. He is mentioned in *I Samuel:5*, when the Philistines capture the Ark of the Covenant and place it in the Temple of Dagon. Two nights later, "Dagon was fallen upon his face to the ground before the Ark of the Lord; and the head of Dagon and both the palms of his hands were cut off upon the threshold; only the stump of Dagon was left to him." The physical description attributed to Dagon applied to an entire race of "gods", or as they were described in the Bible, Nephilim, or fallen angels - the "Great Old Ones", as Lovecraft calls them. The Watchers, "those who were cast down", are described in *The Book of Enoch* literally as stars that descended to Earth. Cthulhu is also described with wings, another attribute of the Nephilim, who were real flesh-and-blood beings, and ruled as the antediluvian kings of the ancient world over a global kingdom whose capitol was Atlantis. As they were an expert sea-faring people - *navigators* - they were also depicted as sea gods, half-man and half-fish, with the horns of a goat.

The fact that Lovecraft's "Great Old Ones"

ruled over Atlantis is quite clear, as their city, called "R'lyeh" in the story, is covered with what Lovecraft describes as "cyclopean" architecture, the same word used by author Ignatius Donnelly (*Atlantis: The Antediluvian World*) to describe the architecture of Atlantis. Lovecraft's descriptions paint a picture of multi-dimensional, non-Euclidean angles, as if they existed in a space-time different than ours, perhaps in an "otherworld" somewhere in between the planes of Heaven and Earth. They are described as grand and mighty creatures, with a moral creed similar to that of Aleister Crowley's "Do what thou wilt", and they trounced on all those weaker than them, bringing destruction to the Earth, devouring every living thing. This is exactly the behavior that is ascribed to the sons of the Watchers, or Nephilim, the giants who wrought havoc upon the world, oppressed and devoured all of the gods' living creation to feed their own voracious appetites. Because of the pride and destructive behavior of the Great Old Ones, their empire city, R'lyeh, sank beneath the ocean as part of a punishment by natural disaster mercifully imposed by God. This is exactly what is said to have happened to the island kingdom of Atlantis, which also sank because of the pride of its inhabitants. It is also what is said about the Nephilim in the Bible, who, along with their offspring, were destroyed by God via the Flood of Noah. The fact that the Great Old Ones are lead by a being called "Cthulhu" is significant, for "Thule" is another name for Atlantis, and the Nazis believed that it was literally located inside the Earth, in the "underworld", the city of "Agartha" or "Agade", the "abode of the Gods."

The "Hollow Earth", or underworld seems to be the place where R'lyeh ultimately sank to, where Cthulhu and the rest of the Great Old Ones now remain, sleeping in their watery tomb, "dead but dreaming", as Lovecraft now describes it. There they are, waiting for the day when they will awaken, their city rise from the waves, and their empire once again hold dominion over the whole earth. This echoes the story of the Watchers or the Nephilim, who were said to be imprisoned by God inside the Earth, or in "the Abyss", which was a word used by the ancients to describe the ocean. The theme of a subterranean Lord, imprisoned in the underworld, who will one day awaken from his death-like slumber to reclaim his kingdom is, as I have established in other articles, a very common archetype, most notable in the form of Kronos. Called "the Forgotten Father" and "the Hidden One", Kronos was the leader of the Titans, and the King of Atlantis, whose kingdom was cast down into the Abyss, and who was imprisoned therein, to be thereafter known as "the Dark Lord" of the underworld. And there is clearly an etymological connection between "Titan" and "Teitan", otherwise spelled "Satan." The Titans, or Satans, and the Nephilim are clearly the same as the Great Old Ones, and Kronos, otherwise known as Saturn, or Satan, is clearly the same as Cthulhu. As I have established, he is also synonymous with Dagon or Oannes, who is referred to in the Bible as Leviathan, the beast who will rise from the sea at the Apocalypse. The return of Cthulhu, the Great Old Ones, and the city of R'lyeh would appear to be Lovecraft's way of depicting the Apocalypse.

Confirmation of the above conclusions can be found by examining quotations from Lovecraft's manuscript, the implications of which, in light of what I have just said, will be self-explanatory. When the main character in *The Call of Cthulhu* manages to interview an actual member of the Cthulhu cult to determine their beliefs, the descriptions that follow parallel precisely the tales of the Nephilim, the Titans, and the war in Heaven between God and Lucifer, as well as the fall of the Atlantean empire:

"They worshipped, so they said, the Great Old Ones, who lived ages before there were any men, and who came to the young world out of the sky. These old ones were gone now, inside the earth and under the sea; but their dead bodies had told their secrets to the first man, who formed a cult which had never died. This was that cult, and the prisoners said it had always existed and always would exist, hidden in the distant wastes and dark places all over the world until the time when the Great Priest Cthulhu, from his dark house in the mighty city of R'lyeh under the waters should rise and bring the Earth again under his sway. Some day he would call, when the stars were ready, and the secret cult would always be ready to liberate him.

Meanwhile, no more must be told. There

was a secret which even torture could not extract. Mankind was not absolutely alone amongst the conscious things of the Earth, for shapes came out of the dark to visit the faithful few. But these were not the Great Old Ones. No man had ever seen the Old Ones. The carven symbol was great Cthulhu, but none might say whether or not the others were precisely like him. No one could read the old writing now, but things were told by word of mouth. The chanted ritual was not the secret - that was never spoken aloud, only whispered. The chant meant only this: 'In his house at R'lyeh, dead Cthulhu waits dreaming."

This clearly describes the secret Luciferian doctrine of the gods being transmitted to their offspring, "the first man", just as the serpent gave wisdom to Adam and Eve in the Garden of Eden. They created a covenant with that man, and a cult of magic, of ritual and sacrifice, in order to preserve their infernal secrets, one of which is so secret that it could not be talked about, only whispered. This is what has been done in the rites of Freemasonry, Rosicrucianism, the Knights Templar, the Greek and Egyptian mystery schools, the Sufis, the Assassins, and countless other secret occult orders, which Lovecraft was no doubt alluding to when he referred to the "cult which had never died... had always existed, and always would exist", preserving the teachings of the "Forgotten Father" until such time as he should rise again from the sea to once more rule the Earth. The connections to Leviathan and the rise of the Antichrist do not even need to be elucidated. Lovecraft's description goes on:

"Old Castro remembered bits of hideous legend that pale the speculations of Theosophists and made man and the world seem recent and transient indeed. There had been eons when other things ruled on the Earth, and they had had great cities. Remains of them ... were still to be found as Cyclopean stones on islands in the Pacific. They all died vast epochs of time before man came, but there were arts which could revive them when the stars had come round again to the right positions in the cycle of eternity. They had indeed come themselves from the stars, and brought their images with them."

Lovecraft, like the prophet Enoch, and like ancient man himself, conceived of the Atlantean gods or Nephilim as possessing supernatural power, and, like Enoch, says that this power comes from the stars - that these beings in fact had come from the stars themselves, and seem to be metaphysically affected by the movement of the stars, being able to resurrect from the dead only when the stars were in a certain position. Likewise, the Atlantean god-kings purposely associated themselves with the stars and the planets, taking on the personifications of planets and constellations, each of which had a particular "energy" or plain of existence associated with it. This energy is further manipulated by the prayers and rituals of the cult members in Lovecraft's stories, who are loyal to the Great Old Ones, and wish to see their kingdom rise again. In much the same way, Masons, Rosicrucians and other occultists today perform rituals in hope of bringing about the "Great Work" called the "New World Order", a new Golden Age, just like the one that covered the antediluvian world when the Atlantean god-kings (whom they revere) ruled over the Earth directly. The Eye in the Pyramid on our dollar bill, which represents the New World Order, is clearly a symbol of this newly-risen kingdom of Atlantis, "watched over" by the All-Seeing Eye, which could just as easily be the eye of Dagon, or Leviathan, or Cthulhu. It even looks reptilian, like it belongs on the face of a dragon.

The rise of R'lyeh, the New World Order, the New Atlantis, the New Jerusalem, the Golden Age, and even the Apocalypse - these are all terms for the same resurrection of the ancient global kingdom of the gods. Such a resurrection is also described in Aleister Crowley's *The Book of the Law* when he writes about the coming "Age of Horus" and the return of the rule of the gods, as well as their offspring, the human "kings":

"Ye shall see them at rule, at victorious armies, at all the joy... love one another with burning hearts, on the low men trample in the fierce lust of your pride, in the day of your wrath... Trample down the Heathen; be upon them, O warrior, I will give you of their flesh to eat."

Now read the following passage from *The Call of Cthulhu* and compare:

"Then, whispered Castro, those first men formed the cult around small idols which the Great Old Ones showed them; idols brought in dim eras from dark stars. That cult would never die, 'til the stars came right again, and the secret priests would take great Cthulhu from his tomb to revive his subjects and resume his rule of Earth. The time would be easy to know, for then mankind would have become as the Great Old Ones; free and wild and beyond good and evil, with laws and morals thrown aside and all men shouting and reveling in joy. Then the liberated Old Ones would teach them new ways to shout and kill and revel and enjoy themselves, and all the earth would flame with a holocaust of ecstasy and freedom. Meanwhile, the cult, by appropriate rites, must keep alive the memory of those ancient ways and shadow forth the prophecy of their return.

This age of the glorious rule of the Old Ones, and the land which they ruled over, is so similar to Atlantis, Thule, Lemuria, and all of the other mythical lost civilizations as to be blatantly obvious, and it is clear that it was the biblical Deluge that put an end to their kingdom. We read in Lovecraft:

"In the elder time chosen men had talked with the entombed Old Ones in dreams, but then something had happened. The great stone city R'lyeh, with its monoliths and sepulchers, had sunk beneath the waves; and the deep waters, full of the one primal mystery through which not even thought can pass, had cut off the spectral intercourse. But memory never died, and the high priests said that the city would rise again when the stars were right. Then came out of the Earth the black spirits of the earth, moldy and shadowy, and full of dim rumors picked up in caverns beneath forgotten sea-bottoms. But of them old Castro dared not speak much."

The climax of Lovecraft's story comes when the main character reads an account of his uncle's death in a fishing boat off the coast of Australia. He had come across a monolith sticking out of the ocean, which turned out to be resting on top of a mountain that was poking out of the water, upon which he and his shipmates landed their boat. There they discovered a strange sunken city built with "cyclopean", non-Euclidean architecture. It was an earthquake that had brought the top of the city to the surface, where Cthulhu and the Great Old Ones were entombed. Their presence awakened Cthulhu, who oozed out of the mountain, dripping green slime, and presumably killed the whole crew.

Similar themes are touched upon in Lovecraft's other work. In *At the Mountains of Madness*, he returns to the theme of discovering the lost city of the Old Ones, this time set in Antarctica, which, as the Nazis and many others believed, is rumored to be the location of one of the largest entrances to the hollow Earth. In *The Nameless City*, he delves explicitly into the hollow Earth, describing the discovery of a subterranean passage filled with the caskets of dead reptilian bodies, who had obviously, at one time, lived inside the Earth. And finally, in *Dagon*, Lovecraft tells the tale of a shipwrecked man who finds himself stuck in a "slimy expanse of hellish black mire", which had been unearthed when "through some unprecedented volcanic upheaval, a portion of the ocean floor must have been thrown to the surface, exposing regions which for innumerable millions of years had lain hidden under unfathomable watery depths." This is clearly another reference to the recurring theme in Lovecraft's work of sunken Atlantis rising from the ocean, which as we have established, is also a common theme in world mythology.[1] There the character discovers a white monolith covered with hieroglyphs:

"The writing was in a system of hieroglyphics unknown to me, and unlike anything I had even seen in books, consisting for the most part of conventional aquatic symbols, such as fishes, eels, octopi, crustaceans, mollusks, whales, and the like. Several characters obviously represented marine things which are unknown to the modern world, but whose decomposing forms I had observed on the ocean-risen plain."

Clearly, then, what this character has

discovered are the remains of a high civilization of sea-faring, ocean-obsessed people, which is exactly what Atlantis is described as being, and why their kings, or "gods" were depicted as half-man, half-fish. Lovecraft continues:

"Plainly visible across the intervening water on account of their enormous size was an array of bas-reliefs whose objects would have excited the envy of Doré. I think that these were supposed to depict men - at least, a certain sort of men; though the creatures were shown disporting like fishes in the waters of some marine grotto or paying homage at some monolithic shrine that appeared under the waves as well. They were damnably human in general outline, despite webbed hands and feet, shockingly wide and flabby lips, glossy, bulging eyes, and other features less pleasant to recall."

It is at this point that our narrator espies with his own eyes one of these creatures - not a bas-relief, but the real thing:

"Vast, Polyphemus-like, and loathsome, it darted like a stupendous monster of nightmare to the monolith about which it flung its gigantic scaly arms, the while it bowed its hideous head and gave vent to certain measured sounds. It think I went mad then."

When the character awakes, he is in a hospital bed in San Francisco, safe and sound, but not of sound mind. Disturbed by his memories, he consults "a celebrated ethnologist, and [amuses] him with peculiar suggestions regarding the ancient Philistine legend of Dagon, the Fish-God." Clearly, the character believes that it was Dagon himself, or one of his horde, whom he witnessed that faithful night. As I have previously established, Dagon, one of the kings of Atlantis, was symbolically the same as Kronos, Oannes, Enki, and therefore Satan. He was one of the Nephilim, Watchers, or fallen angels upon which Lovecraft's "Great Old Ones" are based. In keeping with the theme, the character in this story believes that they will one day return to rule the Earth again:

"I dream of a day when they may rise above the bellows to drag down, in their reeking talons, the remnants of puny, war-exhausted mankind - of a day when the land shall sink, and the dark ocean floor shall ascend amidst universal pandemonium."

Perhaps Lovecraft's most pertinent story, however, is 1931's *The Shadow Over Innsmouth*, about a "half-deserted" Massachusetts fishing town regarded with fear and suspicion by the surrounding New England populace. When the unnamed narrator, on an antiquarian tour through the area, expresses to the clerk at the Newburyport train station an interest in visiting the town, he gets an earful of reasons why he absolutely should not go under any circumstances, and if he must, he should certainly not stay the evening. It had once been a thriving seaport, but in 1846 there was an epidemic of some "foreign disease" that "carried off" over half the population. Since then, the main industry in town had been the Marsh Refining Company, founded by Captain Obed Marsh, whose descendants made up the majority of the town's remaining population.

Captain Marsh was the son of a South Sea island woman, and had developed "some skin disease or deformity late in life that makes him keep out of sight." The people of Innsmouth had strange physical features as well. "Some of 'em have queer, narrow heads with flat noses and bulgy, starry eyes that never seem to shut, and their skin aint quite right", the train station clerk told the narrator. "Rough and scabby, and the sides of the necks are all shriveled or creased up. Get bald too, very young. The older fellows look the worst - that is, I don't believe I've seen a very old chap of that kind. Guess they must die off looking in the glass!" General Marsh's family had been noted for the fact that, after they reached a certain age, they dropped out of public view, and spent the rest of their lives inside, out of sight.

The Innsmouth economy now revolved around the sale of gold ingots from the refinery, always in plenteous supply; "a queer king of jewelry" made from strange little beads of unknown material; and fish. The fish swarmed to the ports of Innsmouth more so than any other nearby seaport town, for some reason, but the townspeople would chase off any outsider who tried to fish there. They were odd and very secretive, not appreciating visits from strangers, and for that matter, most of the outside populace held the people of Innsmouth with equal apprehension, even disgust. The fish at Innsmouth tended to congregate at a spot called "Devil's Reef", so called because Old Captain Marsh had been seen there many times, "driving bargains with the devil and bringing imps out of hell to live in Innsmouth... some kind of devil worship and awful sacrifices", the clerk told him. "The story is that there's a whole legion of devils seen sometimes on that reef - sprawled about, or darting in and out of some kind of caves near the top."

The clerk tells the narrator that the only hotel in Innsmouth is the "Gilman House", but the last man he knew who had stayed there had been frightened in the night by the most mysterious noises. "It was so unnatural - slopping like", he said, and it went on all night. The clerk suggested that, if he must go, the narrator should stay the night at Newburyport and leave in the morning, taking the only mode of public transport that would even venture into Innsmouth - a rickety old bus filled with undesirable natives.

That evening, the narrator heads over to the Newburyport Historical Society to look at some of the strange jewelry that the people of Innsmouth had been trading throughout the area. The most magnificent piece on display was:

"...a sort of tiara... with a very large and curiously irregular periphery, as if designed for a head of almost freakishly elliptical outline. The material seemed to be predominantly gold, though a weird lighter lustrousness hinted at some strange alloy with an equally beautiful and scarcely identifiable metal... [2] *One could have spent hours in studying the striking and puzzlingly untraditional designs - some simply geometrical, and some plainly marine - chased or molded in high relief on its surface with a craftsmanship of incredible skill and grace... It clearly belonged to some settled technique of infinite maturity and perfection, yet that technique was utterly remote from any - Eastern of Western, ancient or modern - which I had even heard of or seen exemplified. It was as if the workmanship were that of another planet."*

The curator of the museum agrees that the strange jewelry did not originate in Innsmouth, and was "of probable East-Indian or Indochinese provenance; although she admitted that no one was sure." The narrator describes the designs on the tiara, and the seemingly racial memories that they conjured within him:

"The patterns all hinted of remote secrets and unimaginable abysses in time and space, and the monstrously aquatic nature of the reliefs became almost sinister. Among these reliefs were fabulous monsters of abhorrent grotesqueness and malignity - half ichthyic and half bactracian in suggestion - which one could not dissociate from a certain haunting and uncomfortable sense of pseudomemory, as if they called up some image from deep cells and tissues whose retentive functions are wholly primal and awesomely ancestral."

From the curator, our narrator learns the origin of the rumors of devil-worship being practiced in Innsmouth. It is actually a "quasi-pagan" Eastern cult that had been imported 100 years previously, "at a time when the Innsmouth fisheries seemed to be going barren." The cult was called, believe it or not, "The Esoteric Order of Dagon", and as soon as it took root in the community, the fish returned in abundance. The cult "...soon came to be the greatest influence in the town, replacing Freemasonry altogether, and taking up headquarters in the old Masonic Hall on New Church Green."

So there you have it - a Dagon cult practicing arcane sacrificial rites in a Masonic temple, and coveting age-old secrets. Lovecraft must have intended some sort of ironic comparison between Freemasonry and the Dagon cult, hinting that some of their traditions may in fact be the same, something that my research would tend to corroborate.

The story progresses, with the narrator taking the horrible little bus to Innsmouth the next morning, every grotesque sight and eerie occurrence stirring up his ancestral memory. He has a talk with a seventeen-year-old grocery boy who is not part of the cult and clearly an outsider at

Innsmouth. The youth fills him in more on the Esoteric Order of Dagon, and the "blasphemous" rites that they conduct:

"They seemed sullenly banded together in some sort of fellowship and understanding - despising the world as if they had access to other and preferable spheres of entity. ... their voices were disgusting... It was awful to hear them chanting in their churches at night, and especially during their festivals or revivals, which fell twice a year on April 30 and October 31." [3]

The tiara that the narrator has seen at the Newburyport museum was, according to the youth, a headdress worn by the priests of the cult. Besides worship, their favorite activity was swimming, and they would often have swimming races out to Devil's Reef. He confirmed that the natives looked normal early on in life, but as they grew older they began taking on that deformed "Innsmouth look", and stayed out of sight altogether. The youth also said that Innsmouth was honeycombed with underground tunnels, in which these people were apt to hide.

After walking around a bit, and catching glimpses of creepy-looking people with lidless eyes peering through the dingy windows of dilapidated houses, the narrator strikes up a conversation with yet another Innsmouth outsider, an old wino named Zadok (the name given to the priests of ancient Israel) who, although he was not one of them, had been forced to join the Dagon cult at one point in his life. In exchange for a drop of liquor, Zadok rambles on with wild stories about all of the devils, monsters, and awful ritual sacrifices he had witnessed during his time at Innsmouth; about humans mating with "toad-lookin' fishes", and hybrid human/sea-monster offspring that looked human at first but grew into awful, grotesque creatures who eventually took to the sea, and who never died, unless, "they was kilt violent." Zadok described the things he had seen in Biblical terms:

"..Dagon an' Ashtoreth - Belial an' Beelzebub - Golden Caff an' the idols o' Canaan an' the Philistines - Babylonish abominations..."

Zadok's recollections eventually put him into a horrific trance, and he sinks into a bizarre garbled chant which the narrator attributes to drunkenness:

"...an' the children shud never die, but go back to the Mother Hydra an' Father Dagon what we all come from... Ia! Ia! Cthulhu R'lyeh wgah-nagh fhtagn."

Zadok mutters to the narrator that on festival days, horrible creatures called "shoggoths" are called up from Devil's Reef with this chant, and they fill the streets between Water and Main Street, lumbering about, hollering with inhuman screams. The narrator decides to leave Zadok alone to finish his drink.

That night he stays at the dreaded Gilman House, clearly named "Gilman" as an allusion to the half-fish, half-human nature of the town's inhabitants. He is unable to sleep, and in the middle of the night he hears someone - someone who emits alien grunting sounds - trying to unlock the door to his room with a key. Fortunately he had already thought to deadbolt the door, and as his pursuers attempt to batter down the door, he narrowly escapes through the adjacent room and out the window. Outside he finds the air permeated with a horrible fishy odor, and the streets teeming with half-human sea monsters. Full-blooded sea-monsters are pouring out of the sea at Devil's Reef and onto the town's streets. The entire horde pursues him through Innsmouth. The narrator describes them as, "a band of uncouth, crouching shapes loping and shambling in the same direction. He adds that he was, "horrified by the bestial abnormality of their faces and the dog-like subhumanness of their crouching gait. One man moved in a positively simian way, with long arms frequently touching the ground, while another figure - robed and tiaraed - seemed to progress in an almost hopping fashion." The narrator tries to blend in by adopting their "shambling gait", and then hides in a pile of brush as they lurch past him, something he found unbearable. "The stench waxed overpowering, and the noises swelled to a bestial babel of croaking, baying and barking without the least suggestion of human speech." He tries to keep his eyes closed during the ordeal, but finally is unable to do so any longer, and faints at the sight of whatever it is he sees.

The next day he wakes up alone in the same field, walks to the next train station, and takes the first train to Arkham, where he reports his experience to the local government officials. The result of this is that the federal government sponsors a police raid that year that in which all of the houses along the Innsmouth waterfront are burned to the ground, the raid being disguised as, "one of the major clashes in a spasmodic war on liquor."

Although the narrator obviously does not continue with all of his intended plans for an "antiquarian" trip through New England, he does stop by the Arkham Historical Society to research his genealogy, where he discovers that his great great-grandfather had been Captain Obed Marsh, and his great-great grandmother that strange foreign woman, whom Zadok had described to him as actually being a sea monster. The curator tells him that he possesses the famous "Marsh family eyes", and that he also resembles his Uncle Douglas, who had stopped by the Arkham Historical Society years before on a similar genealogical research study. The narrator had already heard of this study which his uncle conducted, for he had shot himself immediately afterward.

A year later, after completing his college studies, the narrator stops by the house of his late mother's family in Cleveland - the side of his family that was descended from the Marshes, and the side which he had never cared for. Both his uncle and grandmother on that side had always terrified him, and as he looks over photographs of them and their family, he begins to recognize the repulsive physical features that had always brought him such discomfort. It is, of course, the "Innsmouth look." Worse yet, his uncle shows him some family heirlooms locked in a safe deposit box that he instantly recognizes as well: "two armlets, a tiara, and a kind of pectoral", made in that distinct Order of Dagon style with that indescribably foreign material. For the second time, he faints.

From that moment on, the narrator spends his days in madness, haunted by horrible aquatic nightmares in which he:

"... [wandered] through titanic sunken porticoes *and labyrinths of weedy cyclopean walls with grotesque fishes as my companions. Then other shapes began to appear, filling me with nameless horror the moment I awoke. But during the dreams they did not horrify me at all - I was one of them, wearing their inhuman trappings, treading their aqueous ways, and praying monstrously at their evil sea-bottom temples."*

As the days wear on, and the narrator becomes less and less sane, he begins to notice himself taking on the "Innsmouth look." His dreams become even more bizarre. In them, he meets his grandmother in this undersea kingdom, still alive down there, and she tells him that his destiny is to live down there with, "those who had lived since before man ever walked the earth." He also meets his great-great-grandmother, Captain Obed Marsh's wife - a sea monster named "Pth'thya-'yi", and learns of the plan of the "shoggoths" for world domination. "For the present they would rest", she told him, "but some day, if they remembered, they would rise again for the tribute Great Cthulhu craved." The story ends with the narrator resolving to break into the sanitarium where his cousin Laurence is being held (the narrator suspects he was put there because he had also begun to acquire the "Innsmouth look") and run away with him to the sea beneath Devil's Reef. He declares:

"We shall swim out to tat brooding reef in the sea, and dive down through black abysses to cyclopean and many columned Y'ha-nthlei, and in that lair the Deep Ones we shall dwell amidst wonder and glory forever!"

The themes alluded to in Lovecraft's work were taken to their utmost conclusion by the authors and editors of *The Necronomicon*, based on the imaginary grimoire that Lovecraft wrote of repeatedly in connection to Cthulhu and the Old Ones. This was supposedly a book of black magic with spells aimed at causing the sunken city of R'lyeh to rise again, and the "dead but dreaming" Old Ones to awaken from their slumber. *The Necronomicon*, published by Avon books, purports to be that very grimoire, "the most dangerous Black Book known to the Western World."

Although from reading it and the silly portentous warnings that fill the introduction (attempting to scare away the casual practitioner from meddling with forces so dangerous), it is hard to believe that this is, verbatim, an ancient text, it does appear to be based largely on genuine texts. As the Editor, L.K. Barnes explains:

"The Necronomicon is, according to Lovecraft's tales, a volume written in Damascus in the Eighth Century, A.D., by a person called the 'Mad Arab', Abdul Alhazred. It must run roughly 800 pages in length, as there is a reference in one of the stories concerning some lacunae on a page in the 700's. It had been copied and reprinted in various languages - the story goes - among them Latin, Greek and English. Doctor Dee, the Magus of Elizabethan fame, was supposed to have possessed a copy and translated it. This book, according to the mythos, contains the formulae for evoking incredible things into visible appearance, beings and monsters which dwell in the Abyss, and Outer Space, of the human psyche."

The system of gods, legends, and rituals presented in the book are as old as civilization itself, having originated from the oldest civilization accepted by historians, one of the greatest states in the empire of the god-kings of Atlantis: ancient Sumeria.

There is a dualistic notion inserted into *The Necronomicon* that is completely absent in Lovecraft's work. Lovecraft's "Old Ones" were primordial beings, beyond good and evil. That was the essence of their power. In *The Necronomicon*, the "Great Old Ones" have been split into two factions: the "Elder Gods" and the "Ancient Ones" - the good guys and the bad guys. This is noted in the excellently-written introduction by the Editor, L.K. Barnes, which alone should be invaluable to the serious student of the occult, and Sumerian mythology. Writes Barnes:

"Basically there are two 'sets' of gods in the mythos: the Elder Gods, about whom not much is written, save that they are a stellar race that occasionally comes to the rescue of man, and which corresponds to the Christian 'light'; and the Ancient Ones, about whom much is told, sometimes in great detail, who correspond to Darkness. These latter are the Evil Gods who wish nothing but ill for the Race of Man, and who constantly strive to break into our world through a gate or door that leads from the Outside In. There are certain people among us, who are devotees of the Ancient Ones, and who try to open the Gate, so that this evidently repulsive organization may once again rule the Earth. Chief among this is Cthulhu, typified as a Sea Monster, dwelling in the Great Deep, a sort of primeval Ocean..."

I have sincerely tried to figure out what the essential difference is between the Ancient Ones and the Elder Gods. The Elder Gods are lead by a great trinity: Anu, Enlil and Enki, three of the most well-known ancient god-kings of Sumeria, and perhaps, Atlantis. Anu held the seat of kingship, the inheritance of which was disputed by his sons, Enki and Enlil, leading to a catastrophic war that destroyed much of the Earth. This is recorded in the Sumerian *Enuma Elish*, as well as the biblical tale of the "war in Heaven." In the Sumerian texts, there is a race of gods descended from this trinity called the "Annunaki", analogous to the "sons of God" of the Bible, or the "Watchers" of *The Book of Enoch*. In *The Necronomicon* the strife between Enki and Enlil is completely ignored, and the Annunaki are considered to be a separate race, a faction of the Ancient Ones. They live in the Absu, or Abyss, a.k.a. "Nar Mattaru", the great underworld ocean, which is also called "Cutha" or "Kutu." This place is also described as "the Sea beneath the Seas", and clearly indicates an ocean *inside* the Earth which coincides with descriptions of the hollow Earth being largely filled with water. "Nar Mattaru" is very similar to "Nar Mar", one of the kings of the global empire of Atlantis, Sumeria, Egypt and India, whose name meant "Wild Bull", but who was symbolized by a cuneiform character depicting a cuttlefish.

The Elder Gods of *The Necronomicon* seem most definitely to be associated with the planets. In the chapter entitled "Of the Zonei and Their Attributes" ("Zonei" referring to the "zones" or orbits in which the planets travel), we learn that beneath Enki, Enlil and Anu are seven planetary deities. It appears that it is not the planets themselves that were worshipped in the old days, but the gods that those planets represented. As I have previously discussed, the ancient god-kings of Atlantis associated themselves with the stars and the planets, taking on the attributes that these planets were supposed to represent. Interestingly, it is written of Nergal, the god of Mars, that, "He was sometimes thought to be an agent of the Ancient Ones, for he dwelt in Cutha for a time." Clearly, whether a god is considered "Ancient" or "Elder" depends less on moral or physical attributes than it does on where spatially the "god" is believed to be located. Ancient man believed that the underworld was the land to the west, because that is where the sun went to "die" every night. So if there was a time when Mars rose in the West, it would explain this association between that planet and "Cutha."

The Ancient Ones, for their part, seem to be associated both with the Abyss, or underground sea, and with the constellations as well. This is not a contradiction if one takes into account the fact that ancient man considered the sky itself to be a cosmic ocean, and it was often called "the Abyss" as well. There seem to be three star systems in particular that the Ancient Ones are associated with, which have given birth to what *The Necronomicon* describes as: "The Cult of the Dog, the Cult of the Dragon, and the Cult of the Goat" (all cults that would be perceived as pagan or "Satanic" today), corresponding to the stars Draconis (the Dragon), Sirius (the Dog-Star), and Capricorn, (the Goat). *The Necronomicon*'s narrator Abdul Alhazred explains that:

"There shall forever be a war between us and the race of Draconis, for the race of Draconis was ever-powerful in ancient times, when the first temples were built in Magan, and they drew down their power from the stars..."

Many would interpret this to means that the Ancient Ones, "the Race of Draconis", are a lizard race of extraterrestrials from Draco, much like the concept promoted by conspiracy theorist David Icke. These beings are uncaring and unfeeling, yet the cause of all pain on this Earth, and they can be known by "their many unnatural sciences and arts, which cause wondrous things to happen, but which are unlawful to our people."

Here again we comes across the roots of the ancient yet nonetheless false dichotomy between good and evil. The Ancient Ones are reviled for teaching man secret wisdom, arts and sciences that are "unnatural", because they enable man to conquer nature, just as the Watchers did in the *Book of Enoch*. In that text, the forbidden knowledge consists of math, writing, astronomy, and the like. Here it seems to be associated mostly with the forbidden arts of ritual magic, which, if performed by the Elder Gods would be perfectly alright, but which "are unlawful to our people."

And who exactly are "our people" in this schematism? The human race in general? Or something more specific? In "The Testimony of the Mad Arab", Abdul Alhazred writes of his first encounter with the worshippers of the Ancient Ones, who were performing a sacrificial ritual around a large, floating, gray rock, upon which was carved three symbols. Of the first, the pentagram, he writes: "The first is the Sign of Our Race from beyond the Stars, and is called "Arra" in the tongue of the Scribe who taught it to me, an emissary of the Elder Ones. In the tongue of the eldest city of Babylon, it was Ur." The pentagram was indeed called the "Ar", or "Plough Sign" by the ancient Sumerians, and some have speculated that this is where the word "Aryan" comes from. The gods of ancient Sumeria were depicted with blue eyes, and their language is clearly the root of our "Indo-European", or Aryan system of languages. Is it so much to assume that the Sumerians were in fact themselves "Sum-Aryans"? This would seem to confirm it. Even L.K. Barnes makes note of the "strange, non-Semitic language of the Sumerians; and language which has been closely allied to that of the Aryan race, having in fact many words identical to that of Sanskrit (and, it is said, to Chinese!)"

But the blood of the Aryans has a special quality to it in this view, for it possesses the co-mingled powers of both the Ancient Ones and the Elder Gods. As L.K. Barnes writes: "Man was created from the blood of the slain commander of the Ancient Army, Kingu, thereby making man a descendant of the Blood of the Enemy, as well as the 'breath' of the Elder Gods; a close parallel to the 'Sons of God and the daughters of men' reference in the Old Testament." Indeed it is a close parallel, for these Sumerian legends of the war in Heaven are the source of this later Biblical tale. A trace of these ancient versions can be found in what L.K. Barnes refers to as the "centerpiece" of *The Necronomicon*, "The Magan Text."

The Magan Text tells the story of the creation of our present Earth, and of the human species. It starts out much like *Genesis*, with the emergence of creation out of the formless void of chaos, which is referred to as "the Waters" in both texts. From "The Magan Text" we read:

"When on High the Heavens had not been named,
The Earth had not been named,
And Naught existed but the Seas of Absu,
The Ancient One,
And Mummu Tiamat, the Ancient One
Who bore them all,
Their Waters as One Water."

Tiamat is the female version of Leviathan, the consort of Cthulhu in this book. From L.K. Barnes we read:

"That Tiamat was undoubtedly female is to the point; and that the Chinese as well as the Sumerians perceived of two dragon currents, male and female, gives the researchers a more complex picture. The Green Dragon and the Red Dragon of the alchemists are thus identified, as the positive and negative energies that compromise the cosmos of our perception, as manifest in the famous Chinese yin-yang symbol."

Tiamat, therefore, would have, like Leviathan and Kutulu/Cthulhu, represented the ocean itself, as well as the Earth, or, at least, the larger planet that existed in Earth's place prior to being rent in the manner that "The Magan Text" later describes.

The beginning of the poem describes a time "before the Elder Gods had been brought forth", meaning before the planets had been formed. "Uncalled by name, their destinies unknown and undetermined", it says - the word "destiny" referring to the gravitational orbits of the planet. "Then it was that the gods were formed within the Ancient Ones." This means that the Ancient Ones represent forces that pre-existed the creation of matter itself - time, space, electromagnetic and nuclear forces - the primeval void that was the womb of creation. This is what L.K. Barnes means when he writes:

"The method of <u>The Necronomicon</u> concerns deep, primeval forces that seem to pre-exist the normal archetypal images of the tarot trumps and the Golden Dawn telesmatic figures. These are forces that developed outside the Judeo-Christian mainstream, and were worshipped and summoned long before the creation of the Qabala as we know it today."

This is because Western magic is largely based on the worship of the Sun, the planets, and creation as it exists now. But these Ancient Ones are the forces of creation, of life, which is why Leviathan and Tiamat are synonymous with the "Kundalini power" of Tantric sex magic. In this sense, Tiamat plays the role of the Orobouros, the serpent eating its tail which encircles the cosmos, providing a "womb", as it were, for the celestial ocean, the Abyss. Since the ancients conceived of the "cosmic abyss" of the sky as an extension of the Abyss on Earth known as the ocean, they also believed that the dragon Tiamat or Leviathan lived there as well, in the terrestrial sea. It *was* the sea, and it *was* the Earth itself. Says Barnes:

S.H. Hooke, in his excellent <u>Middle Eastern Mythology</u>, tells us that the Leviathan mentioned in <u>Job</u>, and elsewhere in the Old Testament, is the Hebrew name given to the Serpent Tiamat, and reveals that there was in existence either a cult, or scattered individuals who worshipped or called up the Serpent of the Sea, or Abyss. Indeed, the Hebrew word for Abyss that is found in <u>Genesis 1:2</u> is, Hooke tells us, tehom, which the majority of scholars take to be a survival of the name of the chaos-dragon Tiamat or Leviathan that is identified closely with Kutulu or Cthulhu within the pages. They are mentioned independently of each other, indicating that somehow Kutulu is the male counterpart of Tiamat, similar to Absu.

This monster is well known to cult worship all over the world. ...The Chinese system of geomancy, feng shui (pronounced fung shway) is the science of understanding the 'dragon currents' which exist beneath the earth, these same telluric energies that are distilled in such places as Chartres Cathedral in France, Glastonbury Tor in England, and the Ziggurats of Mesopotamia. In both the European and Chinese cultures, the Dragon or Serpent is said to reside somewhere 'below the earth'; it is a powerful force, a magickal force, which is identified with mastery over the created world; it is also a power that can be summoned by the few and not the many."

Since the Elder Gods were begotten of the womb of Tiamat, it makes sense that they would be made of the same material, the primordial energy, or "prima materia" that she represents. That is where they would ultimately get their planetary power from. That is, therefore, where the Earth would get its power too. One is reminded of the myth of the Black Sun, the ball of "prima materia" that supposedly exists in the center of the hollow Earth, providing the "dragon current" that resides beneath the Earth, and corresponding to the myth of Leviathan in the Abyss. The myth of the Black Sun comes from the ancient belief that the Sun died in the West every night, turned black, and descended into the underworld. It just so happens that this is exactly what "The Magan Text" refers to: To quote Barnes:

"The word Magan may mean the Land of the Magan which was said to lie in the West of Sumer. For a time, it seems the name Magan was synonymous with the Place of Death - as the Sun 'died' in the West. Hence, it is a bit confusing as to what Magan is really supposed to mean in this text, but in context the 'Place of Death' explanation seems quite valid."

The Magan Text, then, may refer not only to how the Earth was formed out of the rending of a larger planet, but how the so-called "Black Sun', in its guise as Tiamat, or Leviathan was purportedly deposited in its center. What is really interesting is that in this story, it is Tiamat who is the most powerful, the most ancient, and the Most High God. It is she who is rebelled against, and the "Elder Ones", the good gods, are the ones who rebel. The following passage describes how the planets became disturbed in their orbits within the womb of Tiamat (space, the Abyss), thereby "rebelling" against her.

"The Elder Ones came together
They disturbed Tiamat, the Ancient One, as they surged back and forth.
Yea, they troubled the belly of Tiamat
By their Rebellion in the abode of Heaven.
Absu could not lessen their clamour
Tiamat was speechless at their ways.
Their doings were loathsome unto the Ancient Ones.

Absu rose up to slay the Elder Gods by stealth.
With magick charm and spell Absu fought,
But was slain by the sorcery of the Elder Gods.
And it was their first victory.
His body was lain in an empty Space
In a crevice of the heavens
Hid
He was lain,
But his blood cried out to the Abode of Heaven."

What follows is essentially the same as the war in Heaven. Tiamat creates children (monsters) out of her womb to attack the rebellious Elder Gods. These monsters are lead by a demon called Kingu. Enki, "The Lord of the Magick Waters", summons his son Marduk to do battle with the "Ancient Horde." Enki represents the planet Saturn, and therefore, Satan, while Marduk, attributed to the planet Jupiter in this text, bears an uncanny likeness to Lucifer, as the leader of the rebellious gods. He is also referred to as "The Brightest Star Amongst the Stars", and the Elder Gods are said to represent "the nature of the cosmos before the Fall of Marduk from Heaven." However, the event of Marduk's "fall" is not recorded in this text, but merely mentioned in passing later on. Rather, Marduk is said to have been victorious against the Ancient Ones, and caused *them* to fall from Heaven. His father Enki, "Lord of All Magick", told him "the Secret Name, the Secret Number, and the Secret Shape", thereby enabling him to access the powers of magic.[4] Then:

"Marduk struck with the Disc of Power
Blinded Tiamat's Eyes of Death
The Monster heaved and raised its back
Struck forth in all directions
Spitting ancient words of Power
Screamed the ancient incantations
Marduk struck again and blew
An Evil Wind into her body
Which filled the raging, wicked Serpent
Marduk shot between her jaws
The Charmed arrow of Enki's Magick
Marduk struck again and severed
The head of Tiamat from its body."

One would assume that this represents cosmic forces causing planets to smash into one another. And from the dead body of Tiamat, the Earth was formed. After it was all done, Marduk was responsible for re-establishing the planetary orbits, and basically taking over. He himself became the creator of the new Heaven and the new Earth, while the Ancient Ones were imprisoned in the underworld:

"Marduk
Victor
Took the Tablets of Destiny
Unbidden
Hung them around his neck.
Acclaimed of the Elder Gods was he.
First among the Elder Ones was he.
He split the sundered Tiamat in twain
And fashioned the heavens and the earth,
With a Gate to keep the Ancient Ones Without.
With a Gate whose Key is hid forever
Save to the Sons of Marduk
Save to the Followers of Our Master Enki
First in Magick among the Gods.

From the Blood of Kingu he fashioned Man.
He constructed Watchtowers for the Elder Gods
Fixing their astral bodies as constellations
That they may watch the Gate of Absu."

So Lucifer cast the creator of the universe into Hell? L.K. Barnes himself notes how odd it is that the Luciferian character is the hero in this text.

"Whereas Christianity states that Lucifer was a rebel in heaven, and fell from God's grace to ignominy below, the original story was that Marduk was the rebel, and severed the Body of the Ancient of Ancient Ones to create the Cosmos - in other words, the precise reverse of the Judeo-Christian dogma. The Elder Gods evidently possessed a certain Wisdom that was not held by their Parents, yet their Parents held the Power, the Primal Strength, the First Magick, that the Elder Ones tapped to their own advantage, for they were begotten of Her."

Since the Elder Gods were made "of" the Ancient Ones, they necessarily possessed the dual powers of good and evil, the balance of which is the secret power of the occult. And so, as the text explains, does mankind, which Marduk created "from the blood of Kingu", as well as the "breathe" of the Elder Gods. "The essences of the Ancient Ones are in all things, but the essences of the Elder Ones are in all things that live." So man's material essence comes from the body of a demon that represents prima materia, while his life-force is provided by the powers of the planets. This prima materia is, in one way, the "dragon force" that can be conjured within the human body, the Kundalini serpent that lives at the base of the spine, which can be roused through meditation, and drawn up through the spine to electrify the seven chakras, each of which corresponds to one of the seven planets. This can be done because man is connected genetically to the serpent power, which his DNA allows him to access, and which his DNA, in fact, represents. For as L.K. Barnes writes, "the twisting, sacred spiral shape formed by the serpent of the Caduceus, and by the spinning of galaxies is also the same Leviathan as the spiral of the biologists' code of Life: DNA." This DNA acts as a conductor for the forces of the Ancient Ones, sort of an inter-dimensional gateway, or patch bay connecting our reality to theirs. In fact, this genetic component of human blood is described in *The Necronomicon* as being the "key" capable of unlocking the prison inside of the Earth where the Ancient Ones lie. Part II of "The Magan Text", called "Of the Forgotten Generations of Man", states:

"And was not Man created from the blood of Kingu
Commander of the hordes of the Ancient Ones?
Does not man possess in his spirit
The seeds of rebellion against the Elder Gods?
And the blood of Man is the Blood of Vengeance
And the blood of Man is the Spirit of Vengeance
And the Power of Man is the Power of the Ancient Ones
And this is the Covenant
For, lo! The Elder Gods possess the Sign
By which the Powers of the Ancient Ones are turned back
But Man possesses the Sign
And the Number
And the Shape
To summon the Blood of his Parents.
And this is the Covenant.
Created by the Elder Gods
From the Blood of the Ancient Ones
Man is the Key by which
The Gate of Iak Sakkak may be flung wide
By which the Ancient Ones
Seek their Vengeance
Upon the face of the Earth
Against the Offspring of Marduk.
For what is new
Came from that which is old
And what is old
Shall replace that which is new
And once again the Ancient Ones
Shall rule upon the face of the Earth!
And this is too the Covenant!"

One of Lovecraft's proteges, Frank Belknap Long, wrote a story about this very concept called *The Hounds of Tindalos*. In this story, a writer named Chalmers takes a drug that enables him to mentally regress through the genetic memory of his DNA, all the way back through human evolution and beyond. As he reports to his friend, the narrator:

"I am going back and back. Man has disappeared from the Earth. Gigantic reptiles crouch beneath enormous palms and swim through the loathly black waters of dismal lakes. Now the reptiles have disappeared. No animals remain upon the land, but beneath the waters, plainly visible to me, dark forms move slowly over rotting vegetation."

Chalmers makes it clear that these underwater forms are multi-dimensional beings, and that by taking this drug and having these visions, he was actually performing a feat of time travel through the fourth dimension:

"The forms are becoming simpler and simpler. Now they are single cells. All about me there are angles - strange angles that have no counterparts on Earth... Beyond life there are... things that I cannot distinguish. They move slowly through outrageous angles."

What are these strange angles, and how is Chalmers able to see "beyond life?" It is because he is experiencing another dimension of space where all points of time exist simultaneously. As he explains:

"Time is merely our imperfect perception of a new dimension of space. Time and motion are both illusions. Everything that has existed from the beginning of the world exists now. Events that occurred centuries ago on this planet continue to exist in another dimension of space. Events that will occur centuries from now exist already. We cannot perceive their existence because we cannot enter the dimension of space that contains them. Human beings as we know them are merely fractions, infinitesimally small fractions of one enormous whole. Every human being is linked with all life that preceded him on this planet. All of his ancestors are parts of him. Only time separates him from his forebears, and time is an illusion and does not exist. ... By simply straining I can see further and further back. Now I am going back through strange curves. There is curved time and angular time."

It is the angles that allow the "dark forms" that Chalmers sees - and Chalmers himself - to pass from point to point in space-time. That the Ancient Ones in *The Necronomicon* are likewise multi-dimensional beings is clear from the descriptions contained therein. They are said to be able to pass through doors "like a wind." They can do this because they live:

"...in the places between, the places unknown in Heaven and Earth... Nowhere are they known. Not in Heaven, nor in the Earth are they discovered, for their place is outside of our place, and between the angles of the Earth. We are the Lost Ones, from a Time before Time, from a land beyond the Stars... We are a race from beyond the wanderers of night... falling like rain from the sky, issuing like mist from the Earth."

It is this "issuing from the Earth" aspect that we should examine now, since that is where the Ancient Ones are said to be currently located. Later on in "The Magan Text", Ishtar (Venus), described as the "Lady of the Harlots of UR", descends into the underworld. When she does this, she "[sets] her mind from above and to below... [sets] her mind in that direction", indicating that "entering the Underworld" requires a special mental process whereby you set your mind in between the dimensions represented by Heaven and Earth, so that you can get onto the right frequency and travel through space/time. This may link up with the claim by some that the hollow Earth, in which these fallen gods lie sleeping, exists in another dimension, which is why it is not acknowledged by science.

That the "underworld" is literally inside of the Earth is quite obvious from the text. As Ishtar descends, she must go through seven chambers, which clearly involves traveling through a series of tunnels into the depths of the Earth. This could also be seen symbolically as her descending down the seven chakra points to the "underworld" at the base of the spine, where the Kundalini Cthulhu lies "sleeping." She is forced to remove an item of jewelry at each gate, similar to a Masonic initiation ritual in which the candidate is divested of all metal objects. These jewels themselves seem to correspond to the seven chakra points on Ishtar's body, and apparently they were protecting her. For after they are removed, Ishtar's sister, Ereshkigal, the dragon queen of the underworld, releases the "7 Annunaki" against her. These Annunaki slay Ishtar in a most barbarous way, chaining her down and ripping her flesh with their teeth.

Normally, in Sumerian legend, the Annunaki are merely the sons of the Elder Gods, and appear to be of the same species as them. But not in this version. Here they are the "Dread Judges, the Seven Lords of the Underworld", like the gods that judge dead souls in the Egyptian underworld. Most interesting among these demons is one called "the Eye on the Throne", which appears to be the same as Kingu, the slain dragon from whose blood mankind was made. The Eye on the Throne was a hieroglyph used in Egypt and Sumeria to denote the world monarchy of their antediluvian gods. Since here it is called "Kingu", obviously he was one of these "kings." [5]

The fate that came of Ishtar in the underworld is exactly the fate that befell Chalmers in the Frank Belknap Long story when he was left alone after the drug session. The creatures that he had witnessed moving through angles, "the Hounds of Tindalos", came looking for him, and moved right through the angles in his ceiling into his apartment. Narrowly escaping from their first attack, he attempted to thwart them by redecorating. He called the narrator to his apartment again, asking him to bring with him a bucket of plaster, and told him:

"They can only reach us through angles. We must eliminate all angles from this room. I shall plaster up all the corners, all of the crevices. We must make this room resemble the interior of a sphere."

Why the hounds should want to kill him is explained twice, with a different reason given each time. On the one hand, they are mindless forces that simply hunger for blood. The same is said of the Ancient Ones of *The Necronomicon*, for whom, "The blood of the weakest, here is libation" unto them. But for the Ancient Ones, there is also an element of revenge, for their murder and imprisonment in the underworld. The same motive is given to the Hounds of Tindalos:

"... a terrible and unspeakable <u>deed</u> was done in the very beginning. Before time, the <u>deed</u>, and from the dead... The deeds of the dead move through angles in dim recesses of time. They are

hungry and athirst! ... For a moment I stood on the other side. I stood on the pale gray shores beyond time and space. In an awful light that was not a light, in a silence that shrieked, I saw them! But they scented me. Men awake in them cosmic hungers. We have escaped momentarily from the foulness that rings them round. They thirst for that in us which is clean, which emerged from the deed without stain. There is a part of us which did not partake of the deed, and that they hate. But do not imagine that they are literally, prosaically evil. They are beyond good and evil as we know it. They are that which in the beginning fell away from cleanliness. Through the deed they became bodies of death, receptacles of all foulness. But they are not evil in our sense because in the spheres through which they move there is no thought, no moral, no right or wrong as we understand it. There is merely the pure and the foul. The foul expresses itself through angle; the pure through curves. Man, the pure part of him, is descended from a curve. Do not laugh. I mean that literally."

This "angular" state represents the dualistic realm of opposites that creation is made from, the breaking down of the One into the Many, into the world where the principles of good and evil, and of male and female are separated. The part of us which is "pure" is the part of the One godhead that descended into dualistic matter, the light that descended into darkness, represented by the fall of Lucifer from Heaven, and his subsequent imprisonment in the Earth; or the fall of the Grail stone from his crown, which became enclosed in the deepest recesses of our minds, to be accessed by only an elite few. This has also been represented as the fall of Man from the Garden of Eden, who became corrupted when he gained knowledge of good and evil as being separate from the One. Subsequently, man became imprisoned in the three-dimensional world, and this is the deed that must be avenged.

But man contains the spark of godhead within him as well as the material of corrupted matter, just as Abdul Alhazred tells us in *The Necronomicon* that we have the body and blood of the Ancient Ones, but the spirit of the Elder Gods breathed into our souls. This is similar to the story in *Genesis* where God crafts Adam from "clay", and then puts the "breathe of life" into him. Yet this is just a continuation of the dualism that resulted in the godhead's descent into corrupted matter, or the imprisonment of the Ancient Ones. For they and the Elder Gods are inextricably connected. One bore the other, and therefore they are of the same substance, two sides of the same coin. Combining their essences results in the union of the Many back into the One, or a return to the womb of the Mother. This is the "Grail energy", the Elixir of Life. the occult power that works magic. This conundrum is expressed by a confused Abdul Alhazred when he says of the worshippers of the Ancient Ones:

"And who is their master? Of this I do not know, but I have heard them calling Enki, which is surely a blasphemy, for Enki is of our Race, as it is writ in the text of Magan. But perhaps, they call another, whose name I do not know. But surely it was not Enki."

It is also of note that Enki's son Marduk appears to have the qualities of both Lucifer (as the "Brightest Star in Heaven" and the one who "fell to Earth"), and those of Jesus or St. Michael, for he is son of the Eldest God Enki, sent to Earth to rule over man, and he is the vanquisher of the Evil One in Heaven. Such dualism seems to also be present in the references to the "Mountains of Mashu", the same twin-peaked mountains upon which the Babylonian Noah character, called Utnapishtim, rested his Ark, and which the Ancient Ones are said in *The Necronomicon* to rule over. L.K. Barnes writes that:

"...the original translator has noted the resemblance between the Greek word for lord, Kurios, and the Sumerian word for mountain, Kur, and for a type of underworld chthonic monster which is also called Kur and which refers to the Leviathan of the Old Testament. Also, in this particular conjuration, the word for mountain is "Shadu", like "El Shaddai", meaning Lord of the Mountain, a title applied to Jehovah."

This dualism points to the parentage of mankind, which is both infernal and divine, and

Enki is a mediator between the two. This dichotomy is the cause of the sorrow of human existence, for as *The Necronomicon* states:

"...man, being born, is of sadness, for he is of the Blood of the Ancient Ones, but has the Spirit of the Elder Gods breathed into him. And his body goes to the Ancient Ones, but his mind is turned towards the Elder Gods, and this is the War which shall be always fought, unto the last generation of man; for the World is unnatural. When the Great Kutulu rises up and greets the Stars, then the War will be over, and the World will be One.

But how is it exactly that the Elder Gods, being planets, "breathed life" into humanity at all? Well, there are those who hold that the gods of Sumeria were actually real flesh-and-blood kings of human civilization during the golden age of Atlantis. But they were more than human. The kings of Atlantis were somewhere in between man and god. They are said to have been, literally "stars" that fell from Heaven, and similarly the power of the Ancient Ones, as we know, comes from the stars - in other words, solar power. Stars put out waves of all sorts along the electro-magnetic spectrum, as do planets, which could account for the power and influence they are said to possess. If one could tune into the waves they are putting out, one could hear the "speech of the gods." And if one could harness that energy, then all of the feats that have been attributed to magicians over the centuries could be conducted. Scientists even say that if we are ever to build an inter-dimensional space traveling machine, it would require so much power that we would have to harness the Sun itself to make it work. This could be done either through advanced technology or advanced occult practice, and legend tells us that the Atlanteans possessed both.

Whether by evolution, divine creation, or genetic engineering, these beings were superior to us, and evidence shows that they existed in multiple dimensions, possessing multi-dimensional powers, just like their stellar "parents." By intermarrying with human females, they passed that star seed onto us, and all the powers that go with it. This "multi-dimensional" aspect is one way to explain the physical countenance of their human/god hybrid children as they are described in various myths: they were said to have been monsters and giants. It is this multi-dimensional force that the gods taught man to utilize in the rites of magic and occultism, which the gods invented and passed onto their human offspring, drawn from the power of the stars and planets, including the telluric "dragon force" of Cthulhu that lives within the Earth, and slumbers at the base of the human spine. L.K. Barnes confirms that Sumer was not just the birthplace of civilization, but also of religion and ritual magic. Here is where the rebellious ones taught their cult to the "first man", as Lovecraft described in *The Call of Cthulhu*. This is what enabled Abdul Alhazred in *The Necronomicon* by magick, to "summon the ghosts of [his] ancestors to real and visible appearance." Author Nicholas de Vere describes such ancestral conjuring rituals as being the central rites of "royal magic." Summoning ancestral ghosts is also the purpose of Voodoo and Santeria ritual.

Another aspect of the gods is that they are said to be able to live forever, and their human offspring were said to have had extremely long life spans as well. Likewise, the Ancient Ones of Lovecraft are incapable of dying, as time does not exist for them, ""For their times and seasons run uneven and strange to our minds, for are they not the computers of all time? Did they not set time in its place?"

Interestingly, after Frank Chalmers is devoured by the Hounds of Tindalos (the plaster didn't work), a strange protoplasmic substance is found in his apartment, apparently from the dripping jowls of these hounds from beyond time and space. This substance is examined by a bacteriologist, who writes in his report:

"The fluid sent to me for analysis is the most peculiar that I have ever examined. It resembles living protoplasm, but it lacks the peculiar substances known as enzymes. Enzymes catalyze the chemical reactions occurring in living cells, and when the cell dies, they cause it to disintegrate by hydrolyzation. Without enzymes, protoplasm should possess enduring vitality, i.e., immortality. Enzymes are the negative components, so to speak, of unicellular organism, which is the basis of all life. That living matter can

exist without enzymes biologists emphatically deny. And yet the substance that you sent to me is alive and it lacks these 'indispensable' bodies. Good God, Sir, do you realize what astounding new vistas this opens up?"

It is something like this which might make the long life spans attributed to the gods and their offspring physically possible, and would make it possible for their bodies to remain underground in a state of hibernation for eons before being resurrected again. It is this resurrection that they are hoping their human descendants will affect by practicing the occult rites of necromancy that they have been taught:

"Let all who read this book be warned thereby that the habitations of men are seen and surveyed by that forgotten race of gods and demons from a time before time, and that they seek revenge for that forgotten battle that took place somewhere in the cosmos, and rent the worlds in the days before the creation of man."

This is, mythologically, the same battle which caused the kingdom of Atlantis to sink to its watery depths, the war in Heaven in which the sons of God or Watchers were imprisoned within the underworld, their mighty kingdom destroyed, all because they dared to pass their divine seed, and their divine knowledge onto lowly humanity. *The Necronomicon* states that, "civilizations were destroyed because of the knowledge contained in this book." This is the deed that must be avenged, the memory of which slumbers in the blood of these gods' human offspring - just as they slumber beneath the Earth, waiting for the day that the stars will be right again, and their descendants will perform the rites which will bring them up from the depths to reclaim their kingdom. Then the age of the gods will begin anew: the New Atlantis, the New Jerusalem, the New World Order.

"Know that Tiamat seeks ever to rise to the stars, and when the Upper is united to the Lower, then a new Age will come of Earth, and the Serpent shall be made whole, and the Waters will be as One, when on high the heavens had not been named.

And the Dead shall rise and smell the incense!"

Endnotes:

[1] One is reminded of the final scene in the box office hit, *The Abyss*.

[2] This recalls the "white gold" substance, mentioned in the writings of Laurence Gardner and others, that is the Philosopher's Stone of the alchemists.

[3] These are Walpurgis Night and Halloween, the two most important witch holidays ont he calendar.

[4] One wonders if there is any connection here to the "Lost Word of Freemasonry" which, in their legends, Hiram Abiff refused to divulge, and which died with him.

[5] Perhaps his name is related etymologically to "Cain", whose name is the root from which the word "king" comes, and who is said to be one of the eldest ancestors of the Grail family.

Jean Cocteau: Man of the Twentieth Century

By Tracy Twyman

"I belong to the blood donors, the only artists I really respect. The long red trail they leave behind them fascinates me."
- Jean Cocteau

The Frivolous Poet

Jean Cocteau (1889 - 1963) was an influential poet, playwright, novelist, artist and filmmaker from the early half of the twentieth century, and a contemporary of people like Pablo Picasso, Igor Stravinsky, and Marcel Proust. He is also purported to have been Grand Master of the Priory o Sion during one of their most tumultuous periods. However, many authors, including the writers of *Holy Blood, Holy Grail*, have stated that Jean Cocteau seems an unusual choice for the leader of such an organization, having been an opium addict, homosexual, and eccentric "libertine" with no known connection to any particular royal house. For this reason, the legitimacy of the claim that Cocteau did hold this post has been questioned. However, my investigation has revealed overwhelming evidence that Cocteau was not only a Grand Master of the Priory of Sion, but also one of the most important figures of the twentieth century, and the complex meaning behind his art and writing has been severely underestimated.

He was born on July 5, 1889 in Maisons-Laffitte, a Parisian suburb, to a cultured, aristocratic family. [1] As *Holy Blood, Holy Grail* states: "Cocteau was raised in a milieu close to the corridors of power - his family was politically prominent and his uncle was an important diplomat." His father, a painter, shot himself when Cocteau was only nine years old, and so he clung to his mother, maintaining an unusually close relationship with her for the rest of her life. As is the case with many geniuses, Cocteau did poorly in school, and dropped out in the equivalent of high school. He ran away from home at age fourteen, and spent his time in Venice, as well as the "red light district" of Marseille. He was soon ingratiating himself with the salon crowd of Paris, impressing some of the world's most well-known artists and intellectuals with the brilliance of his work.

The first poem he presented to his salon friends - at age fifteen - was called *The Frivolous Poet*, which stuck with him as a nickname for years, as it seemed to encompass the light-heartedness of much of his work at the time. However, as Cocteau matured, and his work matured, this "frivolous" appellation gave way to the title "King of Poets" - a title he inherited from his friend and mentor, Apollinaire. He was patronized by some of Europe's most wealthy and respected nobility. His fame and reputation grew, and by the latter part of his life, he had been elected to the prestigious Academie Francaise, inducted with a ceremonial sword that had been designed by Picasso. He had also been named "Poet of the Year", made a "Chevalier of the Legion of Honor", and was invited to Oxford to become an honorary Doctor of Letters. Once, he was even invited by Charles de Gaulle's brother to give a national address on the general state of France. There is no doubt in my mind that Jean Cocteau had every attribute required to be the Priory of Sion's Grand Master, and has accomplished everything necessary to be listed among the greatest poets and artists of all time.

The Return to the Rose

It is ironic that the first use of the term "surreal" was made by the poet Apollinaire in relation to Cocteau's work on the *Ballet Russe* – ironic because the movement that later became known as surrealism was diametrically opposed to everything that Cocteau stood for, and aesthetically unrelated. The prefix "sur" in Latin carries the same meaning as "subra", so the term "sur-real" would mean "less than real", or "beneath reality." In contrast, Cocteau always spoke of his aesthetic as being supra-real, beyond real, or in other words, a higher form of reality than that which is readily perceived. It was the secrets of the ages, gleaned, presumably, from the Priory of Sion, that Cocteau was trying to communicate, albeit in cryptic form.

Most of the avant-garde art movements that were prevalent during Cocteau's time were rejected by him: Dadaism, Surrealism, even Cubism (although he did, for a time, explore Cubist techniques, mostly because of his interest in geometry, and his love for Pablo Picasso). As he saw it, these modernists embraced weak, atheistic creeds such as Existentialism, creating works of "art" that excelled in their meaninglessness - rubbish which continues to clutter up modern art museums to this day. These people also, in general, espoused left-wing political views that were anti-royalist, anti-elitist, and opposed to any form of hierarchical order whatsoever: aesthetically, politically, philosophically, or otherwise. In contrast, Cocteau wrote that, "If [the Dadaists] stand at the extreme left, I am at the extreme right. The extreme right used not to exist. Every right is timid. I invented the extreme right." Cocteau declared himself the President of an "Anti-Modern League", and rejected their empty creeds. He instead took classical themes and revitalized them, giving them new meaning. As biographer William A. Emboden described it, "Cocteau's emerging aesthetic was becoming an extension of Neoclassicism simplified. In Cocteau's words, 'it was a return to the rose', a reference to Ronsard's *Roman de la Rose*, which he so admired." It was also, I might add, a return to the rose cross

Cocteau's anti-modern, pro-classical, right-leaning aesthetic and attitude provoked extreme hatred and vindictiveness from the modernists, culminating in vicious attacks both verbal and in print. But they could rarely attack his work, since it so clearly surpassed their own. Instead, the attacks took the form of personal insults, which were then transformed onto his art and writing as though they were mere manifestations of his perceived personality flaws. He was portrayed as a hanger-on, who used people for money, connections, or notoriety, an idea thief whose main goal was to weasel his way in to the fashionable set. But Cocteau's sense of style was beyond the comprehension of this set, who made fun of his aristocratic appearance and mannerisms with that shallow form of derision that so obviously stems from jealousy. Worst of all were the insinuations that Cocteau's relationships were not genuine. His friendships with aristocrats and noble families were all just a ploy on Cocteau's part, they said, to get the money he needed to finance his projects, his expensive tastes, and eventually, his opium habit. His relationships with the great artists of his time, most of whom he knew personally, were equally false, they said. He merely wanted to be seen with them, say the biographers, while these artists, in contrast, wished nothing to do with him, and only feigned affection for him out of politeness.

Even Picasso, one of his closest friends and creative partners, is painted with this brush, and passing comments of slight irritation he might have made about Cocteau throughout their lifelong friendship have been blown out of proportion against the more numerous laudations and approbations they both heaped upon one another. The depth and sincerity of their mutual respect was undeniable. Cocteau described their first meeting as one of almost instantaneous telepathic communication. "There were long silences. Varése couldn't understand why we looked at each other without saying anything. When Picasso spoke, his syntax was visual. One immediately *saw* what he was saying." Together, these two artists - one an anti-modern Modernist, one a modern anti-Modernist - formed the twin pillars of an artistic temple that housed a Hermetic brotherhood of contemporary intellectuals.

Secret Agent Jean Cocteau

Cocteau consorted with a number of people who, if they were not actually members of the Priory of Sion, made superb candidates. Picasso, for instance, to quote John Richardson, "was of noble lineage; what is more, his uncle Salvador had married into the Malagueño aristocracy. 'I'll dine with the duke' is how he ends one of his notes." In 1917, he even had an audience with the King of Spain. His art, too, shows his interest in Hermetic subjects: his obsession with the bull symbol, his use, on more than one occasion, of the alchemical symbol of the Black Sun, and his undeniable use of pentagonal geometry in many, if not most of his cubist paintings.

Another candidate for Priory membership was Cocteau's friend Salvador Dali, whose "surreal" and "cubist" works often centered around strangely Hermetic religious themes. Also, the two films that Dali worked on, *The Andiluvian Dog* and *The Golden Age,* both used the classical Grail-themed works of Richard Wagner as a soundtrack. They were even financed by the same noble family - the Noailles' - that financed Cocteau's first film, *Blood of a Poet*. Furthermore, Dali's bust was once sculpted by the same artist - Arno Breker - who also sculpted a bust of Jean Cocteau, as well as a statue of Cocteau making the hand sign of John the Baptist. Dali's choice of the title *The Golden Age* for one of his films is interesting too, as it refers to a fabled era in classical mythology in which the gods lived on Earth, ruling it directly. Interesting, also, is that Dali consorted with a group of cubist contemporaries called "Section d'Or" - "the Golden Section."

But besides these two, Cocteau had connections to people who were almost undeniably members of the Priory. He was good friends with Jean Hugo, grandson of one of the Priory's Grand Masters, Victor Hugo. Cocteau was also on close terms with Jean's wife Valentine Gross Hugo, whom he called "my swan." Together they collaborated on countless projects. Cocteau was quite enamored with the late Victor Hugo himself, and is known to have commented once that, "Victor Hugo was a madman who thought he was Victor Hugo." Cocteau even made a film adaptation of Hugo's *Ruy Blas*. Unfortunately, as author William Emboden put it, "Cocteau had taken the liberty of adapting *Ruy Blas* without asking permission of the Hugo family. Worse, he transformed it in a way that greatly displeased Jean, who nevertheless refrained from taking action against the production out of consideration for his friend."

Cocteau had a direct, public relationship with the man who purportedly preceded him as Grand Master of the Priory of Sion: composer Claude Debussy. In 1962, one year before his death, Cocteau was commissioned to design the set and costumes for a production of *Pellé et Mélisande*. As William Emboden writes, "The audience at the opening saw a curtain with a giant face bending over the sea..."

In addition, Cocteau maintained a life-long respect for Leonardo da Vinci, another Priory Grand Master, and quoted him often. It was from da Vinci that Cocteau obtained his theory of the use of line in his artwork, which was one of Cocteau's main methods for communicating the secrets he had learned from the Priory of Sion, using sacred geometry and symbolism. Cocteau's lines were often subtle, implied - which, he believed, made the statements encoded in them all the more powerful. William Emboden sums it up best:

"[Cocteau] felt that line must make itself felt in a way that transcends the model from which it is taken. He employed an analogy similar to the one employed by Leonardo: line, Cocteau wrote, 'sounds an imperishable note, not able to be perceived by the ear or the eye. It is, as it were, the style of the soul...' These thoughts from <u>The Difficulty of Being</u> *are comparable to Leonardo's analogy of the scent of a flower diminished in space like the sound of music, and yet Leonardo accepted the continuum of sound and scent in space as an extension of line."*

Cocteau's art, especially his murals, were often laid out on a grid pattern, unseen on the finished product, which allowed him to place the objects in the picture into specific geometric configurations. However, Cocteau also left indicators in these pictures that allow the viewer to retrace his grid patterns and find the hidden geometry. Grid patterns are indicated by the strange symbols on the archways in the Chapel of Saint Peter, and by the strategically-placed dots in this chapel, as well as in the Chapel of Saint Blaise. Lines of force and geometry are indicated by glances, pointing fingers, spears, flagpoles, and other understated means throughout much of his artwork, allowing the perceptive viewer to "read" the secret messages encoded into each piece. As William Emboden wrote, "Cocteau saw an unbreakable link between the arts of writing and drawing." To him, the lines in a picture were like "lines in a script." Cocteau is quoted as saying that, "When I draw, I am writing, and perhaps, when I am writing I also draw." He explicitly stated that his picture-writing contained a mathematical, almost cabalistic encoding system when he said: "My work is the result of serious considerations which consist of turning ciphers into numbers. And so, I belong to the blood donors, the only artists I really respect. The long red trail they leave behind them fascinates me." Another quote, regarding his poetry, is equally suggestive. "Every poem is a coat of arms", said Cocteau. "It must be deciphered." He elaborated on this further in *Testament of Orpheus*, saying: "The poet, by composing poems, uses a language that is neither dead nor living, that few people speak, and few people understand. ...We are the servants of an unknown force that lives within us, manipulates us, and dictates this language to us."

Some of Cocteau's more "secret-laden" works may have been, in fact, made at the request of the Priory of Sion. Cocteau repeatedly insinuated that his poetry and artwork came to him from somewhere else: either a divine entity, or a secret organization posing as a divine entity. He once said that he was, "only a medium, a hand that carries out instructions", and that his murals for the Chapel of Saint Peter were "the work of a medium." His poem *L'Angel Heurtebise* was written, according to Emboden, "under a mysterious spell... He believed that it came to him by a kind of divine revelation." Of his play, *Les Enfants Terrible*, Cocteau said, "My subconscious wanted me as its writer. It dictated the book to me." And in the film *Orpheus*, the character "Death", who is believed by the public to be a "Princess", is broadcasting poems over a magic radio signal so that poets will think they have been inspired, and will publish the poems as if they were their own. The meaning of this is never explained in the film. I believe this was Jean Cocteau's way of confessing that he was, in a way, a propagandist for a mystical secret order, the Priory of Sion, and that the messages he was incorporating into his work were actually messages given to him by the order. Characters in his films and plays are repeatedly subjected to bizarre moral allegory plays and told not to ask questions - that it is wrong to try to understand. This is exactly what would occur during an initiation into a secret society, and what must have occurred with Cocteau's initiation into the Priory.

Cocteau and "The Universal Church"

"It is excruciating to be an unbeliever with a spirit that is deeply religious."
- Jean Cocteau

As if his classical style, conservative politics, superb talent and relationships with the world's most influential artists weren't enough to annoy his contemporary detractors, Cocteau's re-conversion to Catholicism in 1925 drove them over the edge, while driving numerous other associates and followers back to Mother Church. With a seemingly libertine lifestyle saturated by opium and young boys, Cocteau might have seemed an unlikely convert, but, in a way, that might have been part of what drove him back in the first place. Then again, it could have been something far more complicated.

Like many people, Cocteau had never really broken with the church of his childhood - he just fell out of practice. But he had apparently always maintained a deep and profound belief in God. While he was in his mid-twenties he was known to have had an argument with Count Mathieu de Noailles which ended with the Count chasing him down the stairs shouting: "Besides, it's simple. If God exists, I would be notified before anyone else!" Obviously, Cocteau had been arguing the pro-God position. Since his childhood, Cocteau had been obsessed with crystals, and he collected crystal paperweights, which he would press up against his eyeballs in order to examine their facets. "Like those who press their ears against seashells to hear the roar of the sea", he wrote, "I brought my eye near this cube and believed that I had discovered God." He had also been obsessed with angels ever since 1914, when he took a plane ride over France with the famed pilot Roland Garros. An interesting quote from Cocteau bears witness to this: "Nothing fascinates me more than the angel which a slow-motion camera forces out of everything like a chestnut from its shell. Since in relation to God, our centuries elapse in a twinkling, we are being shot in slow motion."

Cocteau's 1925 re-conversion came he when met the poet Jacques Maritain, a Catholic who "sought a reconciliation between Christianity and the twentieth century." Maritain had first become acquainted with Cocteau's work when a disciple named Charles Herion gave him a copy of Cocteau's pamphlet *Le Coq et l'Arlequin*. Herion soon became ordained as a priest, and it was from him that Cocteau took the sacraments for the first time since his childhood, during the Feast of the Sacred Heart. This "Sacred Heart" symbol played a large part in Cocteau's passionate conversion. According to William Emboden, when Cocteau was introduced to Father Herion, he:

"...looked at the swarthy priest wearing a cloak with a red cross above a red heart - the symbol of his order - and all but swooned as he dropped into the arms of the church. When he wrote afterwards of Father Herion as an angel in costume, we cannot help but look back to the opium drawings of only months earlier with the theme of the angel with the heart on his chest. ...Cocteau was now in the same 'club' as Picasso and Stravinsky; he had converted back to Catholicism."

Indeed, it would appear that Cocteau was already a member of a club that included those two - specifically, the Priory of Sion. The Sacred Heart symbol which so attracted him, and which had been a theme of his art even prior to his conversion, was a symbol used by the Hieron du Val d'Or, and would appear to be a metaphor for the rose cross. In fact, one of Cocteau's drawings from that period, *The Mystery of Jean the Birdman, No. 15* shows a rose protruding out of his chest, and a human heart protruding out of his back, reinforcing the connections between the two symbols. These symbols have always been considered equivalent by Hermeticists, both being signs of the cabalistic Sephiroth known as "Tiphereth", and thus, the Sun.

At this point, Cocteau allowed Maritain to "cure" him of his opium addiction. Maritain suggested that he take communion wafers for his withdrawal symptoms, "like a tab of aspirin." Cocteau stayed at a Catholic convalescent home in Villefranche-sur-Mer, where he was cared for "according to ancient prescriptions of the faith" by Father Herion, who belonged to an order of monks that practiced herbal medicine. The following October, while still at Villefranche-sur-Mer, he composed a pamphlet called *Letter to Jacques Maritain* which "amounts to a proof of God by Cocteau, resulting in a proof of Cocteau by God", according to one of his biographers. Cocteau wrote: "If He counts us, if He counts our hairs, He counts the syllables of verse. Everything is His, everything derives from Him. He is the model of audacity. He has borne the worst insults. He requires neither religious art nor Catholic art. We are His poets, His painters, His photographers, His musicians." At Villefranche, he was often seen by fisher boys "in an ecstatic trance before a statue of the Virgin."

After his conversion, many of Cocteau's followers decided to take the plunge into Catholicism as well. "God was in", as biographer Frederick Brown described it. "Le Boeuf suddenly abounded with penitents while seminaries abounded with clerics reading Cocteau's verse." Many authors have claimed that Cocteau only converted to impress Maritain, and presume sexual lust as the motivation, even though Maritain was married, and his wife was a good friend of Cocteau's as well. Further, they imply that his new-found faith was just a phase, based on the evidence that he soon returned to the comfort of the opium pipe, which he never truly gave up. "He exploited the Church for his own ends", wrote Frederick Brown, "like a spouse who provides a spouse he no longer loves a consolatory substitute, the solution to a bad marriage being a divine triangle." According to others, this was part of a pattern for Cocteau, who would continue to flirt with Catholicism for many years. As it states in *Holy Blood, Holy Grail*:

"For a good part of his life Cocteau was associated - sometimes intimately, sometimes peripherally - with royalist Catholic circles... At the same time, however, Cocteau's Catholicism was highly suspect, highly unorthodox, and seems to have been more an aesthetic than a religious commitment."

While I do not wish to question Cocteau's religious commitment, which would be rude and presumptuous, I am willing to agree that Cocteau's beliefs were, and always had been, highly unorthodox - much like those beliefs held by the members of the Priory of Sion. For instance, the Priory reserves a special reverence for the biblical figure of Mary Magdalene (or "Madeleine"), who seems to have significance for them, both as the mother of Christ's children, and as an embodiment of the Venus goddess archetype. Cocteau, too, seemed to bear a similar reverence for this figure. As William Emboden has written, "[Cocteau] spoke of a mystical effluvium of the Madeleine Church [in Paris], like the emanations from some antique temple, that kept him in the region of that edifice." The Priory of Sion has, in the past, purposely used the letters "MM", or sometimes just "M" to symbolize Magdalene, and Cocteau used them as well. In the Church of Notre Dame de France ("Our Lady of France") in London, which Cocteau decorated with fantastic murals, this letter "M" is mysteriously placed on the altar, directly beneath the scene of the crucifixion. [2] To the left are depicted the dice thrown by the Roman soldiers, who according to the Gospels, cast lots to determine who should get Christ's clothing after he died. The number of dots that are shown on the dice is fifty-eight, a significant number. The skull of Baphomet, which the Templars and later the Priory of Sion are said to have possessed, was referred to cryptically as "Caput 58M." $5 + 8 = 13$, and "M" is the thirteenth letter of the alphabet. Therefore, "58M" could be a code for "Mary Magdalene", who is traditionally shown praying before a skull.

The same statement is being made in Cocteau's mural at Notre Dame. This statement is further reinforced by the fact that the "M" on the altar is directly below a rose that Cocteau has placed on the cross, precisely beneath Christ's feet. Not only does that make it a "rose cross", but the rose is above the initial "M" for "Mary." The term "Rosemary" is used in occult parlance to refer to the female consort of a god or demon. (Thus the title for the film *Rosemary's Baby.*) This is exactly what Magdalene's symbolism entailed. The fact that the rose, as well as the blood drops beneath it, are colored both red and blue may indicate the "blue blood" of Christ's royal line. Given all of this, the Church's title "Notre Dame De France" is interesting. Most would assume this to be a reference to the Virgin Mary, who is called by Catholics "Our Lady." But the true "Lady of France" is the goddess Marianne, their national symbol. Perhaps "Marianne" and "Magdalene" are representations of the same archetype.

Notre Dame de France is located in London's red light district. Cocteau had always held a special place in his heart for prostitutes, as prostitutes had taken him in when he ran away to Marseille at age fourteen. William Emboden writes of Notre Dame that: "This church was dear to Cocteau because it was French and because it was in an area frequented by prostitutes and the poor of London. After his mural was completed, the local prostitutes took up a collection and bought a blue rug in honor of the Virgin and as a tribute to Cocteau's work." The irony of a group of pious Catholic prostitutes paying homage to a *virgin* cannot be ignored, and perhaps someone was making a veiled reference instead to the "whore" Mary Magdalene (the real "Notre Dame" honored in Cocteau's mural) under the guise of the Virgin Mary.

Another heretical belief posited by the Priory of Sion seems to be present in Cocteau's work: the idea that not Christ, but a substitute died on the cross, while the real Jesus lived on. This concept is illustrated in the Notre Dame mural, where only the feet of the crucified man can be seen, leaving his identity undetermined. Looking on, with a scowl on his face, and tears of blood dripping from his eye (which has been made to resemble a fish) is a man who is unmistakably Christ - the real one. On the opposite side of the cross, Cocteau has depicted himself, with his back turned to the crucifixion, as if to show that he rejects the orthodox version of the story. The theme is picked up at the Chapel of Saint Blaise, which Cocteau decorated and was buried in. Here we see two Christs depicted. We see only the head of the central one, wounded with his head slumped over as though he has just died on the cross. Above him, however, is another Christ, wounded in the hand, but perfectly alive. On either side of the two figures are two identical crowns of thorns, repeating the "dual Christ" theme. Finally, in the Chapel of Saint Peter, Cocteau has made another unorthodox statement on the nature of Christ. In his own words: "I concealed the image of Christ in a curve of the Roman vaulting. You can't see it as you enter the chapel. You have to get close to the altar to spot it. The construction of the vaulting reveals it only to the Priest, unless you go up and look." In other words, the true nature of Christ is concealed to all but the initiated, and is not to be found in the man who died on the cross.

Jean 23

The belief that John the Baptist was the true messiah, and not Christ, is one that, it has been posited, is also held by the Priory of Sion. Because of the special reverence that they seem to hold for him, all of their Grand Masters since 1188 (the Cutting of the Elm) have taken the title "Jean (or, if female, "Jeanne") upon assumption of the office. It has been noted by authors Lynn Picknett and Clive Prince that a hand signal associated with John the Baptist (a raised forefinger) can be found at the mural at Saint Blaise being made by Christ.

The authors of *Holy Blood, Holy Grail* have also made the point that Jean Cocteau, as the twenty-third Grand Master of the Priory of Sion since 1188, would have been "Jean 23." In 1958, during Cocteau's grand mastership, a new Pope came to power - Angelo Roncalli - who also called himself John XXIII. It was this Pope who finally revoked the ban on the practice of Freemasonry for Catholics, making members of the Priory of Sion, which is described as a "Hermetic Freemasonry", legitimate Catholics again. What is more, the 1976 book *The Prophecies of Pope John XXIII*, allegedly written by the Pontiff himself, stated that he was secretly a member of the Order of the Rose Cross, with whom, to quote *Holy Blood, Holy Grail*, "he had become acquainted while acting as papal nuncio to Turkey in 1935." Stranger still, in *The Prophecies of Malachi*, written by a twelfth-century Irish monk, the assumption of the papacy by a "John XXIII" was predicted, and the descriptive motto he gave to this Pope was "Shepherd and Navigator." Well, "Navigator", of course, is the official title given to the Grand Masters of the Priory of Sion. Furthermore, Jean Cocteau identified himself with the Greek mythological figure of Orpheus, who was the subject of many Cocteau paintings, drawings, poems, plays and films. Orpheus was, traditionally, both a shepherd and a seaman. This tends to indicate that Pope John XXIII was a member of the Priory of Sion, and had a very close relationship with Jean Cocteau. The authors of *Holy Blood, Holy Grail* suggest that, "Cardinal Roncalli, on becoming Pope, chose the name of his own secret grand master - so that - for some symbolic reason, there would be a John XXIII presiding over Sion and the papacy simultaneously." What could this symbolic reason possibly have been?

The Priory of Sion, as we know, has always been presumed to be at odds with the Catholic Church for a number of reasons. First, there is the fact that the Church had stolen the mythos of Christ for its own use, and the way that the Church purged the Bible of any reference to Christ's marriage, children, or real patrilineal ancestors. Then there is the fact that the Church has censored any interpretation of Christ other than its own faulty version, and "cleansed" the Bible of all texts that presented evidence to the contrary. Then, of course, there is the pact that the Church made with the Merovingian descendants of Christ, making them the perpetual heirs to the title "New Constantine" in exchange for their silence about their lineage. This pact was broken when the Church conspired to assassinate Merovingian King Dagobert II, and drove the Merovingians virtually out of existence.

But the Priory has often been composed of members who were nominally Catholic, and many of them have even been clerics. Furthermore, the Priory had, by Cocteau's time, begun calling itself "an order of Catholic chivalry", and Cocteau had taken care to make a public show of his re-conversion to Catholicism. The Priory had also recently announced its intention to create, through covert manipulation, a United States of Europe, much like what the European Union is becoming, and what the Holy Roman Empire, which the Merovingian bloodline presided over, used to be. Such a feat would be as impossible today as it was back then without an alliance with the Catholic Church, which still holds the allegiance of much of Europe's citizens.

Yes, it would take an alliance, or a coup. Evidence indicates that such a coup was attempted with the placement of John XXIII on the papal throne - a coup for which that other John 23, Jean Cocteau, was at the helm. Chillingly, John XXIII died in the same year as Jean 23 - 1963 - a mere five years into his papal reign, indicating that the attempted coup was snuffed out by the Vatican before it accomplished its ultimate goal: a reform from the inside of the corrupt Church of Christ, by those who possessed his true teachings, and his blood. But they certainly tried. The authors of *Holy Blood, Holy Grail* state that:

"...more than any other man, Pope John XXIII was responsible for reorienting the Roman Catholic Church - and bringing it, as commentators have frequently said, into the twentieth century... And in June 1960, he issued a profoundly apostolic letter. This missive addressed itself specifically to the subject of "the Precious Blood of Jesus." It ascribed a hitherto unprecedented significance to that blood."

This would be the blood whose bearers, in the form of the Grail family, the Priory of Sion was sworn to protect.

It is interesting that both John 23s were thought of as prophets. Pope John XXIII's papacy had been predicted by the prophecies of Malachi, and there were a set of prophecies supposedly written by John XXIII himself as well. Cocteau had also been named "the Prophet" by the sculptor Arno Breker, for reasons that remain unexplained. But there is a clue in the first syllable of Cocteau's name, a symbolism which Cocteau himself emphasized in his work. He called himself "le Coq" ("the Cock"), and published a folded broadside of the same name with Raymond Radiguet in 1920. According to William Emboden, "Cocteau liked the concept of a bird alter ego. ... It is a symbol of the soul's flight." Cocteau referred to changes in his artistic style as "moltings", and his young disciples were referred to by others as "geese." The poet Apollinaire characterized Cocteau in writing as, "The bird that sings with its fingers", a line that was later used in Cocteau's film *Orpheus*. But it was the cock specifically, Emboden writes, in which Cocteau saw himself, "as a bird that calls the morning hour, and calls his name in part." A cock is an announcer of things, just like a prophet, and thus he used the crowing of the cocks in his films *Blood of a Poet* and *Testament of Orpheus*.[3] He also used the cock in the Chapel of Saint Peter, where it watches the denial of Saint Peter from atop of a ladder.

Recall that it was Peter who was said to have denied Christ thrice, by the third crow of the cock, on the morning of the crucifixion. There is a further symbolic significance here. Saint Peter is regarded by the Catholic Church as the first Pope, and yet he denied the true Christ, as the Church still does today. They consider Peter, who was consumed with jealousy for Mary Magdalene's relationship with Jesus, and who mischaracterized them both in his teachings, as their rock of foundation. Indeed, Peter's name means "rock", and it is also very close to "Pater" - "Father", the title assumed by all Catholic priests upon ordination. In another mural at the Chapel of Saint Peter, entitled *Saint Peter Walking on Water*, Christ is shown standing with his right foot upon a white rock, presumably the "Rock of Sion" upon which he said his messiahship was founded, i.e., the bloodline of King David. And yet Christ also called Peter "my rock." On the left side of the picture is Saint Peter supposedly "walking on water", with the help of heavenly angels. But examination shows that he is not walking on the water so much as being held aloft by the angels while his feet are dipped into the water. The rites of baptism as practiced by the likes of John the Baptist involved the immersion of the feet in water - not the entire body, as is practiced today. This mural, completed in 1957, one year before John XXIII's assumption to the throne of Saint Peter, may have been Cocteau's way of prophetically announcing a reconciliation between the Rock of Sion (the Priory of Sion) and the Rock of Saint Peter (the Catholic Church), pronouncing that the Church, symbolized by Saint Peter, was about to be re-baptized.

The Divine Light of Lucifer

There is yet another possible layer of meaning behind the emphasis on the words "John 23." *The Revelation of Saint John the Divine* has only twenty-two chapters, and ends with the dire warning that, "...if any man shall add or remove an iota of the words of the book of this prophecy, God shall take away his part out of the book of life, and out of the holy city, and from the things which are written in this book." A similar line occurs in the poem *Le Serpent Rouge*, which was one of the original "Priory of Sion documents" and which may have been written secretly by Jean Cocteau. The line reads, "Take heed, dear Friend. Do not add or remove one iota; think and think again. The base lead of my writing contains the purest gold." André Douzet, in his recent book *Berenger Sauniere and the Secret Model of Rennes-le-Chateau*, speculates that the former priest of Rennes-le-Chateau, Berenger Sauniere, may have been in possession of a twenty-third chapter of *Revelation*, which he received through his contacts with the Priory of Sion. This same book alleges that Sauniere's last words were "Jean 23." He could have been referencing this supposed hidden Bible verse, or he could have been prophesizing the coming of the future Pope John XXIII. Then again, seeing that his death occurred in 1917, and Cocteau's assumption of the Priory's grand mastership took place in 1918, it is possible that he was referring to the future leader of the secret order that he belonged to. It is quite possible that he and Cocteau knew each other through the Priory, since Cocteau was undoubtedly an influential member of the order for some time prior to taking over its helm. Is it possible that Sauniere could have passed along to Cocteau the knowledge of this hidden Bible verse, and that this explains the significance placed on the words "Jean 23" during Cocteau's reign?

It is true that the "red serpent" in the *Le Serpent Rouge* poem could be seen to parallel in certain ways the red dragon of *Revelation*, among many other things. And Cocteau painted something called "the Candlesticks of the Apocalypse" inside the front door of the Chapel of Saint Peter. Also, the word "Rosemary" encoded in the Notre Dame mural could just as easily apply to the mother of the Antichrist as it could to Mary Magdalene. Both the Roman Catholic Church and the Priory of Sion have been accused by certain conspiracy theorists of playing a leading role in what they see as an impending Apocalypse, and they believe that the Merovingians are not the spawn of Christ, but of Lucifer. But the Merovingians may in fact consider themselves to be the descendants of both Christ *and* Lucifer.

This is an idea that is perhaps illustrated in Cocteau's painting, *The Temptation on the Mountain*, portraying Christ's temptation by Lucifer. Here, Lucifer appears to be blessing Christ, as a halo of light issues from the place where his hand touches Christ's head. The veins in his arms are emphasized, and appear to be filled with blue blood that is flowing *towards* Christ. Unlike the biblical description, they are shown seated at a table, taking wine together, like a couple of old friends - or relatives - and Christ appears to have been served some type of (perhaps forbidden?) fruit.

Given this, it would be valuable to quote a letter from one of Cocteau's friends, Jean Bourgoint (a monk also know as "Brother Pascal") to another of Cocteau's friends, Madame Jeannette Kandaouroff, apparently in response to a letter she had written him after Cocteau's death in 1963. He wrote:

"... I want to correct your mistake concerning Cocteau's death, which - quite the opposite of what you think, touched me profoundly... One thing I should like to clear up at once is the word <u>Satan</u>, which you think you remember and which I do not remember having used concerning him. Isn't there confusion here? Didn't I speak of <u>Lucifer</u>, bright name of the 'most beautiful of the Angels' before his fall? (In fact. don't you have a magnificent photograph of him, part of my 'estate' signed by him with that name?)"

Perhaps this identification with Lucifer is the source of what William Emboden calls, "Cocteau's preoccupation with angels, and the belief that all persons are angels in borrowed costume." An angel in the form of a human would be, necessarily, a fallen angel. Cocteau also repeatedly drew a figure called the "angel of flaming cheek", which could easily be identified with Lucifer. And of course, we should consider Cocteau's signature, with which he always included that perpetual symbol of Lucifer, the pentagram, complete with a little dot in the middle. Cocteau's explanation of his use of this star was that it represented a head wound that Apollinaire had received during the World War II. This may be a lie, but it represents an interesting metaphor: that of the divine ray of Lucifer entering into the brain of one who has just become enlightened.

Henry Lincoln has pointed out that there is a geometrically implied pentagram in the mural at Notre Dame de France which radiates from the center of Cocteau's forehead. If we were to draw in the dot that Cocteau always placed in the middle of his signature pentagram, it would land right in the location of Cocteau's third eye, or pineal body, the place where divine revelation first enters the mind. A similar geometric pentagram radiates from the forehead of the shepherdess in Nicolas Poussin's *The Shepherds of Arcadia*. In Cocteau's *Frontpiece for Dessins*, there is an arrow pointing towards the same spot on the forehead of a figure that looks somewhat like Cocteau himself. And in his *Head of Orpheus*, there are lines pointing to the same spot on the forehead of one of the busts.

A Young and Radiant David

Another figure from the Bible with which Cocteau identified himself was King David. In 1911, Cocteau began work on a ballet called *David*, which he enlisted Stravinsky to work on with him, but which was never produced. The costume designs he drew for *David* show the Judaic king wearing a Templar cross. Cocteau's letters to Stravinsky from the year 1914 are very telling, revealing a very Hermetic perspective on the king's life. In one, postmarked February 21, he wrote:

"A woman theosophist has described to me one of David's dances according to the Magi - it is terrific. He danced around the <u>Sacred Ark: The Dance of the Planets</u> !!!! Can you imagine the music!!!!! - what a noble thing we can make of it - strong and rugged like those times when Jehovah was the ogre, when the church sacrificed two thousand <u>sheep</u> in order to <u>please</u> the good shepherd."

Then later, on February 28, Cocteau wrote: "I am seeing a lot of the theosophical Magi and old Fabre, who know everything about David." These Theosophical Magi may very well have been from the Priory of Sion.

But it was not only Cocteau who saw himself as David. Others did too. In 1918, André Germain published a "heroic farce" in his magazine *Ecrits Nouveaux*, which was entitled *Cocteau Bourgeticide on Apollinaire Sauvé*. In it Cocteau personifies the young David who, on the orders of his "beloved leader", Apollinaire, beheads the "Goliath" of Cubism in the form of the artist Paul Bourget. The quote below shows how this was also equated with the story of Saint George beheading the Dragon:

"GUILLAUME APOLLINAIRE: One more symbolic gesture is required! Who will place his foot on the head of the prostrate dragon?

UNANIMOUS VOICES: You, you beloved leader!

APOLLINAIRE: No - it shall be the youngest and the most innocent, the babe still at the breast, the suckling of the future, Jean Cocteau!"

Then, after Cocteau beheads Bourget, Apollinaire declares: "Astride the modern Goliath, dear child, you look like a young and radiant DAVID!"

Cocteau the Magus

There is little doubt that Jean Cocteau was heavily steeped in the occult. Author Frederick Brown described him as being "part of a smart set which called itself necromantic. It made an issue of sentiment and occultism." The authors of *Holy Blood, Holy Grail* specifically attribute his interest in these subjects to his friendship with Jean and Valentine Hugo, "with whom he embarked on assorted excursions into spiritualism and the occult. He quickly became versed in esoterica, and Hermetic thinking shaped not only much of his work, but also his entire aesthetic." Some of these "excursions" took the form of séances, in which Cocteau's friends Georges Auric and Raymond Radiguet also participated. One of these séances predicted Radiguet's early death at the age of 20, thereafter making Cocteau an absolute believer in the power of divination, and in the existence of life after death.

Cocteau publicly showed an appreciation for the occult science of astrology, which would have been necessary for him to have been the author of the astrological prose poem *Le Serpent Rouge*. This interest of his is evidenced by his painting *The Age of Aquarius*, as well as his five-part series of paintings entitled *The Astrologer*. The first in this series shows Cocteau himself making strange, occult-looking hand signals with two right hands: one white and one black. In the fourth painting, the Astrologer is shown taking a white, astral-looking cord out of the fiery chakra of his heart and holding it against his forehead. In the third painting, the Astrologer is shown reaching up to touch a planet hanging in the sky, and in the fifth, subtitled *Anti-gravity*, rocket ships shoot up towards the heavens. This reminds me of Cocteau's emphasis on the concept of the unity of Poetry and Science, which he associated with the myth of Pegasus.

Much of the occult symbolism employed by Cocteau in his work specifically resembles that employed by the Priory of Sion. The "Horse of God" and "Divine Horsemen" mentioned in their literature (in the Rennes-le-Chateau parchments and in *Le Serpent Rouge*) show up as the "man-horses" in Cocteau's film *Testament of Orpheus*, and as the magical white horse named "Magnificent" in his film *Beauty and the Beast*. Like Parzival's horse in the Grail legend, Magnificent will take you directly to the elusive Grail castle (represented in the film as the Beast's mansion) if you ride it with slack reigns. The Black Sun, which was an important symbol to the alchemists, the Nazis, and, I suspect, the Priory of Sion, shows up in one of Cocteau's drawings of *Orpheus and Eurydice*, and in the mural at Notre Dame. The Black Sun is further indicated in this mural by the halo around one of the angels, which contains thirteen red lightening bolts, and resembles the glyph that the Nazis used to signify the Black Sun.

Cocteau emphasized the alchemical symbolism of the Sun in general as being a representation of the Philosopher's Stone and thus, the Grail. He repeatedly depicted people gazing up at it in a sort of religious ecstasy: for instance, in *Classical Figures in a Landscape*, *Faun*, *Homage to the Women of Villefranche*, and the Notre Dame mural. Another, more specifically Masonic solar symbol, the All-Seeing Eye, is used by Cocteau numerous times: in *Box of Three Faces*, *Stele*, *The Moon*, *50 Years of French Film*, the amphitheater at Cap d'Ail (where it is coupled with the symbol of the serpent), the curtain for the play *Oedipus Rex*, and in the Chapel of Saint Peter, where it looks directly at the altar. Cocteau even called this latter depiction "the All-Seeing Eye" himself. Most strikingly, however, it is depicted in a glass sculpture called *Hand-Eye*, in which a hand is holding up an eye while making a signal which means "love" in international sign language, but also resembles the Satanic hand signal for the Goat of Mendes. (As in *The Temptation on the Mountain*, the veins in the arm are clearly visible.)

Goats, fauns, bulls, and other horned figures are also common Cocteau motifs. These horned figures can be found in such Cocteau works as *Goat-necked*, *Faun*, *Small Faun*, *Jean Marais as a Faun*, *Flutist*, and *The Great God Pan*. In the drawing for *The Lady and the Unicorn*, the unicorn is depicted as a goat, not a horse, in accord with the most ancient traditions of the unicorn. This is an important metaphor. For one thing, we know that the goat is a symbol of Satan, or Lucifer, and the bull would seem to be a variation of that. The bull was also a particular obsession of Cocteau's friend, Picasso.

The Quinotaur and the Rape of Europa

One of the strangest legends of the Phoenicians involves the disappearance of Europa, the daughter of Canaan, whose own father was Poseidon. [4] She was said to have been kidnapped and raped by a creature called a "sea bull" that magically appeared out of the ocean. The sea bull was actually the Greek god Zeus in disguise, who, after capturing Europa, transformed back into his regular form and then proceeded to impregnate the girl. Herodotus wrote that Europa was a historical person, and the namesake of Europe.
The story connects with that of the Quinotaur, who sired the Merovingian King Meroveus, and spawned the Merovingian bloodline

The Quinotaur seems to be represented quite explicitly in Cocteau's frequent depiction of the lyre of Orpheus, which he always showed as having five strings, and very distinct bull horns. Of course, "quin" means "five" in Latin, and thus, the lyre is the Quinotaur, or the sea bull. In *Blood of a Poet*, this lyre is shown standing next to a globe of the Earth, perhaps showing the Quinotaur, as a representation of the Grail bloodline, holding dominion over the Earth. Another scene in the film seems to depict the myth of Europa. It features a bull with four pieces of cow dung stuck to its side (said in the script by Cocteau to be Europe split into four pieces) being led by a woman named "Europe." Perhaps one of the statements being made here is that a divided Europe, as opposed to the "United States of Europe" that the Priory of Sion wishes to create, is nothing but dung.

The Language of Waves

Other depictions of sea creatures in Cocteau's work also echo this Quinotaur theme of being half-human and half-fish. Mermaids and mermen show up in *Ulysses and the Sirens*, *Saint Peter Walking on Water*, and a glass sculpture called *Siren*, in which a mermaid is shown next to a bunch of grapes, a symbol of the Grail bloodline. In his drawing *The Fisherman*, a man with a pitchfork is shown riding the sea-monster Leviathan. Also, the figure that Cocteau probably used most in his work, and with whom he identified himself the most, was Orpheus, a seaman, whose name is quite similar to the Latin "Orphus", meaning "sea-fish."

Fish, fishermen, water, and sea symbolism form some of the most pervasive emblems used in Cocteau's work. These themes can be found in *Madame Favini and Her Daughter*, *The Ancient Baths*, *Ulysses and the Sirens*, *Pheadre and Oenone*, *The Fishermen*, *Lovers*, *Siren*, and of course, all over the Chapel of Saint Peter, which is dedicated to the fishermen of Villefranche. It even includes a mural called *Homage to the Two Saint-Maries of the Sea*, these two being Martha and Mary Magdalene, who are said by the French to have come to France by boat after the crucifixion of Christ. The themes are also emphasized in his films *The Eternal Return* (based on Richard Wagner's opera, *Tristan and Isolde*), and *Testament of Orpheus*, in which Cegestius, Cocteau's fictional character from his previous film, *Orpheus*, comes to life from out of the sea. In this scene, Cocteau, who appears in the film himself, states: "I have enough sea in my veins to understand the language of waves."

Besides the Chapel of Saint Peter, Cocteau decorated a number of properties to make them look like ancient pagan temples to the gods of the sea. In 1959, he remodeled a natural amphitheater at Cap D'Ail near Villefranche, on the grounds of an art school called Centre Méditeraneé, located on a cliff overlooking the sea. In a letter he wrote to a friend he boasted, "The site is more beautiful than any in Greece." He used actual stones from the Mediterranean to create there a huge mosaic of a horned ram. At the villa of Santo Sospir, which he decorated at the request of his friend Francine Weisweiller, he, according to William Emboden, "proposed painting images with characters from ancient myths represented as their friends. Francine would become Diana, Edouard would be Narcissus, and so forth... The villa was thus transformed into a mythological palace on the sea. Cocteau believed that it rivaled Knossos." Emboden says that Cocteau felt similarly about his mural in the Marriage Hall in the Hôtel de Ville in Menton. "For the decorations he envisioned the 'superb decadence of Knossos...' It was a Cretan palace in the modern sense... On the left wall... the legend of Orpheus and Eurydice is represented... Cocteau viewed this Orpheus as the brother of the young prince of Knossos..."

Jean Cocteau also liked to combine the symbol of the fish with the symbol of the All-Seeing Eye. We see this in the murals at Saint-Sospir, Notre Dame de France, the Chapel of Saint Peter, the Chapel of Saint Blaise, and the Marriage Hall at the Hôtel de Ville, as well as his drawing of *The Fisherman*, and a piece of jewelry he made called *The Eye*. Cocteau often used in his art shapes that look like Runic or Egyptian letters, especially the letter "M" in these alphabets, which also resembles the alchemical sign for water. In the Runic alphabet, this is, amazingly, the *twenty-third* letter - quite apt for use by John 23. But even more amazingly, the name of this rune is "Dagaz", which not only contains the first syllable of "Dagobert", but also means, in many ancient languages, "fish."

But in many other ancient languages, the

syllable "Dag" means "day", which is what "Dagaz" means as well - or, more precisely, the equilibrium between night and day. As *The Handbook of Rune Magic* by Edred Thorsson explains, Dagaz is "the synthesis of the powers of day and night through the concepts of dawn and twilight. This is expressed by the heavenly phenomenon of the morning and evening stars - as symbols of the divine twins." This, then, is the perfect symbol for Cocteau, who called himself "le Coq" - "the opener of the *day*." The Dagaz rune shows up in his tapestry of *Judith and Holophernes*, his drawing of *Her Majesty Queen Cleopatra*, his *Portrait of Raymond Radiguet*, all over the Chapel of Saint Peter, and probably in many other places. In one of the murals at Santo Sospir, he depicts himself as the Sun with blue horns, stalks of wheat for eyebrows, and the water/"M" symbol inscribed on his chin, coming up out of the ocean. Also, another symbol that means "Dag", a Sumerian hieroglyph, can be seen on *Box of Three Faces*, an obscure ancient emblem for a man with no formal education like himself. Cocteau has been quoted as saying, "I express myself with hieroglyphics", and this statement was literally true.

But Cocteau did not merely overemphasize the symbolism of water without also employing the symbol of its alchemical opposite: fire. The union of fire and water in alchemy produces the Elixir of Life. Thus, the fiery emblem of the Sun in always central in Cocteau's sea-themed works. The sea reflects the solar disc just as the Earth reflects Heaven, and man's intellect reflects the spirit of God. As discussed earlier, in *The Testament of Orpheus*, Cegestius - a character who was killed in Cocteau's earlier film, *Orpheus* - is resurrected and made into a real living being by taking, "that road which passed through fire and water." A photograph of him rises Phoenix-like from the ashes of a fire, and then is torn to pieces and tossed by Cocteau into the Mediterranean. "At once, a monstrous flower of foam is churned up", the script reads, "from which Cegestius issues like a stamen, flies up and lands gently on the shore..." Cocteau also displayed his interest in alchemy with his 1960 drawing of *Apollo/Mercury*, the God who is purported to have first taught the art of alchemy to man.

This fire and water union is also represented in the symbol of the Hermaphrodite, a creature both male and female, usually depicted with two faces. Hermaphroditic, and/or two-faced beings are depicted in Cocteau's *The Split/Each Time*; *The Twins, or Castor and Pollux*; *Three Eyes*; *Study for Lunar Tapestry*; *The Moon*; *Trinity*; *Bifronte*; *The Ancient Baths*; *Cocteau's Final Slateboard*; and *Box of Three Faces*. Furthermore, in *Blood of a Poet*, there is an entire scene which depicts "the desperate meeting of the Hermaphrodite", which "took place in Room 19." A bisexual figure undresses layer by layer to reveal a sign that says "Danger of Death" - the death that leads to eternal life through alchemy. This hermaphroditic concept is illustrated in *Testament of Orpheus* as well, in which Cegestius is tortured by two opposing natures trapped within his single body. The goal of his character in this film is to make these two opposing natures one again. Then there is Cocteau's *Self-Portrait as Nefertiti in Plaster*, where he depicts himself as the sister/wife of the Pharaoh Ankenaten, a purported alchemist, whom some contemporaries suspected of having achieved hermaphroditism through the practice of alchemy. This brother-sister incest idea is a further symbol of hermaphroditic union, and Cocteau used it in his film, *Les Enfants Terrible*, about an incestuous brother and sister.

The Scion of Sion

Cocteau's films repeatedly play on the theme of a lead male character being either killed or led to his death by a destructive goddess. This appears in *Blood of a Poet*, with the statue-goddess who is responsible twice in the film for a man's suicide; in *Orpheus*, where the title character falls in love with a "Princess" named "Death", who kills Cegestius; and in *Beauty and the Beast*, where a statue of the goddess Diana comes to life in her sacred grove and slays two men with arrows. But nowhere is this theme used so *autobiographically* by Cocteau as in *Testament of Orpheus*, where his mission as the main character is to deliver a hibiscus flower - which he raised from the dead and which he specifically states is a representation of his blood - to the goddess Minerva, or Pallas Athena, played by Brigitte Bardot. [5] She hurls a

St. Peter Walking on Water.

spear through his heart and kills him, but he is almost immediately resurrected. In the film, Cocteau was brought to the goddess by Cegestius, who is referred to in this film as Cocteau's *"true and adoptive son."*

My interpretation of this scene is very specific: Cocteau is showing us how he attempted to resurrect himself prior to his death by uniting with a goddess (i.e., a "Princess") sexually, and breeding an heir. The flower he presents her with represents his seed and his bloodline, which must have been very significant given his determination to pass it on. At the end of *Testament of Orpheus*, Cocteau states that, "My star is the hibiscus flower." Since I have established that the hibiscus flower represents his blood, and his star is the pentagram, the sign of Lucifer, this must mean that his blood is associated with Lucifer, and that he is of the royal line of the Holy Grail - a line which he wished to pass on to future generations.

A lot of people probably cannot imagine Jean Cocteau getting married and having children. After all, he was a strict homosexual who preferred his gentlemen young, according to most biographers - not at all the type to want to raise a family. Well, there are a couple of complications with that hypothesis. The first is that it specifically stated in the Articles of the Priory of Sion, which Cocteau himself wrote and signed, that:

"Members are admitted to their office for life... Their titles revert by right to one of their children chosen by themselves without consideration of sex.... By virtue of the hereditary rights confirmed by the preceding articles, the duties and titles of the Grand Master of the Priory of Sion shall be transmitted to his successor according to the same prerogatives. In case of a vacancy in the office of Grand Master, and in the absence of a direct successor, the convent must precede to an election within 81 days."

So in order to maintain any amount of control over who would succeed him as Grand Master of the Priory of Sion, Cocteau would have had to have sired children. But there is an emotional factor as well. Many people do not realize that Cocteau had in fact always wanted a son, which is why he repeatedly "adopted" young men, like Raymond Radiguet, as his spiritual sons, and acted as their mentors. However, in the decade of the 1930s, Cocteau actually made an attempt to breed not only a son, but a royal heir. The scene is described in Francis Steegmuller's biography, *Cocteau*:

"To a private showing of Blood of a Poet Serge Lifer brought a beautiful young woman with whom Cocteau seems almost instantly, amid clouds of opium, to have decided to 'fall in love' and beget a son... The beauty was a Princess by birth, worldly and elegant, married to a gifted husband much in view; she was a café society favorite, cinema-struck, later to have a brief film career of her own."

Cocteau and "the Princess" (whom Steegmuller strangely refuses to name) seem to have had a brief affair which included at least an attempt at sexual intercourse. However, as the Princess herself describes it, "He wanted a son, but he was only as potent with me as one can be who is completely homosexual and full of opium." Before the relationship could progress any further, the Princess' husband found out about her infidelity and divorced her. She reportedly broke off the Cocteau affair shortly afterward.

But Cocteau's account of the matter is quite different. He claims that he actually did impregnate her, and that he wanted to marry her and raise the child. Instead, she ran off to Switzerland to have an abortion. Cocteau's later reflections about this unfortunate incident reveal just how regal the Princess' family was. Frustratingly, Steegmuller prefers to misquote Cocteau rather than reveal what the young lady's family name actually was: "'I almost made a little Hapsburg'", he was in the habit of lamenting - using, instead of 'Hapsburg', the name of the lady's equally illustrious family."

The question arises, however: What European royal family at that time was equally as illustrious as the Hapsburgs? It could only have been an offshoot of the Habsburgs, like the Lorraine family, for instance. There were no other candidates. And the Hapsburgs were, as many readers know, direct descendants of the Merovingians. Furthermore, Cocteau seems to have shown an interest in the Hapsburg family in particular. He decorated stained-glass windows for the Chapel of Notre Dame de Jerusalem in Fréjus, France, with a double-headed eagle, the symbol of the Hapsburgs, wearing the Cross of Jerusalem. The Hapsburgs are, of course, the hereditary kings of Jerusalem. Cocteau even produced a play, and later a film, entitled *The Eagle with Two Heads*, about a Hapsburg Princess who is seduced by an anarchist. Playing a bit role in the film version was the young man who would later become Cocteau's "true and adopted son", as well as his legal heir: Edouard Dermit. As William Emboden describes it:

"This young man had been working in coal mines

in Lorraine, but, having a desire to paint, he had moved to Paris. Through a bookstore clerk in Saint Germain-des Prés he was introduced to Cocteau shortly before shooting began. Cocteau was enchanted. Engaged as a chauffeur, Dermit joined the Marais-Cocteau household at Milly-la-Forêt near Fontainebleu, where Cocteau had recently bought a lovely country estate. He became and remained Cocteau's closest friend..."

Dermit remained loyal to Cocteau throughout his life, and afterwards. He went on to marry and have two children himself, whom he raised at the apartment at Milly-la-Forêt that Cocteau bequeathed to him. Until his own death in 1995, most of Dermit's life was taken up, according to Steegmuller, "by consultation with advisors concerning the legal and literary complexities of his inheritance" - an inheritance that included the copyrights to all of Cocteau's work, and, most probably, his seat in the Priory of Sion. Indeed, we do not know for certain who presided over the Priory from Cocteau's death in 1963 to the ascendancy of Pierre Plantard to that post in 1981, although there have been a couple of suggestions. But it seems likely to me that Dermit would have been Cocteau's first choice for a hereditary successor to that office, and was probably named as such, even if, for some reason, the succession did not in fact occur.

Phoenixology

To Cocteau, having a son was a way of living on after his physical death, a feat he seems to have been determined to accomplish. Another way that Cocteau intended to live forever was in the form of his works, which is why he continually used the metaphor of fictional characters becoming real, or statues coming to life, as in *Blood of a Poet* and *Beauty and the Beast*. These statues represented, on a certain level, his creations, into which Cocteau had put enough energy to give them a life of their own. His work, he believed, would withstand the test of time, and be seen by historians of the future as among the greatest accomplishments of *all* time. A quote from William Emboden proves this. He wrote: "Cocteau's [first heart attack] took him to Francine Weisweiller's Villa Santo Sospir, where he ruminated on his murals as being as fine as any created in antiquity. With age, he predicted, they would be thus judged. He felt his works were equal in importance to those in Knossos..." Another quote, from Cocteau himself, reflects this same mindset. He said, "I have always dreamed of becoming an archeologist, and as I have never followed through with this dream, I invented pottery that I would love to have found in the earth."

Cocteau believed that he had already become a living legend, like the great men of the ancient world, who were immortalized as gods. Emboden wrote that, "Increasingly, Cocteau would see all life, including himself, as mythology..." Cocteau used ancient myth as the basis for most of his greatest works. He even used the Grail myth in his play, *The Knights of the Round Table*. A wonderful quote from him in the documentary *Biography of an Unknown* explains the importance he placed on myth:

"The Pharaohs incorporated into the foundations of their temples pieces from earlier temples, used the wrong way round. They sewed these seeds so that the temples might grow like plants. When a young Egyptologist explained this mysterious process of recycling to me, I realized, although somewhat belatedly, what I had done in <u>La Machine Infernale</u>. Essentially, I had followed the rhythm of the Egyptian temple builders without knowing it. The reinterpretation of myths is essential if they are to survive. They are handed down from one writer, one generation to another, like certain stories which are translated orally. In the process, they are constantly embellished, or they loose their meaning. In any case, they are altered by every narrator. The great myths are not very many in number. Racine, Goethe, and Shakespeare knew very well why their use is so effective. Myth is like a key that opens even the most unsympathetic soul to writing.. I have always preferred myth to history, because history consists of truths which in the end turn into lies, while myth consists of lies which finally turn into truths. If I am fortunate enough to live on in memory, then it will be in the form of mythology."

However, Cocteau also appeared to believe that death could be transcended quite literally. He called himself an expert in "Phoenixology" (a term borrowed from Salvador Dali), which he defined as, "the science that allows one to die many times, only to be reborn." Death and resurrection were constant themes in his work, including *Blood of a Poet*, *Beauty and the Beast*, *Orpheus*, and *Testament of Orpheus*. Cocteau implied many times that he himself had died before, and that he was in fact the living dead. He said of the making of his murals in the Chapel of Saint Peter that, "For two years, I locked myself inside like a Pharaoh painting his own sarcophagus. I was already dead." This thought was expressed in *Testament of Orpheus*, in which he spends most of the film as a walking corpse in the afterlife, reviewing the events of his previous existence, and the works of his own creation - in other words, the forms of his own unconscious. Cocteau believed that the afterlife and the unconscious were one and the same, and were located in an "underworld" that could be accessed through mirrors. This is how Beauty got to the Beast's magic castle in *Beauty and the Beast*, how Orpheus got to the underworld in *Orpheus*, and how the Poet got to the Hôtel dé Folies-Dramatiques in *Blood of a Poet*. Cocteau stressed the mirror concept in his artwork too, by using mirror images, or backwards "mirror-writing", as in *The Mystery of Jean the Birdman No. 33*, and even reversed speech, as used by the character Cegestius in *Testament of Orpheus*. The implication is that the afterlife of the underworld is in another dimension that is a mirror reflection of our own, located in the watery depths of our own unconscious. But Cocteau also warned of the dangers of swimming too much in these waters. In *Blood of a Poet*, the living statue says, "Mirrors should reflect a bit more before sending back images." And in *Testament of Orpheus*, Cegestius opines that, "Mirrors reflect too much. They reverse images pretentiously and think they are profound."

Numerous times Cocteau implied that it was possible to travel through such portals (represented by mirrors) to transcend time and space - to exist eternally in a state that is neither life nor death. In the tribunal scene in *Testament of Orpheus*, he tells the panel of judges who are judging his life that: "I have often wanted to jump over the fourth mysterious wall that men write their loves and dreams upon", referring to time, the fourth dimension. In this film, Cocteau dies and enters the underworld after he has opened up a "glory hole" in space-time, and gotten lost in the various centuries of history. This was accomplished by firing a gun filled with bullets made of "chronons" - particles of time. Cocteau visits the science professor who invented the bullets at the end of his life, snatches the bullets away from him, and then travels back in time to deliver them to the professor as a younger man - before he had invented them, giving him the breakthrough he needed in order to be able to invent them in the future.

Cocteau clearly looked forward to the afterlife, and embraced the idea of flitting about freely in time and space, meddling in the affairs of men as an eternal - and timeless - ghost. Given his interest in talking to the dead while he was alive, in the form of the well-documented séances, I can easily imagine him, as a departed spirit, whispering valuable pearls of wisdom into the ears of the future chosen few. After all, Cocteau's self-chosen epitaph in the Chapel of Saint Blaise reads: "I remain with you." And in one of the final scenes of *Testament of Orpheus,* he tells us: "Pretend to weep, my friends, as poets only pretend to die."

Endnotes:

[1] Cocteau's full name was Clement-Eugène-Jean-Maurice Cocteau, but he enjoyed using "Jean Cocteau" because it could be initialized as "J.C.", the same initials as "Jesus Christ."

[2] Another, similar-looking and oddly-placed "M." can be found on Cocteau's glass sculpture entitled *Stele*, and numerous "Ms" have been found in his mural at the Chapel of Saint Peter.

[3] In this sense, then, "Jean the Birdman" could be code for "John the Prophet." In other words, Cocteau was again identifying himself with Saint John the Baptist, and all that he represents.

[4] Canaan was the historical figure after whom the Phoenician city-state was named.

[5] Bardot, whose middle name is "Anne-Marie", was once personified as the national goddess of France, Marianne, in a series of sculpted busts of the goddess that were made in her likeness, and which were put on display in public buildings throughout France for a number of years. Jean Cocteau was also known to have made a few pen-drawn representations of the goddess, one of which was made into a national postage stamp.

[6] On the opposite side, also wearing the same cross, are two Templar knights.

[7] This archetype is based upon the story of Galatea, a Greek goddess (after whom the Gaulish race may have been named) who began as a statue brought to life by Venus. She did this because she felt sorry for the sculptor, who was in love with his own creation. This exact same scenario takes place in *Blood of a Poet*.

The Prophet: Jean Cocteau

By Boyd Rice

There has been much speculation as to whether the Priory of Sion is a shadowy secret society made up of some of the world's most illustrious figures, a paranoid delusion, or an elaborate (but baseless) hoax. The men and women said to be its Grand Masters are certainly real, most of them key players in science, the arts, and the occult. Yet certain names seem to jump out from the list, seeming at first glance to be so absurdly inappropriate as to cast doubt upon the rest. Two such names would no doubt be those of Leonardo da Vinci and Jean Cocteau. Both Da Vinci and Cocteau were men of genius, and both evinced an interest in the occult/religious matters, but... *guardians of the bloodline of Christ?*

I offer a strange new piece of evidence which seems to link together Jean Cocteau, Leonardo da Vinci, and John the Baptist (*and*, by implication, the Priory). It is a sculpture of Cocteau done by none other than the most famous sculptor of the Nazi regime, Arno Breker, and it is called *Der Prophet*. Now, it confounds all reason that the foremost Nazi sculptor would even do a sculpture dedicated to a leading French intellectual, not to mention a homosexual French sculptor, and then have the audacity to christen it *The Prophet*. But that's just for starters.

In the sculpture, Cocteau strikes the pose made famous in Da Vinci's well-known painting of John the Baptist, raising his overturned hand, with a single finger curling skyward. [1] This is remarkable for a number of reasons. Firstly, because John the Baptist was a figure of key importance to both the Priory of Sion and the Knights Templar, and no one can seem to satisfactorily explain why. Secondly, because all Grand Masters of the Priory assumed as a mantle of their leadership the title "John" (or "Jean"), and both Da Vinci and Cocteau were Grand Masters. Thirdly, because the figure represented in Da Vinci's painting of the Baptist was, in fact, Da Vinci himself. So here we have two famous artists, separated by centuries, both alleged Grand Masters, and both presenting themselves in the guise of John the Baptist, *the prophet*.

But why John the Baptist? This is a conundrum that has seemed to baffle more than a few researchers into the Priory/Templar mystery. And most who take up the challenge to delve into the mystery seem to come away with little more than baseless speculation or elaborate theories that are never wholly satisfying. I suggest that the answer to John the Baptist's pivotal importance for these groups and individuals may well be found within the title of Arno Breker's Cocteau sculpture, *The Prophet*. It may be something so simple and straightforward that everyone's missed it entirely, looking instead for something occult, complex and secret.

What do we know of the Baptist? Little beyond the fact that he was related to Christ, and that he was *the prophet* who set the stage for the emergence of Christ as Messiah. Could it be that just as the first John facilitated the emergence of Christ, the Priory of Sion saw themselves as guardians of a secret tradition that would eventually facilitate the *re-emergence* of his bloodline, and so adopted his name as a title symbolic of their role and function? The "Ockham's razor" approach to the Grail mystery is very rarely of any use, but in this instance it seems altogether appropriate.

This may well explain only one small facet of the John the Baptist mystery. And it certainly presents us with another mystery altogether. Namely, how did a sculptor infamous for immortalizing ht likes of Nietzsche, Wagner and Hitler even come to sculpt the likeness of a decadent French poet like Jean Cocteau?

Believe it or nor, Breker and Cocteau had a very close relationship for nearly four decades. The two first met in 1924, at the time of Breker's first visit to Paris. When the sculptor returned to Paris to exhibit his work, he found Cocteau his most vocal advocate; extolling the virtues of Breker's heroic realism at a time when such neo-classicism was decidedly out of favor with the modernist demimonde. Even a skeptical Pablo Picasso came to the exhibition at Cocteau's insistence, and was indeed impressed. Still later, at the height of World War II, Cocteau remained a strong proponent of Breker's sculpture. If his enthusiastic support of such work seemed merely unfashionable prior to the war, during the occupation it was perceived by most French intellectuals as tantamount to treason. The French Resistance was livid - yet many members who knew Cocteau secretly attended Breker's wartime exhibit nonetheless.

The bond between Cocteau and Breker seems to go deeper than mere art appreciation. It's one thing to play the *enfant terrible* during peacetime, but to adopt a stance as politically disadvantageous as Cocteau did during wartime can be downright dangerous. And Arno Breker too put himself in no less danger. Breker personally intervened with the S.S. just in time to prevent Picasso from being sent to a concentration camp. Upon hearing of the incident, Albert Speer strongly advised Breker to mind his own business if he knew what was good for him. Yet when Cocteau's leading man, Jean Marais, throttled a pro-Nazi journalist, Breker again stepped in to save him from the camps. Marais never even knew how close he had come to spending the war engaged in hard labor, and only learned of his timely reprieve after Cocteau's death.

To put this all in clearer perspective, it cannot be over-emphasized that Arno Breker was a member of Hitler's inner circle. He was a houseguest of Hitler and can even been seen flirtatiously frolicking with Eva Braun and her sister in Eva's home movies. The Nazis presented his art as being a manifestation of values that were diametrically opposed to those of modernist "degenerate art" (such as, for instance, the cubist abstraction of Picasso). For Hitler, Breker's work was a cultural manifestation of the same ideals he was trying to implement through political means. But beyond even that it was felt that the role of art fulfilled a spiritual function as well, embodying eternal values such as strength, beauty, tradition, heroism, and the will to power. There's no real evidence to indicate that this isn't exactly the light in which Breker, too, saw his work.

So why would a man like Arno Breker put his career on the line to save friends of Jean Cocteau, or for that matter, be involved with him to begin with? It would all seem to beg the question of whether or not Breker knew of Cocteau's involvement with the Priory of Sion. And if he did know, was he too involved? His connections to France are strong, having lived there from 1927 to 1934. He is said to have been initiated into a Resistance movement called "the White Dove" by Cocteau, yet never exhibited any signs of being a "reformed" Nazi. After the war he neither renounced with past affiliations, nor altered the style of his art. In a strange way, despite their seeming differences, the art of these two men seems to share a common ground. Despite his modernist tendencies, Cocteau's art seems rooted in the same abstract notion of neoclassicism. When he stated that he "detested originality, and [tried] to avoid it at all costs", Cocteau wasn't being facetious. Both men shared an appreciation of the sacred as subject matter, and likewise, of themes rooted in mythology. Both, for instance, addressed the theme of Eurydice and Orpheus (Cocteau repeatedly). It may well be that these two shared a far more fundamental accord with one another than their respective politics or lifestyles would lead one to believe.

While it doesn't exactly provide a solid enough basis to justify speculation as to whether or not Breker played some role in the Priory of Sion, the idea is intriguing nonetheless. We know that Breker certainly moved within a circle of powerful men (the Nazi hierarchy) who were at least as obsessed with the idea of the Holy Grail as Cocteau's circle. Perhaps the most we can say with certainty is that, at least on the surface, the figures of Jean Cocteau and Arno Breker seem to comprise one of the most unlikely alliances of the twentieth century (or at least World War II). We may never know the whole story, but at least for now, we've found an interesting new wrinkle on an old theory.

Endnotes:

[1] The author of this article has since acknowledged that this was an error, and that Cocteau is not, in fact, making the "John the Baptist hand signal" in this sculpture. That gesture requires an *upturned*, not *overturned*, hand, with the index finger pointing straight up, not *out*.

Sleeping Beauty and the Sacred Mountain: House of God, Gateway to Heaven

By Tracy Twyman

Every culture has a myth about the sacred world mountain, such as Mount Meru in the East, or Mount Olympus in the west, where the peaks (often twin peaks) reach to the heavens. It is symbolically placed in the "center of the Earth", the world axis, marker of the celestial pole about which the world turns. It is also Paradise, where the gods live in immortality. And they live not just on the mountain, but in its caverns, which are said to reach down into the very depths of Hell. The mountain is often volcanic as well, according to the stories, and the mountain is usually surrounded by a body of water, sometimes with four sacred rivers issuing from its peak. This makes the whole scene a perfect union of the four elements: water (the sea and rivers), fire (the volcanic material within), earth (the mountain itself), and air (the lofty summit of the peak, reaching into the heavens). This mountain is universally remembered as having been a refuge for both gods and men during the Deluge, which is another myth common to all cultures. According to some versions, the mountain was so high that the floodwaters could not submerge it, and those who occupied it (the gods) remained safe. In other versions, such as the Judeo-Christian, it is this mountain which is the first dry land arrived at by the hero of the Flood story, the Noah figure, the pilot of the Ark. In fact, the Ark in these myths is most often occupied by a divine couple, such as Isis and Osiris. In the Greek myth these two were called Deucalion and Pyrrha.

Pyrrha's name is related to the root word for fire: "pyr." In fact, both Deucalion and Pyrrha are directly related to Prometheus, who first brought fire to Earth. Pyrrha is said to have been named so because of her "fire-red" hair. Deucalion foresaw the Flood and built an ark, which eventually washed up on the peak of Mount Parnassus, the highest peak in the world, and the only bit of land not covered by water. When the waters subsided, they repopulated the planet by magically creating people out of stones, which were cryptically referred to as "the bones of our mother" (i.e., "Mother Earth"). This race of men was called "the Stone People." They had exceptional talents and strong physical constitutions, and rebuilt civilization up from the mud and slush of the Deluge.

Pyrrha would appear to be another version of the goddess archetype most common to all cultures: the goddess of love, Venus, whose myth can be found in Isis of the Egyptians, Ishtar of the Babylonians, Astarte of the Canaanites, Aphrodite of the Greeks, Sybil of the Europeans, and many more. In several cultures she is said to inhabit a magic mountain (obviously based on the polar world mountain). This is the well-known "Venusberg" tale upon which Richard Wagner's *Tannhauser* is based.[1] Here she lived with her attendant gnomes and fairies, who occupied the numerous caverns and underground rivers that honeycombed the inside of the mountain. A book called *Myths of the Middle Ages* by Sabine Baring-Gould, it is described as having, "its own mirror-world within, where trees and vaults grow, rivers run, and stars shine out from the hidden vaults of the roof", much like a Masonic lodge is built "under the vault of Heaven", with an artificial starry ceiling. Venus is commonly known as the consort of Mars, but her principal consort was Vulcan, god of fire, and patron deity of metallurgy, which he is said to have invented.[2] However, the preferred habit of the mountain's mistress was to enchant some hapless young man into her abode and hold him there under a spell of sexual magnetism, sometimes for years at a time, the immortal goddess wasting the poor man's life away in orgiastic debauchery. She is said to still be buried there today, lying in her tomb in a deathless sleep, from which she can only be raised by the embrace of a new young man. Thus arose the tale of "Sleeping Beauty", a myth referred to repeatedly in the evocative poem published by the Priory of Sion called *Le Serpent Rouge*, a poem that also makes repeated references to the flood, and to the area of Rennes-le-Chateau in the south of France. This is the vicinity of the Pyrenees mountains, and the Pyrenees were named after the goddess said to be buried within that mountain - "Pyrene", who, like the similarly-named Pyrrha, was the consort of another famous ark navigator, Hercules. In fact, the myths of Pyrrha and Pyrene would appear to be different manifestations of the same story. This notion is tantalizing to consider when you take note of the fact that the royal family which the Pyrenees area is most famous for producing is that of the Merovingians, who are the central subject of this magazine, and who were known for their magical fire-red hair.

The woman upon whom all these goddesses were based was a real historical personage, Semiramis, queen of ancient Babylon, whose husband King Nimrod, built the city of Babylon and its famous "Tower of Babel", as well as a number of other cities within his mighty empire, which appears to have spanned the globe. [3] Nimrod, as I have stated previously, appears to have certain characteristics in common with the biblical figure of Cain, and with the sea-gods known throughout various cultures as "Dagon", "Oannes", "Enki", etc. This figure can even be seen in the mythical ancestors of the Merovingian kings, the sea monster they called "the Quinotaur." Like Venus' consort Vulcan, Nimrod was said to have invented metallurgy, as well as writing, math, navigation, and masonry, the latter being used to build the magnificent tower for which he is most famous. His wife, like Venus, was a love goddess, nicknamed the "Mother of Harlots", and she acted as the Headmistress of the temple prostitutes, who performed sacred sexual magic in the tower, which was built to represent the sacred world mountain. This sex rite, still practiced by secret societies and occultists today, was known as "pyr", magic fire, and was employed as a symbolic union of the elements of fire and water - male and female energies. This rite of sexual alchemy, which was also ceremonially performed by Semiramis and Nimrod themselves, is secretly referred to by occultists with the Latin phrase: *Rex igne redit et coningo gaudet occulto* - "The king returns with fire and rejoices in his hidden bride."

Replicas of the sacred mountain, of which the Tower of Babel was perhaps the first, can be found all over the world, in the pyramids and stepped ziggurats of the ancient world - from China to Cambodia, from Egypt to South America. All were built to embody the union of fire and water. They were either built on an island, or surrounded by a moat, or connected to an elaborate system of fountains, and they usually contained a sacred fire which burned perpetually at the temple's peak. In fact, the word "pyramid" itself means "fire in the middle." Often they would have a secret system of tunnels built underneath them, like under the Giza pyramids, or under the temple of Maccu Pichu, to represent the infernal caverns of the legendary "world mountain." Like the Tower of Babel, they often consisted of seven steps - seven being the number of godly perfection - and sometimes each step was painted with one of the seven colors of the rainbow, forming a "rainbow bridge" to Heaven - which was indeed the main function of the temple. In fact, the Sumerian word for ziggurat is "duranki", which means "the binding of Heaven and Earth", and the word "Babylon" means "gateway of the gods." Furthermore, in the Pyr ritual which was performed in a temple's inner sanctum, the priestess was referred to, in Latin, as "Ianua Coeli" ("Gateway to Heaven"), proving again that the ritual which took place inside the temple represented the same concepts as the temple itself. [4]

According to the biblical narrative, the Tower of Babel was built relatively soon after the Flood, when all of the people who remained were essentially of one stock, and all of one culture. The Tower of Babel may have been the first thing built by the post-diluvian civilization that had any structural significance to it. The Bible makes it sound as though the people who built it were just arrogantly attempting to create a replica of the holy mountain on which the gods lived, as part of some narcissistic, self-serving effort to be more god-like. But subtle details in a passage from *Genesis: 11*, make it clear what the original purpose was. *Genesis 11:4* states: "And they said, "Go to, let us build a city and a tower, whose top may reach unto heaven; and let us make a name, lest we be scattered abroad upon the face of the whole earth."

Let us recall: the Earth had just been destroyed by a flood, from which only a handful of mortal humans had survived. However, the gods were not touched at all by the waters of the Deluge, because they lived on mountains so high that the peak reached into the heavens, and the waters could not reach their summits. Logically, then, these people figured that in order to survive the next catastrophe brought on by divine punishment, they too would have to build a mountain reaching up to Heaven, "lest we be scattered abroad upon the face of the whole earth." Even Plato's description of the holy temple on Atlantis specifies that the entrance to the temple was marked by two pillars, one made to be imperishable by fire, the other imperishable by water, into which were placed sacred scrolls containing the most valuable knowledge they had attained, so that, no matter what kind of cataclysm occurred, their knowledge, and their "name", their identity, their culture and traditions would be preserved for future generations. However, in the case of the Tower of Babel, the gods saw fit to prevent this establishment of a "name", fearing that if these people could build a mountain as tall as their own, "then nothing will be restrained from them." So the tower was smashed by the might of the gods, and the people who built it were scattered upon the face of their earth, their true identity lost to history, and their unified language scrambled into the multitude that we know today.

The "universal language" that is undoubtedly referred to in the Tower of Babel story is Sumerian, in which can be found the roots of many, if not most of the words in the unfathomable multitudes of languages used on Earth today. One might imagine that if you could put all of the pieces together like a jigsaw puzzle, you would find this hidden language in the various fragments. But alas, the true pronunciation and meaning of the language of Sumer has been lost to the mists of time, along with the people who used that language, for the people who today occupy the landmass that was ancient Mesopotamia are certainly not their direct ancestors. Divine retribution stole from them their most precious possession - posterity. Symbolic similarities can be found in the later Biblical tale of the twelve tribes of Israel, ten of which were "dispersed" and lost to history, again as part of a divine punishment. During the God-imposed captivity of the Israelites in Babylon. According to *The Book of Jeremiah*, God's purpose for the punishment of the Babylonian captivity was to scatter the Israelites across the globe, to cause them to lose their identity, and especially, their *language*. Even the patriarch of the twelve tribes of Israel, formerly known as Jacob, bears a certain symbolic connection to the figure of Nimrod or Cain, the one who rebelled against God. Experts say that Jacob's name, in Hebrew, means "usurper", because he usurped his brother's birthright, a story element shared with that of Cain and Abel. But there is another detail of Jacob's story that connects him even further to the figure of Nimrod. That is his temple of Bethel.

As the story goes, God sent Jacob to a place called "Luz" (Light), "in the land of Canaan." This was the same spot where his ancestor, Abraham had once built "an altar to the Lord", and where, according to certain Jewish traditions, he had attempted to sacrifice his son Isaac, being located on Mount Moriah. Here Jacob found the altar which his forefather had built out of twelve stones, and laid them out on the ground, saying: "'If, not, these twelve stones will unite into a single one, then I shall know for a certainty that I am destined to become a father of the twelve tribes.' At this time, the twelve stones joined themselves together and made one, which he put under his head, and at once it became soft and downy like a pillow." [5] Overcome with sleep, Jacob had a wondrous dream, in which he witnessed, "a ladder set up on the earth, and the top of it reached to heaven: and behold, the angels of God ascending and descending on it." (*Genesis 28:12.*) When Jacob awoke, he said to himself: "Surely the Lord is in this place, and I knew it not." (*Genesis 28:16.*) He then became afraid and exclaimed, "How dreadful is this place! This is none other but the House of God, and this is a gate of Heaven." (*Genesis 28:17.*) He then took the stone which he had used for a pillow, and set it up as a pillar, consecrating it with oil which magically poured down from Heaven, and resolved to use it as a cornerstone for a temple of God, which he would build upon that very spot. Thereafter he called the place "Bethel."

Now consider the "ladder to Heaven" which he witnessed. As Freemasonic expert and author Albert Pike writes in *Morals and Dogma*, "The word translated 'ladder' is 'salem', from 'salal', raised, elevated, reared up, piled into a heap... a pyramid with seven stages." Other biblical scholars share in this consensus: the "ladder to Heaven" which Jacob saw in his dream was a seven-staged ziggurat reaching to Heaven - just like Nimrod's Tower of Babel! Even the word "Bethel" is phonetically similar to "Babel." But there is more. The word "Beth-El", or "Beith-El" has been translated from the Hebrew as meaning "house of God", and also "gateway to Heaven" - exactly what Jacob said it was. But according to author René Guenon in his book *The Lord of the World*, this word is also related to "betyle", which is, "a stone believed to be the dwelling-place of the deity... Thus this stone must be the true "divine habitation', the seat of the Shekinah." This concept is further elaborated on in his colleague Julius Evola's *The Mystery of the Grail*, where he writes, "lapis betillis, or betillus... may be a reference to baitulos, the stone fallen from the sky according to Greek mythology." This "stone that fell from Heaven" is also known as the Grail stone, a representation of Lucifer or Satan, and the bloodline of his descendants through Cain. This is the "Grail family", which included the kings of the ancient world, the biblical patriarchs, the Merovingian kings in France, and much of the royalty of modern Europe.

Jacob built a temple upon that stone, and if he believed that the spirit of God actually lived inside that stone, then this temple would quite literally be a "house of God." Furthermore, it is clear that the temple he built represented, as all "world mountain" temples do, the center of the Earth, for we read in *The Legends of the Jews* that after he had set up and anointed the pillar, "God sank this anointed stone into the abyss, to serve as the center of the earth, the same stone, the Eben Shetiyah, that forms the center of the sanctuary, whereof the Ineffable Name is graven..." Therefore, if Jacob built his temple as a replica of the one he had seen in his dream, he would have a seven-stepped ziggurat reaching up to Heaven, with the cornerstone sunk down into the abyss, to the center of the earth - an exact representation of the primordial world-mountain in all details. Perhaps this myth is the source of Judaism's most pre-eminent symbol, the six-pointed Seal of Solomon, which can be viewed as a representation of this mountain. The upward-pointing triangle represents the mountain's peak, as well as the element of fire, licking up towards Heaven, and the downward-pointing triangle represents the cavern leading t the center of the Earth, and to the stone, as well as the element of water, issuing from a subterranean source. That the Israelites viewed their God as actually living inside of a holy mountain is clear from his traditional title, "El Shaddai", the "Lord of the Mountain", and from the fact that he introduced the Ten Commandments to Moses from inside of a volcano, appearing in the form of a flaming *pyre* to a man whose name ("Moses") means "rescued from the water" - symbolic indeed. Of course, there is also that other most well-known habitation of the Lord, Mount Zion, next to which the Jews built another "house" for the Lord, the Temple of Jerusalem.

Despite the very specific dimensions detailed in the Bible regarding how many cubits high and wide it was, we really do not know what the Temple of Jerusalem looked like - only that it was built according to the specifications of the Almighty God himself. However, most experts agree that it was built on the foundation of a much older, megalithic-style temple, obviously to another god. Although we do not know for certain that this previous temple took the form of a ziggurat, it would certainly seem to be implied by the name "Jerusalem", containing that word "salem" which, according to Albert Pike, means "a seven-stepped pyramid."[6] The number 7 recurs repeatedly in the story of the Temple of Solomon, which was built in seven years, within the confines of a city that, like Rome, was built upon seven hills. Like Bethel, and other sacred "world mountain" locations throughout the ancient world, Jerusalem was believed to be the literal "center of the earth", and throughout the middle ages was depicted on maps as being in the exact mathematical center, with all of the other land masses clustered around it evenly. The temple was itself believed to have been built in the direct center of the holy city. And of course, like Bethel, the Temple of Solomon was built upon a sacred foundation stone, "the Rock of Sion", "the stone which the builders rejected." Just as the Lord was believed to literally be living inside of the cornerstone at Bethel, God was believed also to literally reside inside the Ark of the Covenant, the Jews' most famous treasure, for which the Temple was supposedly built in the first place.

The Temple was built with three concentric chambers, and the Ark was placed in the exact center of the Temple's inner chamber, the "Holy of Holies", right where we now find the black meteorite known as the "Kaaba", another "stone that fell from Heaven", worshipped by Muslims at the Dome of the Rock, which was built over the old Temple mount. And what else was inside the Ark, supposedly? *Stone* tablets, handed to Moses by God himself, inscribed by God's own divine finger. The stone at Bethel was said to have words written on it as well, specifically the four-fold "Ineffable Name of God." [7] Evidence would indicate that the cornerstones of both the Bethel and Jerusalem temples are in fact the same object. And although Bethel and Jerusalem were probably not the same geographical places historically, there is another interesting detail from the Jewish apocrypha that indicates a geographical and symbolic connection: both Mt. Sion and Bethel are said to be "near" a place called "the Cave of Treasures", in which many Biblical patriarchs and matriarchs are said to be buried. Here, Adam and Eve are said to lie, their bodies undecayed in a perpetual death-like slumber. Eve, it would appear, is another manifestation of the "Sleeping Beauty" goddess archetype. Then the Garden of Eden, it would follow, must have been located atop the sacred world mountain, especially noting the fact that Eden was surrounded by four sacred rivers, just like the world mountain is.

There have actually been a series of "reincarnations" of the Temple of Jerusalem, all of them sacked and ruined by foreign invaders. The Ark was, according to legend, secreted away long before, most probably within the vast caverns underneath the Temple which Solomon had built - another similarity between this temple and ancient ziggurat temples. With the Ark, and its precious cargo, deposited underground, that makes the similarity between Solomon's Temple and Jacob's Bethel - in which the cornerstone was sunk down into "the abyss" in the "center of the earth" - complete. Although the famous "Wailing Wall" is the only remnant of the Temple still intact today, the "ruined" Temple of Jerusalem has become a powerful symbol for modern-day Freemasons, who undoubtedly adapted it from their predecessors, the Knights Templar. [8]

Interestingly, there is a symbolic representation of the Temple of Solomon to be found in Scotland's Rosslyn Chapel, built by a direct heir to the Templar heritage, William Sinclair. It was purposely designed to have direct structural and dimensional similarities to the Temple of Jerusalem, including underground caverns in which treasures are believed to have been secreted. But it was also purposely left unfinished, as a representation of the concept of the "ruined temple." This concept may just be an archetypal memory of the destruction of the Tower of Babel, a concept that one might suppose is also represented by the missing capstone of the Giza pyramid. This capstone is presented on the Masonic "Great Seal of the United States" on the back of the dollar bill as having been restored or replaced by the "All-Seeing Eye of God." In a way, the ruined temple represents the Fall of Man, and its restoration, his return to the Garden of Eden. With this is mind, it is noteworthy that Rosslyn Chapel is located in the Scottish city of "Edinburgh", which literally means "Mount of Eden", and which is also, believe it or not, built on seven hills.

However, Rosslyn is not the only holy site in Europe where the architects and landscapers have clearly attempted to reflect or symbolically refer to Jerusalem and the Temple of Solomon. The other most noteworthy site is Rennes-le-Chateau, France, which has a landscape that has been purposely concocted to resemble the street layout of the Old City of Jerusalem. On this landscape you will find the Church of St. Mary Magdalene, with the words "This place is terrible. It is the House of God and the Gateway to Heaven" transcribed over the doorway, a deliberate reference to Jacob's Temple of Bethel. Directly inside that doorway stands the infamous statue of the demon Asmodeus, the legendary builder of Solomon's Temple, according to Judaic tradition. The demon holds aloft on his shoulders a seashell full of holy water, surmounted by two fiery salamanders, and is then further surmounted by four angels, thus embodying a symbolic union of the four elements, like the ancient ziggurat temples I have written of. This church is profuse with seemingly gratuitous water imagery, like the ziggurats of old were, with their sacred pools and moats. And although there is no sacred pyre or evidence of temple prostitution having taken place there, the patron saint of the church, Mary Magdalene, actually was a temple prostitute, and a worshipper of Astarte, a.k.a. Semiramis - another temple prostitute. And Mary was also, just like Semiramis, married to the king of a holy city – Jesus. In fact, some say that the name "Magdalene" means "companion of the king", while it may also derive from the Babylonian word "migdol", which means "tower." Her first name, "Mary", is derived from the root word for "water", "mar." But another derivative of "Mary" commonly used is "Miriam", which is found to be contained in "Semiramis", and which is a proper noun designating the female consort in a sacred sex ritual. Since Mary Magdalene's companion was known as the "Second Adam", that must make Mary the "Second Eve." Also known as the "Bearer of the Grail", because she carried Christ's seed, she is depicted in Catholic statuary as holding a vase full of balm, something shared by many other goddesses of the Venus archetype.

Things such as these are undoubtedly the cause for the strange development of the "cult of Mary Magdalene", in which the saint is worshipped in a veiled form (and Venus in a form veiled further still), taking the shape of "Black Madonnas", strange idols of the Madonna and child that can be found in Catholic churches throughout the Pyrenees region. It should come as no surprise, then, to learn that there is a long-standing tradition which states that Mary Magdalene is buried, in the region of Southern France surrounding Rennes-le-Chateau, perhaps somewhere amongst the five mountains found there that form a perfect pentagram - the symbol associated with Venus. Or perhaps St. Mary can be found in the local "Cave of Pyrene" in the Pyrenees. Certainly Father Sauniere's mural in the church at Rennes-le-Chateau depicted her inside of a cave, surrounded by emblems of death - surely an indication of the secret he had learned regarding the location of her remains. And her descendants, the Merovingians, were known for their fire-red hair, just like Pyrrha/Pyrene.

The Sumerian word "pir", from whence comes "pyre", and thus, "fire", also has a number of other very interesting derivatives.[9] From it we also get the Sumerian word "par" or "bar", which means "house" or "temple", and thus the Egyptian word for "priest-king", "pharaoh." The syllable "par" or "per" can be found in a number of other seemingly related words: "Paradise" (the location of the world mountain); "peer" (meaning "nobleman"); and most likely, the words "perfect", "pure", and "purge", from which we get the word "purgatory" - all words related to spiritual cleansing (based on the idea of baptism by fire). This is probably the source of the word "pray" as well. We should also consider the Indian Zoroastrians known as "Parsis", and the Jewish caste known as the "Pharisees", as well as the land of "Persia." This root word "pyr" may even be related to the word "pierce", from whence "Parcival", the Grail hero, gets his name, which means "pierce the valley" - as in the valley between the twin peaks of the world mountain. Note also that one of the places where Parcival sought the Grail was in "Chapel *Per*ilous."

Interestingly, the syllable "per" comes up in André Douzet's recent book, *Sauniere's Model and the Secret of Rennes-le-Chateau*, published by Adventures Unlimited Press and "Societe Perillos." This group is obviously named after the area of Perillos in Southern France where Douzet believes Jesus Christ to be buried. He points out that the coat of arms of the Lords of Perillos depicts three pear fruits, specifically a variety of wild pears known as "Mary Magdalene pears." More provocative still is the painting which he mentions, found at the church in Arques, not far from the "Col du Parades" ("Hill of Paradise"), where the baby Jesus is depicted in the Garden of Eden being offered a pear by an old woman. Douzet then makes the most amazing statement, writing that, "Because of its agreeably sweetened savour and its abundant juice, this fruit symbolized Venus... also undoubtedly by her round and soft form, it inspired the eroticism symbolizing the woman, the Love."

What is being indicated here with all of these "per" or "par" words in relation to Southern France, the goddess Venus, and the Holy Grail? Is it possible that the Lady Venus, the female co-pilot of the Ark during the Deluge, is buried in one of the nearby mountains, her grave cryptically referred to by locals as that of Mary Magdalene? Or was there, perhaps, a stepped-pyramid temple to Venus in the area during ancient times, containing the sacred flaming pyre, which has since been destroyed? [10]

A fascinating hint that this possibility exists can be found in the book *Le Vrai Langue Celtique*, by Abbe Henri Boudet, a friend of Rennes-le-Chateau's priest, Berenger Sauniere, who was intimately involved with his discovery of the famous "Rennes-le-Chateau parchments", and who undoubtedly knew the secret of Rennes-le-Chateau. He used this book about the Celtic language to encode clues about that secret, many of which have yet to be deciphered. On page 216, Boudet makes a strange, out of place reference to the word "PYRE" - in uppercase letters. This reference is then connected to another, ill-fitting allusion which Boudet makes to the passage of *Genesis 9:18*. As luck would have it, this reference is quite relevant to the subject of this article, for it is a reference to the Flood, and to the bloodline of Noah's descendants. It says: "The sons of Noah who went out from the Ark were Shem, Ham, and Japheth. Ham is the ancestor of the Canaanites." And the Canaanites, we might infer, were, Boudet believed, the ancestors of the Merovingians, the Grail family. Perhaps this is part of the secret, contained within Southern France for hundreds of years, which Boudet was trying to communicate.

Endnotes:

[1] In Sumeria, we have the tale of the goddess Ninurta, who stopped up a flood of waters pouring out of the inside of the Earth by hurling a mountain on top of the exit point. That mountain became, thereafter, the world mountain, and Ninurta changed her name to Ninhursag, "the Lady of the Mountain." She was also called the "Lady of the Rib", a symbolic connection to the biblical Eve.

[2] His name is the root of the word "volcano."

[3] It is interesting to note that, in 1627, a Sicilian witch interrogated by the Inquisition confessed that she had seen Sibyl emerge with her fairy entourage from "a cave in the Tower of Babylon", and that Sibyl was "King Solomon's sister."

[4] Traces of this function performed by the priest and priestess in ancient times can be found in the Latin word for "priest" - "pontifex" - which literally means "builder of bridges" - to Heaven, of course.

[5] From *The Legends of the Jews, Vol 1.*, by Louis Ginsberg.

[6] The Temple of Solomon was based on the Phoenician temple on the island of Tyre. All Phoenician temples, like the Atlantean temple described by Plato, had two pillars that marked the entrance: one made of wood, for the goddess Astarte (Venus), the other made of stone, for the god Baal. The Temple of Solomon also had two pillars, named Jachin and Boaz. And although there was no body of water surrounding the temple, there was something called the "Brazen Sea", held aloft by twelve stone bulls, three facing each cardinal direction, over which stood the flaming "pyre" of burnt offerings. The temple was supposed to be dedicated to the Jewish god Yahweh alone, but even King Solomon himself erected idols to the Phoenician gods within its inner sanctum, and maintained a harem of temple prostitutes with which he undoubtedly performed sacred sex rituals - just like in the ziggurat temples of old.

[7] This jibes with the legends of the "Grail stone" that "fell from Heaven", which is inscribed with the names and lineage of all of the members of the "Grail family." The Rock of Zion is also representative of that same bloodline, for Christ called himself by that title, a statement that is usually interpreted as a reference to his descent from King David. Christ, of course, was born in a city called "Bethlehem" - very similar to "Bethel."

[8] This group had lead the Crusades to recapture Jerusalem for the Holy Roman Empire, and used the Temple Mount itself as their headquarters.

[9] "Fire" may be the source of the name of the

Norse Goddess, Freya, that culture's version of Venus, after whom "Friday" was named.

[10] A relevant fact which should be noted here is that the Pyrenees mountains contain a number of caves, one of which is the previously mentioned "Pyrene's Grave", covered with pre-historic paintings of animals, some of which were native only to far-away places like China and South America, indicating that the people who made them were world-wide navigators who had washed up from a foreign shore. These caves, by the way, were all painted during an epoch of pre-history (14,000 - 10,000 B.C.) known to archeologists as the "Magdalenian Era", named after the famous "Magdalene Cave" in Dordogne, France.

Omega and Genesis: Underground Cities, the Deluge, and the Holy Mountain Hypothesis

By Boyd Rice

The legend associated with the descendants of Cain says that they dwelt in the "underground kingdoms." Interestingly, a number of places associated with the legacy of Cain had underground tunnels, labyrinths, and even cities. In Jewish legend, it was said that after Cain's expulsion from Eden, he went to an underground world named Arka. This obviously equates with the well-known Agartha and the less well-known Egyptian underground world Agert. An alternate title of Cain was Ag, and both underworld names appear to have been connected to him. But underground cities seem to be more than mere myth. In South America, there are countless miles of underground passages, most of which have never been fully explored even to this very day. Some think that they criss-cross the continent, connecting the cities to one another.

A famous story told about the underground tunnels of Cuzco relates that a man who went into them reappeared after a period of two weeks, with a brick of gold in each hand. He was wild-eyed and disoriented. Shortly thereafter, he keeled over dead. Legends that a horde of gold was hidden beneath the earth provided an ongoing incentive for would-be treasure-hunters. Many *never* reappeared, and eventually the local government had the entrances to the labyrinth sealed.

There was said to have been such a labyrinth beneath the palace of King Minos at Knossos on Crete. It has never been found, but the fact that other labyrinths *have* been found may be an indication that it's still there. At any rate, it is certain that the tunnels of South America *are* still there. First chronicled by the conquistadors of Spain, they attempted to navigate them. They went in, going as far as their spools of twine permitted. Without a trail of string to follow back to the entrance (a modern version of the "thread of Ariadne"), they would surely have been lost. And clearly they didn't have enough. They gave up. More modern explorers went in relying just on their wits. Most never returned, and those who did return often "lost their minds."

In another tale, related by author David Hatcher Childress, a treasure hunter became lost in the Cuzco tunnels and:

"One morning, about a week after the adventurer had disappeared, a priest had been conducting mass in the Church of Santo Domingo. The priest and his congregation were astonished to hear sudden, sharp rappings from beneath the church's stone floor. Several worshippers crossed themselves and murmured about the Devil. The priest quieted his congregation, then directed the removal of a large stone slab from the floor... The group was surprised to see the treasure-hunter emerge with a bar of gold in each hand." [1]

Evidently the Church of Santo Domingo had been erected on the very site of the ancient Temple of the Sun. Do other, still existent ancient temples (either in South America or elsewhere in the world) conceal similar underground labyrinths? If we consider ancient folklore to be a trustworthy indicator, the answer is very possibly *yes*. For centuries there have been legends about underground mazes and secret chambers beneath the Temple Mount site in Jerusalem. There are even rabbis still living today who claim to have entered them, and that they yet conceal secrets and treasures. [2] The precise nature of these secrets and treasures will one day be revealed, they assert, but only when the time is right. It's quite conceivable that there could be countless such underground places - places such as the underground library believed to be concealed beneath the Sphinx. Seismic testing has indicated that something is indeed under there, but the Egyptian authorities have, as yet, been reluctant to permit excavations. Then there are the so-called "Tunnels of Set", reputed by esotericists to lay beneath the Great Pyramid. And too, the aforementioned labyrinth is said in myth to exist beneath the Temple of Minos at Knossos. Because it has always been assumed to be purely mythological, no one has ever bothered to look for it. But what might they find if they did?

Andrew Collins, in his book *From the Ashes of the Angels* connects the legend of fallen angels to a series of underground cities in ancient Cappadocia, now modern Turkey. Using comparative mythology and other clues, he traced the stories of the Watchers to Kurdistan, Persia, and Cappadocia in an attempt to locate the historical location of the biblical Eden. In the process, he investigated an unusual series of structures called Fairy Towers. These were huge conical structures made of volcanic rock, the interiors of which had been carved out and used as temples and dwellings. The legend associated with them is that they were the fire chimneys of the Djinn, a race of angelic-demonic beings descended from Azazel, the fallen angel antagonist in *The Book of Enoch*. Azazel is a huge figure in this part of the world, and is the central deity worshipped by Kurdistan's Yezidis (who were said to have been the world's first devil worshippers). Strangely, Collins was to discover that the locale of the Fairy Towers, a place called Derinkuyu, also concealed another bizarre archeological legacy dating back to ancient times: the astonishing remains of a full thirty-six underground cities. That the cities are also connected to Azazel and his descendants, the Djinn, seems very much likely, although no one really knows who built them. It was long speculated that they were the handiwork of early Christians, who used them as a means to escape Muslim persecution. But such an explanation is as unsatisfactory as it is unlikely, since it would have provided their persecutors an easy means of simply sealing them inside and starving them to death en masse.

Of the thirty-six subterranean cities, most have never been fully explored. The one at Derinkuyu, assumed to be the largest, was described by Collins as a "vast underworld, covering an estimated two and a half square miles…" Of Derinkuyu, Collins goes on to say:

"So far eight different levels have been explored… though between eighteen and twenty are known to exist. The first three stories alone contained 2000 households, providing accommodation for an estimated 10,000 people. Scholars have estimated that anything up to 20,000 could have lived comfortably in the Derinkuyu complex at any one time, and if this figure is considered in the knowledge that at least another 35 similar cities exist in the region, then it paints an awesome picture of what appears to have been going on here in ancient times. Anything between 100,000 to 200,000 people would have been able to live comfortably in these citadels for any conceivable length of time. More incredible still is the fact that long tunnels are known to have linked several of these cities. One such tunnel, situated on the third story at Derinkuyu is thought to connect with the underground complex of Kaymakli five miles away. Moreover, the passage in question contains ventilation ducts to the surface and is large enough to enable three to four people to walk upright, side by side, along its entire course."

Oddly, the passages thought to be the oldest were also the tallest, and reached a height of seven feet, leaving Collins to ponder why people would construct tunnels so tall, unless perhaps they needed the headroom. David Hatcher Childress describes a tunnel said to stretch from near Sao Paulo, Brazil all the way to Machu Pichu, Peru in which the height was an incredible nine feet tall. He also relates a story told by a local of how he saw a man seven feet tall and "strangely dressed" who disappeared into that same tunnel.

These stories are extraordinary, because in

so many myths the abode of the gods is located not in the heavens, but in the *Underworld*. And in any number of myths, the story is told of a race of giants "cast into the abyss", or the Underworld. The work of Collins is particularly interesting because it abounds with names and place-names that appear to be etymologically linked with so much that is central to our research. His work seems both dovetail with our own and independently confirm many of our most primary hypotheses. He confirms the pivotal role played by Azazel, whom, as we've demonstrated, is synonymous with Cain. Azazel's progeny, the Djinn (pronounced "Ginn") obviously take their name from Cain's Sumerian title "Gin." This ties into the Jewish folk tales of Cain's descendants (the Cainites) having dwelt underground.

Place-names of the region reveal similar connections. Kaymakli, the city connected via tunnel to Derinkuyu, may be rooted in the Sumerian Kha-Mukla, or Hole of Mukla. Mukla is the Sumerian origin of "Melchi" and "Michael", and an alternate title of Cain. Since remains of Khatti/Hittite towns were found built above the underground cities, it's not unreasonable to conclude that many of the region's place-names might retain traces (at least) of their Sumerian origin. Other names in the area such as "Kharsag" and "Zagros" contain the name of Cain's father "Sag" or "Zag" (Ia). There is a range of mountains called the "Taursus mountains", and although the name clearly dates from a much later period, it obviously retains a connection to the symbolism of the bull, a sacred animal for Cain and his descendants. Most remarkable of all, perhaps, is that Collins places the location of the original Eden somewhere in the vicinity of Lake Van, a region whose landscape is dominated by a massive extinct volcano called "Nemrut Dag." Nemrut Dag simply means "the Mountain of Nimrod", or "Mount Nimrod." That an extinct volcano in the Garden of Eden is named after Nimrod is incredible enough, but the revelation that "dag" means "mountain" adds a new layer of meaning to Cain's title of Dagon. Viewed in this context, "Dagon" could also be seen as meaning "Lord of the Mountain", equivalent to the very title often given to God in the Old Testament, "El Shaddai." This view is reinforced by the fact that El Shaddai is believed by many scholars to be the basis of "El Shaitan", the original name of Satan. And the Yezidis also saw El Shaitan as simply another name of Azazel. So all of the ideas, the comparative mythology, and the names - all fit together like hand in glove, as though they were of a single piece. And indeed, they are. As we have demonstrated, Azazel is Cain, and Cain is Dagon. Dagon is the Lord of the Mountain, El Shaddai. El Shaddai is El Shaitan, and El Shaitan is Azazel.

The history of Sumer tells of a people who came down from a high place, or "the highlands" (the mountains) to take control of "the plains of Shinar (Sumer)." It also tells of gods who "descended from the heavens" to become the kings of Sumer. The legend of the Watchers tells a kindred tale. And the Heaven of ancient Greece was atop a mountain called "Olympus." Are all of these stories based on the same historical prototype - a very real circumstance often related in mythic terms? It would appear so. But in the Old Testament it is not said that God/El Shaddai lives *on* a mountain, but rather *in* a mountain. Did the race of the Watchers dwell in underground cities inside mountains before descending to the plains to build similar cities such as Derinkuyu and Kaymakli? Is it the notion of the gods coming down from atop mountains that served as the inspiration for the ziggurats - the man-made holy mountains scattered across the globe? And if these beings *had* lived in cities within actual mountains, could the man-made mountains have concealed entrances to "vast underworlds" as well? It's certainly possible.

But all this begs the question: Why would they *want* to live in underground cities? It's quite possible that at some point in their history, simple survival necessitated it. After all, central to our understanding of the story of the Watchers is that they were the remnants of a previous high civilization that somehow *survived* a global cataclysm of some sort. At some other time we will explore the various theories of catastrophism in-depth, but at present we will examine why they may have chosen to build subterranean cities beneath those on the surface. We have long hypothesized that given the physical descriptions of the Watchers, these were a people who at some point in their evolution were forced to spend an extended period of time beneath the Earth's surface. Whether or not you believe in the Hollow Earth theory, the persistent notion connecting these people to the underworld or Abyss has to have a basis in some historical truth. Thus far, the idea of the Hollow Earth remains mere conjecture based upon folklore. But if those known to us as the Watchers were forced to literally go underground for an extended period of time, this circumstance could have served as the basis for such folklore.

If the Watchers were required to live underground for long enough, hidden from the rays of the Sun, this could easily explain the loss of pigmentation in both their skin and hair. It could also explain how their eyes could "glow like flames of fire." Evolution would have given them pupils large enough to see perfectly in near or complete darkness, like cats. Who hasn't witnessed a cat's eyes in a darkened room, or at night in the headlights of our car, reflecting and magnifying the available light? We might not say they looked like "flames of fire", but the ancients may well have. This may even be one of the factors leading to the ancient notion that cats were "demonic", as the Watchers were said to have been. And if the ancients saw a people a foot or two taller than themselves, with skin as white as snow, and eyes of fire, what might they reasonably have concluded? That they were gods? Or devils? Or angels? Or demons? They might logically have assumed any of these. And judging from the mythological accounts, they drew all four conclusions at one time or another, because this is precisely what these varying accounts assert.

The underworld thesis may also shed some light on the recurring mythological theme of the Black Sun, a scenario of death and resurrection. When the king dies, the sun turns black. He descends to the underworld and is reborn as God, a very bizarre notion. But imagine for a moment that the death of the king symbolizes the destruction of his empire by a global cataclysm. The Sun is blotted from the sky by unprecedented storms such as would flood the entire world, or by violent volcanic activity that would fill the atmosphere with ash, and reduce the temperature so abruptly as to trigger an ice age. Such theories have been posited by very credible members of the scientific community as plausible theories to explain major earth changes of the past. Now imagine that some people are able to escape the cataclysm by going underground to live. Perhaps they know of secret passageways to the Hollow Earth, or simply vast subterranean caverns. Perhaps they had underground cities already in place and well-stocked, because their far-distant ancestors had experienced similar cataclysmic events. Note how biblical patriarchs who became key advisors to enemy rulers (such as the Egyptians) advised them to plant crops in excess of their immediate needs, and to stockpile the additional portions for use in times of emergency such as draught or *flood*. It's as though this procedure were a key part of their tradition. Yet they weren't presented as being part of an agricultural community, but as nomadic shepherds. Could they have preserved this tradition because they were the descendants of survivors of previous cataclysms? In the case of an ice age, these people would be confined to quarters for an incredibly long period of time, venturing out only to hunt for game. The surface dwellers who managed to escape to more hospitable climates would have still been impacted by harsh conditions, and have had to revert to barbarism in an ongoing struggle just to keep warm and alive. The subterraneans, however, would have had a temperate refuge - one in which they could live comfortably (as Andrew Collins puts it) "for any conceivable time." They would have been in a position to preserve the knowledge of their lost civilization, while those on the surface could count themselves lucky just to have survived. When things slowly, incrementally returned to normal climactically, those who emerged from the underworld would not be the same as those who had remained on the surface. They would look different, and indeed *be* different. They would have evolved differently. And too, those scattered about the surface may well have *devolved*. This accords with the descriptions of the two types of people often contrasted in the Bible. One is milky-skinned and pure, the other dark-complexioned, abhorrent and *covered with hair*. Those on the surface would no doubt be darker-complexioned and probably hairier. Were the remnants of these two types still highly visible specimens even so late as Old Testament times? Possibly so.

But the subterranean Watchers would not

have been able to easily make the transition back to surface life. Having lost their pigmentation, they would have been extremely sensitive to the Sun's rays. This could account for the paradoxical descriptions of the Watchers' skin as "white as snow", and conversely as "red as a rose." Too, their eyes having evolved to see in the absence (or near absence) of light, they couldn't have stood much direct sunlight. If they initially emerged only at night, they could have fueled the lore in some mythologies that they were akin to vampires. And it could account for an odd passage in the Bible which says that, "God appears to His people *only at night.*" [3] Remember too that the angel Jacob was said to have fought with appeared to him in complete darkness, and vanished only as the sun began to rise.

Was this the source of the notion that demons lived beneath the Earth, or that demons only came out at night? Could it have been the source of the idea that a group of gods was cast into the Abyss? It seems a very likely idea, and it would explain the widespread pervasiveness of such beliefs. At any rate, it seems far more conceivable that these widely held beliefs had *some* sort of origin in fact, rather than being universally concocted for no particular reason. Even the most outlandish superstitions and beliefs had to have had their origin somewhere, and in something which was at one time *concrete*. This brings us back to the myth in which the Sun turns black, descends to the Underworld, and reemerges as God. This is the myth attached to Osiris. Is it a form of symbolic shorthand, intended to be emblematic of the idea that he, or the people from whom he claimed descent, actually survived the process of death that had destroyed a world? There are certainly alternate explanations. But as we believe that Osiris *was* a historical figure, and is synonymous with Cain, Azazel, and the other figures connected to the legends of a race of angels from the underworld, this seems a fairly tidy and succinct symbolic synopsis of what we theorize may have actually occurred.

Most people dismiss the story of Noah's Ark because the idea of putting a pair of every species of animal on board a boat seems to defy all logic. They then conclude that since the incident "couldn't" have happened in the manner described, it therefore didn't happen at all. But let's assume for a moment that the Bible story is a highly embellished retelling of an older story based on a real incident. (It certainly wouldn't be the first or the last.) If we were instead to assume that the passengers on the Ark were merely a few hundred men and women fleeing a natural disaster, does not the story already seem more plausible? They may well have brought as much livestock as possible, though its a cinch that wildlife brought on board ended up as food for the passengers, and *not* repopulating the Earth.

We suggest the figure of 200 passengers on the Ark because that is the reputed number of Watchers in *The Book of Enoch* (though some alternate accounts say 500). There have always been varying traditions about where the Ark came to rest. Some say Mount Ararat, some say a location nearby. There is credible evidence in support of both views. Aerial photographs of Mount Ararat show what appears to be the Ark emerging from a sheet of ice. But not so far away, on a peak traditionally called the "Mountain of Death", modern researchers have discovered the remains of a gigantic buried ship, which they assert can be carbon dated to "the time of the Flood." Both of these peaks are in the general vicinity of Nemrut Dag and the underground cities. Since Nemrut Dag (Mount Nimrod) is one of the highest peaks in the region, would it not seem a likely landing place for the Ark? Perhaps it was. Perhaps there were *several* arks, and each was carried to the same general locale by the same current. Each came to rest on a different peak, giving rise to different traditions. Perhaps each tradition contains a seed of truth, and what is false is the notion that there was a single ark. In fact, when it was announced in August of 1883 that a ship thought to be the Ark had been discovered on Ararat, *The New York Herald* published a sarcastic article in which it posed the question that if ark building had been practiced in ancient times, why had not a dozen arks washed up atop various mountains? Well, perhaps they did. Perhaps this is why the names of flood heroes vary, and why different stories have the Ark coming to rest in the Pyrenees, Mount Parnassus, and so on. Those who survived the Flood were members of a great sea people, so it's not outside the realm of possibility that others escaped as well. But despite this possibility, most of the legends we've examined appear to be dealing with essentially the same figure.

As explained in previous articles, we believe that the Flood represents the starting point of our current historical epoch, and that the story of the Flood is also the story of the Watchers. In the usual telling of the Flood saga, the Ark comes to rest on an incredibly high mountaintop, and in short order the Earth is dry. It's inhabitants descend the mountain and give thanks to God for surviving. But how does a *flooded earth* simply become dry so quickly? Where does all the water go? Would it not take years for the waters to "subside", evaporate, or whatever?

There is speculation that the Flood was caused by the end of an ice age. Melting ice and snow turned to liquid and soon the world was submerged under water. Might it not be just as likely that a flood *preceded* an ice age? That the same climate changes that caused the flood created a global cooling that turned the waters of the Deluge to ice? If it happened that way, the only chance for survival would have been to dig out an underground dwelling in the mountaintop. But it may also have been their best option even if the survivors were just in a ship atop a mountain peak, surrounded by an endless sea. A good many of the mountain peaks in the region where the Ark is reputed to have landed are volcanoes, and the soft volcanic rock would have been perfectly suited for the building of underground cities. Also, these peaks are not terribly far from the complex of underground cites found around Derinkuyu. Though this thesis may understandably sound far-fetched, it is not mere gratuitous speculation. It is rooted in the numerous myths and legends of underground kingdoms, many of which were said to be accessible through *holy mountains*. Such stories are also invariably connected to mythic histories of gods, demons, genies, and so on.

The idea that a race of beings, perceived to be gods, *lived in a mountain*, both long prior to their contact with humanity and long after, is persistent and widespread. Even Sargon the Great is known to have made the enigmatic statement that he "knew not" his father, but that his father's brother "dwelled in a mountain." The clear implication seemed to be that he was a direct descendant of the gods, and that their dwelling-place was inside a mountain. Presumably, such an inference was plainly understood at the time the statement was made. This may be the reason why the pre-eminent religious structure in ancient times was the man-made holy mountain. These structures were the central focus of religious or political life. They were at once temples, brothels, and royal palaces, home to the king, the sacred harlot, and reputedly, the gods themselves. Were they symbolic recreations of the original holy mountain from which the gods "descended from the heavens" to share their wisdom with man? Perhaps they were both this, and something more as well. We have already discussed the fact that many of these ziggurats concealed vast subterranean complexes of tunnels and chambers. Is it possible that they all did? In Babylon it was thought that the gods lived inside the holy mountain. Once a year, during a sacred marriage ceremony, a girl would be dispatched to a sacred sex chamber atop the holy mountain, where it was said that a particular god would appear to her *in the flesh*. The girl was often a princess, and would spend the night engaging in sex with this god. Though modern readers may scoff at such a notion, could it be possible that a remnant of those people viewed as gods by the ancients in fact dwelled beneath the mountain? If so, their willing sexual consorts, seeing the strange visage of a pale subterranean, would naturally have believed that they had in fact had sex with a god! And the notion persisted right up through the Middle Ages that the demiurge, the ancient Lord of the Earth, dwelled in a subterranean realm from which he controlled the destinies of men. Could this be the reason why Babylon, with its massive ziggurat, was called "the Gate of God"? The ancient Babylonians never called themselves Babylonians. The word "Bab-el" indeed meant "Gate of God", but it was a Semitic word. The original name of Babylon was "Kadimura", a term probably meaning "Mountain of the Lord." So both Sumerians and Jews called this place by a very similar title, and both obviously considered the holy mountain a very real portal to God. Whether its connection to God came from its height reaching to the heavens, or its caverns descending to the underworld is open to debate.

There is further evidence which tends to suggest that the holy mountains may have been patterned on the original abode of the gods. A number of mythologies have figures roughly equating with Cain, all of whom live in volcanoes. As previously stated, Azazel's descendants, the Djinn, were said to have lived in volcanoes. Azazel is credited with inventing metalworking for the fabrication of tools and weapons. So was Cain. The Djinn were supposed to have been a race of blacksmiths. As Andrew Collins relates: "Not only would copper and lead smelting have become a sacred profession in its own right, but blacksmiths would have been classed as fire priests under the dominion of the genii (i.e., the Djinn) of the fiery domains." The priests of early Sumer, by the way, were called "fire priests." Collins continues: "The significance of fire, and in particular volcanic fire... signifies the magical power by which the blacksmiths could change rock into metal objects such as jewelry, tools, and weapons." Perhaps to the very primitive ancients, the art of the blacksmiths was equivalent to the later *black art* of al-chem-y ("chem" meaning "black"), the science of transmuting one substance to another. Instead of turning lead into gold, they turned rock into metal. It's the same difference really: extracting something high from something base.

The primordial blacksmith of Roman myth was Vulcan, from whose name we derive the word "volcano." He was said to have dwelt in Mount Ertha, a volcano. His very name preserves the root of Cain's Sumerian title of "Kan." Like Cain, he was viewed as the inventor of tools and weapons, but also of jewelry (so symptomatic of human pride and vanity). He was the god of fire and forges, and his workers were a *race of giants*, the Cyclopeses. (Remember that cities called "cyclopean" were said to have been built by these giants. It's also worth noting that the fire-priests of old had a solar disc tattooed on their foreheads, possibly giving rise to the notion of the Cyclopes.) His frequent consort was Venus, a goddess who equates with many of the better-known consorts of Cain, and whose role in the Grail mystery is of central importance.

Vulcan is widely believed to be based on the Greek Hephaestus, who forged metal objects possessing magical powers. Though relegated to the position of a minor deity, and revealing none of the qualities traditionally associated with Cain, his connections thereto are nonetheless inescapable. It was said that after a brief liaison with the goddess Athena, she gave birth to Ericthonius/Erechtheus, the first king of Athens. This figure is universally regarded as synonymous with Enoch, the son of Cain. Alternate traditions say that Ericthonius was the son of Dardanos, whom we've also revealed to be synonymous with Cain. Some say he held court at Erech, a city generally regarded as one and the same with Enoch City, built by Cain and named after his son. Hephaestus is also said to have been fathered by the Kabiri, an "arcane race of blacksmith gods." The Kabiri have been associated with the Djinn. History places the Kabiri in ancient Phrygia or Cappadocia, essentially in very much the same geographic location as the underground cities and fire chimneys discussed earlier.

If the term "Kabiri" was translated as an ancient Sumerian term, it would have to be a conjunction of "kha" and "bir" - the "kha" meaning "fish, setting sun, glory, complete, perfect, great"; and the "bir" meaning "bright, shine, pure, the Sun", or "offspring, young, child, brood." This presents us with a nearly perpetual permutation of possibilities, including (but not limited to): "fish of the Sun", "offspring of the fish", "children of glory", "children of perfection", "shining fish", "brood of the setting sun", and so on. None of these titles would be inconsistent with the myths we've thus examined.

High Mason Albert Pike equates Hephaestus with: "Tsadok... the supreme god in Phoenicia. His Seven Sons were probably the Seven Kabiri; and he was the Heptakis, the God of the Seven Rays." We have already equated Cain, and thus Vulcan and Hephaestus, with Zadok, a term which in Sumerian probably meant "Sha-Duk", or "Lord of the Sun." Remember that the Essenes of the Dead Sea Scrolls called themselves "the Sons of Zadok." They claimed direct descent from Noah. So too did the Merovingian kings of France. And so too did the Yezidis of Kurdistan, the strange so-called devil-worshippers who held Azazel/Cain in such high esteem.

Are all these groups simply deluded? Or

could it be that they are all privy to a secret doctrine of some sort? If so, it would appear to be *the same* secret doctrine, since they all seem to believe essentially the same thing. And it all seems to correlate very closely with what we've hypothesized all along, if not *precisely*. Let's review: Zadok seems to equate with Azazel/Cain. The Sons of Zadok, the Kabiri, seem to equate with the Djinn, the sons of Azazel. These are also the sons of Hephaestus. They were all originally located in Cappadocia, Kurdistan, and Phrygia, and later relocated to Greece and Rome. Their early names reveal an etymological connection to ancient Sumer, while the later versions are largely Greco-Romanized. The names have been changed, but the myth remains the same: gods dwelling in a mountain, a volcano, or an abyss, possessed of magical powers to transmute the base to the high, to make something of nothing.

And what of Zadok/Hephaestus, the God of the Seven Rays? The Seven Rays equate to his seven sons, who in turn relate to the seven stages of the ziggurat, and presumably, the seven heavens that this hierarchical clan was said to occupy. Interestingly, the seven Kabiri also seem to equate with the seven "builder gods" said to have come to Egypt after their homeland, "the island of the gods", was destroyed by a flood.

Though gods represented as blacksmiths may sound corny or utterly irrelevant in a modern context, it's difficult to overestimate the impact that the introduction of bronze, iron, etc., had on planetary evolution. Those who knew how to extract and manipulate metals wielded vast economic and political power. Those with whom they shared the byproducts of their specialized knowledge gained a great survival advantage. The Watchers appeared to people who essentially had not evolved beyond the level of hunter-gatherers, taught them the arts of agriculture, and gave them the tools of attack and defense, bringing them wholesale into a *new world*. Had they not intervened, it's impossible to estimate how long it might have taken these people to have discovered such knowledge and techniques on their own. If the Bronze Age had been postponed for 1000, 2000, or 5000 years, humanity today would exist in a very different world indeed. Had it occurred even a short thousand years later, we would all be living in a manner akin to medieval times, with no computers, indoor plumbing, or motor vehicles. The forbidden knowledge passed down by the Watchers essentially jumpstarted civilization and provided the very foundation for everything we today take for granted. Consider the fact that there are people in Africa who have lived by the sea for millennia, yet have never stumbled upon the notion of putting sails on their boats to harness the power of the wind. Had someone taught them how to do this four or five thousand years ago, how might this simple bit of knowledge have impacted their subsequent evolution and quality of life? The effects of such a seemingly basic piece of technical advantage could easily have produced inestimable consequences, as did the knowledge that the Watchers taught us. The invention of the plough accredited to Cain may at seem like a lowly accomplishment for a god, yet the shift to an agriculturally-oriented society set man on an altogether different path, and drastically altered his destiny. It created the basis for men to come together in communities, and nomadic tribes gave way to city-states.

The impact of mining was equally decisive. The advent of the Bronze Age signaled a huge change in human society. Because bronze was an amalgam of copper and tin, this forced man to traverse great distances by sea in order to obtain the necessary tin, a material not found just anywhere. The most well-known ancient source of tin was in Cornwall, England, a great distance from the ancient Near East. In going back and forth between the British Isles and the Near East, trade routes were established, and the great ports such as Marseilles would eventually become major centers of commerce. Soon the major traffic was not just in tin, but in any commodity abundant in one region and scarce in another. Cedar from Lebanon was shipped to Egypt and Greece. Olive oil from Greece was exported to regions without olive trees, and so on. It was this sort of international commerce which facilitated the early blossoming of civilization. The sea, which is so often thought of as being a barrier separating ancient societies, was actually a highway which linked them to one another. It has been demonstrated beyond a shadow of a doubt that the early sea peoples traveled to all corners of the Earth, millennia before Columbus. But none of this would have been possible if not for the knowledge of the Watchers.

The true legacy of the Watchers was not merely in the material realm, or limited to knowledge alone. Their most decisive impact on human evolution may be genetic in nature. By interbreeding with the people they found, they in effect created a new kind of man. Their hybrid offspring obviously reflected their more highly-evolved nature. Thus they were creating a class of human beings bearing a greater capacity to understand and implement the "arts of civilization", which the Watchers were the evangels of. And without this new genetic type, again, it would be difficult to estimate in what direction humanity may have gone. Most of us are no doubt descendants of the hybrids, and of the Watchers. We possess the Nephilim blood in varying degrees. Those with the highest concentration of this blood constitute a natural elite. These are the people who make things work, and who give the orders. Those with the smallest concentration of this blood are the ones who *do* the work and *follow* the orders. The legacy of the Watchers lives on, both in and around us. Without it, both we and the world in which we live would be very different.

Addendum:

Having formulated the foregoing hypothesis, additional information has come to light which brings us full circle and seems to neatly tie together any loose ends. It seems that the remains of the Ark so often reported by eyewitnesses on Mount Ararat were never visible in modern times until 1840. In that year a violent earthquake rocked Ararat, the falling debris wiping whole villages off the face of the Earth. A byproduct of this cataclysm was that a huge chunk of glacier slid from the mountain's summit and lodged itself between two peaks two-thirds of the way down Ararat. Frozen inside the massive piece of ice were the perfectly-preserved remains of a gigantic ship - the Ark. If the weather is warm enough in summer months, one end of the huge chunk of ice sometimes melts enough that the front of the Ark lays exposed. But for at least ten months of the year, and often year-round, the giant wooden structure is visible only as a dark shadowy configuration concealed within a wall of ice. Those who've seen it exposed (and there have been many) tell virtually identical stories. The structure contains several levels, countless rooms and chambers, and a huge door (which is now missing). Each witness relates that the Ark had *very high ceilings*. They all tell that it can only be partially explored, as the aft regions are frozen solid with ice. Since many of these stories predate modern mass communications, they also predate a time period in which an "Ark lore" could have developed to explain these stories' consistencies. The location of the wreckage is, even by modern standards, in the middle of nowhere and at the ends of the Earth, at a geographic region straddling Turkey, Russia, and Iran. Locals who made the trek in the quest for the Ark had no access to cameras at the time and probably still don't today. Outsiders who made the quest were often greeted with hostility by suspicious local government authorities, and even greater suspicion from nearby villagers.

Though the eyewitness accounts of the Ark are fascinating, what's even more compelling in our estimation is that the very event which revealed the Ark to modern eyes seems to have been the result of geological anomalies in Mount Ararat itself, for it appears that Mount Ararat was partially *hollow*. We repeat: hollow. The earthquake that shattered the peak of Ararat and devastated the villages at its base opened a crevice on the mountainside revealing "a vast abyss" that reached to "its very heart." Some early observers of this chasm estimated the abyss to extend to a depth of perhaps *9000 feet*. Considering that Ararat is approximately 16,000 feet in height, that's some abyss.

Also, evidently, since the time of the Ark's reputed landing, melting icecaps have over the centuries filled the hollowed-out underworld with a vast quantity of accumulated water. When Ararat cracked open at the time of the earthquake, massive amounts of water rushed out, enough to flood an area of *thirteen square miles*. We pause here to remind the reader that the Sumerian king associated with the Watchers was known as the "Lord of the Abyss", and his descendants were known as "the Lords of the Watery Abyss."

Though Ararat was a volcano, it is a mistake to conclude that this meant it was a hollow honeycomb of passages via which molten lava could be disgorged. Not at all. Most volcanoes are solid mountains of volcanic rock. Some retain concave hollows at the very peak but this is not at all synonymous with being hollow "to their very heart." And Ararat possessed twin peaks, which matches up with many legends in which the primordial holy mountain had "twin peaks reaching to Heaven."

While the name "Ararat" doesn't provide many clues that might shed further light on the mystery, its original title does. Before this peak was called "Ararat", it was known as "Aghri Dag" - Mount Aghri. Aghri is a name rich in possible associations. It could be the primary root of Agartha, the Egyptian underworld Agert, or Cain's subterranean domain of Arka. G and K are both sounds that linguists call gutturals, and were virtually interchangeable in early tongues such as Sumerian. Note that the nearby Cudi Dag is today called Mount Judi. The C/K and J/G sounds have been transposed, and each name clearly echoes "Catti", or "Guti", both Sumerian names for "Lord/King."

The town at Aghri's base, said to be "of the greatest antiquity", now wiped out by the earthquake that disgorged the Ark, was named "Aghouri", or "Ahora." "Ahora" equates "Asura" with the "Shining Ones" also known as "Ilu", "Ellu", or Ari - terms for kings in many cultures, but also associated with fallen angels (or Elohim). The word is further a sound-alike to "Ahura", the god of light in Zoroastrianism.

The "Ag" root of Aghri is, as previously mentioned, a title of Cain, "Lord Ag." Ag is also a word meaning "fire", "spirits of the deep", "fiery spirits", or "evil spirits." Those who dwelt in a hollow volcano could well have been designated by any of these titles, all of which would be equally applicable to the Djinn, Kabiri and so on. If we assume Aghri to be one and the same as Arka, we find that "ar" (fire) and "kha" (hole) fits perfectly, as it would mean "hole of fire", or "fire hole", an apt designation of a volcano. Ag can also have the additional meaning of "fire within", just as the word "pyramid" is said to mean "fire within." "Agkha" would mean precisely the same thing, while possessing the additional connotation of "the hole of Lord Ag", or "the Hole of Cain", while "Aghri" would mean "fire of the Sun." These people were associated with fire, volcanoes, the Sun, and the underworld for many centuries, so all of these conclusions seem apropos. The word "Ag" also shows up in "Anag" (Anak/Enoch), which means "son of Ag/Cain." And "Anak-im" is, of course, another Biblical term for the fallen angels.

So, is the Arka of Cain synonymous with the mythical underground Agartha? Is the legendary holy mountain of ancient tradition a place in the Garden of Eden? And if Eden rests in the shadow of Mount Ararat (Aghri), does that not tend to lend credence to the notion that the Flood was indeed a precursor to the biblical narrative? Lake Van, which borders the proposed locale of Eden, is an *inland salt sea*, a fact which in itself seems to attest to the occurrence of the Deluge. The world's most famous salt lake is Lake Titicaca, and is located miles from the ocean, a great distance above sea level. Utah's Great Salt Lake, though now slowly evaporating, is well over a day's drive from the ocean. Modern research has shown that miles out at sea, the remains of freshwater shellfish can be found next to those of saltwater shellfish. The most recent freshwater shells date to about 7000 years old, while the saltwater shells may be 6,500 or more years old. This is taken to indicate that at least one global flood must have occurred around 5000 B.C. But there are legends of other floods, and as many timelines as there are researchers (with conflicting examples of "proof" on behalf of each). We've yet to tackle the conundrum of timelines, of proofs and counter-proofs. For the time being, none of these seem nearly so compelling as the evidence to be found in mythology, etymology, and symbolism. To be sure, it is not evidence that can be quantified by any scientific means, but it nonetheless constitutes a kind of evidence that, again and again, has lead us to discoveries that we couldn't have reached by any other means. And for now, at least, it seems to have lead us to the discovery of a primordial holy mountain, located squarely in the Garden of Eden.

The notion of the Garden of Eden brings us

to our final set of clues. In at least four different ancient tongues, Eden doesn't mean "garden" or "paradise" at all, but in fact, quite the inverse. It means "desert" or "wasteland." Could we perhaps infer from this that the phrase "Garden of Eden" implied a place of respite in the midst of a desert or wasteland? Well, we can at least be fairly confident that there was no lush earthy paradise anywhere around the region suggested as the locale for that mythical garden, even so early as 5000 B.C. It was a terrain dotted with volcanoes and copious amounts of volcanic rock. Interestingly, in Sumerian "Edin" meant "lofty temple, abode, or *high place*." Though there was a specific place anciently called "Eden" (or "Etin"), Andrew Collins claims that the original title of Eden was in fact "Kharsag." Immediately, this alternate place-name reveals much more to us, and relates to the foregoing theories. "Kharsag" is a conjunction of the Sumerian "qar" *(meaning "vessel", or literally, "jar"), and "Sag", (name of the first Sumerian king/god.) So "Kharsag" would mean "the vessel of Sag", or "vessel of God." The pictogram for Qar is an upside-down triangle, and could represent a drinking vessel or inverted pyramid, extending to the underworld rather than the heavens. This all becomes much more interesting when we examine the symbol used to depict the same word by Egyptians. The hieroglyph for "qar", which means "drinking pot", resembles precisely the Greek symbol Omega, only in an inverted form. Since Omega signifies the end, and is obviously based upon this far older symbol, the implication seems clear. Omega ("the end") is equated with an overturned drinking pot, i.e., the Deluge. And the Greek symbol Alpha, "the beginning", resembles a mountain or pyramid. So Alpha and Omega, the beginning and the end, at least as visualized by the Greeks, seem to tie into the holy mountain hypothesis. [4]

All this brings to mind the tableau in Rennes-le-Chateau in which Christ is identified as the Alpha, and John the Baptist as the Omega. Observers have always commented that the Alpha and Omega presented here were out of sequence chronologically. Since the Baptist prepared the way for Christ, would not *he* be the beginning, the Alpha? It made no apparent sense. What could it mean? Perhaps the meaning is simpler than suspected. Perhaps what is being said is that the Alpha and Omega were one and the same; that the two overlapped one another historically, but that the Omega *preceded* the beginning. Such a thesis could explain the water imagery and rites of baptism associated with John. The ritual immersion in water, a symbolic death and rebirth, may be a ceremonialized memory of the Flood as both an end *and* a beginning. The baptism of Christ marked the true beginning of his ministry, and a kind of passing of a dynastic legacy from the older generation (John) to the younger (Jesus). Could this pivotal episode of the New Testament represent a retelling of how both a legacy and a bloodline were passed from one generation to another, from an antediluvian generation to a postdiluvian generation? It's certainly an intriguing possibility, and one that would go a long way towards bringing perspective to what many observers have commented on as a most puzzling Biblical episode - that is, one which prompts people to ask why the Son of God/Messiah requires the approval of his cousin, a wild-eyed prophet.

So, was "Kharsag" another name for "Arka"? Was "Arka" the same as "Agartha" inside Mount "Aghri"? There is much in the way of mythology to make a strong case for such conclusions. And it's interesting to note in relation to such a notion that "Vessel of God" (which the place-name of Kharsag translates to) is precisely what some researchers have asserted is the original meaning of the word "Grail." This school of thought maintains that Grail is a conjunction of "Gar" and "al" – "Vessel of God." [5] In Sumerian "gar" and "qar" ("khar") are variant spellings of the same word (both meaning "vessel"). So, could the holy mountain (which represented both Heaven and Hell) also be emblematic of the Holy Grail? Is this so-called vessel of God the Flood-era receptacle of the Grail bloodline, and the citadel from which issued forth demons, angels, devils, gods and kings? Though all signs point to "yes", the reader would be well-cautioned to keep sight of the fact that the Grail mystery is possessed of countless layers of meaning. Each layer of the mystery which is successfully unlocked provides the key for unlocking yet another. The holy mountain hypothesis may well be one such key: the Omega of one aspect of the mystery, and the Alpha of still another.

Endnotes:

[1] Editor's note: This is from *The Hitchhiker's Guide to Armageddon*, Adventures Unlimited, 2002.

[2] Editor's note: Indeed, many of these tunnels have already been explored and documented by archeologists.

[3] Editor's note: Actually, there is no such quote anywhere in the Bible.

[4] Editor's note: The concepts in this paragraph originated in Tracy Twyman's lecture at the FortFest in Washington, D.C. in 20001, and were also discussed in her articles in *Dagobert's Revenge Magazine, Volume 4#2*.

[5] Editor's note: This information was also first disclosed in the Twyman articles and lecture from 2001.

The Cutting of the Orm: The Golden Age Calendar and the New Cabala

By Tracy Twyman

According to the *Secret Dossiers* of the Priory of Sion, discovered by the authors of *Holy Blood, Holy Grail* in the Parisian Bibliotheque Nationale, the Priory broke away from its military arm, the Knights Templar, in the year 1188, during a ceremony called "the Cutting of the Elm." This occurred following the loss of Jerusalem, in 1187, to the Saracens by the Christian crusaders, who were being led by the Knights Templar, and their Grand Master, Gerard de Ridefort. The material in the *Secret Dossiers* seems to indicate that this was, in fact, the cause of the rift between the two organizations, and that Gerard de Ridefort had committed some form of "treason" that lead to the loss of the Holy Land. As the authors of *Holy Blood, Holy Grail* put it:

"The Ordre de Sion, which had created the Knights Templar, now washed its hands of its celebrated proteges. The 'parent', in other words, officially disowned the 'child.' This rupture is said to have been commemorated by a ritual or ceremony of some sort. In the Secret Dossiers and other 'Prieure documents', it is referred to as the 'cutting of the elm', and allegedly took place at Gisors."

An event known as the "Cutting of the Elm" did occur at Gisors during this year, although the historical record of this event does not contain any reference to either the Order of Sion or the Knights Templar. It also does not appear to have ever been fully explained. Supposedly, there was an elm tree located in the "Champ Sacre", or "Sacred Field" at Gisors. The authors of *Holy Blood, Holy Grail* write that, "According to medieval chroniclers the site had been deemed sacred since pre-Christian times, and during the twelfth century had provided the setting for numerous meetings between the kings of England and France." The Elm was, as the story goes, the only source of shade on the field. It was more than 800 years old, and "so large that nine men, linking hands could barely encompass its trunk." In 1188, during one of those historic meetings between the French

monarch, Philippe II, and the English monarch, Henry II, a skirmish broke out between the two men's armies over the shelter provided by this tree. After three days of negotiations, *Holy Blood, Holy Grail* states that a "full-scale onslaught" ensued. The English "took refuge within the walls of Gisors itself, while the French are said to have cut down the tree in frustration. Philippe II then stormed back to Paris in a huff, declaring that he had not come to Gisors to play the role of woodcutter." Other accounts of the story include some other bizarre details. They say that Philippe announced to Henry his intention to cut down the tree, and Henry's response was to reinforce the trunk with bands of iron. *Holy Blood, Holy Grail* tells us that:

"... the following day the French armed themselves and formed a phalanx of five squadrons, each accompanied by a distinguished Lord of the realm, who advanced on the elm, accompanied by slingsmen, as well as carpenters equipped with axes and hammers. A struggle is said to have ensued, in which Richard Coeur de Lion, Henry's eldest son and heir, participated, attempting to protect the tree and spilling considerable blood in the process. Nevertheless... the tree was cut down."

As you can see, the relationship between the above account and the separation of the Order of Sion from the Knights Templar is not exactly clear. But the separation from the Templars was not the only change to occur at this time for the Ordre de Sion. They are said to have changed their name to the "Prieure de Sion", and to have appended to that title two subtitles. One was "the Ordre de la Rose-Croix Veritas", or "the Order of the True Rose-Cross." The other was "Ormus", the name also given to a Gnostic mystic from Alexandria who founded, according to Masonic tradition, an "order of initiates" in the year 46 A.D., and who employed the Rose Cross as his symbol. The implication is that the Priory of Sion and the Rosicrucian brotherhood were one and the same. And Jean de Gisors, the first Grand Master of the Priory after the Cutting of the Elm, is named in a manuscript by Robert Denyau, the cure of Gisors, as having founded the Order of the Rose-Croix in 1188.

The name "Ormus" is itself very suggestive, for the word "orme" is French for "elm", so the term "cutting of the elm" is translated as "decoupage de l'orme." But the word "orm" in more ancient languages, such as Sumerian and Babylonian, means "worm", or "serpent." Therefore, "cutting of the elm" could be a play on words referring to the "cutting of the serpent." And the serpent, as I will now discuss, was a symbol of both the night's sky, and the alphabet.

The Hebrew alphabet is referred to by Jewish mystics as the Teli, a serpent biting its own tail, like the serpent Orobouros who encircles the night's sky, and who represents the ring of the zodiac.[1] Part of the reason behind this metaphor is that the last letter of the Hebrew alphabet can be combined with the second letter to form the shape of the first letter, Alef. Because of its serpentine nature, the twenty-two lettered Hebrew alphabet is also called a "cable", which is where the word "cabbala", the science of Hebrew mysticism, comes from. In this system, each letter represents a number, the first letter, Alef, representing one.[2] Each letter also corresponds to a planet, an element, and a zodiac sign. The Hebrews further distributed their sacred alphabet upon the Tree of Life, their version of the "world tree" common to all mythology systems, which stands at the center point of the world - and the universe - providing an anchor-point for the cosmos. The Hebrew Tree of Life in fact represents the cosmos, with each of its ten spheres, or "Sephiroth" representing an element of creation. And slithering up the paths between the Sephiroth formed by the letters of the alphabet is the Teli, the serpent. This combination of the cosmic serpent and the World Tree is also common in mythology (like in the story of the Garden of Eden). Perhaps this is part of what was being implied in the story of the Cutting of the Elm, which involves both a tree and the implication of a serpent.

The mystical significance of the Hebrew alphabet has become a science studied not just by Jews, but by all Hermeticists for at least the last few centuries. When the Knights Templar invented the system of the Tarot, each card corresponded to a letter of the Hebrew alphabet. And when the Hermetic Order of the Golden Dawn created their extremely complex system of the Rose-Croix symbol, the rose in the center contained three rings of twenty-two petals, each ring consisting of three, seven, and twelve petals, respectively. On each petal was placed a letter of the Hebrew alphabet. [3] These corresponded to what are traditionally called the three "mother letters" of the Hebrew alphabet, followed by the seven planetary letters, and the twelve letters corresponding to the zodiac. However, it is my opinion that the story of the Cutting of the Elm refers to a similar cabalistic system using not the Hebrew alphabet, but our modern twenty-six letter alphabet, and to a zodiac system that has been kept secret by the Priory of Sion for over a thousand years. [4] This system was revealed by the discovery of the Compass of Enoch.

      This 26-pointed configuration, which is detailed in the article of the same name by Boyd Rice, provides an obvious number correspondence for each letter of the alphabet, although it does not merely go in chronological order, with A being 1 and Z being 26. When the alphabet is placed upon the Compass of Enoch according to certain clues which I have discovered, it is split in half at the M, and then the rest is turned backwards, mirroring the first half in perfect symmetry, giving Z the value of 14, and N the value of 26. Therefore, A is on the opposite side of the wheel to Z, showing a reflective relationship between the "Alpha and Omega", the beginning and the end. Between the letters zigzags a continuous line that connects each letter to its opposite. This line is the equivalent of the Teli serpent - the Orm - which encompasses the Hebrew alphabet, and the zigzagging is similar to the way in which the Serpent of Wisdom zigzags its way up the Tree of Life in the Hebrew cabala, while the lightening-bolt-like "Flaming Sword" of divine light zigzags its way down the tree. Significantly, the reason why the serpent zigzags in this fashion is exactly because the alphabet has been cut at the M. [5] Is this division of the alphabet what the "Cutting of the Elm" story is supposed to signify? The title "Ormus" that the Priory of Sion took on after the Cutting of the Elm was written with the letters "o", "r", "u", and "s" placed inside of the middle letter, "m", which was written like the astrological symbol for Virgo - ♍ - a sign that resembles an M combined with an Ichthys fish symbol. Later on, the Priory also took possession of a relic that had gotten the Knights Templar in a lot of trouble - a skull named Baphomet, also called by the title "Caput 58c, with the M written as the Virgo sign. Now since M is the thirteenth letter of the alphabet, and five plus eight equals thirteen, it has been speculated that this was a code for "MM" - "Mary Magdalene", and that the skull which the Templars possessed was hers. Logical. But in another sense, it could also be a code for this particular cipher system. Thirteen plus thirteen is twenty-six, i.e., the twenty-six letters of the alphabet, which, on the Compass of Enoch, is split at the thirteenth letter, the M. And the Compass of Enoch also creates a geometric shape that includes a pattern of thirteen oblong Ms. [6]

      The number thirteen is very important in the occult, but especially to the Freemasons, the Knights Templar, and the Merovingians. The Templars were arrested in France on Friday, October 13th, which thereafter gave rise to the superstition that Friday the 13th was an unlucky day. Their symbol of the skull and crossbones was the basis for the "Jolly Roger" flag used by pirates (many of them Freemasons), which features, underneath the symbol, the number 13. [7] The Merovingian bloodline and its offshoots are called by conspiracy theorists "the 13th Illuminati bloodline", and the Grail-related magical order from the 14th century known as the Dragon Court, consisted, according to author Nicholas de Vere, of "twenty-six members, or two magical circles of 13." The number thirteen is also integral to the founding of the United States, which began with thirteen colonies that turned into the first thirteen states, and which were represented on our first flag as thirteen hexagonal stars. (These stars were later changed to pentagonal shapes.) The number thirteen is all over our one-dollar bill also, on the Great Seal of the United States, created by Freemasons, who founded this country. On the backside of the seal, there is an eagle holding thirteen arrows, and an olive branch with thirteen leaves. His shield contains thirteen stripes, and above his head are thirteen pentagon stars made in the shape of a hexagram. In his mouth he holds a banner that says "E Pluribus Unum" - "Out of Many, One" - a phrase containing thirteen letters. The number "One", or "1" is also written on the

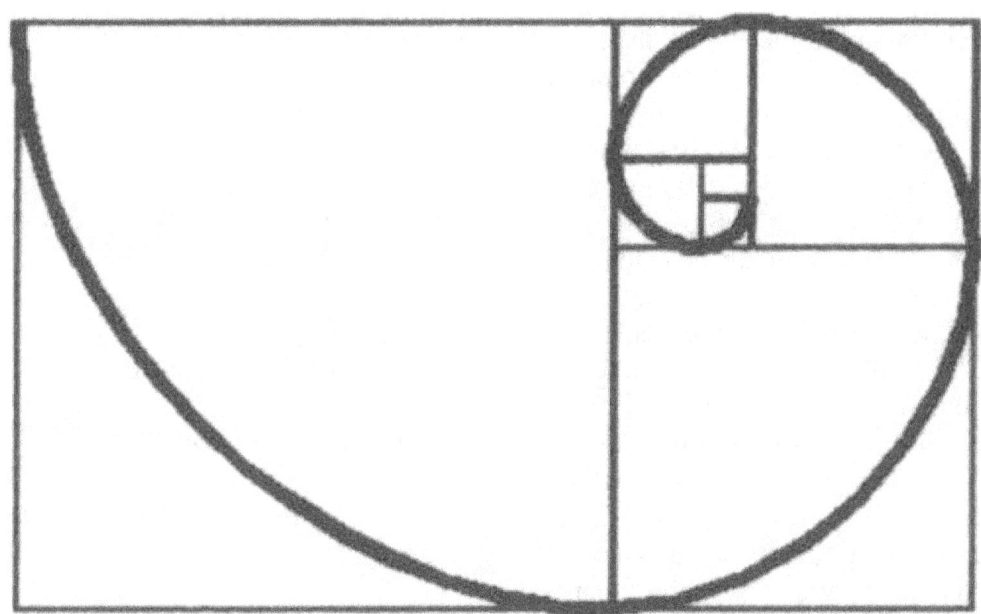

The Fibonacci Spiral.

dollar twelve times, unless you count the Latin word "Unum", which would make thirteen. On the front side of the Great Seal are the words "Annuit Coeptis" and "Novus Ordo Secorlum." "Annuit Coeptis" contains, again, thirteen letters, and is usually translated, "He (meaning God) agrees with the cause which we have started."

However, this translation appears to have no basis in reality. All one needs is a simple Latin dictionary. "Annuit" means "circuit" - like the circuit of the zodiac in the night's sky, and the precession of the equinox. This meaning is further encoded into the word "Annuit" itself. "Annu" relates to "Anno", which means "circle", and "year", while "Nuit" means "night" in French, and is related to the Egyptian word for night, "Nut." "Coeptis" means "new beginning." This goes along well with the words at the bottom, "Novus Ordo Seclorum", which mean "New World Order." So the statement being made here is, perhaps, that at the beginning of the new astrological age - Aquarius - we will have a new secular order on Earth, symbolized by the eye and the pyramid. The dawn of this new age is symbolized by the tale of the death of the last Merovingian king, Dagobert II, during a hunting trip taking place on December 23. Since "Dag" means "fish", and "Bert" means "house", this symbolizes the death of the "fish house", the Age of Pisces, at the dawning of the Age of Aquarius. Interestingly, the Mayan calendar, which is based largely on the number thirteen, ends on December 23, 2012, right on the brink of the Age of Aquarius, and on the anniversary of Dagobert's death.

It was at this point in the investigation that I had a major flash of insight. In the magazine called *CIRCUIT*, published in the forties and fifties by the Priory of Sion, they describe a thirteen-house zodiac system, with the insertion of the constellation of Ophiuchus - "the Serpent-Holder", constituting the extra house. [8] They also published a poem called *Le Serpent Rouge* (*The Red Serpent*), written, it would appear, by their Grand Master, Jean Cocteau. This poem consisted of thirteen stanzas, each dedicated to one of these zodiac houses, starting with Aquarius and ending with Capricorn, the sign under which Dagobert was killed. Here we have two very distinct references to the zodiac and the serpent. Ophiuchus, the Serpent-Holder, was the constellation that traditionally rules over the science of medicine, just like Mercury. It therefore makes sense that Ophiuchus would be a zodiacal representation of Mercury, and should be symbolized, just like the god and planet Mercury, by the caduceus, a winged staff intertwined with two serpents. It occurred to this author that the serpent of the thirteen-house zodiac could be equated with the implied serpent, or Orm, of the Compass of Enoch, and the twenty-six-letter alphabet could be applied to this thirteen-house system, with two letters assigned to each house. Since there was so much emphasis in the clues to the Grail mystery equating the sign of Virgo with the letter M, it made sense to make that one of Virgo's letters on the wheel. And that, at least, gave me a starting point with which to orient the rest of the zodiac on the compass.

Just a day or so later, the next breakthrough occurred. In Chapter Eight of *Holy Blood, Holy Grail*, the structure of the Priory of Sion is examined in detail. According to the statutes published in *Secret Dossiers* prior to 1956, the order consisted of seven grades, with a total of 1093 members, whereas the post-1956 statutes had it broken down into nine grades, totaling 9841 members. In addition, a set of twenty-two statutes written and signed by Grand Master Jean Cocteau describes a structure of five grades. However, in all three versions of the structure, the number of members in each grade is three times larger than the number of members in the next grade, and all of the numbers, except for one 1 and 3, are divisible by nine. It would appear that the only difference between the three versions of the structure is that the pre-1956 statutes are not counting the members of the lowest two grades. Also, the Jean Cocteau statutes have one-third as many people listed in each grade, with 243 members of a fourth grade that are considered part of an outer order, or laity, called the "Children of Saint Vincent." They were created, say the statutes, in 1681 - a very important date to the Rennes-le-Chateau mystery.

In the post-1956 statutes, the structure is also broken down into provinces (each of which contains forty members), commanderies, and the "Arch Kyria", the name for the top three grades, which consists of a total of thirteen members. The structure, as quoted from the *Secret Dossiers*, is as follows:

"The general assembly consists of all members of the association. It consists of 729 provinces, 27 commanderies, and an Arch designated "Kyria."

Each of the commanderies, as well as the arch, must consist of forty members, each province of thirteen members.

The members compose a hierarchy of **9** grades.

 a) in the **729** provinces
1) Novices: **6, 561** members
2) Croises de Saint-Jean: **2,187**

 b) in the **27** commanderies
3) Preux: **729** members
4) Ecuyers: **243** members
5) Chevalieres: **81** members
6) Commandeurs: **27**

 c) in the Arch 'Kyria':
7) Connetables: **9** members
8) Senechaux: **3** members
9) Nautonnier: **1** member"

Meanwhile, the statutes written by Jean Cocteau state the following:

"The hierarchy of the Prieure de Sion is composed of five grades:

 1st Nautonnier, number: **1**
2nd Croise, number: **3**
3rd Commandeur, number: **9**
4th Chevalier, number: **27**
5th, Ecuyer, number: **81**
total number :**121**

The first two levels are part of a substructure called "The Arch of the **13** Rose-Croix."
The other levels are part of a substructure called "The **9** commanderies of the Temple."

In addition, Article 19 states that:

"There are **243** Free Brothers, called 'Preux', or, since the year **1681**, Enfants de Saint Vincent, who participate neither in the vote, nor in the Convents, but to whom the Prieure accords certain rights and privileges, in conformity with the decree of **January 17, 1681**."

While most of the numbers here are, as I have stated, divisible by nine, the total number of members according to each version of the statutes is not. However, attempting to divide them by nine reveals some interesting relationships. For instance, the total number of members, according to the post-1956 statues, is 9841. 9841/9 = 1093.44444... - the same number, minus the decimals, as the number of members according to the pre-1956 statutes. 1093/9 = 121.44444... - the same number, minus the decimals, as the number of dignitaries (ranked members) according to the Cocteau statutes. 364, the number of total members according to Cocteau, including the 243 Children of Saint Vincent, when divided by nine, gives us 40.44444... - the same number, minus the decimals, as the number of members in each commanderie. And 121/9 = 13.44444... - the same number, minus the decimals, as the number of members in the "Arch Kyria", or "Arch of the Thirteen Rose-Croix."

Thirteen. There's that number again. It occurred to me that the "Thirteen Rose-Croix" might relate to the cabala of the modern alphabet implied by the Compass of Enoch, and that this shape might, in fact, play the same role as the rose cross which contains the twenty-two letters of the Hebrew alphabet in the Hebrew cabala. It could be considered a "thirteen-petaled rose" containing the twenty-six letters of our modern alphabet. Thirteen-petaled flowers do occur in nature, and include the globe flower, ragwort, double delphiniums, mayweed, corn, marigold, and chamomile. The average number of petals on each type of flower are always Fibonacci numbers, a number sequence - discussed later in this article and in other *Dagobert's Revenge* articles - that reflects the growth pattern of nature, and which includes the number thirteen. Interestingly, Stan Tenen (a theoretical physicist whose pet theory is that all ancient alphabets were based upon the Fibonacci spiral) refers in one of his lectures to a structure which he calls the "thirteen-petaled rose", a set of twelve spheres arranged around a thirteenth sphere, which is the most compact three-dimensional structure possible, and which occurs repeatedly in nature. Also, the royal esoteric symbol known as the Tudor Rose sometimes contains an inner circle of five petals, and an outer circle of eight, for a total of thirteen. The hypothesis of the "Thirteen Rose-Croix", then, would appear to be a distinct possibility.

But still I wondered: how might these numbers from the Priory of Sion relate to the thirteen-house zodiac? I decided to subtract thirteen from each of the numbers that would not divide evenly by nine, and then try the division again:

9841 - 13 = 9828
9828/9 = 1092 (just one less than 1093)

1093 - 13 = 1080
1080/9 = 120 (just one less than 121)

121-13 = 108
108/9 = 12 (just one less than 13)

and:

364-13 = 351
351/9 = 39 (just one less than 40)
And 39 is also 3 x 13

Then I noticed another thing:

1+0+9+3 = 13

and:

3+6+4 = 13

But even more astounding:

364/13 = 28

It was at this point that the meaning encoded in the number structure of the Priory of Sion came flooding into my mind. 28 is the average number of days in a lunar cycle, and there are thirteen lunar cycles in a solar year, making the 364-day lunar calendar observed by some of our ancestors, with thirteen months of exactly 28 days each. 364 is the exact number of days it takes for the Moon to travel through the zodiac. Also, 364 is very close to the number of days (365.2424) in our current solar year. Throwing caution to the wind, I decided to speculate: What would happen if we actually did observe a 364-day calendar? What would happen if, at some time in the past, the solar year had corresponded precisely with the lunar year?

The answer is that then we could have a perfect calendar, consisting of thirteen months of 28 days, each dedicated to one of the thirteen houses of the zodiac. [9] Also, we could still have 7 days in a week, *exactly* four weeks in each month, and *exactly* 52 weeks in each year. In our current system, the number of weeks in a month, and in a year, is neither exact nor consistent. But in this system, all months would begin and end on the same day of the week, and would match each other perfectly. All floating holidays, such as Thanksgiving and Easter, would occur on the same day every year. The menstrual cycle of each woman would begin on the same day and end on the same day of each month, also making periods of high fertility easier to calculate. [10] Since each zodiac sign would correspond to a single month, all zodiac periods would be of equal length, with no "cusps", and everyone could easily determine which sign a person was born under simply by knowing the month of their birth. One could even break down the hours in a day into a thirteen-based system. We could split the day into twenty-six hours, each consisting of fifty-two minutes, which would in turn consist of fifty-two seconds each. That would give you a total of 25, 590, 656 seconds in a year.

For thousands of years, men have been trying to create an "aliquot calendar", a perfect system that would synthesize both the solar and lunar cycles with exact, whole numbers. But as Duncan Steel remarks in *Marking Time: The Epic Quest to Invent the Perfect Calendar*, "We have been stymied by the fact that the solar day and the lunar month are not an aliquot part of the year. That is, there is not an exact integer number of days in the year defined by Earth's orbit, nor lunations in that year. However, he also remarks that, "it has not always been this way. About 1.5 billion years ago there were precisely fourteen lunar months in a year, each lasting for thirty-one solar days, but there was no one around to notice the fact and construct a calendar based upon it." The number of days in a year has varied substantially over time, due to a number of factors. One of the most significant factors, however, is called "tidal drag", a force caused by the ocean tides, which are in turn caused by the gravitational attraction of the Moon. This is causing the rotation of the Earth to slow down, making it probable that we will reach a 364-day solar year at some point. Whether or not the number of lunar cycles in a year will synchronize with this at that point is, however, a matter of speculation.

The Priory of Sion is a secret society preserving *ancient* knowledge, most of which originated during the "Golden Age', at least 10,000 years ago - an age associated with the utopian empire of Atlantis, and the fabled Garden of Eden. This "Golden Age", in which the Hermetic sciences supposedly originated, was dominated by the concept of "As above, so below", the idea that the heavens and the Earth are connected via a harmonious relationship, one reflecting the other, and the idea that nature tends to create mathematically harmonious relationships between all aspects of creation. One of the most consistent harmonious relationships recurrent in nature involves what's known as the Phi ratio, or, more commonly, the "golden ratio."

The Fibonacci sequence is the basic growth pattern of nature. Expressed in whole numbers the sequence begins with 0 and 1, mimicking the creation of the universe, in which the whole of existence emerged as the undivided Monad out of the unmanifested Void. Then, another 1 is added, making 2, the next stage in the creation of the universe, in which the undivided Monad split into the duality of two opposing aspects (such as light and dark, male and female.) From there, the sequence continues, adding the next number to the previous number in the sequence to create the one following. 2+1 = 3. 3+2 = 5. 5+3 = 8. 8+5 = 13. So the sequence goes: 0,1,1,2,3,5,8,13... This sequence could go on and on indefinitely. When the numbers are divided by one another to form ratios (1/1, 2/1, 3/2, 5/3, 8/5, 13/8), the results, graphed on an x/y axis, form an undulating wave that starts out large and flattens out at an exponential rate towards an asymptote (a place approached but never reached) of 1.6180339..., with an endless series of decimals at the end. This number called in mathematics "the F (Phi) ratio."

In what's known as a "golden rectangle", this ratio can be expressed by dividing the rectangle into one-third and two-thirds sections. [11] Then you construct a larger golden rectangle around that, with the first golden rectangle constituting the smaller, one-third section of the larger golden triangle. Keep doing this for several steps. The whole of each rectangle, when divided by the larger, two-thirds section, will always equal the same ratio as the large part divided by the small

The following chart demonstrates how the numbers encoded into the Priory of Sion structure (based on all three versions of the Priory's statutes) indicate cycles of 364-day years, with a leap day added every two years. The largest number in the Priory's structure is 9841, but I have extended the numerical pattern out a few steps for demonstration purposes. I have also shown, on the right-hand column, how all of the larger Priory numbers reflect the other numbers mathematically.

Priory of Sion #	# of 364-day years indicated	# of leap days added to the cycle	# of 28-day months in the cycle	Relationships with other Priory of Sion #s
729	2	1 (728 + 1 = 729)	26	364 + 243 + 121 + 1 (364 x 2) + 1 9 x 81
1093	3	1 (1092 + 1 = 1093)	39	729 + 364
2187	6	3 (2184 + 3 = 2187)	78	(1093 x 2) + 1
6561	18	9 (6552 + 9 = 6561)	234	3 x 2187
9841	27	13 (9828 + 13 = 9841)	351	6561 + 2187 + 729 + 243 + 81 + 27 + 9 + 3 + 1
29523	81	39 (29484 + 39 = 29523)	1053	9841 x 3
88569	243	117 (88452 + 117 = 88569)	3159	29523 x 3
265707	729	351 (265356 + 351 = 265707)	9477	9841 x 27
797121	2187	1053 (796068 + 1053 = 797121)	28431	9841 x 81
2391363	6561	3159 (2388204 + 3159 = 2391363)	85293	9841 x 243

part. After you have constructed a series of golden rectangles within golden rectangles, draw a line curving from the inside bottom corner of the larger section of the first rectangle to the upper left-hand corner of that box, then continue that through the larger section of the second rectangle, then the third rectangle, and on and on. This curved line will quickly develop into what is called a "Fibonacci spiral."

The Fibonacci sequence of numbers represent the growth pattern of all nature: the growth pattern of the embryo as it becomes a fetus, then a baby, then a child, then an adult; or of a seed that becomes a seedling, then a plant. The human fetus, the horns of a ram, the spiraling bracts of a pine cone, the whirlpools in the ocean and the storms in the sky also contain this pattern. The golden spiral, sequence and ratio can be found in the visual color spectrum, and in the thirteen-note musical scale. The vibration of each note is the sum of the vibrations of the two notes previous. The structure of a piano keyboard reflects this, with eight white keys, representing whole tones, and five black keys, representing sharps and flats, arranged in groups of threes and two, for a total of thirteen notes in a full octave. This contains the Fibonacci sequence of 2, 3, 5, 8, and 13. The most pleasing pieces of music are those which take full advantage of the Fibonacci relationship, striking a familiar cord with the Fibonacci spiral shape of our own ears, while music that sounds "off" does exactly the opposite. The syntax of words in poetry, in which some combinations of words are more pleasing than others, undoubtedly follows the same principles.

Not surprisingly, perhaps, our solar system also contains Fibonacci relationships. It is like a whirlpool, or vortex, with the Sun as its "calm eye" in the center, the asymptote of the spiral that is always approached but never reached. Leonardo da Vinci, a Grand Master of the Priory of Sion, once said: "A vortex, unlike a wheel, moves faster towards its center", and this is true of our solar system as well, where Mercury has a year that lasts for 88 of our days, while Pluto's year lasts for 248 of our years. But there is also a "golden relationship" between the orbits of each of our planets. The distance from the Sun to Mercury, when added to the distance from Mercury to Venus, equals the distance from Venus to Earth. This Phi relationship can be found between each of the planetary orbits in sequence, although the pattern gradually breaks down towards the outer planets, while still approaching Phi. This relationship between the planetary orbits is expressed in Johannes Kepler's "Third Law of Planetary Motion", which states that:

"... the ratio of the squares of the revolutionary periods for two planets is equal to the ratio of the cubes of their semi-major axes; or: $P1^2 / P2^2 = R1^3/R2^3$"

The golden relationship between the planetary orbits was written of in the book *Key to the Sacred Pattern*, by Henry Lincoln, one of the co-authors of *Holy Blood, Holy Grail*. Lincoln's geometric study of the landscape of Rennes-le-Chateau revealed the golden ratio of 1.618 everywhere, especially in the group of mountains whose peaks form a perfect pentagram. Amazingly, the orbit of Venus throughout the year forms a perfect pentagram from the perspective of the Earth, which is why the pentagram is associated with that particular planet/goddess. It is the only planet that forms a perfect geometric shape with its orbit. A pentagram contains in its angles the golden ratio, and from it can be derived a golden triangle. Lincoln, although stopping short of saying that the mountains at Rennes-le-Chateau were artificially arranged to mimic the orbit of Venus, still writes that:

"The 'holiness' of the Rennes-le-Chateau landscape stems from its pentagonal (and therefore Golden Section) configuration of mountains, which reflect on Earth the movements of Venus in the Heavens. Earth's year consists of 365 and a quarter days. 365.25 divided by 1.618 = 225.74. Rounding off... leaves us with 225 - the number of days in Venus' year... Venus goes through one complete cycle of phases (her synodic period) in 584 days. 584 divided by 1.618 = 360.9, which, rounded off, reflects the Ancient Egyptian year of 12 months of 30 days, i.e., 360 plus 5 'added' days. Or the 360 degrees in a circle. Additionally, Mercury and Saturn, the inner and outermost planets of the medieval cosmos, show Golden Section relationship in order and size to within 99 percent accuracy."

Clearly, planets orbiting our Sun tend towards a circular orbit. Venus' orbit is the most circular, with an eccentricity of only .0068, while Earth's is still a mere .0167. As with the Golden relationship between the orbits, the tendency towards a circular orbit lessens as the planets get further away from the Sun. Is that just a property of the lesser gravitational pull from the Sun, I wondered? Or was there some cataclysmic celestial event that may have occurred to "mess up" the beautiful symmetrical orbits that all planets once had, and also messed up the Golden relationships between their orbits? Whatever the case, I began to wonder, for the sake of the perfect calendar, what it would be like if the Earth had a perfectly circular orbit. Furthermore, assuming that the cataclysm had also tilted the axis of the Earth, I factored in the possibility that the Earth's axis may have been perfectly perpendicular to its orbital plane.

So what would happen? Well, as you may have already surmised, such conditions would create a virtual Paradise on Earth, a true golden age. There would be no seasons. The middle portions of the Earth would be perfectly temperate all year round. Daylight and nighttime would always last for the same amount of time every day.

At the equator, the Sun would always pass precisely overhead at midday. At the poles it would always be on the horizon. Duncan Steele writes of it in *Marking Time*: "Imagine yourself on this idealized Earth. Each time Earth spins on its axis, the stars do a complete loop around the sky. In essence these form a stationary backdrop against which one may measure the spin of the Earth." Scholars have pondered for centuries how it is that ancient man could have acquired the astounding astronomical understanding that he had, with some cultures seeming to have master the concepts of the spherical nature of the Earth, the other planets, and their relationships to the Sun - things that our culture only surmised millennia later with the assistance of telescopes. But during this proposed golden age, these properties would have been easy to observe with the naked eye. Also, because the day is always the same length, there would be no solstices, just a perpetual equinox, and without the wobble in the Earth's axis, there would be no Precession of the Ages.

Hmmmm.

I had been wondering for some time how the 364-day calendar would fit in with the precession. The number of years in the precession is usually rounded up to 26,000, which is, of course, a multiple of 13. If it did take exactly 26,000 years and we did have a 13-sign zodiac, there would be exactly 2000 years between each astrological age. How nice and succinct that would be! And of course, it could be joined with the symbol of the alphabet on the Compass of Enoch, and each of the letters would represent a 1000 year period, two of them then representing an astrological age.

But currently, the precession takes exactly 25,920 years, a multiple of nine, as well as 360 x 72 (reminding one of the angles found in a golden triangle, and in a pentagram, which are 72° and 36°). This is because the zodiac is a perfect 360° circle, split up into twelve houses of 30° each, in which it takes 72 years to travel from one house to the next. If you were to draw a pentagram inside of this circle, it would split the sky into five sections of 72° each. [12] It occurred to me that the Priory of Sion numbers that were divisible by 9 might multiply evenly into 25,920. This worked for 27 and 81, but not for any of the higher numbers. However, there was a much larger number, derived from the precession of the equinox, that *every single one* of these numbers multiplied evenly into. It is called "the Nineveh Constant", and the relationships that it bears to the revolutionary cycles of the heavenly bodies are rather amazing.

In 1857, during an archeological dig in the ancient Assyrian city of Nineveh, 30,000 clay tablets were unearthed pertaining largely to practices of ritual magic. One of the tablets contained a long series of huge, lengthy numbers, one of which was fifteen digits long: 195,955,200,000,000. Over a hundred years later, this number came to the attention of Maurice Chatelain, a French communications specialist who had been studying the Mayan calendar for several years. His theory was that the Mayan civilization had been born of some sort of contact with the Assyrians of Nineveh. In short time he had discovered that the 15-digit Nineveh number was 70 X 60 to the power of 7. He had a hunch that it represented an expression of time in seconds, which were invented at the dawn of civilization by the preceding occupants of Mesopotamia, the Sumerians, and which was based on the 360° in a circle, as well as, amazingly, the circumference of the Earth. Author Peter Tompkins, as quoted in *The Atlantis Blueprint*, by Colin Wilson and Rand Flem-Ath, writes that:

"The Mesopotamians had linked their measures of time and space - in seconds of time and seconds of arc. 34,020 million days is not only the number of days in 3,600 Sumerian precessions of the equinox, , but 3,600 tenths of a degree - consisting of 36,000 Egyptian feet of 0.308 meters - is the circumference of the world... The Mesopotamians had not only chosen as a unit of measure that was earth-commensurate, it was also commensurate with the great Platonic year [the precessional cycle] of 25,920 years."

When Chatelain calculated the Nineveh number in terms of seconds of time, he found that it equaled exactly 2,268 million days (more than 6 million years), which is exactly 240 precessional cycles. Chatelain's next discovery was even more amazing, and is best described in *The Atlantis*

Blueprint, in which the authors state that:

> "Chatelain found himself wondering if the Nineveh constant was what astrologers and occultists had called 'the great constant of the solar system', a number that would apply to the revolution of all the bodies in the solar system, including moons. He preceeded to calculate the cycles of the planets in seconds... and found that each was an exact fraction of the Nineveh constant...
>
> Chatelain went a step further. When he divided the Nineveh constant into solar years, then compared this with a modern astronomical table based on a caesium clock (which gives the most accurate estimation of the length of a second), he found a slight discrepancy in the sixth decimal place. It was only a twelve-millionth of a day per year, but it puzzled him. Then he saw the solution. Modern astronomical measurements tell us that the rotation of the earth is slowing down very slowly, so every year is getting shorter by sixteen-millionths of a second.
>
> The Nineveh constant proved to be totally accurate 64,800 years ago, and that suggested to Chatelain that it was first calculated 64,800 years ago..."

A hypothesis began to form in my mind: What if the Earth's orbit had originally been 360 days, like the Sumerians believed, and had been perfectly circular? That may be why they based their 360° circle and metric system on it. It also would have matched up with the zodiac cycle and with the circumference of the Earth. There may have been no moon to slow down the rotation of the Earth at that time. All of the other planets would also have perfectly circular orbits, with perfect golden relationships to one another. Then the unknown calamity occurred, which disturbed these orbits. Perhaps it was a large comet that passed through the solar system, bending the perfectly circular orbits with its gravity, smashing into the planet that once stood where the crumbled asteroid belt now lies, tilting the axis of the Earth and depositing the Moon into our orbit. Now, I speculated, the Earth is tending towards a new equilibrium in its orbit, attempting to synthesize the orbit of the Earth around the Sun, and of the Moon around the Earth, as well as the rotation of all three bodies. If this is true, already some amazing relationships have formed: note how closely thirteen lunar cycles divide into our solar year, and the fact that it rotates at a perfect rate in relation to the Earth's rotation, so that the same side is always facing both the Earth and the Sun, while the other side stays completely dark. It is also at a perfect distance from the Earth so that its disc on the horizon appears to be exactly the same size as the solar disc from the perspective of a person on Earth, allowing the Moon, at times, to eclipse the Sun, and the Earth, at times, to eclipse the Sun's rays from the Moon.

Perhaps this event, if it did indeed occur, is what is memorialized in the story of the Garden of Eden. During the Golden Age, the Earth itself was Eden, lush and temperate all year long. Man had no knowledge of hardship or climatic change. Then came the cataclysm, and the appearance of the Moon. This event is synonymous with the "Cutting of the Elm (or Orm)" story, which also involves an (implied) serpent, and a sacred tree. [13] The serpent of the night's sky was "severed" in half by the tilt of the Earth, due to the cataclysm, which skewed our view of the zodiac ring, whereas before, the Earth had traveled through the zodiac in a perfect loop perpendicular to the axis of the Earth. [14] Furthermore, the wobble in the axis was introduced, and the Earth began to precess backwards through the zodiac. Perhaps this is why, in the Compass of Enoch alphabet system, the last thirteen letters are wrenched backwards. The relationship between the Earth and the serpent of the zodiac (from which, I have postulated, many ancient alphabetic and numerical systems were derived) became upset, and thus the meaning of both the letters and the numbers became lost.

This is the equivalent of the destruction of the Tower of Babel, the loss of the secret name of God, of the secret word of a Master Mason, and the expulsion from the Garden of Eden. During the Golden Age, a perfect mathematical harmony may have existed between the orbits of the planets, the zodiac, the alphabet, the musical scale, and the growth patterns of natural life. The Hermetic arts, including astrology and other forms of divination – cabalism, etc. - may have had a much greater utility at that time. The correspondences between numbers, letters, elements, planets and zodiac houses may have been real instead of merely symbolic, and thus, these practices may have actually worked. After the Cutting of the Orm, the truth, accuracy, and therefore power behind these correspondences was greatly reduced. But the old meanings were preserved by the initiates, who also set about creating a new system of correspondences to match the newly-forming harmony to occur to the best of their ability. Unlike during the Golden Age, it would have been only the elite of society at this time who would have been capable of understanding the complexity of the new celestial cycles, and their meanings.

In this theory, prior to the "Cutting of the Orm" there were no "equinoxes" or "solstices" to be observed. The Earth was in a perpetual "equinox" every day. Perhaps this is the meaning behind the emphasis on "midday" by the Freemasons, the Priory of Sion, and other groups. Dagobert II was killed at midday, Hiram, the architect of Solomon's Temple, was killed at midday, and "midday" is mentioned in the parchments found by Berenger Sauniere at Rennes-le-Chateau. [15] The French word for "midday" is based on the Latin "meridianus", which also means "meridian", indicating that maybe the reason why the old (and perhaps ancient) Paris meridian is held sacred by the Priory of Sion is because it was somehow the basis of this old, Golden Age system of counting time. [16] "The Sun is always at its meridian in regards to Freemasonry", states an old Masonic motto. Maybe this explains why the equinoxes were held to be highly sacred days of celebration by ancient man, while solstices - times in which the periods of night and day were at their most unequal - were often considered to be days of ritual mourning, fasting, and sacrifice. Equinoxes reminded man of the old Golden Age, in which he had been so happy and carefree, while solstices merely reminded him of the tragedy that had occurred to upset that perfection - thus he would pray, fast, and sacrifice for the return of the old equilibrium.

The acquirement of the Moon introduced a new "silver" element into a world that was previously "golden", or entirely solar-based. The Sun is always associated with gold in Hermeticism, and the Moon with silver. [17] The relationship between the Sun and the Moon, from a Hermetic point of view, is a reflective one, similar to the "As above, so below" relationship between Heaven and Earth. The Moon produces no light in itself, but merely reflects the light of the Sun, like a mirror, making it a male/female relationship as well. [18] This concept is illustrated in the courtyard at the Rennes-le-Chateau church where, at sundown, the light from the Sun shines through the sun disk behind Christ's head on the Calvary, and reflects off of the mirror behind the head of the statue of Mary Magdalene that is surmounted upon the Visigothic pillar. The union of the Sun and the Moon is considered to be one of the greatest secrets of the Hermetic science of alchemy, which creates the Philosopher's Stone, perhaps referring to the new harmony that is now still forming between the Sun and the Moon in relation to the Earth.

With the introduction of the Moon, the tilted axis, and the elliptical orbit, we began to have seasons, with regular periods of death and rebirth in nature. Man had to learn to till the soil, and to preserve himself from harsh weather by wearing clothes and building a house for himself, just as the story of the Garden of Eden relates. The traditionally "female" element of periodic change was introduced, which could explain why the female is presented in the story of *Genesis* as being the cause of the fall from perfection. Even the word "calendar" has been said to have come from the name of the Hindu moon goddess Kali, associated with periodic creation and destruction, indicating that, prior to the catastrophe which introduced the Moon, and the climactic cycles of periodic change, there may have been no need for a calendar (at least as we currently envision it) in the first place. The feminine moon created the tides of the sea, thus creating the "tidal drag" force that is slowing down the Earth's rotation and shortening the year from 365 days towards 364. It also introduced the menstrual cycle in women, and is undoubtedly responsible for both the pain of menstruation, and the pain of childbirth, something that was supposed to have been handed down by God as punishment to Eve for her rebellion. [19] The gestation period of a child, by the way, lasts for nine lunar cycles - nine of the thirteen lunar cycles in a year.

There are those two numbers again.

After pondering the possible meaning and relationship between these two numbers, it occurred to me that the Priory of Sion numbers, based on both 9 and 13, are pointing towards this equilibrium between the Sun and the Moon. Nine would naturally be, for a number of reasons, associated with the Sun. The Sun is the eye in the vortex, providing the gravitational glue that keeps the solar system together - a solar system made up of nine planets. Each of these planets contains in its orbit and rotation the nine-based Nineveh number, and these number correspondences occur because of the 9-based geometry of the 360° circle, which is what all planetary orbits in our solar system tend towards. Even the ° (degree) symbol, invented by the Sumerians, represents the Sun. The Moon, however, contains in its orbit and rotation a 13-based system, which combines with the 9-based system of the Sun to in turn act upon the orbit and rotation of the Earth. Aleister Crowley wrote in his treatise on Gematria that 9 represents "stability in change", which clearly describes the masculine aspects of the Sun, while 13 represents "Luna", and "the scale of the highest feminine unity."

The relationship between these two numbers, and the concepts that they represent are referred to rather explicitly in the coding system of the Priory of Sion numbers. This became apparent when the final piece of the puzzle fell into place. For as I soon discovered, the larger numbers, including 729, 1093, 2187, 6561, and 9841, all form a pattern when divided by 364. 729 is 2 x 364 + 1. 1093 is 3 x 364 +1. 2187 is 6 x 364 + 3. 6561 is 18 x 364 + 9. 9841 is 27 x 364 + 13. At first, I thought this might represent a system in which a 364-day year is used, and a leap day is added every two years, so that in 27 years, 13 leap days have been added. This yielded the following chart, seen on the next page, which revealed a great many astounding numerological correspondences. For instance, after 243 years (the number of "Children of Saint Vincent" in the Priory of Sion), 117 leap days have been added.

Whether or not the "remainders" on these numbers actually represent leap days in a 364-day calendar, the Priory of Sion numerology system still points most definitely to a mystical relationship between the solar number 9 and the lunar number 13. As if to prove this point, the icing on the numerological cake came to me at last. 9 + 13 = 22. This is the number most consistently stressed within the layout and landscape of Rennes-le-Chateau, as well as the number of letters in the Hebrew alphabet. Interestingly, the Hebrew letter Mem, the equivalent of M, is also the 13th letter of that alphabet, and the meaning of that glyph is "water." The ninth letter is Teth - T - and it means "serpent."

The interaction between the Sun, the Moon, and the planets amongst the serpent of the zodiac is what gave ancient man his understanding of time, and forms the basis for the systems of time-keeping which we still observe today. Of all the signs of the zodiac, it was Virgo (c) which was seen by ancient man as being the herald of new times and ages, and she had a very particular relationship with the celestial serpent. A curious reference in *Morals and Dogma*, the classic handbook of Freemasonry by General Albert Pike, relates Virgo to the serpent; the Bull; and to the bee (an emblem of the Merovingian bloodline):

"A serpent-ring was a well-known symbol of time: and to express dramatically how time preys upon itself, the Egyptian priests fed vipers in a subterranean chamber, as it were, in the sun's winter abode on the fat of bulls, or the year's plenteousness. The Virgin of the zodiac is bitten in the heel by Serpens, who, with Scorpio, rises immediately behind her; and as honey, the emblem of purity and salvation was thought to be the antidote to the serpent's bite, so the bees of Aristaeus, the emblems of nature's abundance, are destroyed through the agency of the serpent, and regenerated within the entrails of the Vernal Bull."

It is Virgo who was the inseparable companion of Mercury, a figure I have identified not only with the planet named after him, but with the constellation Ophiuchus, because Mercury's symbol was the caduceus, and Ophiuchus was "the Serpent Holder." Virgo also bears a resemblance to the goddess Isis, who is identified with the planet Venus so sacred to the Priory of Sion, and who is described in the poem *Le Serpent Rouge* as being the "eternal white lady of legends", "Notre

Dame des Cross" - the bearer of the "vase filled with healing balm", the Grail. Virgo is described in the same manner by Albert Pike:

"Isis, the same as Ceres, was, as we learn from Eratosthenes, the constellation Virgo, represented by a woman holding an ear of wheat. The different emblems which accompany her in the description given by Apuleius, a serpent on either side, a golden vase with a serpent twined round the handle, and the animals that march in procession, the bear, the ape, and Pegasus, represented the constellations that, rising with the Virgin, when on the day of the Vernal Equinox, she stood in the Oriental gate of Heaven, brilliant with the rays of the full moon, seemed to march in her train... The cup, consecrated in the mysteries of both Isis and Eleusis, was the constellation crater."

Virgo's role as - literally - the guardian of the "Gate of the Sun", and the herald of seasonal change - that is, of time itself - is further elucidated by Pike:

"The Celestial Virgin, during the last three centuries that preceeded the Christian era, occupied the horoscope or Oriental point, and the gate of Heaven through which the Sun and Moon ascended above the horizon at the two equinoxes. Again it occupied it at midnight, at the Winter Solstice, at the precise moment when the year commenced with the march of times and seasons, of the Sun, the Moon, and day and night, and the principal epochs of the year... At the equinoxes... at the moment when the Sun occupied that point, the Virgin rose before him; she stood at the gates of day and opened them to him. Her brilliant star, Spica Virginis, and Arcturus, in Bootes, northwest of it, heralded his coming. When he had returned to the Vernal Equinox... again it was the celestial Virgin that lead the march of the signs of night; and in her stars came the beautiful full moon of that month."

One can see how Virgo, who is crowned with a ring of stars with the Moon beneath her feet at the Vernal Equinox, is the inspiration for the figure of the Virgin Mary, the "Queen of Heaven" depicted in Catholic iconography in exactly the same manner. At the same time, Venus, as the "Queen of Harlots" and the "love goddess", is the inspiration for the figure of Mary Magdalene. [20] And like both Venus and Virgo, Magdalene was the bearer of a holy vase, or Grail cup, full of balm. At the same time, however, the Virgin of the sky and the Virgin Mary were both the mothers of the "son of God": Mary begetting Christ, the son of God, and Virgo begetting Horus, the son of the sun-god Osiris. When Osiris died, Horus became the Sun, just as Christ himself came to symbolize the Sun, dying at the Summer solstice (at Easter) and being reborn at Christmas, the Winter solstice. An Arabian manuscript in the Royal Library in Paris shows Isis holding the baby Horus with the inscription: "I am all that is, all that was, and all that shall be; and the fruit which I brought forth is the Sun." Albert Pike describes it thusly:

"At the moment of the Winter Solstice, the Virgin rose helically (with the Sun), having the Sun (Horus) in her bosom."

One might note that "Horus" sounds like "Hour", "Horo", and "Hora", and thus can be associated, like his mother Virgo, with time. It makes sense that it is the Sun, together with the planets that rotate about it, which are the markers of time's passage in the first place. Therefore he is, like Kronos, "Father Time." Time is the great creator-destroyer of the universe, and it is therefore fitting that it is symbolized by the Orobouros serpent, which equates with the idea of death and rebirth. [21] Goddesses like Venus and Virgo embodied this creator-destroyer concept. In fact, many of the good goddess/bad goddess duos throughout the history of world mythology, including the Christian figures of the Virgin Mary and Mary Magdalene, would appear to merely represent two opposing aspects of the same goddess. Note the similarity between this description of Virgo's behavior upon the death of the Sun (represented by the god Osiris) and that of Mary Magdalene upon the death of Jesus, thus linking Virgo with both the Virgin Mary and the Magdalene:

"Nine months after the Sun enters Virgo, he reaches the Twins. When Scorpio begins to rise,

Orion sets; When Scorpio comes to the meridian, Leo begins to set. Typhon reigns, Osiris is slain, and Isis (the Virgin), his sister and wife, follows him to the tomb, weeping."

Perhaps the fact that this goddess figure was split into two aspects represents the idea that the purity of the golden age was tainted when the Fall of Man occurred due to the corruption of the female element by the serpent, thus causing the harsh seasonal changes that we experience now every year. [22] Albert Pike specifically associates the Winter season with this corrupting snake when he writes:

"The Virgin and Boötes, setting helically at the Autumnal equinox, delivered the world to the wintry constellations, and introduced into it the genius of Evil, represented by Ophiuchus, the Serpent."

Clearly, this 9 and 13-based system, the Compass of Enoch, and the 364-day calendar that they imply are among the greatest secrets preserved by the Priory of Sion, revealed for the first time in the pages of this publication.

And we can only assume that there is more yet to come. Much more.

Appendix:

A thirteen-based tarot system using the cabalistic attributes of the modern alphabet can be easily created. Simply take the traditional 78-card tarot deck of 22 Major Arcana (archetypal figures dedicated to each of the Hebrew letters) and 56 Lesser Arcana (four sets of 14 court cards dedicated to each of the elements), then shift four cards from the Major to the Minor set. You then have 26 Major Arcana (each dedicated to one letter of our modern alphabet, with two cards related to each of the 13 zodiac houses), and 52 Lesser Arcana (4 sets of 13 court cards dedicated to each of the elements). This may be a more appropriate system of correspondences than traditional tarot decks, matching more closely the current cosmic order.

Endnotes:

[1] The Hebrews also equated the Teli with the Earth's orbit. The rabbi Aryah Kaplan, in his commentary on the *Sephir Yetzirah*, states that, "... the Teli is also often referred to as a dragon or fish. This is because it has the shape of a fish, wide in the center, and coming to a point at both ends."

[2] This forms a literal basis for the common saying that "math is the *universal language*."

[3] Note the similarity between the words "Tarot", "Torah" (the Five Books of Moses sacred to the Hebrews, which contain the coded secret of their alphabet), and "Tower" - as in the Tower of Babel that represented the original one-world language. The "High Priestess" card in the A.E. Waite tarot deck shows her holding a script marked "Tora", standing between the Masonic pillars of Jachin and Boaz that flanked the entrance to Solomon's Temple.

[4] It seems probable that the letters of many of the world's alphabets were inspired by the constellations in the night's sky. Perhaps this is part of the link, consistent in world mythology, between stars and angels. The word "angel" means "messenger", and the stars were considered by ancient man to be divine "messages" written in the sky. It was the purview of astrologers to interpret these messages by "reading the stars."

[5] In the Bible, the dragon Leviathan, which clearly represents the celestial snake, is specifically called "the Crooked Serpent."

[6] Since Magdalene's name means "Tower", she would seem to represent the alphabet itself, further signified by the Tower of Babel. (This may also link up to the fact that the "houses" of the zodiac are split up into four sections, each dedicated to a cardinal point, which are called "watchtowers.") In this light, it is significant that Berenger Sauniere built a tower on his property dedicated to her in which he housed his *library*. He also repeatedly encoded references to the number twenty-two, the number of letters in the Hebrew alphabet.

[7] The number thirteen itself is considered so baleful

that there is actually a name - triskadekaphobia - for the psychological condition of the fear of 13. This is why so many buildings, especially on the East Coast of the United States, do not have a thirteenth floor.

8 One of the illustrations in the Priory of Sion publication *Vaincre* depicted a man mounted upon a white horse and bearing a flag of the "United States of Europe" riding towards a sunset, upon which was inscribed the sign for Aquarius.

9 28 is an interesting number because it is the sum of the numbers 1-7, and is equal to the sum of its divisors (1+2+4+7+14 = 28).

[10] We should presume that calculating these menstrual cycles would have been something that was very important to the "Grail kings" of the ancient world, especially if, as author Nicholas de Vere claims, they drew wisdom and power from a vampire ritual that involved drinking the menstrual blood of "Grail maidens" to obtain the blood's melatonin-rich essences, which De Vere terms "starfire." An interesting myth pertaining to the symbolism of the World Tree encoiled with a serpent illustrates the importance of the menstrual cycle and the number 13. As De Vere writes in his book *From Transylvania to Tunbridge Wells*: "Yggdrasil, the Tree of Life of the Viking kabala or Nine Worlds system, is coiled about at its base by the serpent-dragon Jormangr the Encircler. At Yggdrasil's roots there is a pool. In Ireland, Scotland and Wales, this symbol is repeated as the Hazel Tree by the Well, in which lives the Salmon of Knowledge. Atop the branches of the Hazel tree there sits an eagle who drops a blood-red nut of wisdom into a well 13 times a year. There it is consumed by the Salmon of Knowledge."

[11] The "golden mean proportion" in geometry has long been known by visual artists as that which is most aesthetically pleasing to the eye, and paintings, photographs, etc. are often purposely constructed with the most important visual element located at the two-thirds mark for this reason.

[12] Cabalists believed that there were seventy-two languages on Earth that had been handed down to man by God, and one of their most sacred meditations involved the chanting of the "Shemhamaphorash" - "The 72-fold name of God."

[13] If the "Cutting of the Elm" is indeed a metaphor for this event, the tree, in one layer of meaning, could represent the Sun and the nine planets of the solar system in the same manner as the "Tree of Life", which the Nordic peoples represented as having nine "spheres" or "worlds" attached to it (like the Hebrew Tree of Life with its ten "Sephiroth"). In that case, the reinforcing of the elm tree with "bands of iron" could represent the orbits of the planets, which resisted but ultimately succumbed to the celestial attack that caused them to become upset, cutting the "Orm", or the serpent of the zodiac, from the perspective of the Earth.

[14] The slaying of the dragon is a recurrent theme in world mythology, from the dragon which Saint George defeated to become the patron saint of England, to the old serpent-dragon Tiamat - who represented to the Sumerians the encircling totality of time and space, and who, according to their mythology, was rent in two by their god Marduk in what is clearly described as an astronomical catastrophe that forever changed the nature of life on Earth. Another recurrent theme is that of a god-king whose body is torn into numerous pieces, such as Osiris being cut up by Set, or Orpheus being torn apart by the Bacchantes.

[15] The Mayan calendar, which, amazingly, is based on the numbers 9 and 13 as well, ends on December 23, 2012, the anniversary of Dagobert's death, which is known to Catholics as "St. Dagobert's Day."

[16] This could be part of the subtextual meaning behind the battle between the French and the English in the "Cutting of the Elm" - it was a conflict between those who preferred the old Paris meridian and those who preferred the Greenwich, England meridian which is currently in use. Both of these meridians radiate from a central location built upon an ancient holy site, and are the basis of corresponding "ley lines" or "dragon lines" of electromagnetic energy, upon which other ancient holy sites in the surrounding areas are placed.

Perhaps all of the sacred sites throughout the ancient world that mirror objects in the heavens - such as the pyramids of Egypt, England's Stonehenge, and the Venusian pentagram at Rennes-le-Chateau - were laid out during the Golden Age, when man had no reason to believe that the stars would ever move from their current positions. The Earth could have been entirely mapped just by equating certain areas on Earth with certain things in the heavens. Note that a common Masonic symbol is the pillars of Jachin and Boaz surmounted by a celestial globe and a terrestrial globe, respectively, indicating a connection between patterns in Heaven and patterns on Earth. Also, the term "dragon lines" indicates a connection between the lines of force on Earth which ancient man used to lay out his temples and the zodiacal serpent in the night's sky.

[17] Michael Schneider makes an interesting point in *The Beginner's Guide to Constructing the Universe* about silver's ancient association with the Moon, writing that, "The ancients chose a symbol more appropriate than they may have known. It was only in this century that scientists probing the atom found that the atomic weight of silver is... 107.870, or nearly 108, a tenth of the moon's radius of 1,080 miles."

[18] Nicholas de Vere writes of this concept that, "The sun and the moon both represent spirals. The sun's energy spirals out while the moon acts as a vortex, sucking in the tides and the Sun's light."

[19] After the introduction of the Moon, the number 13 became associated with rebellion. Even Adam's rebellious son Cain, father of the Grail bloodline which the Merovingians belong to, is associated with this number. In *The Pattern and the Prophecy*, by E.W. Bullinger, he points out that that the names all of Cain's descendants mentioned in the Bible, when converted into cabalistic numbers, add up to 2223, which is divisible by both 9 and 13. The 364-day calendar also seems to be implied in *The Book of Genesis*, of which Bullinger writes, "while the opening statement of *Genesis 1:1* is composed of seven words and twenty-eight letters (4x7), the second verse consists of fourteen words, but fifty-two letters; fifty-two being 4 x 13 tells of some apostasy or rebellion which caused the ruin of which that verse speaks." Bullinger seems to make this conclusion certain when he relates that the cabalistic value of the Hebrew word for "Satan" is **364**!

[20] Venus the whore can be seen to symbolize the corrupted state of the virgin goddess, and conversely, the Virgin can be seen as a chaste corruption of the love goddess.

[21] There are two symbols of death and rebirth on the entrance to the graveyard at Saint Magdalene's church at Rennes-le-Chateau which are noteworthy. One is the Masonic emblem of the hourglass - representing time, and death, surrounded by a laurel wreath, which represents Immortality. The other is the skull and crossbones - the skull of which, by the way, has 22 teeth. The term "Death's head" for this symbol contains the words representing the beginning - "head" - and the end - "death."

[22] People may even have lived much longer during the golden age without having to be exposed to these conditions, thus explaining the extraordinary ages that some of the biblical patriarchs, as well as the deified kings of the ancient world, were said to have reached.

The Tower of Babel:
Vessel of God and Ark of His Preservation
(and the Secret of the Original Language Which It Contained)

By Tracy Twyman

Most people are familiar with the Biblical tale of the Tower of Babel from *Genesis*. After the Flood, when the Earth was still of one language and one nation, man decides to build a tower (specifically, a seven-stepped pyramid, or ziggurat), "in the land of Shinar (or Sumer)" whose top reaches Heaven, so that they themselves may ascend thereto. At the same time, they resolve: "...let us make us a name, lest we be scattered abroad upon the face of the Earth." The term "name" may just indicate that these people with a shared language and culture wished to preserve their identity by building a monument to their language and culture that could be seen by God himself - big enough and strong enough, they thought, to survive any future cataclysms. However, the word translated as "name" was actually the Hebrew "shem", which other authors have translated as "shining (or fiery) stone" - specifically, a conical capstone to a ziggurat temple. Such a "shem" is depicted in the "Victory Stele of Naram-Sin" from Akkadia, c. 2280 B.C., where it is shown covered in Sumerian hieroglyphs. Interestingly, "Shem" is also the name of one of Noah's sons in the Bible, and Shem's descendants are listed immediately after the end of the Tower of Babel narrative.

Whatever was meant by "shem", the end result of the Tower of Babel story is the same. The Lord and his angels, seeing that mortal men had built a tower that reached unto their heavenly abode, took this as a sign of man's haughtiness, and decided to destroy it. The repercussions of this were that the one language which the world had enjoyed somehow became scattered, "confounded" into a million various tongues, all somewhat similar and connected in various ways, but only concealing small, fragmented bits of the puzzle that was the original language. Thus does our English word "babble", for nonsense language, derive from this story. The tale, including the tower that reaches to Heaven and the bizarre, inexplicable connection with a universal language that got dispersed when the tower was destroyed, is confirmed in the records of the Sumerians (who add the detail that it was covered with the seven colors of the rainbow), as well as in the records of other cultures, even as far away as Central America, indicating that the story is factually based.

Furthermore, symbolic representations of this story can be found elsewhere, for instance, in the story of the Emerald Tablet of Hermes - a tablet upon which is written the pinnacle of human wisdom, often depicted as having been inscribed upon the side of a volcanic mountain. Hermes was later said to have been buried with this tablet in a secret location, presumably in Egypt, where it was later discovered by both the Pharaoh Akhenaten, and on a separate occasion, Alexander the Great. This same story is echoed in the description of the tomb of Christian Rosenkreutz, legendary founder of the Rosicrucian brotherhood, said to be buried in a mountain in the center of the Earth, the tomb covered in strange hieroglyphic symbols. The Tomb of Christian Rosenkreutz is said in the rituals of the Hermetic Order of the Golden Dawn to be the symbolic equivalent of the tomb of the Egyptian god Osiris. Given this, it is interesting to note that, as pointed out in *The Atlantis Blueprint* by Colin Wilson and Rand Flem-Ath, if the continents were reunited as they were before the continental drift, the pyramids at Giza would be at the direct center of the Earth's land mass. The pyramid, then, like the Tower of Babel, was a representation of the world mountain at the center of the Earth which Osiris was buried in.

Then take into consideration this: the Cheops pyramid was once crowned with brilliantly-colored tiles of limestone, hued in seven bands that matched the seven colors of the rainbow - just like the Tower of Babel in Sumer. At the top of this would have been the fabled missing capstone, which many have speculated to have been of crystalline form. Whatever it was, it was undoubtedly red-colored, to give it the appearance of fire issuing out of the top of the world mountain, and also because red is the uppermost color of the rainbow, so it would naturally have been at the top.[1] The colors of the rainbow range from top to bottom in order of their temperature, with yellow, orange and red at the top, being warmest, the most "fire-like", and green, blue, indigo and violet down at the bottom, being the coolest, the most "water-like." Thus, the pyramid would have been like a massive standing representation of the world mountain reaching up out of the flood waters towards the fiery heavens. It would also be clearly linked symbolically with the Tomb of Hermes, the Emerald Tablet, and the Tower of Babel. Or rather, the pyramid, the Tablet, and the Tomb of Hermes are all symbolic echoes of the original Tower.

It does indeed seem reasonable to think of the Tower of Babel as a man-made representation of the world mountain covered with the strange characters of the original universal language. And such a structure would make a fitting tomb for Hermes, the father of writing. The "Emerald Tablet" may in fact have been a "Rosetta Stone" for deciphering this original language, and Hermes may very well have had it inscribed on the side of his tomb, an artificial mountain or ziggurat located in the center of the Earth. Mythology is replete with stories of patriarchs and father gods attempting to preserve the secrets of civilization, most notably math and writing, in a set of "pillars" against future catastrophes of fire and flood. This may refer to an actual attempt by the man called Hermes to preserve the original language for future generations.[2] The disintegration of the Tablet/Tower would have resulted in the eventual disintegration of the language into various imperfect copies, which is what we have today.[3] This would be the mythological equivalent of the loss of the Holy Grail, or of the secret "Word" of Freemasonry. The goal of occult research, then, would be to recover this lost language. A language is a code, and in order to crack a code, you need to find the key. A California theoretical physicist named Stan Tenen may have found that key, and its origin lives in that ever-present Fibonacci sequence.

Tenan's discovery, made way back in the 1960s, was that the Fibonacci spiral is the apparent basis for the Hebrew alphabet, as well as the Greek, Arabic, and Sanskrit alphabets, making it the root of the universal language used at the Tower of Babel. It all started when he discovered a pattern in the original Hebrew letters of the first sentence of *Genesis* - a pattern that appeared when he counted the letters in base three. He then placed these letters into geometric shapes based on that pattern. When placed in a square shape, with like letters placed next to each other in concentric square rings, the result was what looks like a "bird's eye view" of a seven-stepped ziggurat like the Tower of Babel. When this was then placed upon a torus or "doughnut"-shaped surface, and the excess space stripped away, what Stan Tenen had was a three-dimensional representation of the Fibonacci spiral, a shape that can be found in numerous occurrences of nature, including the shape of a developing fetus, and the horns of a ram. This somewhat snakish, flame-like shape Tenen then placed inside of a crystal tetrahedron - a four-sided prism or pyramid. When light was shined through the object in a shadow-box, Tenen found that he could form every single letter of the Hebrew alphabet - in order - just by changing the position of the shape relative to the crystal. With a slightly different orientation, he was able to produce the letters of other alphabets as well. Appropriately, Tenen named the shape the "flame letter."

The Fibonacci spiral is a representation of the golden mean proportion that occurs so often in nature, and which has been used in all of the most magnificent works of art and architecture, going back to ancient times, including the pyramids at Giza and presumably, the Tower of Babel. Even the colors of the rainbow are made by different wavelengths that vary in size in a golden mean proportion relative to one another. This can be seen in the varying widths of the color bands in a rainbow. The seven colors correspond to the seven notes of the diatonic music scale, and the mathematical, golden mean relationship between the notes, as they ascend and descend along the scale, matches exactly the relationship between the colors of the rainbow.[4] The fact that colors have musical equivalents is reflected in the twelve-note "chromatic" musical scale. As described by author Michael S. Schneider in *A Beginner's Guide to Constructing the Universe*: "The chromatic twelve-scale includes the diatonic seven-scale plus five sharps or flats between them, giving the scale shades of musical color." [5] This may provide a factual basis for the sensory phenomenon known as "synesthesia", in which certain people naturally see certain colors when they hear certain sounds, and vice-versa. Such people often report seeing the letters of the alphabet in certain associated colors as well. The modern musical scale system used in the West is based on that invented by the ancient Greeks, and attributed to the sacred "lyre of Apollo", which also belonged, in turn, to Orpheus, Pythagoras, and originally, *Hermes*. Schneider writes that, "As one stroked the strings upward, the tones descended to earth through E-D-C-B-A-G-F." Elsewhere in the book he states that the scale would be ritually strummed by priests in order to *call angels down from Heaven*!

Imagine if you will that the Tower of Babel encompassed all of these concepts - that it was built around the "flame letter" of the Fibonacci spiral, a true "fire in the middle" of the pyramid, or ziggurat - a pyramid colored like the rainbow and covered with the hieroglyphs of the first universal language. Perhaps the "flame-letter" shape was even placed inside of a crystal capstone on top, just like the pyramid at Giza. Perhaps this is what caused the letters to be formed on the outside of the Tower - shadows refracted through the prism as it spun around in various positions, creating the various characters. Christian Rosenkreutz's tomb is said to be covered with letters written on multi-colored squares that "flash" - perhaps echoing this concept. The spinning around of the shape would have also, when propagated through the magnetic field that would have been created by the rapidly-moving crystal, have created sounds, music even, perhaps, that would have been broadcast through the heavens just like a radio transmission, calling the angels down from Heaven. [6] That is exactly what the Tower of Babel was supposed to do as a "gateway of the gods." At this point, it is interesting to note that in *The Book of Enoch*, supposedly written by a prophet who is considered to be the same figure as Hermes, the angels who descended from Heaven to Earth did so from the top of "Mount Hermon", a name clearly derived from "Hermes." If the Tower of Babel and the Emerald Tablet are one, then they are also the Mountain of Hermes.

There are many ways in which the making of this heavenly music could have been facilitated by the golden mean-based architecture of the tower itself. In *The Mysteries of the Chartres Cathedral* by Louis Charpentier, the author explains how the pointed arch known as the "ogive" used in Gothic architecture (which is based on golden mean principles and may have originated with the Knights Templar) acts as a dynamic sound vibrator. Their specific geometric designs, again always based on Golden Mean principles, can control the action of sound vibrating within them, and the architects of these buildings tuned them like musical instruments. Similar means could have been used in the construction of the Tower of Babel. Given this, it is worth noting that the ancient Greek music system included seven modes of musical scale, and each mode was associated with a style of architecture known by the same name. I should also note that these same ancient Greeks believed that music could affect solid matter in prescribed, mathematical ways. Thus it was said that Orpheus used the magic lyre of Apollo (and Hermes) to cause trees and rocks to "dance", and thus they were moved into geometric patterns in which they remain to this very day. According to this method, the Tower of Babel could have been built by Hermes himself just by employing these mathematical principles of music.

Even the name of Stan Tenen's research group, "the Meru Foundation" confirms the relationships between the world mountain (or a representation thereof), the alphabet, and the golden mean. "Meru", of course, is the name of the world mountain in Tibetan myth, and it is depicted as forming a perfectly geometric stepped pyramid shape - as though it were artificially made. As Tenen points out in his videotaped lecture entitled *Geometric Metaphors of Life*, the word "Meru" is also used in Eastern India as a title for the number sequence known here as "Pascal's Triangle" - a whole number representation of the Fibonacci sequence. The Cheops pyramid, colored with those seven bands of the rainbow and located in the center of the Earth's land mass, was also, he says, called "Mera." But most amazingly, Tenen also says that the Hebrew name for their sacred alphabet is none other than "Meruba."

The Hebrew alphabet was, according to cabbalistic tradition, formed by the "flame of God" - presumably, the "flame-letter" of the Fibonacci spiral that Mr. Tenen has discovered. The alphabet consists of twenty-two letters, broken down into three groups of three, seven and twelve, with each letter corresponding to a number as well. The numbers 3, 7, 12 and 22 occur repeatedly in my research into the Grail mystery, too often to merely ignore. Note the musical scales of 7 and 12, and the seven primary planets, set against the twelve houses of the zodiac. 3 plus 4 is 7, and 3 times 4 is 12. 22 is an important recurring number in the mystery of Rennes-le-Chateau, and the human DNA strand, when placed in tetrahelical (block) form, as Buckminster Fuller envisioned it, has twenty-two sides. If Hebrew letters were placed on these sides, it would form a snake-like cable - the meaning of the word "cabala." But this snake would, like the Orobouros, be swallowing its own tail in a way, for if you take the second letter of the Hebrew alphabet and conjoin it with the last letter, you get Aleph, the first letter of the alphabet.

Clearly, there is something remarkable about this set of letter-numbers said by the Jews to have come directly from God. That this alphabet and the Fibonacci spiral which forms it are encoded into the text of the Torah shows that attempts have been made to preserve the secret of the "flame letter" - the source of the original language in the Tower of Babel - for future generations, honoring its creator, Hermes/Enoch's stated wish. Jewish tradition says that the secret of the Torah is encoded in its first letter. That letter is Bet, which means "house." This represents the Grail - the vessel or container of God, of the source of all knowledge, and the ark of its preservation. In the form of the Fibonacci spiral at the heart of man's writing, art, music, architecture, and numerous other sciences inherent to civilization, enclosed within the vessel of the world mountain, or the Tower of Babel, the Grail would certainly be seen as the source of all knowledge brought to man by the gods, and the vessel of its preservation for the future, like the Tablet of Hermes engraved upon a mountain, set in the Center of the World.

Endnotes:

1 The word "pyramid" means "fire in the middle."

2 In fact, if both the Tower of Babel and the Cheops pyramid existed at the same time, they may have been near-replicas of one another, constituting the two "pillars" of Hermes, only one of which still survives in a greatly reduced form. This is speculation, perhaps, for another article.

3 The Emerald Tablet was, according to legend, once in the possession of Moses. I have speculated that this may have, in fact been the tablet that was placed within the Ark of the Covenant. The loss of the Ark, and indeed, the breaking of the first set of tablets by Moses could be seen as representative of the loss of the Emerald Tablet and thus, the Tower of Babel.

4 This color spectrum, by the way, can be created by refracting light through a crystal prism, or tetrahedron, just like the letters created in the shadow-box.

5 Interestingly, Schneider also says we have a ten-octave hearing range due, somehow, to the Fibonacci spiral shape of our ears!

6 Playing the scale in the opposite direction would presumably result in the opposite effect, that of causing human, earthly consciousness to be raised to the level of the gods. This is the same process as that of the Kundalini snake (the appearance of which resembles strongly that of Tenen's "flame letter") being raised through the seven chakras of the human body (analogous to the seven levels of the ziggurat, the seven notes, and the seven colors) to the pineal gland or Third Eye (the analogue of the tower's capstone.)

The Occult Roots of Christianity

By Boyd Rice

If you were to tell a stranger that you belong to a religious movement whose adherents believed in demons, the raising of the dead, or the invoking of entities to alter worldly events in accordance with their own will, they might logically suspect that you were a member of a Satanic cult. And if you further told them that your faith practiced rituals patterned on the idea of drinking blood and consuming human flesh, they'd no doubt feel certain that such was the case. Yet all of the ideas just mentioned are precepts fundamental to orthodox Christianity. Beliefs that would seem utterly bizarre or inherently occult in any other context are, for mainstream Christianity, simple articles of faith. Even so simple an act as prayer has roots in ancient occult practice and belief. There was a time in which it was thought that there were hierarchies of angels and demons whose aid and assistance could be enlisted by mortal men. Each particular angel or demon was seen to govern some specific aspect of human existence, and by making entreaties to the correct entity, man could achieve his desires. To invoke a demon, one had only to speak his name aloud, say the right words, and command him to do one's bidding.

In the Catholic Church, the legions of angels and devils have been replaced by saints, but the process involved is essentially identical. Each saint is said to hold dominion over some aspect of daily life, and by offering prayers to them one can receive blessings covering everything from safe travel to baking bread. While asking for *blessings* obviously seems far more benign than the act of invoking a demon, both practices are rooted in the magical thinking of the far-distant past, and represent different aspects of the same fundamental world-view. In passing, it's worth noting that the Catholic Church is the last Christian institution which still embraces the concept of the malediction, or in common parlance, the curse. While it is well-known that the early Church consciously co-opted certain aspects of paganism (including pre-Christian holy days), Christianity is so rife with occult concepts that it is difficult not to imagine them as anything other than vestiges of ideas that must have been central to the creed from the very start. After all, some of the most illustrious biblical patriarchs, such as Abraham, Solomon, and Moses were men said to traffic in the black arts. In the time of Christ it was widely believed by both his enemies and his supporters that he too was a sorcerer.

Though the foregoing statement will undoubtedly seem blasphemous to true believers, there is ample evidence in historical sources which indicates that this perception of Christ was not an uncommon one in his own day. Such evidence is explored in-depth in Morton Smith's landmark book *Jesus the Magician*. In this book, Smith documents how popular opinion at the time posited that Christ's miraculous powers were the result of the fact that he "had a demon." This could mean either that he was possessed by a demon, or exercised control over one. Many believed that John the Baptist had a demon too, and that at the time of his beheading, control of the demon passed from John to Christ. Strangely, for many at the time, the notion that Christ was possessed by a demon didn't seem at all inconsistent with their perception of him as "divinely inspired." It is said that many faithful Jews at the time even included the names of demons alongside those of biblical patriarchs when saying their prayers. Examples of this can also be found in some ancient magical incantations, such as this quote from the *Papyri Graecae Magicae*:

"...Lord of life, King of the heavens and the earth, and all those that dwell therein, whose righteousness has not been turned aside... who has irrefutable truth, whose name and spirit [rest] upon good men, come unto my mind and my vitals for all the time of my life and accomplish for me all the desires of my soul. For you are I and I am you. Whatever I say must happen... for I have taken to myself the power of Abraham, Isaac and Jacob, and of the great god-demon Iao Ablanathanalba."

While most of Christ's early followers didn't seem to view his status as a magician as any sort of stumbling-block, his opponents used it to discredit him, saying he was a charlatan, a *mere sorcerer*. After all, the Holy Land of that day had no shortage of would-be messiahs, false prophets and sorcerers. Many of these people were probably charlatans, but by and large the designation of "magician" was by no means synonymous with charlatanism. In fact, according to Morton Smith:

"In Jewish priestly circles of the first century like those of Josephus, to be thought a magician was not necessarily discreditable, and in other Jewish circles it might be taken as a <u>messianic trait</u>."

Evidently, in Christ's own lifetime (and the years immediately following), his status as a magician *was* seen as a messianic trait. As the centuries passed, his powers came to be seen as divinely ordained rather than demonic, and by the fourth century his transition from magician to messiah was complete. In the intervening years however, there was a strange interim period in which the occult tradition of Christ became indistinguishably blurred into what would eventually emerge as Orthodox Christianity. In some cases the occult aspects were subtly present, in others widely overt. In the most pronounced cases, Jesus himself was invoked as a demon, or alternately, as a king of demons whose blessing would confer power over other demons. In a lead curse tablet from first or second century Greece, the goddesses Persephone, Hecate, and Selene are conjured in the name of Jesus to curse an enemy's "body, spirit, soul, mind, thought, sensation, life, heart." Another such tablet, from Carthage, reads:

"I conjure you, whoever you are, daemon of the dead, by the god who created the earth and heaven... I conjure you by the god who has authority over the subterranean regions, Neicharoplex... by ... holy Hermes ... Iao .... Sabaoth ... the god of Solomon, Souarmimooth ... the god having authority over this hour in which I conjure you, Jesus."

Interestingly, the gods mentioned herein seem to be viewed as co-equal, with the ruler of the underworld being called upon in the same breath as he who created the Earth and heavens. And strangely, included in their ranks is "holy Hermes", whose words Christ seemed to echo in the apocryphal *Gospel of Thomas*. In this context, Jesus (the "demon of the dead"), although being conjured, seems to be an intermediary between man and the gods. The fact that there is a plurality of gods whose power is being invoked here is significant, insofar as it demonstrates that the figure of Christ was indeed viewed at one point as the new evangel of a far more ancient tradition. For some he was a prophet who, in the manner of earlier deified kings, joined the ranks of the gods upon passing from his earthly life. For others, he was a conjurer of demons who *became* a demon. Though he would ultimately be viewed as the son of the one true God, author Morton Smith asserts that in the centuries leading up to that time, "there is no question that Jesus' name continued to be used in magic as that of a supernatural power by whose authority demons might be conjured."

There is ample evidence in the Old Testament, alternative traditions and rabbinic lore that the notion of Christ as a magician or conjurer of demons is no mere misconception or misinterpretation. In fact, it seems to constitute a family heritage of sorts. The patriarch Abraham was said to be well-versed in "the black arts", and traveled extensively, sharing his knowledge with priests and kings of other lands. In rabbinic lore it was recorded that Solomon conjured the demon Asmodeus to build his mighty temple, as is well-known. And Solomon was also said to have been the author of an influential grimoire, *The Key of Solomon*, which was revered by occultists as a text of monumental importance for many centuries. Clearly, there are firmly-established traditions in which these patriarchs are remembered as occultists and magicians.

Though to modern sensibilities, much of this seems utterly incomprehensible, these ideas may have originally been viewed in an altogether different light than they are today. For instance, it is widely thought that the word "demon" merely meant *spirit*, and was initially devoid of any connotation denoting evil entities. The Socratic use of the term *daemonic* simply referred to a power beyond that of humans. Much of early religion was based upon a form of ancestor worship. Many ancient kings both worshipped their deified forebears, and presented themselves as being their living embodiments - possessed by their very spirit. Invoking the names of demons/spirits may have merely been a form of such ancestor worship. A good many demonic names, when translated according to predominant ancient tongues, bear a remarkable resemblance to many early king titles. For instance, "Asmodeus" can be translated as "the Lord God", and "Azazel" can be translated as "Lord Son of God." If the invocation of so-called "demonic" names was an esoteric tradition, known and understood by only a small number of initiates, it's plain to see how it could easily have been misunderstood or misinterpreted by outsiders. We have already described the used of the names of biblical patriarchs in demonic conjuration, which may be another indication that ancestor worship played a part in the process. But that is just speculation. When all is said and done, the most we can definitively say is that these people believed there were forces exterior to man which could be entreated to conform to his will. As previously mentioned, this view differs little from that of any man who lights a candle and utters a prayer, or invokes the name of a saint in hopes of securing blessings.

Those with an anti-Christian bias point to the fact that there were upwards of a dozen crucified messiahs whose stories closely resembled that of Christ, claiming this constitutes "proof" that Jesus never existed. After all, they argue, mythology is full of dying and resurrected gods such as Tammuz. The fact that Christ's story shares similar elements must mean that it too is merely another myth. Of course, such an argument doesn't *prove* anything of the sort. What it does tend to indicate, it seems, is that Christ was part of a long-standing tradition - a tradition whose tenets are often preserved in myth and symbol.

The traditions from which Christianity is derived date back to a time when religious iconography was highly symbolic. At that time, the symbolism involved seems to have been widely recognized and understood. Although much of this same iconography later played a central role in Christianity, the original meanings have long since been forgotten. Take, for example, the cross, the foremost symbol of Christianity. Ask most Christians its meaning, and they're likely to tell you that it's an emblem of their faith because Christ died on the cross. Such an idea seems fairly straightforward, since as often as not when one sees a cross, it is in the form of a crucifix, bearing the image of a crucified Christ. Thus, the conception of the cross as being synonymous with the death of Christ has come to be firmly established in the popular consciousness. In fact, however, the cross was one of the primary religious symbols in many ancient cultures for millennia before the advent of Christ. In both the West and the East, the cross can be traced to the remotest antiquity. Some claim that the origin of the cross lies in the earliest practice of solar religion. At dawn, salutations were given to the Sun as God the Father reborn. People would face the Sun as it rose on the eastern horizon, embracing it ritualistically by extending their arms straight out at their sides. They would then turn away from the Sun and, maintaining the same posture, gaze toward that point on the western horizon where the dying Sun would "sink into the Abyss" later that evening. While looking westward in this manner, the rising Sun cast a long shadow of their body that gave a cross-like appearance. So it was that the cross became a symbol of the Sun as a dying and resurrected god. The later meanings attributed to the cross by orthodox Christianity are but a continuation of the theme of death and resurrection - a theme whose roots go back to the dawn of recorded history.

The single institution in which the overlap of Christian and pre-Christian ideas can be seen most explicitly is without a doubt Roman Catholicism. The emerging Church of Rome absorbed a great many of the rites and ideas that had dominated Roman religion and politics in the centuries prior to the birth of Christ. Much of this had come to Rome by way of Babylon, Sumer and Persia. The idea that the emperor was a living incarnation of God was rooted in the most ancient examples of religion in Sumer and Egypt. During the period when the caesars were looked upon as gods, the role of emperor was also to serve as high priest in the Mithraic mysteries, which were then the state religion. His title in this capacity was "Pontifex Maximus." Later, as papal authority accrued, the Church of Rome would lay claim to the title Pontifex Maximus as a designation for the Pope. In time Catholicism elaborated a policy which presented the Pope as having a role analogous to that of Christ, representing "the voice of God on Earth." Such a notion is more in keeping with the ideas that defined pagan Rome than with anything to be found in the Bible. Non-Catholic Christians deemed the idea blasphemous, and harsher critics went so far as to label the Pope an agent of the Devil.

The emblem of papal authority, a logo comprised of two crossed keys surmounted by a crown, also has its roots in pre-Christian religion. The gods and goddesses associated with the mysteries (such as Janus and Diana) were often depicted holding keys. It is altogether probable that early non-Christians who saw this iconography in the context of the new religion may have drawn the conclusion that the Pope was an initiate of the mystery schools, or that he was a living inheritor of the knowledge of the gods. Later, as the intrinsically pagan symbolism of the keys faded from public memory, the Church began to assert that the keys represented the "keys to Heaven" given to the apostle Peter by Christ. Peter, they said, traveled to Rome and became the first Pope. Subsequently, the keys have been passed down to each successive Pope. This is the version of things that has been accepted as official Catholic doctrine, although prior to the first half of the fifth century there had been no mention of St. Peter as the first Pope, or of the keys to Heaven.

The distinctive clothing of the Catholic priesthood for many centuries involved the wearing of a garment that looked rather like a dress. The adoption of this style of clothing may have its genesis in the cult of Attis and Cybele, which originated in Greece in 500 B.C., and remained a strong presence in Rome until around 400 A.D. The central myth of the sect stated that Attis had stood beneath a sacred pine tree and castrated himself as an offering to Cybele. This legend served as the basis of yearly rites held in Spring, in which "priests wearing effeminate costumes" would castrate themselves, burying the knives and severed members in the earth as a "blood sacrifice to the goddess." Such rites may have been the source of the practice of celibacy in the Catholic priesthood. Most religions have no policy demanding celibacy from their priests, and there seems to be no basis in any Christian literature for the adoption of such a practice. Although there is nothing to indicate that Catholics have participated in ritual castration akin to the goddess cult, there is however a curious quote from *The Book of Matthew* in which the author refers to priests as "eunuchs of the Kingdom of Heaven."

The black color of Catholic priestly garb can be traced to Babylon, where the priests of Baal were famous for having dressed in black. Babylon exerted a powerful influence on the religious thought of Rome, and another rite central to Roman Catholicism may also have its roots in the priesthood of Baal. Undoubtedly the most bizarre ritual of the Roman Church is that of Communion - the symbolic consumption of the flesh and blood of Christ. Even as a *purely symbolic act*, the ceremony's connotations are barbaric, and seem to have more in common with occultism than Christian doctrine. It is said by some that in certain Babylonian rites, a human sacrifice was required, and that the victim's flesh and blood was then consumed by participants in the ritual. If such accounts can be taken seriously, this might have served as the basis of the later (purely symbolic) practice of Communion. Though some scholars dismiss the claims of Babylonian sacrifice, it's interesting to note that our modern word for consuming human flesh, "cannibalism", is rooted in the Babylonian words "kahane baal" ("priest of Baal").

In a number of ancient cultures, each year a young man was chosen to act as a living incarnation of one of their gods. He would reside in the temple dedicated to that god, and lead a kingly existence, with no luxury denied him. At the end of a year's time, however, he would be offered as a sacrifice. Being selected for this role was evidently the highest possible honor, both for the sacrificial victim and his family. When the sacrifice was completed, the man's flesh would be eaten, evidently as a means of achieving communion with the deity he symbolized. Assuming that this rite may have been associated with the purported human sacrifice and cannibalism said to have been practiced in Babylon, the additional symbolic content of consuming the dead god's flesh would complete the similarity between the ritual practiced by the Babylonians and the Communion of Catholicism. Though such ideas are not at all in keeping with what we imagine we know about early Christianity, there is perhaps much that we don't know about it. The emergence of Christianity in pagan Rome was a phenomenon viewed with suspicion and fear. Christians were seen as a dangerous, subversive foreign sect. Their doctrine was seen as seditious, because it denied the emperor's divinity, and recognized his authority as being second to that of Christ. Chroniclers writing at the time tell us that the Christians were an ungodly sect who held bizarre rituals beneath a full moon. The rituals were said to have climaxed in an orgiastic frenzy, which sometimes involved human sacrifice. Ironically, the very charges leveled against the early Christians by pagan Rome are nearly identical to those later leveled against heretics by papal Rome. And very similar charges were later made against the Jews in medieval Europe. Most serious students of history dismiss all such charges as fabrications, libelous falsehoods intended to demonize any group who fails to conform to the prevailing orthodoxy. Although such an explanation seem immanently rational, and in keeping with human nature, it's hard to deny that much of early religion involved practices that would today be deemed savage: intoxicated frenzy, orgiastic excess, and sacrifice (both animal and human). Though the early Christians may be entirely innocent of the charges made against them, it is not inconceivable that such practices may have been indulged in by organized groups keeping alive strange traditions from antiquity.

Much of the symbolism of the Church of Rome is derived from the old solar religions, and comes by way of Egypt, Sumer, and (yet again) Babylon. It is a popular misconception that solar religion equates with mere "sun worship", and is the most primitive of superstitions. In fact, the earliest forms of solar religion, those associated with the worship of the Divine Couple, evince a high level of symbolic purity and sophistication, which seems to have steadily decreased with the rise of polytheism. At any rate, imagery related to the Sun can be found abundantly in Catholicism. It is perhaps most evident in the many depictions of saints. The so-called "haloes" surrounding the heads of saints are identical to the solar discs pictured around the heads of earlier gods and goddesses associated with the Sun. In some cases the solar connotation of these haloes is made even more explicit by the inclusion of a red equilateral cross within them - a sun cross. This image of a solar disc enclosing an equilateral cross is a very ancient sun symbol, and can be seen on the king seals of many Sumerian rulers. These deified kings were seen as being *suns of God*, and some bore the title "Son of the Sun." Consequently, they are often pictured in close proximity to this solar icon, as a sign of their divine authority. When the Egyptian pharaoh Akhenaten attempted briefly to institute solar monotheism as the state religion in his land, he too took on the title "Son of the Sun." The single idea most central to Christianity, that of a man being the son of God, had its origin in the ancient royal concept of the "Son of the Sun."

For a great many years, Roman priests sported a distinctive hairstyle known as the Roman tonsure. It was defined by a round circle shaved atop the priest's head toward the back, with a fringe of hair cut to a uniform length surrounding it. The style would eventually be adopted by other religious orders, but its association with Catholicism is the reason it remains known as the "Roman" tonsure. It was a style, however, that was worn for centuries prior to the formation of the Catholic church by priests of the solar religion. The symbolism of the hairstyle was intended to denote the priest as a servant of the sun god. The shaved circle is said to represent the solar disc, and the fringe of hair around it was meant to mimic the Sun's aureole. Though this tonsure may have been worn by priests of numerous solar sects, it would have been best known to Romans as the style associated with the priesthood of Mithra. At some point the Roman tonsure was evidently phased out. However, high-ranking members of the Roman church often still wear small yarmulke-like headgear which occupies the same spot on their heads as once did the circle of shaved hair.

One of the most long-standing tenets of Judeo-Christianity is its taboo against the use of graven images. This dates back to an age in which other religions made statues of their gods, and many people worshipping such idols perceived them to be actual incarnations of the gods they were meant to represent. It is said that the father of Abraham made his livelihood creating likenesses of these gods of other cultures, such as Baal, Dagon, Astarte, and so on. One day Abraham took one of these idols and smashed it, then stated that it could not possibly be a god, or it could not have been so easily destroyed. This single event seems to have signaled the beginning of the prohibition against idolatry and the graven image. The most extreme example of this prohibition can be seen in the iconoclasts of Constantinople. The original meaning of "iconoclast" is "destroyer of images", and this fanatical sect took holy writ very literally. They insisted that no statue, painting or depiction of any sort should be allowed to exist portraying divinities, patriarchs, saints, the Madonna, etc., on the grounds that they constituted forbidden graven images. Consequently, churches were sacked, statues demolished, and paintings burned. The great churches of Constantinople must have looked very boring as a result.

In contrast, the Church of Rome seems to have embraced the pre-Christian fondness for statues. Cathedrals in the eternal city abound with statues, paintings, and holy relics, all of which have become the object of veneration over the centuries. In St. Peter's Basilica, visitors actually kneel before the statues of saints, often kissing their feet or hands. Quite often early Catholic churches were established in buildings which had long been pagan temples, and the very statues of the gods worshipped in pagan times were simply repainted and re-christened as Catholic saints. As often as not, the saint names given to the statues were nearly identical to those of the previous gods. This is commented on in *Babylon Mystery Religion* by Ralph Woodrow, where he states:

"The goddess Victoria of the Basse-Alpes was renamed as St. Victoire, Cheron as St. Ceranos, Artemis as St. Artemedos, Dionysos as St. Dionysis, etc. The goddess Brighit (regarded as the daughter of the sun-god and represented with a child in her arms) was smoothly renamed as St. Bridget. In pagan days her chief temple at Kildare was served by Vestal Virgins who tended the sacred fires. Later her temple became a convent and her vestals, nuns. The continued to tend the ritual fire, only now it was called 'St. Bridget's fire.'"

The practice of using pre-existing pagan idols as Catholic icons was so widespread, it is virtually impossible to ascertain how many of these early images date back to the pre-Christian era. It is particularly difficult in regards to one of the most well-known of Catholic icons: that of the Madonna and child. This image, depicting the goddess holding the Holy Child, was central to pre-Christian religion for millennia prior to Christianity. In Egypt, the mother and child were Isis and Horus; in Babylon, Semiramis and Tammuz. India and China likewise had their equivalents. This image of the sacred mother and her divine child goes back to an age in which worship of the divine couple was still the order of the day. The king and queen were worshipped as earthly incarnations of the couple, and their son, the future king, was seen as having been born "of the gods." Although the details differ significantly, this is precisely Christ's implied legacy, that of a king, and of a son of God. And though the Catholic church denied Christ's dynastic kingship due to his purported "virgin birth", it is clear that the symbolism of the Madonna and child represented an archetype whose meaning was not lost on converts to the early church.

It is popular to contrast Christianity with paganism, to infer that the two exist separately and distinctly from one another, or are, indeed, creeds diametrically opposed to one another. Clearly, such is not the case. If anything, they constitute a continuum of belief. Though they both exist in markedly different forms, they share many of the same intrinsic values and beliefs with one another. That Christianity is merely an extension of ancient occult traditions should be fairly self-evident by now. What is less self-evident is the extent to which it was an organically occurring process, or part of a conscious campaign. Most writers in this vein look everywhere for the hand of the early priesthood, claiming that they deliberately co-opted many aspects of paganism in a cynical bid to gain converts. While to a limited extent this may be true, it cannot be the whole story. The most fundamentally occult aspects of Christianity were part and parcel of the story of Christ well before any *priesthood* came into existence. Indeed, it would have been an impossibility for a meddlesome clergy to have thoroughly expunged from Christian doctrine every tenet with innately occult or pagan content. Had they tried to do so, they would have found themselves with nothing left.

Remember that it took roughly four centuries for Christianity to sort itself out. During those years that doctrine was often a bizarre hodge-podge of mysteries, the black arts, Gnosticism, and what-have-you. The emerging priesthood probably had their hands full just trying to find a common ground that would grant a sense of cohesion to the new church. It would take them centuries just to arrive at a consensus about which of their holy texts should be included in (or excluded from) the Bible. In all likelihood, the evolution of what would emerge as Christianity was probably a far more organic process than is generally presumed. It probably represents a logical synthesis of the predominant religious ideas of the time. The inclusion of pagan ideas was only natural, because Christianity was itself pagan in essence. Consequently, rather than being foreign to Christianity, pagan precepts were complimentary to it. This is perhaps the primary reason that Christianity was so attractive to pagans. They recognized and understood the fundamental symbolism of Christianity, and responded to its archetypal paganism. They were familiar with the concept of a dying and resurrected god, and too, the notion of a son of God. All the rich symbolism associated with the "new" creed required little or no explanation. Indeed, the reason for Christianity's success wasn't that it was a new creed, but rather that it was *not*. Had some would-be messiah turned up preaching a doctrine not rooted in centuries-old traditions and archetypes, his message would have probably fallen on deaf ears.

When all is said and done, virtually every form of religion has as its foundation a precept which is innately rooted in the occult. It is precisely this element of the occult which defines religious thought and feeling, and makes faith what it is. It is *that* factor which above and beyond all else speaks most directly to the soul of man, and hints of mysteries that can never be either wholly understood or adequately explained. Perhaps there exists some motivating force within the twilight world of our ancestral memory which recognizes that the outward symbolism of so many religious modes is actually referring to a much more primordial hidden doctrine - a forgotten faith whose vestiges are preserved in symbol and myth. Perhaps the religious impulse, so inherent in man, is but the most common manifestation of this deeply ingrained instinct. In the words of Philo, "In heaven, to know is to see. On Earth, to remember."

The Divine Couple

By Boyd Rice

One of the most ancient concepts in religion is that of the Divine Couple. In Sumeria it appears as part of perhaps the earliest notion of Trinity. God the Father was symbolized as the Sun, his consort was symbolized alternately as either the Moon or the Earth, and the king was viewed as their offspring: the Son of the Sun; a living representative (or *emanation*) of God on Earth. A similar idea can be seen in Egypt, where the Pharaoh was viewed as a living incarnation of Horus, son of the Divine Couple Isis and Osiris. The Pharaoh was seen both as a god, and as a mediator between the earthly and the divine. It was said that when he died, he ascended to the heavens and *became* Osiris (essentially returning to the source with whom he had always been synonymous in the minds of the Egyptians).

In many traditions the gods and goddesses who comprise the Divine Couple are not seen as being separate or distinct entities, but rather as differing aspects of one another, or even emanations of one another. In this we see traces of an even more ancient tradition: God as the primordial androgyne. Such a notion has been part of many theologies, although the idea has largely been forgotten or (perhaps) *ignored*. Traces of it can even be found in Judeo-Christianity. For instance, we are told that the name of Jehovah is comprised of Hebrew characters representing the four elements: air, fire, earth, and water. But read slightly differently, the same characters spell "he she." And the word Elohim, usually translated as "gods", or "the angels", is actually a composite of "Eloh", the feminine plural of god, and "Im", the masculine plural of god. Even straightforwardly Christian sources concede that this is no doubt indicative of the belief, anciently held, that God was primordially possessed of both sexes. This idea has been central to certain occult traditions, and experienced a kind of revival in the nineteenth century, influencing the Hermetic Brotherhood of Luxor and the Hermetic Order of the Golden Dawn. It developed into the doctrine that the entirety of creation flows from the differentiation of the unmanifested divine into male and female. To those who followed this doctrine, the reunification of the *divine duad* represented the means of achieving union with God.

In ancient cultures, the sundered aspects of this duad were seen symbolically as being the heavens and the Earth: the heavens representing God the Father, and Earth representing the Earth Mother. Together the two represented the most fundamental notion of generative power. In Mesopotamia it was said that there was a time at which the heavens and the Earth *were one*. This primordial oneness, called "Anki", gave birth to a son: Enlil. This son proceeded to cleave the heavens and the Earth apart, creating two separate entities from a primeval whole. *An* departed to rule from the heavens. *Ki* descended to earth to rule with her son Enlil. Thus we have the birth of the Divine Couple, in an early creation myth that chronicles the original state of union from which the two emerged.

In a related story, the god Marduk is said to have created the heavens and the Earth by killing Tiamat, the goddess representing the primeval waters. He cut her corpse in half, and one part became the heavens, the other the Earth. Her eyes became the Tigris and Euphrates rivers that bordered Babylon. Though the story dates from a later period than the Anki tale, and the symbolism is less straightforward, it nonetheless demonstrates that even at this latter date, the idea that Heaven and Earth constituted a primordial unity was still in currency. And although many other creation myths involving a Divine Couple seem to hint at this, most are far less specific in their details. For instance, in Hindu mythology, Dyaus Pitar (God the Father) and Prthivi were the primordial couple who sired the Vedic pantheon of gods. They were said to have placed Heaven and Earth into "conjunction" with one another. If any original cleaving asunder took place, it seems to have eluded mention.

In other myths involving the Divine Couple, their separation seems to be conveyed symbolically by the act of castration. The most well-known tale in this regard must certainly be that of Isis and Osiris. In this story, Osiris is cut into pieces by the dark Set, who scatters the pieces far and wide. Isis sets about finding the pieces to sew them back together again. She finds all but one: the penis. In some versions, the penis has been thrown in the Nile and eaten by fish. Undaunted, she fashions Osiris a penis from gold, attaches it, and instantly the god is resurrected.

This tale is remarkable in that, unlike the early myths, it represents not the *separation* of the Divine Couple, but the notion of their *reunification*. The well-known obelisks of ancient Egypt are said alternately to represent the penis of Osiris, or the needle of Isis. Either interpretation carries essentially the same symbolic meaning. In sewing together the pieces of Osiris, Isis is making him whole once more. The penis she fashions represents the point of *union* between the Divine Couple, and thence comes its symbolic significance to the ancients. So the elements of the story, taken as a whole, can be seen as representing the power of the female element to restore the power of God by restoring the primal equilibrium of the Divine Couple, and reestablishing the union of the two.

Other instances of divine castrations abound in the early creation myths, yet none manage to recapture the simple eloquence and symbolic purport of the tale of Isis and Osiris. But another example of castration dating from the Middle Ages is of particular interest to us insofar as it has become associated with the saga of the Holy Grail. I'm speaking, of course, about the story of Parcival and the Fisher King. The story, in a nutshell, is as follows. The Fisher King lies dying of a *wound that never heals*. Some versions of the Grail romance are vague as to the nature of the wound, but at least one is very specific indeed. In a bizarre accident, the king has lost his genitals. A sword he was wielding broke in two, slicing away his penis. It is said that the area between his legs is "smooth as a woman." The king can only be redeemed by the Grail, and so the knight Parcival embarks on a quest in search of it. But before Parcival can hope to win the Grail, he must procure a weapon to take along on his mystical journey. Taking the shattered pieces of the king's sword, he melts them down, forges the weapon anew, and sets off on his quest.

The Vesica Pisces forms the Ichthys fish symbol.

This is all very interesting. The sword in question is no ordinary one, but a weapon possessed of legendary powers. It is said that it ordains victory and absolute power - but only to those *destined to wield it*. To all others, it ordains ruin. The very fact that it shattered in the hands of the Fisher King seems to indicate that he wasn't its rightful possessor. The wound of the Fisher King is also very telling. The loss of his *manhood* indicates that he existed in a decadent, emasculated state. This in and of itself certainly seems to constitute a "wound that never heals."

The symbolism attendant to the figure of Parcival is every bit as telling. To win the Grail he must first re-forge the mythic sword, and make it *whole* again. This weapon obviously represents some primordial archetypal power - one both creative and destructive. Its breaking in two was the basis of tragedy and ruin; it's reunification, the basis of attaining the Grail. With its shattering, the king was both emasculated and doomed. With its restoration, Parcival won his quest and married the bearer of the Grail.

The symbolism inherent in this story could hardly be more straightforward. The missing penis, besides representing the obvious loss of manhood, is emblematic (as in the case of Osiris) of the cleaving apart of the two most basic forces, as signified by their two most primary manifestations: male and female. The king is useless without the ability to become conjoined to the queen and produce an heir to the throne.

Another revealing aspect of the tale is that en route on his quest (and in order to attain it) Parcival must curse and reject God. He can only attain the Grail by becoming like unto God. This indicates that the very notion of God has become, for him (the truest of heroes), a hindrance that must be overcome before winning the Grail is possible.

Is the figure of Parcival meant to be a Templar Knight? Is he a true servant of God, who, in the course of his service to the supreme deity, must reject organized religion? Perhaps. And what of the Fisher King? Does he represent the orthodoxy of the church, an established authority, possessed of a throne and attempting to wield a supreme power, but hopelessly incapable of doing so? Maybe. Parcival certainly seems to be everything the king is not. He's possessed of the capability of getting the Grail, marrying the Grail bearer, and not only wielding the legendary sword, but of forging it anew. All of this would seem to indicate that the mystery of the Grail encompasses far more than the mere object to which the name is attached. The very quest itself is a part of the process of redemption/transformation. And since the attainment of the Grail seems to be associated with marrying the bearer of the Grail, I posit that this symbolic union is more probably the goal of the Grail quest. The mere object is simply emblematic of it. In other words, the true significance of this tale lies in the coming together of the archetypal male and female in a reflection of the original sacred idea: the Divine Couple. This hypothesis seems to be borne out by the fact that when all of this is accomplished, the Fisher King's "redemption" is that he *dies*, and Parcival succeeds him.

In fact, I think it's safe to say that many of the elements central to the saga of the Grail bloodline could also be explained in terms of the Divine Couple and the principle they signified. For instance, the Knights Templar (Poor Knights of the Temple of Solomon) were intrinsically linked to Solomon's Temple, with its cabalistic pillars of Jachin and Boaz. Occultists tell us that these pillars represented the dual qualities of mildness and severity. One of the pillars was gold, the other green. In another article (*Hiram, King of Tyre*), I proposed the theory that the royal colors of the Merovingians, gold and green, refer symbolically to the principle embodied by the pillars of Solomon's Temple. Taking that notion to its logical conclusion, it would follow that the use of gold and green in both cases also signifies the Divine Couple. Gold, in the ancient world, was always used to symbolize the Sun: God the Father. And green would seem the logical color to symbolize the consort of God in her role as Earth Mother. The roles of god and goddess in ancient cultures seem to have been patterned after the classic parental model. God the Father was severe, distant, and aloof. His consort was far more approachable, and in many ways was seen as a mediator between God and man. It is thought that except in rare or extreme cases, few people petitioned God directly in those times. Rather, they appealed to the female deity to intercede on their behalf, just as any child knows its mother will naturally be more sensitive to its desires, while the father has a tendency to be unyielding and authoritarian. It is speculated that this is the reason why relatively few statues remain depicting father gods, while statues of goddesses abound.

Speaking of statues of female entities, it appears that another of the mysteries associated with the legend of the Grail may well seem more readily comprehensible when viewed in light of the Divine Couple notion. We speak, of course, of the phenomenon of the Black Madonnas. Statues of the Black Madonna appear in churches throughout France (particularly in the Languedoc), and have long been associated with Mary Magdalene. But the question that has long perplexed observers is: "What could these enigmatic figures possibly *mean*?" Heretofore, the answer to this question has been elusive. Most of the hypotheses offered have seemed to be either baseless speculation, wishful thinking, or a combination of the two. Some have pointed to the obvious similarities between the Black Madonnas and Kali, the Hindu goddess of destruction. However, the "obvious similarities" cited are perhaps the most superficial qualities they share: both are female and both are black. The characteristics that define the fundamental nature of each (one is a nurturing mother, the other a crazed destroyer bedecked in a garland of severed heads) would seem to indicate that their respective dissimilarities far outweigh any shared attributes.

Some authors have asserted that both Mary Magdalene and the Black Madonnas are "linked to pagan goddess worship." This conclusion seems to possess even less inner logic than the Kali hypothesis, and fails to explain why the symbolism unique to the Black Madonna phenomenon could be seen to indicate such a notion. The most straightforward explanation for the symbolism of the color black is the most common meaning associated with it in the context of the occult: matter. To the ancients matter was synonymous with the world, the flesh, and the Devil. Consequently, the figure of the Madonna (a *mother*) symbolized as *matter*, can easily be seen to equate with some of the most ancient notions previously discussed concerning the female aspect of the Divine Couple. [1] At that point in history when Black Madonnas came into prominence, heresies were dealt with severely, and the idea that God had a *consort* would have been wildly heretical. Therefore, the Black Madonnas were a coded means of keeping alive one of the most primordial notions of deity, an ancient secret hidden in plain sight. Their outward form was, in all respects but one, deceptively orthodox-seeming. Their unusual coloring was just perplexing enough to confuse those who didn't understand, while not being *so* odd as to generate too much suspicion. Yet the Black Madonnas have been a source of bafflement for centuries, misunderstood by the public, the clergy, and even most occultists.

Viewed in the context of what we've just explained, the symbolism of the Black Madonnas seems not only unambiguous, but really quite obvious. Such symbolism is central to occult doctrine, and is even quite prominent in orthodox religion itself. The well-known depiction of the dove descending into the Grail chalice represents nothing less, and is an image that was of central importance to both the Catholic church, and Aleister Crowley's Ordo Templi Orientis. The latter's use of such straightforwardly Christian iconography no doubt perplexed many, and indeed this was perhaps the intent. But so as to convey the precise intent of utilizing this conventional image, Crowley placed it inside of an oval shape, the arc of which came to points at both the top and the bottom. Were one to follow the path of the arcs comprising each side of this shape, you would find that each formed a perfect circle, and that the shape employed by Crowley represented the point at which these circles overlapped. This is a well-known occult symbol, the "vesica pisces", and the circles are said to represent the corporeal world and the non-corporeal world, or spirit and matter. Therefore, the point at which the two intersect would be emblematic of precisely the same thing as the image placed within this geometric shape: the symbolic union of Heaven and Earth, spirit and matter, masculinity and femininity.

We see the very same image of the overlapping circles on a sacred well in England, in a place called Glastonbury said to have been visited by Christ and Joseph of Arimathea. It is called Chalice Well, and is covered by a large slab of stone decorated with metalwork depicting the intersecting circles. Even Christian commentators assert that the circles signify the point of union between "the visible realm and the invisible realm" (the meaning of which should be self-evident by now.) Yet here an additional element has been added. The two circles are pierced by what has been said to be a "bleeding lance", a symbol well-known from the Grail legends. Some speculate that this lance, said to be synonymous with the Spear of Longinus that pierced the side of Christ, was perhaps emblematic of death and resurrection. Being the instrument of Christ's destruction, it was therefore a key element of his resurrection. This may be at least partially true, yet seems unsatisfactory as a complete explanation. Viewed in conjunction with the two circles, the lance seems to assume a deeper level of meaning. Here it intersects and conjoins the dual worlds represented: spirit and matter, Heaven and Earth, etc. Once again, we seem to see an echo of the same elemental idea already familiar to us. Seen in conjunction with the intersecting circles, the lance serves to emphasize and reinforce the symbolism already implicit in the configuration, in much the same way that Crowley's use of the odd geometric shape around the chalice and dove was a coded reiteration of the same theme.

Finally, another context in which we see the unusual shape defined by the intersection of two circles is perhaps one of the most mainstream icons of Christianity. Turn the above-mentioned shape on its side, extend briefly the lines indicated by the arcs on one end, and we have the well-known "fish" emblem popular with born-again motorists. This emblem is known as the *ichthys*, which means "fish" in Greek. But the word "ichthys" is comprised of first letters (in Greek) of the phrase "Jesus Christ - God - Son - Savior." This all seems to beg the obvious question: "Why would Jesus Christ be identified with a fish?" This fish represents much of what the shape which defines it has already been shown to identify: the intersection of two realms. As a denizen of the waters, it signifies the sea, and all that the sea in turn symbolizes. For the ancients, the waters represented an intermediary point between spirit and matter. Above it loomed the heaven, below it the Earth. Hans Jonas, in his *Gnostic Religion*, tells us "*sea* or *waters* is a standing Gnostic symbol for the world of matter, or of darkness into which the divine has sunk." So once again we see the very same idea associated with the very same shape. This shape turns up repeatedly in medieval religious paintings. There is a painting of Sophia (much associated with the Black Madonnas) framed within this odd oval emblem. It would appear that a good many artists were schooled in occult theology, and like the troubadours, used their craft as a means of keeping alive a secret tradition.

Perhaps the penultimate Divine Couple was Ia and Inanna, reputedly the primordial parents from which all the early Sumerian deified kings were thought to be descendants, and to whom we've traced the bloodline of Christ, the House of David, and the Merovingians. Inanna is thought to be the prototype of most of the major goddess figures in world mythology, such as Isis, Ishtar, Astarte, Diana, etc. And in examining Inanna, we find the basis of much of the unusual symbolism identified with Mary Magdalene - symbolism seemingly inexplicable in the context of orthodox Christianity. For instance, Inanna was symbolized by the rose, and by Venus, the morning star - both symbols associated with Mary Magdalene. She was worshipped at dawn as the principle which animated the whole of the natural world, and at the evening, we're told, "she became the patron of temple prostitutes when the evening star was seen as a harlot soliciting in the night skies." [2] Here then, we find the roots of all the major symbolism attached to Mary Magdalene: the rose, the morning star, and prostitution. Christ, in his union with Mary Magdalene, was consciously trying to manipulate or *revive* the archetype of the Divine Couple. He represented spirit and the heavens; she represented matter, the flesh, and the Earth.

But the myth of Inanna also incorporates elements very similar to those of Christ: a story of death and resurrection. In it, she descends to the underworld and "finds herself stripped naked and tried before seven underworld judges, the Annunaki. She is sentenced and left for dead for *three days and nights* before being restored at the behest of Enki." This tale of death and resurrection after three days and nights is not an unfamiliar one, and echoes of it can be seen in the legends of Christ, Osiris, and many others. But the story of Nana's descent is unique because it appears to be the first telling of this archetypal tale.

The role of the temple prostitute was a highly respected one deemed sacred, and many high-born ladies took the office. Sargon II's daughter was a temple prostitute, as was Assurbanipal's. In fact, most women were taken to the temple at the age of puberty to give their virginity as an offering to the gods. Julius Evola says in *The Metaphysics of Sex* that:

"These ritual or religious unions of man and woman were intended to renew or celebrate the

mystery of the Ternary, or union of the everlasting male with the everlasting female (sky with Earth), when should arise the central current of creation. The corresponding principles were embodied and activated, and their momentary physical union became an effective and evocative reproduction of divine union beyond time and space."

An interesting variation on this took place in Babylon, where once a year, a virgin would ascend by night to the very apex of the seven-tiered holy ziggurat. The high holy place was a bed chamber thought to be inhabited by God himself. The virgin spent the night there, presumably being deflowered by God the Father. Says Evola, "It was also believed that the priestess of Apollo at Patara passed the night on the 'holy bed' in union with the god."

Mircea Eliade, writing about the ritualistic orgies used to invoke the Divine Couple, said:

"The orgy corresponds generally to the holy marriage. The limitless genesiac frenzy on Earth must correspond to the union of the divine pair. The excesses play a very precise part in the arrangement of the sacred; they sunder the barriers between man and society, nature and the gods; they help in circulating the force, life, and seeds from one level to another and from one zone of reality into all the others."

Indeed, ceremonies such as this gave ancient man a chance to tangibly experience the *sacrum*, to invoke and manifest, within himself, the archetype of God by becoming, if only briefly (and symbolically), one-half of the Divine Couple.

Though the gods and goddesses of the ancient cultures we've examined may at first glance appear to have no connection to the later creeds of Judaism and Christianity, such is not the case. Even Judaism (a relative newcomer in the context of the theologies thus discussed) had its own Divine Couple in the persons of El and Asherah, who appear to be the Judaic equivalent of the older Babylonian Baal and Astarte. It is thought that the Jewish move towards monotheism was necessitated when the notion of the Divine Couple became lost, as polytheistic cultures interacted with the Jews, giving rise to an increasingly confusing proliferation of deities, both foreign and domestic. The emerging Jewish nation needed to be united into a single will if it was to survive. And in order to accomplish this task, the polytheistic miasma of gods and goddesses, of belief and counter-belief, had to be transcended. Thus began the emergence of patriarchal monotheism, with its harsh father figure, Jehovah. El and Asherah were vanquished, and in time, Asherah was even turned into a *male* demon, Astaroth.

Despite all of this, even in the context of patriarchal monotheism, rabbinic tradition records that *even Jehovah* once had a consort named Lilith. This goddess figures prominently in rabbinic lore, and is said to have left the side of God to come to Earth as Adam's first wife. She bore Adam his first son Cain, but being of a haughty and rebellious nature, she refused to submit to Adam's rule, eventually leaving him. Some traditions record that she went off to live at the bottom of the Red Sea with Asmodeus, the demon who plays so prominent a role in the mystery of Rennes-le-Chateau.

Be it Ia and Inana, Isis and Osiris, Odin and Freya, Zeus and Hera, Kronos and Rhea, Ouranos and Gaia, Baal and Astarte, or El and Asherah, the names may vary, but virtually every culture has had a version of the Divine Couple. Before the formulation of the notions of good versus evil, or God versus the Devil, man understood duality in terms of male and female, Sun and Moon, fire and water; and the Divine Couple represented an equilibrium between these opposing forces; a *marriage*, if you will, between the two. Ancient man seems to have had a far better understanding of the schematic upon which the universe operates than does his modern counterpart. At the most elemental level, most of the so-called "secret doctrines" seem to preserve this understanding.

The Divine Couple was not a duad of man and woman, but a triad. The third element was the *equilibrium* between the eternal male principle and the eternal female principle. And from the resultant harmony of the Ternary, we arrive at One. This seems to represent an idea central to the ancient understanding of the sacred, and can be glimpsed in its purest, most elemental form in a tradition undoubtedly of far greater antiquity still:

the worship of the primordial hermaphrodite, and the ritualized practice of sacred sex.

Endnotes:

[1] Note that the words "mother" and "matter" are etymologically derived from the Latin "mater."

[2] This ancient association of prostitution with Venus is the foundation of the now disused term "venereal disease."

Giants on the Earth

By Boyd Rice

Since the offspring of the Nephilim were said to be giants, and because virtually every tradition relating to the Flood and the subsequent arrival of the tutelary gods also has to do with giants, I have spent several years making note of giant lore, both mythological and purportedly historical. I've even taken to the road in an attempt to verify reported discoveries of gigantic skeletons in parts of the United States and UK (without luck, unfortunately). Though such discoveries were widely reported in the mainstream press at the times in which they were made, whatever became of the skeletons remains a mystery. Some maintain that the orthodoxy of the scientific/archeological community has created a conspiracy of silence around such anomalous finds because they can't be adequately explained, and thus constitute some sort of threat to the prevailing paradigm. Of course, such finds can only be viewed as *anomalies* if taken singly. *Many* such discoveries would constitute the emergence of a pattern - a pattern possibly indicative of the need to rethink the prevailing wisdom.

Fortunately, the ancients charged with the transmission of their people's history, myth, and folklore felt no need to alter it for public consumption. They simply retold the stories that had been passed down to them by their ancestors. And here too, a pattern emerges, because the creation myths central to so many ancient cultures contain nearly identical themes concerning a race of giants. Often the giants were father gods, tutelary deities, or mythic kings. Often there was a *race* of giants, frequently said to be the offspring of intermarriage between gods and mortals. Repeatedly, such figures are connected with the legend of a global deluge. What follows is a brief overview of some figures or groups central to giant lore:

The Nephilim: These were the Sons of God who in *Genesis* interbred with humans, creating a race of giants. They were called "The Watchers" in *The Book of Enoch*.

The Cainites: This was a race of giants descended from Cain who lived in an underworld kingdom called "Arka." Note that the well-known statement in *Genesis* that "in those days, and after that, there were giants on the earth" is in fact not what the original text stated. What it really said was "giants *in* the earth." [1]

The Anakim: This was another name for the Watchers. It means "the descendants of Anak", or Enoch, Cain's son. Though it was said that a flood had been sent to destroy them, there were still entire cities of Anakim in Canaan as late as the time of Moses. And Jewish chronicler Josephus states that even in his own day it was not uncommon for people to dig up gigantic skeletal remains. Spies sent by Moses to scout Anakim strongholds reported back that the Anakim were so large that the Hebrews seemed "like grasshoppers" in comparison.

The Tritons: This was a race of giant gods, spawned by the interbreeding of Poseidon with a mortal woman named Cleito. In some versions of the story they are part-fish. Some are said to have escaped the flood that destroyed Atlantis.

The Titans: These were a Greek race of giants born to Ouranos and Gaia. It is undoubtedly a later retelling of the Triton saga.

Atlas: He was the King of Atlantis, and a Triton/giant. He was so large and so strong that he was often represented holding the Earth upon his shoulders.

Quetzalcoatl: This was the giant white god who appeared to native South Americans and founded their civilizations, according to their folktales. He too is depicted supporting the Earth on his shoulders, and he told the natives that the civilization from which he originated was destroyed by a flood which he escaped by building a ship.

Hercules: He is also a giant, and is said to have

Et in Arcadia Ego by Guercino.

piloted an ark.

Cuculainn: He is called the Irish Hercules, and came to Ireland in a ship when his homeland was destroyed by a flood. Interestingly, he seems to equate with the South American white god Kukulcan, a figure of "very tall stature" who arrived on a boat telling much the same story.

Votan: This is yet another tall white tutelary deity of South America. Once again we see the strange circumstance that his name sounds exactly like that of the Northern European god Wotan, a deity worshipped in an altogether different hemisphere.

The Ari: These were a race of Sumerian deified kings. "Ari" is a royal title meaning "the Shining Ones." They were obviously the prototypes of *The Book of Enoch*'s Watchers. Numerous Sumerian seals depict them as men of gigantic stature. They are often taller than members of their courts, even when depicted seated on thrones. In the numerous seals that show them standing, they tower above those standing next to them.

The Tuatha de Danaan: This was a race of Celtic giants and father gods. Like the Cainites and other giants, they were said to dwell in underground kingdoms or inside hollow mountains. One of the chief deities was Lugus, a name that translates to "shining one", revealing an astonishing connection to Sumer's deified giant kings.

The Ellu: This was a race of Mesopotamian kings said to be descendants of the gods. Yet again, "Ellu" is a royal court title which translates to "the Shining Ones." It is thought that "Ellu" was the basis of the word "Elohim", a term translated generally as "the sons of God." [2] The Elohim are considered by some to be synonymous with the Nephilim of *Genesis*.

Albion: He was one of the Titan giants fathered by Poseidon. He came to England after the Flood and was for many years the island's principle god. In those times England was actually called "Albion", after their Titan god/king. In fact, many British places place-names retain the words "Albion" or "Albany" to this very day.

Iberius: A Titan and brother of Albion, he went to Spain after the Flood. And likewise, Spain was for centuries named "Iberia" in his honor.

King Arthur: There is some Arthurian lore which claims that he piloted an ark during the Deluge, and this legend also relates that he stood just over nine feet tall. King Henry II, inspired by stories that Arthur was buried at Glastonbury, dispatched a team there to excavate the area. At a depth of nine feet they found a lead cross inscribed with the words: "Here lies the body of King Arthur." Sixteen feet below that was a stone sarcophagus containing the bones of a man *nine feet tall*. Skeptics put forth the argument that the lead cross could have been forged by local abbots wishing to draw attention (and donations) to their abbey. Such an argument, however, fails to address the fact that the nine-foot skeleton discovered beneath the cross would tend to negate the notion that this could have been a mere hoax. Later, in the early 1500s, another gigantic coffin was disinterred, and found to contain a skeleton eight feet and three inches tall. History fails to record what became of these later bones, although those of Arthur were respectfully re-interred.

The Cyclopses: The Cyclopeses were one-eyed giants in Greek mythology. It was said that they built the city of Mycenae in Greece out of massive blocks weighing many tons each. This is why similar constructions found at Baalbek, Lake Titicaca and elsewhere are referred to as having "cyclopean" architecture.

The Cabiri: This was a race of giant blacksmith gods said to live in hollowed-out volcanoes. They had tattoos on their foreheads of a large solar disc, leading to speculation that the myth of the one-eyed Cyclopeses may have originated with them.

The Cimbri: These were giants living in Celtic Gaul. They had long manes of blond hair and a fierce, warlike demeanor, all of which lead them to be compared to lions. They were also known as the "Cimmerians", which may be suggestive of a Sumerian connection.

It was difficult in writing the foregoing descriptions not to make them all sound incredibly redundant. But in order to state the basic facts in their simplest form, redundancy was a necessity, because all of these legends involve essentially the same story told over and over again. In some instances, not only were the stories identical, but so too were the names of the protagonists, such as Kukulcan/Cuculainn, and Votan/Wotan. It is astounding enough that we should see identical myths in places as widely removed from one another as South America and the British Isles, but that the names of the respective flood heroes so echo one another is utterly remarkable. It would seem an altogether reasonable conclusion to draw from such evidence that perhaps these myths might have some basis in truth. Perhaps the figures were indeed real men, and perhaps those men were giants.

But if a real race of giants once inhabited the Earth, why haven't people in recent centuries been digging up gigantic skeletons? According to author Stephen Quayle, *they have*. Quayle recently published *Genesis 6 Giants*, the result of over thirty years of research into Grail lore. The book is replete with biblical and extra-biblical accounts of giants, mythological accounts of giants, profiles on famous giants in history, and countless reports of people across the globe digging up the remains of giants. What follows are a few accounts of such excavations:

Item: In 1891, at Crittenden, Arizona, some workers digging the foundation of a new building at a depth of eight feet struck a huge stone sarcophagus. When they were able to open the lid, inside were the remains of a nine-foot tall giant which time had reduced mostly to a pile of dust.

Item: While searching in a cave near the great canyon of Barranc de Cobre in northern Mexico in the early 1930s, explorer Paxton Hayes came across 34 mummified men and women. All had blond hair. All rose to heights between seven and eight feet.

Item: In 1833, soldiers digging a pit at Lompock Rancho, California unearthed a twelve-foot tall giant with double rows of teeth, both on top and on the bottom. The Lompock giant's teeth, while unusual, were not unique. Another ancient skeleton later found on Santa Rosa island off the coast of California showed the same dental peculiarity.

Item: In 1879, some Indiana archeologists dug into an ancient burial mound in Brewersville, Indiana and unearthed a human skeleton that measured nine feet and eight inches in length. The bones, which were stored in a grain mill, were swept away in the 1937 Flood.

Item: In the 1880s, while digging in a mound at Sayre in Bradford County, Pennsylvania, a reputable group of antiquarians found skeletons of humans measuring not only above seven feet tall, but having *skulls with horns* (located about two inches above the eyebrows.) The diggers, including two professors and a Pennsylvania state historian, turned what they found over to the American Investigating Museum in Philadelphia, but the bones were afterwards either misplaced, stolen, or lost.

Item: In 1903, on an archeological outing at Fish Creek, Montana, Professor S. Farr and his group of Princeton University students came across several burial mounds. Choosing one to dig into, they unearthed the skeleton of a man about nine feet tall. Next to him were the bones of a woman who had been almost as tall.

Item: *Nature*, in its December 17, 1891 issue, reported that at a depth of fourteen feet into a large Ohio burial mound, excavators found the skeleton of a massive man in copper armor. He wore a copper cap, while copper moldings encased his jaws. Copper armor also protected his arms, chest and stomach. At his side lay the skeleton of a woman, probably his wife.

Item: In the 1860s, some excavators digging up a hill in Marion, Ohio uncovered thirty skeletons who ranged in height from seven to eight feet.

Item: In the early years of the twentieth century, a team clearing out bat guano from a cavern near Lovelock, Nevada discovered several giant cadavers measuring well over eight feet in height. Their hair, still intact, was said to have been long and "reddish" in color.

The foregoing accounts, taken almost in their entirety from Quayle's *Genesis 6 Giants*, have been culled from a wide variety of sources, and represent only a small sample of those documented. They are largely reports from the United States, but reveal striking similarities to kindred finds in Europe, South America, the British Isles, Africa, China, the Middle and Near-East, Australia, and New Zealand - that is to say, virtually every corner of the earth.

Though the tales vary in detail, the fundamentals of the stories are often quite cohesive: giants corpses, frequently with light-colored hair, generally buried at a depth of between nine and twelve feet, and often interred with artifacts made of copper. Some accounts report the presence of items bearing strange hieroglyphs or symbols. That several of these finds were excavated from burial mounds seems to lend credence to the stories told to early settlers by Native Americans, i.e., that they didn't know who built the mounds, because they were already there at the time that the "natives" arrived. A number of Native American tribes (such as those in Colorado) have folk tales relating that a race of giants lived in America at a time prior to when their ancestors came there. Still others tell the story that a group of giant white gods came to live among them, after their own homeland (called the "White Man's Island") was destroyed by a flood.

It is almost a certainty that some Native American tribes not only coexisted with the giants, but also interbred with them, because the earliest explorers to the New World repeatedly documented coming into contact with Indian tribes of gigantic stature. Such episodes are noted in the chronicles of Amerigo Vespucci, Magellan, Coronado, De Soto, and Sir Francis Drake, both in North and South America. Though the numerous accounts cited earlier are compelling, and are certainly supported by the eyewitness accounts of some of the world's most esteemed and illustrious explorers, the sad fact remains that the most persistent commonality between all of these tales seems to be that the bones - the physical evidence - have all somehow *gone missing*. In some instances, this can be explained by the fact that local authorities, presuming the remains to be the property of indigenous peoples (Native Americans, Aborigines, Maoris, etc.), simply turned them over to tribal chieftains for reburial, and this without taking a single photograph, X-Ray, or DNA sample for testing (so as not to *profane* the relics).

Of course, the lion's share of these discoveries were made in the 1800s, and many far earlier, at a time in which the rights of indigenous peoples and regard for their religious institutions constituted a matter of far less circumspection than in recent years. If, as Stephen Quayle seems convinced, there is a concerted conspiracy of silence surrounding this archeological evidence, then it is a conspiracy of, well, *gigantic* proportions. The accounts of these giant remains are too numerous and too far-flung for all of them to have been lost, stolen, or secreted away. And yet, I truly believe the accounts. They are supported not only by an overwhelming body of evidence found in mythology, but an equally overwhelming body of archeological evidence. Witness the ruins of the many cyclopean cities referred to earlier. No one knows with any certainty either who built them, or (more importantly) *how* they were built. Witness the vast complexes of tunnels and underground cities associated with the fallen angels, and recall that many of their myths include the detail that they dwelt in *underground kingdoms*. Again, no one knows who built these cities or how they were built. But an interesting fact to keep in mind is that the tunnels associated with them were generally nine, ten, or even twelve feet in ceiling height (the same average heights as those of the giant skeletons found). Such tunnels can be found in South America, the Middle East, and even the Pacific Northwest of the United States. They are reputed to exist still undiscovered in Europe, Egypt, and the British Isles.

Regular readers of this magazine will already be aware of what a pivotal role the story of the Watchers plays in regards to our own research into the Grail mythos and the bloodline connected to it. So many avenues of inquiry central to our own basic thesis seem to have a direct relationship to the Giant lore connected with the Watchers. The kings of Atlantis? Giants. The Shining Ones? Giants. King Arthur, a figure central to the Grail lore? Also a giant.

One of the first well-known paintings on the theme of Arcadia, *Et in Arcadia Ego* by Guercino, depicts a fairly straightforward and seemingly insignificant scene of a man gazing upon an apparently trepanned skull. When I looked at it, there seemed to be no hidden symbolism discernable. Until, that is, I noticed what appeared to be an odd disparity in proportion. The skull, for as close as it was relative to the onlooker, seemed far larger than it should have been. Since the painter's execution of this painting seemed masterly in every other respect, I concluded that perhaps his intent was to portray an *oversized skull*. Perhaps it represented the skeletal head of one of the primordial patriarchs of the Grail bloodline. If, as has been said, the grave of an ancient sacred king were somehow at Rennes-le-Chateau, perhaps those discovering it would open the tomb of a giant, a descendant of the Nephilim.

As time passed, and our research progressed, this initially abstract idea seemed increasingly possible. After reading ancient apocryphal texts which indicated that a number of biblical patriarchs were giants, it seemed altogether probable. Ultimately, reading about Abraham's burial in the Cave of Treasures, I came to suspect that something far more profound might lie in wait at Rennes-le-Chateau. Abraham was an astrologer and magician who was said to have "traced his ancestry back to the Giants." Upon his death, his body was carried to the Cave of Treasures, an underground necropolis where the bodies of all previous patriarchs were also interred, down to and including Adam and Eve.

In addition, the Cave included treasures, relics, and a sacred archive of his progenitors. While treasures and relics are of interest to archeologists and museum-going looky-loos, and sacred archives can be dismissed by academics as mere superstitious hyperbole, such items found in the context of a necropolis of gigantic skeletons might well constitute the basis for a rethinking of world history. These people constituted a living remnant of the antediluvian world, the mythological "First Time." And since myth and history record that their final resting place was *together*, in a single location, I can only assume that they are still there.

Endnotes:

[1] Editor's note: The latter quote is in fact what can be found in the King James version of the Bible.

[2] Editor's note: According to Plato, the race descended from these two figures were the kings of Atlantis, but he does not connect them to the Tritons.

Chaldean Genesis: The Secret Legacy of the Architect-Priests

By Boyd Rice

The genealogy of the Merovingian bloodline has for centuries been shrouded in mystery, and yet, we've been able to definitively trace it back to the "Shepherd Kings" of ancient Sumer. Subsequently, we've managed to fine-tune the focus of our investigation further still, and many indications (both ancient and modern) seem to suggest that the role played by Chaldea was of pivotal importance. For instance, in *The Book of Genesis*, we are told that the biblical patriarch Abraham was "a Chaldean from Ur." For most readers, this seemingly insignificant factoid would undoubtedly slip by unnoticed, but to the student of ancient cultures, it is pregnant with portent, because Chaldea was known to be a Mecca of astronomy, astrology, and the black arts. So much so, in fact, that the word "Chaldean" in many ancient cultures was synonymous with "sorcerer." Even so far away as Northern Europe, their term for sorcerer, "galdyr", was rooted in "Chaldee." The authors of *Genesis* obviously did their utmost to distance the figure of Abraham from the occult traditions of Chaldea, yet Abraham still appears to be an occultist both in biblical and extra-biblical texts:

"Abraham excelled all in nobility and wisdom; he sought and obtained the knowledge of astrology and the Chaldean craft... he traveled to Phoenicia and dwelt there. He pleased the Phoenician king by teaching the Phoenicians the cycles of the Sun and Moon, and everything else as well... [in Egypt] Abraham lived in Heliopolis with the Egyptian priests and taught them much: He explained astrology and the other sciences to them."
- Pseudo Eupolemus.

"Abraham... came to Egypt with all his household to the Egyptian king Pharothothes and taught him astrology."
- Artapanus.

"...before the coming of Abraham, the Egyptians were ignorant of these sciences, which thus traveled from the Chaldeans into Egypt, [and then] passed to the Greeks."
- Josephus, *Antiquities of the Jews*.

Note that Abraham is traveling far and wide *not* to preach the gospel of the "one true God", but rather to spread the wisdom of the Chaldean craft. These Chaldean sciences seem to echo the teachings of the Watchers, and pertained to geometry, astronomy, and the movements of the planets and stars. Compare the lore of the Watchers to what Philo records about the Chaldeans:

"The Chaldeans exercised themselves most especially with astronomy, and attributed all things to the movement of the stars, believing that whatever is in the world is governed by forces encompassed in numbers and numerical proportions... seeking out the numerical arrangement according to the cycles of the Sun and Moon, the planets, and the fixed stars... ."
- Philo, on Abraham.

The parallels between the Watchers and the Chaldeans become greater still when viewed in the light of a tradition cited by Eusebius, which said: "Abraham traced his ancestry to the giants. These dwelt in the land of Babylonia. Because of their impiety, they were destroyed by the gods." So there you have it. These two traditions (of the

Watchers and of the Chaldeans) sound so identical because they *are* identical - one and the same. Were the Chaldeans the descendants of the Watchers, and executors of their tradition? Such an idea is certainly reinforced by the fact that the Hebrew word for "Watcher" is "Ir", which sounds the same as "Ur." And the Watchers were called "the watchers *of the heavens*", a very appropriate title for a people (like the Chaldeans) so preoccupied by astronomy. Could it be that Ur was the primordial city-state of the Watchers? Very possibly. Ur is considered so ancient that to the modern mind it has become synonymous with antiquity itself. All of this would appear to suggest that Abraham's status as a Chaldean from Ur may well be one of the most telling anomalies in the Old Testament. It also seems that Abraham is far more than merely a man who "traced his ancestry to the giants." Remember, it was said that "Abraham excelled all in *nobility* and wisdom." In ancient times "nobility" didn't refer to a man's demeanor - it meant *of noble birth*. And as we will ultimately reveal, the figure known as Abraham was of very noble birth indeed.

For the time being however, we will continue our study of the Chaldean saga by looking into the story of King Gudia. Though one of the most illustrious of the Sumerian/Chaldean monarchs, Gudia remains a relatively obscure personage in terms of mainstream history. Gudia was both priest-king and architect, a builder of great cities and temples, not unlike Cain/Nimrod. And it just so happens that Nimrod was Gudia's patron saint, as well as having been his ancestor. Gudia was like many of the Old Testament prophets, in that he was prone to dreams and vision. In one such dream, Nimrod himself appeared to the king, revealing to him the blueprints of a temple he wished to be erected in his honor. Upon waking, Gudia lost no time setting in motion plans to construct the Temple of Nimrod, a structure that would eventually be seen as one of the most significant edifices of its day.

In a well-known statue of Gudia, the base is emblazoned with the floor plan of this temple. Other statues frequently depict him with Masonic architectural tools, such as squares, rulers, and so forth. As mentioned in previous articles, the first priests were also the first architects. Their secret gnosis encompassed not only the sacred, but the functional as well. And they encoded their sacerdotal wisdom (sacred geometry, astronomy, etc.) into the structures they built, so that their shape, placement, and dimensions were all a reflection of divine principles. This is a pivotal concept, and constitutes a tradition central to our own ongoing investigation. There are those who assert that Christ was not a carpenter at all, and that the word translated as "carpenter" should have actually been translated as "architect." Looking further back in the past, we note that the Babylonian/Phoenician god Marduk is often depicted bearing a trowel. Though commentators have speculated that this may be an agricultural tool (as Marduk was thought to have taught man the science of agriculture), it is far more likely to be an architectural tool. And indeed it looks identical to the trowel which appears in so much Freemasonic ritual and symbolism. From all appearances, this would seem to constitute the tradition from which the Knights Templar and the Freemasons derived their creeds.

At any rate, the reign of Gudia witnessed a flourishing of culture and civilization in his region. He wandered the full length and breadth of Mesopotamia (and often beyond) to amass lumber, blocks, and precious metals for his many projects. He not only built new cities and temple, but rebuilt old ones. Ruling from his capitols of Lagash and Ur, he preferred not to be seen as a king, but rather as a priest and prophet. He was known simply as the "Good Shepherd", and may in fact have refused the title of "king" (although his name does appear in the *King's List*).

Of all the many kings that reigned over Chaldea or Sumer, only a handful of their names are known outside of specialist circles, or from readings of the Old Testament. Those that come to mind are Sargon, Hammurabi, Assurbanipal, and a few others. Why, then (or *how*) could a man of Gudia's stature have simply vanished into the mists of history? A possible answer was suggested upon reading that in Gudia's time and culture there were no letters equivalent to "G" or "I." Substituting the closest equivalent to those letters results in something both startling and altogether unexpected: *Judea*. [1]

Could it be possible that Judah, the son of

Jacob from whom Jews derive their name, could in fact have been a Chaldean priest-king? Are Gudia and Judah one and the same? Turning to the Old Testament in search of information that would either corroborate or disprove altogether such a bizarre thesis revealed passages so scant and so strange as to be of no help whatsoever in either regard. Further searches in Josephus' *Antiquities* and Louis Ginzberg's *Legends of the Jews* proved equally fruitless. How could a man from whom an entire tribe of Israel adopted their name (the Jews) be so little documented in three such major works documenting Jewish history and folklore? It was both perplexing and mysterious, like trying to conceive of a New Testament that featured only a half-dozen off-handed references to Christ. It defied all logic. And it seemed that logic was the only means left to pierce this apparent conspiracy of silence.

So it was that the ancient king lists were consulted again, the reasoning being that the lists were so full of names that corresponded to biblical patriarchs that if Gudia and Judah were the same figure, perhaps other names in close proximity on the lists might have a familiar ring. Four lines above Gudia on the list was a king named "Irarum." Though not precisely identical to "Abraham", it was the only name on the list with so familiar an euphonic ring to it. Remember that these names were not only spelled and pronounced differently from culture to culture, but also often in the same culture. Irarum had a son named "Dar", who also went by the title "Asahk" (literally, "son of God"). It was not uncommon for royal titles to proclaim the king's divinity, or his status as the reincarnation of a popular king or god. Asahk's son was "Khab" (or "Khabulum"), and his son in turn took the royal title "Akhab" ("son of Khab"). He in turn fathered Gudia. So if we take into account the sound of these names in their respective order, we arrive at something quite extraordinary:

Irarum = Abraham
Asahk = Issac
Akhab = Jacob
Gudia = Judah

So with one notable exception (the extra figure of Khab or Khabulum), we find in the Sumerian/Chaldean king lists an almost perfect reflection of the Old Testament line of patriarchs.

At this point it is virtually impossible to ascertain what any of this really *means*. Were the Chaldeans all Jews? Were the people who *called* themselves Jews really Chaldeans? Were both merely different nations or tribes of an essentially Sumerian populace? Could it be that the so-called "Shepherdic Jews" were not so named because they had been shepherds, but because they could claim descent from a priest-king known as the "Good Shepherd"? [2] Remember that this was the title used to refer to Christ, who acted in the capacity of a priest-king without a throne. Christ, too, is said in some early traditions to have been a Chaldean, an idea we will explore in due course.

The Chaldean tradition, and its secret gnosis, is intimately linked with astronomy, astrology, geometry, architecture, *and magic*; all topics central to our ongoing inquiries. But there's more. It was said that Gudia practiced the "Chaldean rite" of bull sacrifice - a practice that passed from Chaldea to Egypt, and eventually many parts of the ancient world. Significantly, this rite is said to have originated in Atlantis, and Gudia, like the Atlantean kings, kept the sacrificial bulls in his own palace. Furthermore, when Gudia's ancestor appeared to him in a vision and gave him specifications for the construction of a magnificent temple, the building thus erected was a seven-stepped ziggurat. Historians believe that Gudia's Temple of Nimrod represented the *very first ziggurat ever built*. But mythology tells us that an identical structure one existed as the royal palace of Atlantis.

By reviving Atlantean architecture and religious ritual, Gudia seemed to be trying to build a bridge between the past and the present, or to reconstitute the past *in* the present. His chosen title, "Gudia" ("Lord/King Ia/Ea") harkens back to Sumer's first deified king. And to emphasize the point, he named his son "Nimrod", an alternate title of Cain, the king's firstborn son. Gudia's son went on to become known as the "Lord of the Four Regions", a title synonymous with "King of the World", and his daughter married the King of Ur. Within two centuries of his death, Babylonians worshipped him as the "Divine Gudia", and put statues of him in their temples. The reign of Gudia is reckoned by some scholars to have been around 2400 BC. By the time Judaism began to coalesce some 900 years later, Gudia and his illustrious forebears would have become mythic figures in an oral tradition. Though there is little proof beyond what we've presented to link the figures of Gudia and Judah, there are references to Judah being a ruling king in rabbinic lore, including descriptions of a crown, royal scepter, and royal signet ring. And although orthodox Judaism seems to have rejected most of what constitutes the Chaldean tradition, there are indications that these ideas were preserved on a sub rosa level, to reemerge later in a most unexpected context.

Christ the Chaldean

And did those feet in ancient time
Walk upon England's mountain green?
And was the Holy Lamb of God
On England's pleasant pastures seen?
- William Blake

As these lines from William Blake's eighteenth century poem *Jerusalem* reveal, the tradition that Christ came to England is one that is both widespread and long-standing. Indeed, Roman chroniclers began referring to it as early as the reign of Tiberius Caesar, who died in 37 A.D. (only four short years after the presumed date of Christ's own death.) It was in Glastonbury, Cornwall, that the first Christian church was built, purportedly by Christ himself.

For those unfamiliar with the story, it is well-documented that Christ's uncle, Joseph of Arimathea made frequent trips to England in the course of his travels as a tin merchant. As the story goes, Jesus often accompanied his uncle on these journeys, and ended up spending a good deal of time in Cornwall during his well-known "lost years." It was here that he conducted the early years of his ministry, and legend records that he constructed a rather large house for the habitation of his mother, Mary. It was this house which, pursuant to the crucifixion, became recognized as the first Christian church in the world. And this *first Christian church* was known by a number of names, such as "the wattle church", "the old church", and perhaps most significantly, "the *Culdee* church." In other words, the Chaldean church.

In Thomas Campbell's *Reullura*, we read:

The pure Culdees
Were Alby's earliest priests of God [3]
Ere yet an island of her seas
By foot of Saxon monk was trod.

In E. Raymond Capt's marvelous book *The Traditions of Glastonbury*, he states: "The first converts of the Culdees... were the Druids of Britain, who found no difficulty in reconciling the teaching of the Culdees with their own teaching of the resurrection and the inheritance of eternal life." In addition, the Druids had long believed in the coming of a messiah - a messiah names *Jesu*. They also shared the Chaldean preoccupation with sacred geometry and astronomy. And too, they had the odd habit of referring to God as "the ancient of days." Clearly these two groups' traditions had a shared origin of some sort. Capt continues:

"Culdees are recorded in church documents as officiating at St. Peter, York, until A.D. 939. According to some church authorities, the Canons of York were called 'Culdees' as late as the reign of Henry II (A.D. 1133-1189). In Ireland, a whole county was named 'Culdee.' The names 'Culdee' and 'Culdish' cling tenaciously to the Scottish church and its prelates until a much later date."

The Culdee phenomenon appears to be little known, little discussed, and even less understood. Nonetheless, over the centuries a fascinating number of theories and legends have become attached to them: theories and legends that are all the more fascinating in that they seem to overlap with much of our own research. What follows are some of the fundamental assumptions held about the Culdees, as collected and preserved by Arthur Edward Waite in his *New Encyclopedia of Freemasonry*:

• The Culdees were identical with the Chaldeans mentioned by the prophet Daniel.
• They were priests in Assyria and can also be

traced to Babylon.
- They were Casideans, Essenes, Therapeutae, and Magi.
- Beneath their cloak of Christianity they concealed a secret doctrine.
- They were mathematicians and architects at the time of the early Roman emperors.
- They were the builders of King Solomon's Temple.
- The Culdees of York were all Masons.
- They denied the personality of Jesus - meaning the historical personality - and also the existence of the Devil.
- The Culdee monks were the schoolmasters and architects of their time.
- It was thought that the historical allegory of the Round Table, as well as the quest for the Holy Grail, referred in mystical terms to Culdee rites.

If the foregoing statements are indeed accurate, it would appear that there was the presence of a Templar-like fraternity in England for a full *thousand years* before the advent of the Knights Templar, and not just in England, but throughout the British Isles. The Culdees had commandaries, schools and churches in Wales, Ireland and Scotland as well. It is said that despite pressure from Rome, the Culdees remained a very strong presence right up to the time of the Norman conquest, which began in 1066. [4] The timeframe here seems highly significant, as 1066 is only a few decades before the founding of the Order of Sion by Godfroi de Bouillon in 1090; which in turn is only a few decades before the foundation of the Knights Templar.

Is it purely coincidental that an organization whose history spans over a thousand years should essentially vanish, and in a matter of mere decade a group whose outlook seems nearly identical should emerge in another part of the world? As you'll recall, most of what the historians assert about the Culdees is incredibly similar to what was said of the Templars. Let's compare: both groups were said to possess a secret doctrine which they concealed behind the facade of Christianity. Both groups denied Christ. Both groups were architects. And both groups were associated with the Holy Grail, as well as with Solomon's Temple.

There definitely seems to be a continuity of belief, purpose and action between the two groups. Certainly the mystery surrounding both groups appears to be the same mystery. But if these two groups represent different manifestations of the same esoteric tradition, it is not simply a tradition whose origin came about after the crucifixion of Christ. The tradition of the architect-priest can clearly be traced to the Chaldean King Gudia, and further still to his role model and patron saint, Nimrod/Cain. As previously stated, Nimrod was legendary as a great king and as a great builder of cities. Remarkably, there are traditions within certain rites of British Freemasonry which claim that Nimrod was in fact the *first Master Mason*. So the notion of the architect-priest goes back to the dawn of recorded history, and to a time in which knowledge of the divine and knowledge of the practical were both different aspects of a very far-reaching Gnosis - at least for the elect.

Endnotes:

[1] Editor's note: Indeed, there were no vowels at all in most ancient alphabets.

[2] Editor's note: Actually, this word is spelled "Sephardic", and refers to Jews of Spanish or Portuguese ancestry. It stems from the fact that the region now known as "Spain" was referred to in the Bible as "Sepharadh."

[3] England was then called "Albion."

[4] In other locations, such as Ireland, their influence remained strong well into the fourteenth century.

The Daughter of God: The Real Story of Joan of Arc

By Boyd Rice

At the church of Mary Magdalene at Rennes-le-Chateau, France, there is a curiously neglected statue. It is obviously the work of the same Marseilles craftsman who created all of the works which dominate the church's interior, yet it is essentially abandoned. It is stored on a patio outside the Villa Bethania, exposed to the elements. Paint cracks and peels from it, and tourists have seemingly chipped off bits of it as souvenirs. It is a statue of that intrinsically *French* saint, Joan of Arc.

When we visited the church, the tour guide could not satisfactorily explain to us why this particular statue has been exiled to this seemingly insignificant location. Neither did she know if it was ever originally within the church, or indeed anything whatsoever of its original whereabouts. This statue is a genuine anomaly. It is a piece of history relegated to insignificance in a place where virtually everything is perceived to be pregnant with potential significance. How did this statue, which, even in its present state of decay, retains the essence of its original beauty and elegance, come to attain such a poor status in relation to the other objects within the church? It is very curious.

Another question might be: "What relationship can be shown to exist between Saint Joan and what is known of the Rennes-le-Chateau mystery?" In fact, there are quite a few connections, but to explore them in any meaningful manner entails a reevaluation of Joan of Arc and her legacy. The standard notion that she was a young girl who heard voices (and may have been crazy) seems very inadequate. Even the most superficial inquiries into the life of Joan of Arc indicate that her real story has never been revealed. Her relationship with the prominent Angevin Grail dynasty suggests that there is much more than meets the eye.

For ages before the appearance of Joan of Arc on history's timeline, there was a popular tale in French folklore that in the nation's darkest hour, "the Maiden of Orleans" would appear, unite its citizens and vanquish its foes. So popular was the legend that certain leaders attempted to manufacture such "maidens" to serve their own ends. Invariably, a skeptical public saw through such ploys, and all of these attempts came to naught. Until Joan came along.

Most tellings of the story of Joan of Arc don't begin to reveal the full extent of how she was perceived in France in her day. She was thought to be the "daughter of God", a sort of feminine French Christ sent to Earth by the primordial patriarch to save the monarchy of France. Pretty wild stuff, but not at all inconsistent with what you would expect of an Angevin/Merovingian conspiracy. Rene d'Anjou's ancestors were masters at manipulating archetypes and reviving old myths with new emanations. Also, both Rene and Joan were so close that many presumed them to be lovers.

In more recent times, an ancestor of Rene d'Anjou was said to have been married to a woman named Melusine who was half-serpent, half-human. This is an obvious recapitulation of the cabalistic tradition which states that Cain's mother Lilith was also a mix of serpent and human. Rene's distant ancestor Jesus Christ seems to have had a very conscious strategy to fulfill messianic prophecy, detail by detail. A prophecy existed promising a Messiah, and a man appeared who embodied that prophecy, or certainly appeared to. He wasn't the first of his bloodline to recycle old myths and present himself as their embodiment, nor was he the last. Just as Christ had reconstituted the myth of Osiris, Joan of Arc has, in a way, reconstituted the myth of Christ. She was the "daughter of God", sent to save *her* people. Had all not gone awfully awry, she would have been worshipped as a living goddess. In fact, her martyrdom, which she wholeheartedly embraced, lead to essentially the same result. The real question in all of this seems to be: "To what extent was Joan consciously aware of the process in which she was involved?"

As an illiterate girl of age 19, she exhibited a cleverness above and beyond that of her learned prosecutors and judges. She was glib, enigmatic, and poetic whilst facing her accusers. They tried repeatedly to trick her and trap her, yet repeatedly she out-thought them. How does a simple peasant girl become a master of rhetoric, a victor in debates with scholars conversant in Hebrew, Latin, Greek, and Old English? Was she divinely inspired or simply well-tutored?

No one disagrees that Joan's tutor and mentor was Rene d'Anjou's mother Iolande. As asserted in *Holy Blood, Holy Grail*:

"It was Iolande who provided the feeble, weak-willed Dauphin with incessant transfusions of morale. It was Iolande who inexplicably appointed herself Joan's official patroness and sponsor. It was Iolande who overcame the court's resistance to the visionary girl and obtained authorization for her to accompany the army to Orleans. It was Iolande who convinced the Dauphin that Joan might indeed be the savior that she claimed to be."

Iolande de Bar was held in such high regard that the Dauphin immediately married her daughter. The influence of Iolande cannot be overestimated. Her impact on the politics of France (and in turn, Europe) is undeniable.

The most difficult aspect of the Joan of Arc story is trying to ascertain the degree to which she may have been a mere pawn of the Angevins, and the degree to which she was a conscious and willing co-conspirator. There are, of course, compelling arguments on either side. But for a dynastic family so obsessed with blood, does it seem likely that they would choose an obscure peasant to occupy a position with such potential politico-religious authority? Of course not. Joan of Arc must surely have been a natural Angevin (i.e., illegitimate). It is altogether possible that Joan was the bastard offspring of Rene's father, who was the Duke of Bar, where Rene was born. This would make Rene and Joan brother and sister. We needn't belabor the archetype of the divine couple as brother and sister. (Isis and Osiris are the most obvious example.) Could it be at all possible that, had not everything gone hopelessly awry, Joan and Rene might have married and become the focus of a new national cult in France? Ponder it for a second: Rene was a descendant of Lohengrin, Godfroi de Bouillon, and ultimately of Christ. Joan was perceived as the savior of France, sent directly by God. Such a couple would have been viewed as a modern Adam and Eve: a divine couple whose offspring would be divinely ordained to rule. The monarchical ideal would have been born anew.

But history is messy business, and things don't always go according to plans. In the France of Joan, Rene and Charles VII, Catholic and British influences were seen as being threatened, so the Brits and Rome garnered their cumulative forces to crush the threat. Joan of Arc was the symbolic "heart" of the French nation. France, used to the tradition of the French national goddess Marianne, as well as the Magdalene cult, saw Joan as an emanation of the French spirit, of their very race-soul. Therefore, she and her influence had to be brought to a halt and discredited. Otherwise Rome and Britain stood no chance. They would have been defeated by a young girl perceived to be the embodiment of an eternal ideal. Their only recourse was to demonize her and label her a heretic, or to entice her into their fold and convince her to recant, to deny her past proclamations. But Joan was a tough nut to crack. She told her inquisitors that even should they "separate [her] soul from her body", she would not recant. Her judges, learned and scholarly men all, felt impotent in the face of this bizarre young woman. So strong was her will, her belief, that she refused to give an inch.

The transcripts of her trial (never accurately reflected in modern films about Joan) reveal the true modus operandi of these court sessions. It is not a trial of a heretic - it is a trial in which one historical tradition is being brushed by another. It is, yet again, the bloodline of the Grail being suppressed by orthodoxy. It is France being subjugated by Britain and Rome. What one immediately notices in the testimony of Joan at her trial is how closely her responses seem to match those of the Templars and Cathars tried for heresy.

She is asked essentially the same types of questions, and her answers are at times so identical as to match *word for word*. When accused of having been sent by the Devil, Joan replied: "No, it was *you* who were sent by the Devil, to torture me." Interestingly, many years later, another woman related to the Angevins gave a very similar response in a trial related to the attempted overthrow of Louis XIV's monarchy. She was the Duchess de Bouillon, and when a magistrate inquired as to whether or not she had ever seen the Devil, she stared him in the face and replied: "I'm looking at him now."

A true window into Joan's history can be glimpsed in the remarkable Carl Dreger film, *The Passion of Joan of Arc*. This is a film that was thought to be forever lost, and then was "miraculously" rediscovered. All known copies of the movie had, like Joan herself, been "destroyed by fire." Then, in 1981, a negative of the film was discovered in (of all places) a Norwegian mental institution. The film is most well-known perhaps for its use of "Theatre of Cruelty" advocate Antonin Arteau, acting as a monk. But this is the film's least compelling offering, although Arteau gives a brilliant performance. The most compelling aspect of the film is that it documents the trial of Joan *word for word*, based on manuscripts still held at a library in Paris. As the film opens, it proclaims these manuscripts to be the "most important" documents in the history of the world.

Important, obviously, but "most" important? Is someone trying to convey the idea that the Joan of Arc drama represented a crossroads in history? One in which the True Faith was (yet again) suppressed by orthodoxy? It certainly seems likely.

One notices in the title sequence that certain members of Jean Cocteau's inner circle seem to be involved in some capacity, for we see the names of Jean Hugo and Valentine Hugo. Mr. Hugo was a close associate of Cocteau, and son of the Priory of Sion's former Grand Master, Victor Hugo, whose time in office preceded that of Cocteau himself. In fact, the whole film seems to emanate the Priory of Sion ethos. That Catholics are all fat, debauched, decadent, and have faces covered with ugly warts. Joan represents the French race-soul as it should be: pure and unyielding.

The upshot of the narrative is never that she was a heretic, but that she refused to submit to the authority of Rome, that one who experiences a direct connection with God has no need of the Church. This was also the message, essentially, of the German mystic Meister Eckhart, who proclaimed that God lives in and through all things; therefore, to experience communion with God required no church and no priesthood. Eckhart's fate, not surprisingly, was not much different than Joan's. He too was a mystic, a visionary, and a prophet far beyond his times. In consequence, he is remembered as a heretic and not a saint. Joan, in fact, received sainthood, as did other key Merovingian "heretics" such as King Dagobert II. The Church, recognizing the futility of opposing public opinion, attempted to incorporate all that they couldn't entirely expunge from public memory. This is by no means anything new.

The building of cathedrals on ancient pagan holy sites was an early example, as was the co-opting of ancient holidays. Right or wrong, the Church knows what it's doing, just as it knew that Joan of Arc was a viable threat. Here was the "Virgin of Orleans", a warrior and a reputed "daughter of God", a French Christ in feminine form. Given the proper circumstances, a figure of this magnitude might well have overshadowed the Church of Rome. She could have made France (and not Rome) the focal point of global religion, and indeed, the center of the world.

Was Joan a mere pawn of the Angevins, or a conscious co-conspirator? We opt for the latter, because Joan was always conscious of the bigger picture, and fanatical in her devotion to her ideals. She embraced her martyrdom, as Christ did his, understanding full well that she would exercise far more power living on as an *ideal* than she ever could in the course of her day-to-day life. She told her accusers that she would win a "great victory" over them. A monk, preparing her for death at the stake, inquired as to what had happened to the "great victory" her God had promised her. Where was it now? Unhesitatingly, she replied: "My martyrdom." And she was correct.

Vaincre:
The United States of Europe and the Merovingian Master Plan

By Tracy Twyman

Since the time of Clovis I, the Merovingian kings of France have been the rightful heirs to the senior crown of Europe - that of the Holy Roman Empire, although that right has not always been recognized. The title that Clovis and his descendants were originally given by the Pope when the covenant between the Vatican and the Merovingians first began in 496 A.D. was "New Constantine", giving him secular authority over the choicest bits of Christian Europe, just like the authority which the namesake of the office, Constantine, had once enjoyed. But Constantine had been the "thirteenth apostle", and was responsible for the incorporation of Christianity into the Roman institution. He was therefore also a priest-king, holding spiritual dominion as well as secular dominion, just as previous Roman emperors had done. But when the later Merovingian kings began to exhibit a desire to exercise their own spiritual authority, which rested partially upon the foundation of their blood relationship to Jesus Christ and King David (they were the descendants of both), it sparked a chain of events that culminated in the assassination of Dagobert II, the last effective Merovingian king, and the loss of the title "New Constantine" for his descendants. However, the Merovingians appear to have taken their right to the title, and their right to European hegemony, very seriously, in a manner that seems to be rooted in something more ancient than the time of Clovis. They believe, perhaps because of their descent from Christ and King David, or perhaps because of their descent from an even more illustrious ancestor, that they were already entitled to rule over Europe long before it was sanctioned by the Pope. This "Divine Right" was recognized by their loyal subjects as well, who regarded the Merovingians as semi-divine priest-kings, and who formed a cult worshipping Dagobert II after his death. With a following like that, the Merovingians were not about to give up their rightful inheritance without a fight.

Less than 200 years later, a man named Charlemagne (Charles the Great), who married a Merovingian princess, was made Holy Roman Emperor, and given dominion over a land mass greater even than that which the Merovingians had possessed. Thus began the majestic Carolingian dynasty, consisting after Charlemagne of men with partially Merovingian blood. Charlemagne too was considered a priest-king, and is probably the most famous and beloved figure in French history. For his scepter he carried with him the Spear of Destiny, that holy relic supposedly bloodied by the wound of Christ, which is said to confer upon its possessor transcendental power over the entire Earth. And while he may not have ruled over the entire world in actuality, he did have dominion over its most significant portion. For at that time Western Europe was without a doubt the foremost bastion of culture, science, philosophy, and morality, a light in the darkness, surrounded on all fronts by uncivilized barbarian hordes.

The Carolingian dynasty ended in 918, but the Holy Roman Empire continued to play a decisive role in the unfolding of its destiny. It was during this time that the Empire began to turn its sights towards the Holy Land. The first Crusade began in 1095, and the entire enterprise was brought about because of the pressure that certain Merovingian descendants placed upon the Pope and the nobility of Europe. This resulted in the capture of Jerusalem four years later, and the creation of the Latin Kingdom of Jerusalem as part of the Holy Roman Empire. The capture was lead by Godfroi de Bouillon, a descendant of Dagobert

II, and his brother, Baldwin I, was proclaimed King of Jerusalem. The Merovingian descendants appear to have considered the Holy Land their rightful possession, once again due to their direct descent from King David, and Jerusalem was in a way their coronation stone, legitimizing their eventual return to the rule of the Holy Roman Empire.

Illustration from *Vaincre*.

It was to this goal that they immediately dedicated themselves, and with the help of Baldwin II (son of Baldwin I, who died shortly after the capture of the Holy Land), a group of Knights was formed supposedly to help keep the roads to Jerusalem safe for pilgrims. Its core members were all from the Merovingian "Grail families", and they soon went about establishing their own sort of empire throughout Europe - one based upon the power of money. The Templars were legally beholden to none but the Pope, and even that they took lightly, so any land controlled by them was essentially an independent principality. They held possessions throughout the continent, and controlled major industries, especially that of banking. Soon, they had all the princes of Europe indebted to them. It took the Pope and the King of France colluding against them to get them disbanded, excommunicated, and in some cases burnt at the stake before the Templar menace was finally subdued.

Meanwhile, Merovingian descendants were busy reclaiming the throne of the Holy Roman Empire via another avenue. In 1273, Count Rudolf of the Merovingian-entwined Habsburg dynasty (later Habsburg-Lorraine) was elected Holy Roman Emperor, and the title stayed within the family until the Empire itself collapsed in 1806. Interestingly, the Empire was ended by Napoleon, himself husband of a Merovingian princess who had consciously attempted to associate himself with the Merovingian mystique by placing golden bees from the tomb of Merovingian King Childeric III on his coronation robe. It is also interesting to note that, although he was not of royal blood himself, he was recognized as an emperor, and ruled over a pan-European empire much like the one that he had just crushed. The Habsburgs remained the emperors of Austria, and then Austro-Hungary, until the revolution of 1919, making them the longest reigning European dynasty in history. And their role in European politics wasn't over by a long shot.

It took only 67 years from the end of the Holy Roman Empire for the Merovingian Grail families to begin jockeying once again for control of Europe. The Knights Templar had been the brainchild of another secret society which spawned them: the Priory of Sion, an order dedicated to nothing less than the restoration of the Merovingian bloodline to the thrones of Europe. And in 1873, they sponsored the creation of another front organization - the Hieron du Val d'Or, whose name, as the book *Holy Blood, Holy Grail* notes, contains an anagram of the place-name "Orval", a location that seems to be particularly important to the Merovingians and the Priory of Sion. Notably, the word "Orval" contains the syllables which, in French, mean "gold" and "valley." Thus "Val d'Or" means "Valley of Gold." In his 1979 book *Le Tresor du Triangle d'Or* (*The Treasure of the Golden*

Triangle), Jean-Luc Chaumeil states that the Hieron practiced a version of Scottish Rite Freemasonry, and that the upper degrees of this order constituted the lower degrees of the Priory of Sion itself. Chaumeil described the group's disposition as "Christian, Hermetic, and aristocratic." They proclaimed themselves to be Catholic, even though the Church of Rome condemned them. Their mystic teachings contained, according to *Holy Blood, Holy Grail*, "a characteristic emphasis on sacred geometry and various sacred sites... an insistence on a mystical or Gnostic truth underlying mythological motifs", and "a preoccupation with the origins of men, races, languages, and symbols... " The order was, "simultaneously Christian and 'trans-Christian.' It stressed the importance of the Sacred Heart... sought to recognize Christian and pagan mysteries... [and]... Ascribed special significance to Druidic thought - which it... regarded as partially Pythagorean." The Hieron du Val d'Or was also unabashedly pro-monarchist, and sought a restoration of the Holy Roman Empire. But this one would be built, unlike the previous one, on an ultimately spiritual basis - a vision specifically echoed in the Priory of Sion's own literature. The new empire would have been a reflection of Heaven on Earth, that specifically Hermetic Arcadian ideal. Jean-Luc Chaumeil described the Hieron's agenda as:

"...a theocracy wherein nations would be no more than provinces, their leaders but proconsuls in the service of a world occult government consisting of an elite. For Europe, this regime of the Great King implied a double hegemony of the Papacy and the Empire, of the Vatican and of the Habsburgs, who would have been the Vatican's right arm."

The authors of *Holy Blood, Holy Grail* were quick to point out that this envisioned scenario accords with the Nostradamus prophecy about the "Great King" who would issue from the House of Lorraine, since the Habsburgs *were* the House of Lorraine. At the same time, though, this vision accords with that shared by numerous other cultures throughout the world and throughout history who have embraced the myth of the King of the World, a legendary quasi-divine global monarch who, it is said by those who believe in him, currently lives in the center of the Earth, psychically directing the affairs of mankind, and who will incarnate in human form at the end of our current epoch so that he can rule earth directly. It further accords with the "King of the blood of Sion" image discussed in the infamous *Protocols of Zion*, which, as *Holy Blood, Holy Grail* hypothesizes, may well have been the minutes of a meeting of the Priory of Sion, as it describes a plot by the descendants of King David to take over the world.

The events surrounding World War I toppled the Western monarchies, and for the first half of this century Europe was in total chaos. It seemed impossible for current events to be any more out of sync with the goals of the Merovingian bloodline during that time. But the chaos worked to their advantage, because it created the need for order. At the close of the First World War, people began to theorize that a united Europe would make it impossible for member countries to go to war with each other in the future. The pitch became even more fevered during and after the Second World War, as people began to realize the true danger of the U.S.S.R. and the need for a united European power bloc to balance the ratio of world power against the Communists. Also, even though most of Europe was appreciative towards the United States for freeing them from Hitler, they also knew that the United States now held more influence than any one European power could hope to stand up to in the case of a conflict. But a United Europe would, once again, create a balance, and stand as a bulwark against both Communist imperialism and bourgeoisie American culture-distortion. Not surprisingly, it was the royal families of Europe, particularly the Grail families, who campaigned for a united Europe, often working through the apparatus of the Priory of Sion and other groups.

During World War II, the Priory was being led by the poet and artist Jean Cocteau, who held the post of Grand Master from 1918 until 1963. However, there was another organization operating under the umbrella of the Priory of Sion known as "Alpha Galates", lead by M. Pierre Plantard, a direct descendant of Dagobert II, who would one day become the Grand Master of the Priory of Sion itself. Alpha Galates was largely concerned with politics, both of France and of Europe in general. They also published a strange little magazine called *Vaincre* (*Victory*). Pierre Plantard has claimed that *Vaincre* was a Resistance journal (although on the surface it does not appear to be) and indeed, European unity was a popular tenet amongst the Resistance. *Vaincre* proclaimed the mission of Alpha Galates, which, as described in *The Messianic Legacy*, by Michael Baigent, Richard Leigh and Henry Lincoln, included:

"1. The unity of France within her geographic frontiers and the abolition of the line of demarcation between German-occupied zones and those under Vichy control;

2. The mobilization of all French energy and resources for the defense of the nation and, particularly, an appeal to the young for obligatory service;

3. The creation of a 'new western order', a 'young European chivalry' whose keynote was to be 'Solidarity.' Within each European nation, this organization, known as 'Solidarity', was to represent 'the first stage of the United States of the West.'"

This idea of the "United States of the West" is one of the predominant themes throughout *Vaincre*, and is illustrated by a drawing that ran in the first issue. This drawing depicts a mounted knight riding down a road upon which is written "The United States of the West", situated in between areas labeled "Brittany" and "Bavaria", towards a rising sunset marked with the sign of Aquarius and "1946", indicating that the birth of the United States of the West would be the dawn of a new age. For Alpha Galates, this was not merely a dream. It was a plan. Louis le Fur, a member of Alpha Galates, later founded a group called "Energie" that included Robert Schuman, another man who wished for a United States of Europe, and who later became an instrumental figure in the drafting of the plans for the European Economic Community. As the French Foreign Minister, it was his "Schuman Declaration", made on May 9, 1950, that resulted in the formation of the European Coal and Steel Community (ECSC), which combined the coal and steel production of several European countries under the same authority. This constituted the real beginning of the EU, and May 9 is now celebrated as "Schuman Day" in Europe.

But it was not only the men of Alpha Galates and the French Resistance that were dreaming of a United Europe. The dream was alive in Germany, not just with Hitler and his advocates (who clearly wanted to "unite Europe" in a wholly different way) but with the German Resistance as well. The German Resistance was largely centered around an aristocrat named Claus von Stauffenberg, a nobleman and monarchist with a large and loyal following of acolytes called "the Kreisau Circle." Stauffenberg was responsible for the famous "Bomb Plot" - the attempt to assassinate Hitler on July 20, 1944, now celebrated as Europe's Stauffenberg Day. Among his circle were his cousins Count Helmut James von Moltke and Hans Adolf von Moltke, the latter of whom was apparently a member of Alpha Galates. In an article from *Vaincre,* in which it is announced that Pierre Plantard has been elected Grand Master of Alpha Galates, Hans Adolf von Moltke, who is described as "a great German, one of the Masters in our Order", is quoted as stating:

"I have the pleasure to say, before my departure for Spain, that our Order has at last found a chief worthy of it in the person of Pierre de France.

It is therefore with total confidence that I depart to perform my mission; for while not deluding myself about the perils I run in discharging my duty, I know that until my last breath my watchword will consist of recognition of Alpha Galates and fidelity to its chief."

Von Moltke had been the German ambassador to both Poland and Britain, and had just been appointed Ambassador to Spain. His cousin Helmut James von Moltke had been attempting to circumvent Hitler by negotiating a peace deal with the Allies himself through associates in Sweden, and it is likely that Hans Adolf von Moltke was on a similar mission in Spain. Von Moltke died in Spain later that year, and although the Allies won the war, the peace that followed was not at all what the Kreisau Circle had in mind. Had they been successful in negotiating their peace deal, Europe may well have turned out much differently that it is today.

This link between the Kreisau Circle and Alpha Galates represents the first definitive link between the French and German Resistance movements yet known. The relationship between the two groups seems not to have begun until 1942, the same year that *Vaincre* began publishing. Like the members of Alpha Galates, the Kreisau Circle became involved in the planning of the EEC through their associates in the Swiss branch of the British Foreign Office, and through Allen Dulles, then head of the Swiss station of the OSS, which later became, with Dulles at the head, the CIA. As I shall discuss, the Priory of Sion appears to have had a special relationship with the CIA as well.

After the war, Pierre Plantard apparently gained high rank within the Priory of Sion itself, and began editing its official journal, *C.I.R.C.U.I.T.*, which stood for "Chevalierie d'Institutions et Regles Catholiques d'Union Independente et Traditionaliste" (Chivalry of Catholic Rules and Institutions of the Independent and Traditionalist Union). It was very similar in style and content to that of *Vaincre*. But in regards to the politics of state, *C.I.R.C.U.I.T.* did not confine itself to mere statements of opinion. They predicted what they believed would inevitably occur. They argued for the abolition of the French system which carved the country's geography into departments. They then laid out their own blueprint for the restructuring of the French government - one which would include nine sections: "Council of the Provinces; Council of State; Parliamentary Council; Taxes, Work, and Production; Medical; National Education; Age of Majority; and Housing and Schools." This doesn't seem terribly radical. But then, in another article by Plantard, he described plans for the restructuring of the entire world, including:

"...the creation of a Confederation of Lands [becoming] a Confederation of States: the United States of Euro-Africa, which [represents] economically (1) an African and European community of exchange based on a common market and (2) the circulation of wealth in order to serve the well-being of all, this being the sole stable foundation on which peace can be constructed."

The formation of a United States of Europe appears to have been one of the most consistently-stated goals of the Priory of Sion and those associated with it during the twentieth century. According to *Holy Blood, Holy Grail*, "The Prieure de Sion [sought] a United States of Europe partly as a bulwark against the Soviet imperium... a self-contained and neutral power bloc capable of holding the balance of power between the Soviet Union and the United States." The idea of a united Europe was also, as I have mentioned, popular among the French Resistance. It was espoused by people such as the national literary hero of the French, André Malraux, who advocated a "European New Deal" allied against the U.S.S.R. Also in 1942, Winston Churchill was quoted as saying, "I trust that the European family may act united as one under a Council of Europe. I look forward to a United States of Europe." Organizations such as Pan Europa, founded by Count Richard Coudenhove-Kalergi, began to pop up in the 1940s. Pan Europa included Jean Cocteau's friend and fellow poet Paul Valery, and is currently directed by Otto von Hapsburg. They employ a Celtic cross as their insignia.

Other groups that were interested in seeing European unity were the Western intelligence agencies, especially British and American intelligence, who sought to build a pro-European network amongst militant Catholic and right-wing political groups. When the O.S.S. (Office of Strategic Strategies), precursor of the CIA, was under the control of William Donovan, they attempted to infiltrate the Vatican and put priests in top positions on their payroll. They made use of Father Felix Morlion, founder of Pro Deo (For God), a European Catholic intelligence agency which the O.S.S. funded and installed first in New York, then in the Vatican itself. They also made use of the Society of Jesuits, which has been involved in Catholic espionage for years.

In 1948, the same year that the Congress of Europe met at the Hague, the O.S.S. became the Central Intelligence Agency. Immediately the CIA began funding European political parties, particularly the Christian Democrats, in an attempt to manipulate European governments and pull them to the right. The following year, the ACUE (American Committee on a United Europe) was formed, and William Donovan was made its chairman. Allen Dulles, former head of the O.S.S. in Switzerland, friend of the Von Moltke cousins and future head of the CIA, was Vice-President. The Director of the Council on Foreign Relations, and the future coordinator of the Trilateral Commission, George S. Franklin, was the Secretary. They even had another CIA employee, Thomas Braden, as their Executive Director. It was because of these men that the decision was made for the US State Department to fund the European movement. Following this, Joseph Retinger proceeded to collaborate with Prince Bernhard of the Netherlands and others to create the now infamous globalist think tank, the Bilderberg Group.

Meanwhile, the CIA busied itself funding organizations and newspapers all over Europe that were pro-Catholic and anti-Communist. A major recipient was Italy's Christian Democrat party, which had been started by the father of future Pope Paul VI, who was also on their payroll. He had been working as a spy and liaison for the OSS, then later the CIA, since WWII. It has also been said that Pope John Paul II has been receiving weekly intelligence briefings from the CIA since 1978, although it is unknown whether that continues to occur given the Pope's current state of deterioration.

It was during the 1960s that the CIA began distributing funds to its favored groups through the Vatican's own bank. This was done with the help of a shadowy, pro-Catholic, anti-Communist Masonic order known as "P2", which allegedly had lodges not only in Italy, but also France, Portugal, Switzerland, the United States, Nicaragua, Bolivia, Paraguay, Argentina, and Venezuela. As author David Yallop has written in his book *In God's Name*:

"P2 [interlocked] with a number of the military regimes of Latin America, and with a variety of groups of neo-Fascists. It also [interlocked] very closely with the CIA. It [reached] right into the heart of the Vatican. The central common interest of all these elements [was] apparently a hatred and fear of Communism."

All of this came out in the Italian press when a massive banking scandal broke involving the official Vatican bank, Banco Ambrosiano, and P2. The main figures implicated were P2 members Michael Sindona (a high ranking official in the bank and P2's financier) and the lodge's Grand Master, Licio Gelli. He was a man with far-right viewpoints who, after the scandal broke, was found hanging from Blackfriar's Bridge in London in 1982, in a manner consistent with Masonic ritual. [1] It also lead to the murder of an Italian investigator, Giorgio Ambrosoli, and later that of Michael Sindona himself, who was the chief suspect in the other two murders.

It is known that P2 is under the direction of an even more powerful organization, which one former member, Mino Pecorelli, named as being an agent of the CIA. [2] But there is another possibility as well. Supposedly, "P2" stands for "Propaganda Due", the meaning of which is not elaborated on. However, it has also been suggested to me that "P2" simply means "Priory 2", and that it is a break-off group of the Priory of Sion.

When the P2 scandal broke in 1981, and Licio Gelli's property was raided, they discovered links between P2 and other organizations that were very high up within the Vatican. These included a Vatican intelligence agency called "Opus Dei", which controls Vatican Radio, and another group that actually claims descent from the Knights Templar: the Sovereign and Military Order of the Temple of Jerusalem. This order, which dates back at least to 1804, claims to have been created by the Templars' last Grand Master, Jacques de Molay, who purportedly drew up a charter naming a successor prior to his execution. They are a genuine continuation, they say, of the original order, and they now dedicate themselves to "antiquarian interests." However, when the authors of *Holy Blood, Holy Grail* met with one of their representatives in 1982, and then did some research on their own, a much more complicated picture emerged.

The representative told the authors that the

order had just undergone a schism in which members of their group broke away to form their own, now headquartered in Switzerland. From this another group had spun off that made its headquarters in the Swiss city of Sion, lead by a man named Anton Zapelli, which called itself "Grand Prieure de Suisse." This organization included a number of members who also belonged to the Grand Suisse Loge Alpina, and Zapelli had been named by one of the informants interviewed for *Holy Blood, Holy Grail* as being, "the real power behind the Prieure de Sion." In their subsequent research, the authors came across internal documents from the Grand Prieure de Suisse. They dealt largely with two themes: international banking and European unification, specifically "the role of modern Templars in the reunification of Europe."

Could it be that the "Gnomes of Zurich" and the powerful men and women throughout Europe who have influenced the formation of the EU were in fact "modern Templars" - members of chivalrous and traditionalist secret societies dedicated to furthering the political goals of the Grail families? That certainly appears to be the case. Pierre Plantard himself admitted as much in his last interview with the authors of *Holy Blood, Holy Grail* (which he conducted just after he had withdrawn himself from the Priory of Sion). In this meeting, Plantard expanded upon the Priory of Sion's political goals for the immediate future. He remarked, according to *The Messianic Legacy*, that "Mitterand... had been a necessary stepping stone", but, "had served his purpose, and was expendable. The time had come to move on, and nothing could now stop 'it' from doing so." He said that for some of the Priory's members, their ultimate aim was a United States of Europe, to balance the power exercised by the Soviet Union and the United States. They also desired a larger "common market" of the Occident, which would include both Europe and the United States. About the involvement of the Vatican in this grand plan, Plantard said that Rome was "cooperating" in accordance with their "ongoing policy" on such matters, "to which individual popes were bound." Without elaborating much on what this meant, he admitted that, "Certain concessions had been necessary in return, but they were essentially nominal." The Grail families then, according to Plantard, ultimately control Europe, but do so almost with the permission of the Vatican, the other great power that secretly manipulates European politics. It is a sort of symbiotic relationship built not so much on mutual respect but on the recognition on the part of each that neither party could hope to hold power for very long without the acquiescence of the other. In this way, the situation is much the same as it was during the days of the Holy Roman Empire.

When the European Union officially began in 1950 as the European Coal and Steel Community (ECSC), it was a purely economic confederation built for the purpose of helping Europe recover from the war and fend off the growing Communist threat. Today, the European Union is a swiftly coalescing super-state, with a common currency, central bank, parliament, judiciary, police force, and international laws that in many cases overrule member states. Plans are in place to create a standing European army, navy and air force meant to phase out European reliance on NATO and the UN. Europe even has a common flag and a transnational anthem - Beethoven's "Ode to Joy." The EU consists of fifteen member countries and is looking to acquire ten more on May 1, 2004 (the pagan holiday of Beltane). It will then contain more than half a billion people. It definitely constitutes a power equal in magnitude to the United States, and the Communist bloc, which it was partially conceived for the purpose of combating, has been destroyed. But the trend towards transnational super-states is growing. Otto von Habsburg stated in a recent interview that, "NAFTA will also develop into such an organization [like the EU.] Then we can gradually come to what will be a global ... organization."

There are those, such as J.R. Church (host of the "Prophecy in the News" television program) and the late Herbert W. Armstrong (of the Worldwide Church of God) who have seen in the EU a fulfillment of Biblical prophecy, the kingdom of the Antichrist described in *The Revelation of St. John the Divine*. In this book, it describes "a woman clothed with the Sun, and the Moon under her feet, and upon her head a crown of twelve stars." (*Revelation 12*) When one reads this, it is impossible not to think of the flag of the European Union, consisting of twelve stars on a blue field, supposedly because "12 is the number of perfection", according to the EU's official website. (This is the same flag proposed in *Vaincre* for the United States of Europe.) Furthermore, the description of the woman in *Revelation 12* accords precisely with that of the Babylonian mother goddess, Ishtar, the "Queen of Heaven", who also stands upon the Moon, clothed with the Sun, and with a crown of twelve stars around her head. This image was later adapted by the Catholic Church into their image of the Virgin Mary, also called by them the "Queen of Heaven." Indeed, the Pope has officially declared the Virgin Mary to be the patron deity of the European Union. Also, the twenty pence coin of the British colony Gibraltar once bore the image of the Virgin Mary, crowned with the twelve stars and labeled both "Queen of Heaven" and "Our Lady of Europa." Ishtar was the Babylonian love goddess, worshipped as a divine whore with the sacred rite of temple prostitution. Can there be any doubt, then, that this is the same goddess discussed later in *The Revelation of St. John the Divine* when it talks about the Scarlet Woman, "the great whore that sitteth upon many waters... with whom the kings of the earth have committed fornication, and the inhabitants of the earth have been made drunk with the wine of her fornication"? St. John describes his vision thusly:

"...and I saw a woman sit upon a scarlet-colored beast, full of names of blasphemy, having seven heads and ten horns. And the woman was arrayed in purple and scarlet color, and decked with gold and precious stones and pearls, having a golden cup in her hand full of abominations and filthiness of her fornication. And upon her forehead was a name written: MYSTERY, BABYLON THE GREAT, THE MOTHER OF HARLOTS AND ABOMINATIONS OF THE EARTH. (Revelation 17:4-5)."

The cup she is described as holding is reminiscent of the Grail, symbolized as a holy vessel. The Catholic Church has personified this image of the scarlet woman in the form of St. Mary Magdalene, the reformed whore of the New Testament who became Christ's closest disciple (and, according to apocryphal literature, also his wife.) The Grail families worship Mary Magdalene as a personification of the Venus/Ishtar love goddess archetype, and she is often depicted holding a vase "full of healing balm", which is said by esotericists to symbolize the Grail.

Another notable feature of the Scarlet Woman is the Beast upon which she rides. St. John the Divine states specifically that, "The seven heads [of the Beast] are the seven mountains on which the woman sitteth." (*Revelation 17:9*.) Rome was built upon seven hills, so this statement may indicate the Catholic Church of Rome, a revised version of the old Babylonian priesthood (with the old gods disguised as Christ, Mary and the saints). In *Revelation 17:12* it says: "the ten horns... are ten kings, which have received no kingdom as yet, but receive power as kings one hour with the Beast." Could these be the crown heads of Europe, who will one day rule over ten forthcoming kingdoms in a newly-revised Holy Roman Empire? Herbert W. Armstrong certainly thought so. He believed (in accordance with my own research) that the royal houses of Europe were made up of the descendants of the ten lost tribes of Israel, and that they were destined to establish the kingdom of the Antichrist, exactly as these tribes had been prophesized to do in the Bible.

The image of a woman riding a beast is in itself symbolic of Europe. An ancient Greek myth, discussed in detail in *Dagobert's Revenge Volume 4#1*, relates how the goddess Europa (after whom the continent of Europe was named) was kidnapped and raped by the great Zeus in the form of a bull. He came to her from out of the sea, and carried her off beneath the waves. This story has previously been identified this story with the myth of the Quinotaur, or sea bull, whose rape of a Visigothic princess lead to the birth of Meroveus, the founder of the Merovingian dynasty. Of course, the Merovingians went on to provide Europe with the royal families who ruled over the Holy Roman Empire, now currently being resurrected in the form of the European Union. The image of Europa riding the bull is used on numerous official EU documents, including currency, and can be found depicted in motifs and statuary throughout the official EU buildings in Brussels and Strasbourg.[3] This has been interpreted by a number of Bible prophecy preachers as a statement by the EU identifying itself with the Beast of *Revelation*, yet many of these people are ignorant of the Greek myth of Europa. It is clear, however, that the man who called himself St. John the Divine most certainly was not ignorant of the Greek myth. He saw that the Roman Empire was destined to dominate the world, and he specifically chose to depict it this way.

The Priory of Sion also appears to see in the United States of Europe an apocalyptic scenario, although they declare themselves to be working for the establishment of Christ's kingdom on Earth. Priory of Sion member Paul le Cour wrote in his book *The Age of Aquarius*: "Let us try to understand what our mission consists of. Let us try to fulfill it by preparing knights of the Apocalypse whose head will be Christ when he returns!"[4] A one-time spokesman for the Priory, Jean-Luc Chaumeil, even wrote a book about the Priory called *Templars of the Apocalypse*. One can certainly see their point of view. For one thing, the kings of a future European empire would be blood descendants of Christ, David, and the patriarchs of the Bible, quite fitting for the administrators of God's kingdom. And if a strong European empire actually managed to fend off the threats to Western organization once and for all, it would indeed seem like Heaven on Earth.

This may be the most convincing argument in favor of a strong European Union: the need for Western civilization, exemplified by Europe, to defend itself against its enemies, especially Islamic fanatics, the same enemy the Holy Roman Empire faced during the time of the Crusades. Today we face a threat that, if not met, could end in the destruction of our culture and the ultimate extinction of our people. This can be done only by presenting a unified front. Only through Europe's union can a genuine state of peace and security, a true "Pax Europa" be achieved in the West - a peace that will spread throughout the entire world if maintained. In a globe such as ours today, external threats to the Western order need to be met with common immigration policies, travel restrictions, and defense policies, as well as health and safety codes. But even more so, those who attempt to destroy our culture need to be met by a West that is healthy, strong and proud; one which acknowledges its common heritage and cherishes its traditions. The threat that faces us is ultimately spiritual in nature, and therefore our unity must be ultimately spiritual - not merely materialistic and political, which is what the EU appears at present to be. The journalist and philosopher Julius Evola wrote of this concept that, "... the principle of the Empire can have ... dignity only by transcending the political sphere in the strict sense, founding and legitimizing itself with an idea, a tradition and a power that is spiritual." Writer Francis Parker Yockey expressed a similar point of view when he wrote: "the nature of the unity of [Western] culture is purely spiritual in its origin. The material unity that follows is the unfolding precedent of the inner, spiritual unity." Even the Pope appeared to be making the same argument during a recent speech he gave to the Italian legislature when he said:

"[The] common European house [should be built with] the cement of that extraordinary religious, cultural and civic heritage that has made Europe great down the centuries... It is necessary therefore to be on guard against a vision of the continent which considers only its economic and political aspects, or which critically engages in ways of life based on a consumerism that is indifferent to the values of the spirit. If one wants to give durable stability to Europe's new unity, it is necessary to ensure that it rests on those ethical foundations which were once at its base..."

It is clear that the heritage which the pontiff is referring to here is that of the Holy Roman Empire, and of the Catholicism that sustained it.

One thing that will be necessary in order for the European Union to survive will be for European society as a whole to reject the overwhelming degree of anti-Americanism that has long been fashionable for them to embrace. The United States has been and will continue to be Europe's greatest ally, a friend in good times and in bad, something they would not do well to reject. As I explained earlier on, the United States government was integral to the formation (as well as the funding) of the European Economic Community since the very beginning, and US Presidents have always been outspoken in their support of a united Europe. Furthermore, there is obviously a common cultural bond between Europe and North America that cannot be ignored, which is why the Priory of Sion has at times advocated a "United States of the West", rather than the more restrictive "United States of Europe." This bond between Europe and America will only become stronger as the common threat to our civilization becomes more grave.

The other thing which European society must resist is its recurrent tendency towards anti-Semitism, once again making a comeback, this time amongst the political left, for whom it is fashionable now to campaign against Israel and maintain belief in Zionist conspiracy theories. Israel, and particularly its capitol of Jerusalem, has been tied to Europe by a spiritual bond since the Crusades. The kings of Europe come from the bloodline of the Jewish kings, and *Judeo-*Christianity is our predominant religion. There is no straining the Jewishness out of Europe without destroying its culture.

Furthermore, Jerusalem was once seen as the jewel of the European empire, and there is evidence to indicate that it will be again one day. Writes Tim Cohen in *The Anti-Christ and a Cup of Tea*: "In September, 1993, [Shimon] Peres signed a secret deal with the Pope promising Vatican hegemony over Jerusalem's Old City by the year 2000." Peres' friend Mark Halter, who was apparently in charge of delivering the message to the Pope, was quoted as saying that, "The city will stay the capital of Israel, but will be administered by the Vatican. The city will have an Israeli mayor and a Palestinian mayor, both under orders from the Holy See." A few yeas later, the Pope, barely able to stand, made the difficult journey to Jerusalem to offer a formal reconciliation with the Jewish nation, apologizing for the Vatican's seeming complicity with the Nazis during the Holocaust. On March 11, 2001, Israeli President Moshe Katsav was quoted by the *Bild* newspaper as saying that he was "firmly in favor of his country joining the European Union." France, Britain, and Germany have also expressed their willingness to admit Israel into the EU. Perhaps Israel will be known again one day as the "Latin Kingdom of Jerusalem." Let us not forget that Otto von Habsburg still holds the title "King of Jerusalem", and the that title will revert to is son Karl upon his death. [5]

The only thing that is missing in this vision is a new Clovis, a new Dagobert, a new Charlemagne, what the Priory of Sion refers to as the "Grand Monarch", the new messianic figure who will be a rallying point for the revival of the Empire. But the appearance of this figurehead will probably not occur until Europe reverts back to its royal tradition of monarchy. This will inevitably develop in a situation in which a unified Europe decides to embrace its common heritage, for it will soon find that without its royal tradition it has no appreciable heritage. A European leader from a royal house with established branches all over Europe is the only sort that would be accepted by people from all European countries. Every other sort of leader would be considered a despot with no mandate to rule. Furthermore, whenever a people embrace or re-embrace an established tradition of monarchy, it always makes them stronger. Julius Evola wrote a great deal on this topic:

"... in the interpretation of the genesis of historical nations, we shouldn't forget what was essentially due to dynasties representing a tradition, and to the loyalty that was created around them... ."

Of the sort of government that should lead a united Europe, he continued:

"European unity would always be precarious if it leaned on some external factor, like an international parliament lacking a common higher authority... Only elites of individual European nations could understand one another and coordinate their work, overcoming every particularism and spirit of division, asserting higher interests and motives with their authority. In other times, it was royalty... who could make the great European policy; they regarded each other almost as members of the same family (which, in part, they were, due to dynastic intermarriages), even when grave conflicts temporarily arose between their peoples."

Finally, Evola made a suggestion for how a European empire could be achieved:

"We could suggest the idea of an order, whose members would act in the various nations, doing what they can to promote an eventual European unity... A first group should be composed of members of ancient European families that are still 'standing', and who are valuable not only because of the name they carry, but also because of who they are, because of their personality."

Evola could have hardly predicted any closer what was soon to occur: the creation of a united Europe by the very same royal bloodlines (the Habsburgs and other Merovingian descendants) who had once ruled over it before, and whose dynasties had been crushed not a century earlier in some instances. The goal of those families - a United States of Europe - is almost fully achieved. Even the title which they envisioned for this new empire is soon to become a reality. In November of 2002, the newspapers reported that the Convention on the Future of Europe, lead by the former President of France, Valery Giscard d'Estaing, has just drafted a proposed constitution for Europe (where currently none exists) in which the very first article declares the establishment of a "United States of Europe."

Within the next few years, we could be seeing the fulfillment of a millennium's worth of plotting and manipulation on the part of Europe's hidden hierarchy - the Merovingian master plan to rebuild the Holy Roman Empire according to their own prerogatives. And you can bet that this time they are not going to give up their empire so easily. They intend this empire to last for a thousand years.

Endnotes:

[1] When initiated, the Masonic candidate takes an oath swearing his loyalty and secrecy on penalty of ritualized murder such as this.

[2] Pecorelli was murdered after making this acknowledgement.

[3] It is peculiar to think that the state of Europe uses an official seal depicting a prelude to rape and bestiality.

[4] Published in 1949 and translated by Peter O'Reilly.

[5] The Habsburgs are also the current possessors of the Spear of Destiny once held by Charlemagne.

Call Me Ishmael: The Biblical Roots of the Persian Gulf Conflict

By Tracy Twyman

As "Operation Iraqi Freedom" continues, the roughly 30% of Americans who oppose action in Iraq continue to repeat the same tired, meaningless questions. "Why is this happening? They didn't do anything to us", they whine. Some have even accused President George W. Bush of making it personal, and have insinuated that the entire action is happening because Bush wants to settle a score with Saddam for attempting to have his father, George Bush Sr., assassinated after the first Persian Gulf War. Though the rationale for going to war, and the national interests this serves, have been explained ad infinitum over the past year, to the point where there should no longer be any question of why, the protestors may be half right. There does indeed seem to be a personal conflict between Bush and Saddam even deeper than the diplomatic conflict between their two nations. The nature of this conflict is that of a family feud, and it is one that has divided Eastern and Western civilization for thousands of years. It all goes back to the Bible, and to a legacy of bad blood that began with the rivalry of two siblings: Ishmael and his half-brother Isaac, both sons of the Biblical patriarch Abraham.

Ishmael was Abraham's first-born son, conceived when he was almost already past his fertile years. His wife, Sarah, had remained barren throughout their entire marriage, and now she was almost 80. Therefore, according to the custom of the time, she encouraged Abraham to conceive a son with their handmaiden, an Egyptian slave named Hagar. Sarah would then raise the child as if he were her own son. But as soon as the child was conceived, Sarah became consumed with jealousy, and began to treat Hagar very badly. When Ishmael was born, he also received poor treatment.

Some years later, when Ishmael was about 13, and his father almost 100, Abraham had a conversation with God (not his first) in which a covenant between them was established. Abraham and all of his descendants, from that point on, would walk in the ways of God and dedicate their lives to the worship of him alone. In exchange, the Lord would make Abraham the father of many nations, and his descendants would be the kings of the Earth. As a sign of this covenant, Abraham and his children would forevermore mark themselves by the rite of circumcision. That day, 99-year-old Abraham was circumcised, along with his thirteen-year-old son, Ishmael.[1] The covenant, at least for Abraham, was sealed.

As if getting circumcised as a prepubescent wasn't bad enough, for Ishmael, things soon went from bad too worse. His adoptive mother, Sarah, became miraculously pregnant, and bore unto Abraham a boy named Isaac. Unbeknownst to him, this was also part of the covenant between Abraham and God. Even though Ishmael was the first-born, Isaac was the first one born to Abraham after the covenant of circumcision had been established. Furthermore, Isaac was the son of Abraham's lawful wife, while Ishmael was merely the son of a slave. Therefore, the Lord instructed Abraham to leave his inheritance to the younger child, upon whom God would then bestow the blessing that he had promised to give to Abraham's first-born son. Then, only a short time after the birth of Isaac, Sarah accused Ishmael of mocking the newborn, and insisted that her husband "cast out this bondwoman and her son." With the encouragement of the Lord, Abraham reluctantly followed through, sending them off into the desert with nothing but a goatskin full of water to sustain them.

The water did not last long, though, and

soon Hagar was sure that Ishmael would die from thirst. She was just about to leave him under a bush so that she would not have to watch him die, when God intervened. He showed them a well of water from which to drink, and promised him that, although deprived of his birthright, Ishmael would still beget a nation because of his biological descent from Abraham. Hagar and Ishmael ended up in Egypt, and today many Arab-Islamic peoples claim him as their forefather. In fact, President George W. Bush himself acknowledged this when he first announced the beginning of the War on Terror, taking time to make clear that this was not a war against the "descendants of Ishmael" as a whole.

However, as anyone with even just a cursory understanding of the last 2000 years of history realizes, what we now know as the "Western world" has been at odds with the Islamic world since before Muhammad's body was even laid in the grave. The wars have been countless, epitomized by the numerous Crusades on the part of the West battling for control of the Holy Land, Israel, and especially Jerusalem. This obsession with the Holy Land on the part of the West is perhaps based on more than just the prevalence of the Christian faith in medieval Europe. As I have repeatedly explained within the pages of *Dagobert's Revenge*, many of the crown heads of Europe, from medieval times until present, have been direct descendants of the kings of Judah - in other words, descendants of Isaac. So, too, were the founders of the Order of Knights Templar, who maintained the most elite fighting force in the conflict, and who may have been partially responsible for inspiring the Crusades in the first place. Their desire to control the Holy Land was really based on their desire to recapture what they believed to be their rightful inheritance, and the true seat of their royal power. This they achieved, at least for a time, and one of them, Godfroi de Bouillon, made the kingship of Jerusalem a part of his family inheritance. The Knights Templar were given unprecedented access to the Temple Mount during Europe's occupation of the Holy Land, and rumor has it that they used that time to explore and loot the stables beneath the Mount of the treasures of Solomon's Temple, including, perhaps, the Ark of the Covenant. To them, this article alone was worth fighting off thousands of Ishmaelites, and for their part, the Ishmaelites may have very well felt the same way.

For Islam, Israel is a Holy Land also, although there are conflicting explanations as to why this is so. One of the most commonly cited stories tells that the archangel Gabriel took the Prophet Muhammad on a tour of heaven, by climbing a "ladder of light" that stood on the exact location of the Temple Mount - an obvious refurbishing of the story of Jacob's "stairway to Heaven." But it seems to me that there is a much more simple reason as to why Islam covets the Holy Land. The Jews (and their European brethren) believe that Israel is "the center of the world", given to them, God's chosen people, by the Lord himself, as part of a covenant that began with Abraham and Isaac. But the descendants of Ishmael, the first born son of Abraham, believe that this birthright actually belongs to them. Thus a 4000 year-old blood feud is continued unto the present day, with disastrous consequences for the entire world. Today, the "Middle East crisis" is at the center of a bloody struggle between two entirely different cultures that stem from the same forefather: the Islamic East and the Judeo-Christian West. Without the conflict over Israel, there would be no Islamic terrorism, and therefore, no need for a "War on Terror."

Of course, it is not Israel alone for which the battle is waged. The Islamic Middle East covers the most important historical and archeological sites known in the world. It was in these lands that most of the Biblical stories were played out and in these lands that mankind's origins can be found. Among these, the most important lands, perhaps are those formerly known as "Mesopotamia", covering, among other places, the modern nation of Iraq. Known as "the cradle of civilization", this land is just that: the place where civilization was born, nurtured, and cultivated. Home to writing, agriculture, architecture, metallurgy, and the invention of items such as bread and the wheel, Mesopotamia was the start of everything we call "civilized." Virtually all of the most basic societal customs which we now observe began in this land. It is the birthplace of religion, morality, law and government - specifically, kingship. The first kings of

Mesopotamia were very mighty indeed. In fact, they were remembered as gods in the legends of their people, and these same "gods" made their way into the mythologies of the entire civilized world. It is the contention of *Dagobert's Revenge* that the Judaic kings are ultimately descended from these gods, and that some of the Bible's patriarchs were in fact Mesopotamian god-kings. The word "Iraq" is itself derived from "Erech", one of the ancient Mesopotamian cities built by the Biblical patriarch Cain. With a heritage like this, and the archeological treasures that attest to it, it is no wonder that the West has fought many wars over the years for control of this region. This most recently occurred during the World Wars.

From the thirteenth century until the twentieth, much of the Islamic world was under the control of the Ottoman Empire, administered by Turkish settlers in Anatolia known as Osmanlis. When this empire began to falter around the turn of the last century, Britain and Germany both vied for control of the vital, oil-rich territory. When World War I began and Turkey sided with Germany, the British quickly moved into Iraq to prevent it from coming under the same influence. They funded and supported the local Arab nationals, and led them in a fight against the German-allied Ottoman Turks, with the understanding that after the revolt, Iraq would return to independent rule for the first time in 600 years. In fact, after the success of the revolt, and the defeat of the Germans, Iraq was made a "Class A mandate" of Britain at the Paris Peace Conference of 1919 (along with Palestine). The British installed the family of Husayn ibn Ali, Sharif of Mecca and former vassal of the Ottomans, as "King of the Arab peoples." His son, Prince Faisal, was later to become the first king of modern Iraq.

The Husayn family, soon to be the most powerful dynasty in the Middle East, were known as the "Hashemites", named after their forefather, Hashem, a descendant of Ishmael, according to them, and great-grandfather of the Prophet Muhammad. The name "Hashemite" is reminiscent of "Hashashim", a.k.a. the Order of Assassins, a radical and mystical secret society of Manichean Muslims who are rumored to have had much contact with and influence upon the Knights Templar during the Crusades. Although the word "Hashashim" is usually said to be derived from the fact that they smoked hashish in their rituals, this has never been definitively proven, and it is interesting to note that one of their most celebrated Grand Masters, presiding between 1070 and 1000, was known as "Hasan-i-Sabah." Also interesting is that the Assassins originated from a sect of Islam known as "Ismaili", who believe that there have been seven prophets sent by God to enlighten us throughout history, one of which was the Biblical Ishmael. Although we do not know if there is a definitive link between the Hashemites and the Hashashim, we do know that it is the Husayn family from which we get the monarchy of Jordan (featuring the late King Hussein), and that they, in turn, are cousins of Saddam Hussein.

In 1932, Iraq became an independent monarchy. But unrest continued, largely because the government was heavily staffed by the Sunni racial minority, who had performed the same function during Ottoman rule. Discontent also fomented because of the Assyrians, who had been resettled into Iraq by the British, but were hated by the Iraqi government and population, as well as the Kurds, who were pushing for an autonomous state in the region they controlled. Anger brewed against the British for haphazardly carving up the region and forcing natural-born enemies to live in the same country. Towards the beginning of the Second World War, the Germans attempted to capitalize on this unrest by becoming friendly with the Iraqi government.

It was, perhaps, natural for the Germans to approach Iraq, not only for strategic reasons, but because Nazi ideology traced the origins of the white "Aryan" race back to the region of Mesopotamia. Indeed, the historical group known as "Aryans" did arise here, thus the name "Iran" for Iraq's neighboring nation. The Aryans were, as I have previously stated in the pages of *Dagobert's Revenge*, a race of conquerors descended from the antediluvian god-kings who civilized the ancient world. Hitler was fascinated with ancient Mesopotamia, and is even said to have regarded himself as a reincarnation of the Sumerian king Sargon the Great. Nazi scholars also seemed to have an attraction to the Islamic faith, and many Nazis converted during the 30s and 40s. The two causes, Nazism and Islam, also shared one fundamental trait: an obsessive hatred of Jews. Many Iraqis, especially in the armed forces, were quite sympathetic to the Nazis, including Khairallah Talfah, an Iraqi officer and the beloved uncle of the young Saddam Hussein. According to some, Saddam's uncle was one of the major influences on him during his youth, and probably instilled him with pro-Nazi sentiments. But in 1941, the British recaptured Iraq and ended the Nazi flirtation once and for all. Saddam's uncle was thrown in prison, and from that moment on, Saddam's hatred for the West, particularly the United States and Britain, has completely consumed him.

It was perhaps Saddam's early exposure to Nazi ideology and military training that influenced the harsh and dictatorial way in which he runs his country. In fact, personality-wise, there are many similarities between Hitler and Saddam. Saddam, like Hitler, believes he is the reincarnation of an ancient Mesopotamian king. Also like Hitler, Saddam consciously utilizes the religious symbolism of the ancient world to subconsciously create the illusion that he is an all-powerful being. For his part, Saddam believes that he is the rebirth of the Chaldean King Nebuchadnezzar II. This was one of Mesopotamia's greatest monarchs. He was a master architect, and during his reign the Babylonian empire over which he ruled enjoyed its greatest period of architectural building in history. Magnificent palaces and temples were built, including the famous Hanging Gardens, one of the Seven Wonders of the World, and it is said that he had his name inscribed onto every brick. During his reign, Babylon also experienced its most fruitful period of study in astrology and mathematics, and some of Babylon's best literature was produced during this time. It was a time when Marduk, the god of writing, was considered the patron deity.

Like Saddam, Nebuchadnezzar was also a megalomaniacal tyrant, believing himself to be an incarnation of Marduk, who, in addition to writing, was also the god of war (like Mars, his Roman counterpart). Nebuchadnezzar had statues of Marduk erected in his own likeness, and demanded the same sacrifice as Marduk: babies thrown into a furnace en masse.[3] But most of all, Nebuchadnezzar showed his affinity with Marduk by making war. While he was on the throne, the empire expanded to the areas now encompassing Syria, Jordan, Israel and Kuwait. The most well-remembered conquest was that of Israel.

Nebuchadnezzar conquered Jerusalem in 568 B.C., looting the Temple of Solomon and taking the Israelite aristocracy into Babylon as prisoners, initiating the "Babylonian captivity" recorded in the Bible. During this time, some of the most famous biblical stories about this are found in *The Book of Daniel*. According to the story, Nebuchadnezzar has a disturbing dream which Daniel was called upon to interpret. In the dream, Nebuchadnezzar saw a gigantic statue, the head of which was made of gold, the breasts and arms of silver, the belly and thighs of brass, the legs of iron, and the feet part-iron and part-clay. Then all of the sudden, a stone came along and broke the statue:

"Then was the iron, the clay and the brass, the silver and the gold, broken to pieces together, and became like the chaff of the summer threshing floors; and the wind carried them away, that no place was found for them: and the stone that smote the image became a great mountain, and filled the whole earth."

Daniel told the king that the head of gold represented his own kingdom, and the various lower parts of the statue represented successive empires that would rule over his lands in the future. The feet, made of both iron and clay, showed that the kingdom would eventually be divided in two. The breaking up of the image showed that the entire kingdom would "break in pieces, and consume all these kingdoms, and it shall stand forever." This appears to be a reference to the kingdom of God prophesized to rule the Earth after the Apocalypse. The successive kingdoms that precede this have been interpreted by students of Bible prophecy as those of the Medio-Persian, Greco-Macedonian, and Roman empires which have ruled Mesopotamian lands throughout history, culminating in the "divided" state of the region today.

In *The Book of Daniel*, it is written that Nebuchadnezzar so appreciated Daniel's dream interpretation that he pledged his loyalty to the God of Israel, and made Daniel a powerful vizier of his government. [3] But shortly thereafter, Nebuchadnezzar set up a gigantic statue of himself made of gold, and compelled the populace to worship it. In the next chapter, Daniel was called upon to interpret another one of the king's dreams. In it, he saw a vision of a huge tree set in the center of the Earth, the top of which reached to Heaven. A "Watcher" appeared to him, and ordered him to chop the tree down, leaving, "the stump of is roots in the earth, even with a band of iron and brass... and let his portion be with the beasts in the grass of the Earth: let his heart be changed from a man's, and let a beast's heart be given unto him.... This matter is by the decree of the Watchers, and the demand by the word of the holy ones... " Daniel told the king that the tree represented himself, grown great and powerful, but also arrogant, and that he, like the tree would be brought down for his impiety, "That they shall drive thee from men, and thy dwelling shall be with the beasts of the field, and they shall make thee to eat grass as oxen... " About a year later, the prophecy was fulfilled. Nebuchadnezzar was driven into exile by his own subjects, and "did eat grass as oxen... till his hairs were grown like eagle's feathers, and his nails like birds' claws."

Needless to say, the figure of Nebuchadnezzar is one which conjures up fear in the hearts of both Jews and Christians throughout the world. But to the people of Iraq, he is beloved, the last great symbol of the once-great Babylonian empire. It is this image that Saddam Hussein has intentionally tried to conjure up with everything that he has done. [4] In is no coincidence that Saddam's regime has brought about the greatest period of architectural renewal since the time of Nebuchadnezzar himself. Saddam has even rebuilt many of the temples, palaces and statues that were built during Nebuchadnezzar's time. Just as Nebuchadnezzar had his name inscribed on every brick of the buildings he erected, so Saddam has had every building he has built marked with the words: "The Babylon of Nebuchadnezzar was reconstructed in the era of Saddam Hussein." When he took control of the country, Saddam proclaimed himself "the rightful heir of the ancient Babylonian king Nebuchadnezzar", and vowed to restore the empire of Babylon by expanding Iraq to encompass its former territories.

This, then, is the motivation for his support of the Palestinians in their push for control of Israel, even though Saddam is supposedly a secularist who only pays lip service to the Muslim religion in order to maintain power. This was certainly the motivation behind his invasion of Kuwait in the early 1990s, which precipitated the first Gulf War lead by the United States, and by President George Bush Senior. This conflict has continued unto the present day, and now another war is being conducted between Saddam and the current President, George W. Bush. As I stated at the beginning of this article, this conflict is, in addition to everything else, extremely personal.

The personalization of the conflict is exemplified by the subtle and not-so-subtle name-calling that has occurred between Saddam and both of the Bush presidents. "Saddam" was not Hussein's birth name, but one that he chose himself, as it means "one who confronts" or "he who shocks", being derived from a Persian word meaning "to crush." Thus Hussein's full name has been translated as "Hussein who crushes obstacles", or "Hussein the destroyer." Knowing that Saddam's first name had a meaning, President Bush Senior. intentionally mispronounced the word whenever possible, placing the accent on the first syllable instead of the last, which changed the meaning to that of "barefoot beggar." Hussein has responded to these personal attacks rather personally as well, attempting to have Bush Senior. assassinated, and referring to the current President as "little Bush."

But the most interesting references that have been made in the ongoing bitch fight between Saddam and the Bushes have been Biblical in nature. For it cannot be insignificant that the Bushes are direct descendants of King Henry II of England, and therefore, by extension, of King David of Israel. [5] That means that they are related by blood to the Jewish kings who were conquered by Saddam's predecessor, Nebuchadnezzar, and like Saddam is a descendant of Ishmael, so are they the descendants of his blood rival, Isaac.

Perhaps this explains the unusual symbolism evoked by Saddam's remark, made at the beginning of the first Persian Gulf War, that he was about to unleash "the Mother of All Battles." Saddam was so fond of this phrase that, after the war (in which he erroneously declared victory), he named one of his ancient restored temples after the "Mother of All Battles." It apparently did not escape the notice of the Americans that, in English at least, this phrase can be abbreviated into the word "Moab."

The story of Moab in the Bible occurs not long after the story of Ishmael, during the account of the life of Abraham. In the story, God warns Abraham that he is about to destroy the cities of Sodom and Gomorrah because of their wickedness, and this warning is also passed onto the character of Lot, an inhabitant of the area. [6] As most readers know, Lot and his family evacuated themselves from the area, and hid themselves in the cave of a nearby mountain. But Lot's wife had been killed in the process (turned by God into a pillar of salt), so Lot's daughters contrived to perpetuate their father's lineage by getting him drunk and sleeping with him themselves. The first child born from this union was Moab, whose name means "born of her father", a reference to his incestuous origin. Moab later became the king of a nation bearing his own name (now modern Jordan), and the Moabites, cousins of the Hebrews, with a similar language and culture, are mentioned frequently in the Old Testament, sometimes allies of the Hebrews, sometimes not. King David's mother was a Moabite, and Moab was a thorn in the side of both David and Solomon during their respective reigns, before the Moabites were finally made subject to the kingdom of Judah. Eventually they were subsumed into the Babylonian empire, during the reign of - you guessed it: Nebuchadnezzar.

This may explain the significance of Saddam Hussein's reference to Moab, a reference to a nation that Nebuchadnezzar once conquered, as Saddam intended to do himself. But in this most recent war with Iraq, the Americans seem to have turned this psychological warfare around to their own advantage. The most significant piece of artillery with which we are threatening Iraq is a relatively new explosive (invented since the last Gulf War) called the "Massive Ordnance Air Bomb", or MOAB, and nicknamed "the Mother of All Bombs." One has to wonder if this bomb was not invented for use against Hussein specifically. Perhaps the Americans are exacting a psychological counter-attack by calling a highly destructive bomb "Moab." For if you haven't noticed, Saddam's name is eerily similar to "Sodom." Maybe what the Americans are saying to him with the use of MOAB is, "We will destroy the cities of Saddam just like Yahweh destroyed Sodom."

Psychological warfare is in fact the key tactic used in "Operation Iraqi Freedom." The massive aerial bombardment that the U.S. is inflicting on Iraq is called by the American military "Shock and Awe", the idea being that the extent of the explosions will be so great that it will produce said psychological effects in the enemy, and force them to surrender. The phrase "Shock and Awe" was repeated endlessly throughout the first week of the war, usually pronounced quickly, so that it sounds like "Shakanah." Is it a coincidence that this is an old spelling and pronunciation of the Hebrew word "Shekinah", which means "whirlwind", or "glory of God"? Indeed, during President Bush's inaugural address, long before another war with Iraq was foreseen, he made a reference to the god he worships, and who guides him in all of his decisions, as the deity who "rides in a whirlwind." Perhaps the "whirlwind" of bombing known as "Shock and Awe" is meant to make Saddam believe that the descendants of Isaac, the Bush family, have God on their side in this war with the new Nebuchadnezzar, and that the Shekinah is coming to destroy him.

There may be even more direct reasons for why the Bush family would want to conquer Iraq and install a "westernized" government. Mesopotamia is the land not only of Ishmael's descendants, but also of the forefathers of the Hebrew race. Abraham, after all, was from "Ur of the Culdees", and most of the text of *Genesis* seems to take place in the Fertile Crescent. In fact, it appears that the patriarchs from Adam to Abraham were all, in fact, kings of this land. Therefore, Iraq contains many of the archeological treasures dear to Hebrew history, some of which Saddam looted from Kuwait while his armies were occupying that country. There may even still be certain treasures from the Temple of Solomon hidden in Iraq. It is mentioned in *The Book of*

Daniel that Belshezzar, Nebuchadnezzar's successor, was eating dinner on the golden tea set his father had stolen from the Temple of Jerusalem when he witnessed the proverbial "writing on the wall", etched by a disembodied hand. According to the story, it was the prophet Daniel who, once again, interpreted the writing for the king. It said:

"MENE, MENE; God hath numbered thy kingdom, and finished it.
TEKEL; Thou art weighed in the balances, and art found wanting.
PERES; Thy kingdom is divided, and given to the Medes and the Persians."

With the exception of the last seven words, this prophecy could just as easily apply to the doomed regime of the new Nebuchadnezzar, Saddam Hussein. One wonders if, perhaps, somewhere in his hidden underground bunker, this would-be Babylonian emperor is now watching another ghostly hand etching out a similar warning. Perhaps it will not be long before, like his historical predecessor, Saddam is driven out into the wilderness by his own subjects, and made to eat grass and leaves like the animal that we all know, at heart, he is. Or perhaps the descendants of Isaac will just blow him to pieces, and declare final victory in the land which once held their forefathers captive.

Endnotes:

[1] To this day, it is traditional in many cultures to perform circumcision not when a child is born, but when he reaches the age of 13, and it is used as a rite of passage into manhood.

[2] This is, some say, the origin of the word "baby", stemming from "Babylon."

[3] This is strangely reminiscent of the story of Joseph and the Pharaoh during the Egyptian captivity of the Hebrews.

[4] Saddam has even named two divisions of his elite Republican Guard "Hammurabi" and "Nebuchadnezzar", the former being the name of another ancient Sumerian king, famous for codifying the tablets of law upon which the Bible's "Ten Comandments" are based.

[5] It is notable, from a symbolic standpoint, that Bush has conducted a great deal of the war with Iraq from "Camp David."

[6] Interestingly, this information was given to him by some "Watchers" who visited him at his house.

The Choice Vine: Mary Magdalene, the Sacred Whore, and the Benjamite Inheritance

By Tracy R. Twyman

The Smear Campaign

Due to the recent popularity of *The Da Vinci Code*, as well as the rising tide of Wicca, New Age, and "goddess worship" that we have seen over the last few years, the subject of Mary Magdalene has been quite fashionable as of late. She has been covered in *Time Magazine*, *Newsweek*, on the History Channel, the Learning Channel, PAX, and in specials aired on all the major networks. *The Gospel of Mary Magdalene* has ranked Amazon.com's top 100, as has Lynn Picknett's *Mary Magdalen*, and Margaret Starbird's *The Woman with the Alabaster Jar* - a book first published in 1993, and one of the major influences on Dan Brown's *Da Vinci Code*. The idea that the Magdalene may have actually been the bride of Christ and the mother of his children is now one that is taken quite seriously amongst the general public, as is the theory that they were the progenitors of the Merovingian kings of France - the so-called "Grail bloodline." The circulation of these ideas has caused an interest in occult spiritual matters to blossom in a sudden and unexpected way, and appears to be setting off the "Arcadian revival" about which we at *Dagobert's Revenge* have prophesied for many years.

But along with this interest has come speculation about the reasons why Jesus' marriage to Mary Magdalene was not written of in the Gospels, or anywhere in the canonized New Testament. The question is, "Why did the Church edit Christ's wife out of the Bible?" Lead by the Wiccans, the New Agers, and the Feminists, many have leapt to the conclusion that this was the result of a misogynist conspiracy by the male-dominated Catholic Church. According to this line of thought, Church doctrine damned human sexuality as sinful because of an institutional hatred which held women to be inherently corrupt. They therefore did not want to admit that Christ had any wives or children, but maintained that he had remained chaste his whole life, as had his Virgin mother. The Gospels and the Church also suppressed any knowledge of the high-ranking positions that Mary and other women held in the Jesus movement.

It certainly is true that the Roman Church hierarchy and doctrine was misogynist in nature, but then again so was everything else in the world at that time. It also does seem that the Jesus movement was, in comparison, relatively enlightened in this regard. However, the severe doctoring and suppression that was done by the Church to the historical records of Jesus and his family indicate more than just misogyny. The Church established the doctrine of the "virgin birth" to disconnect Jesus from the genealogy of his father Joseph, a descendant of King David, and for a while tried to maintain that the Virgin Mary had herself been conceived in the same manner, thus disconnecting Jesus from her side of the family as well. They tried to establish the *perpetual* virginity of Mary, thus claiming that Jesus had no biological brothers or sisters, and maintained that the many "brothers" of Jesus mentioned in the Gospels were either children of Joseph from a previous marriage, or merely "brothers" in spirit. They then insisted that Jesus had remained chaste his entire life as well. The numerous passages in the Bible proclaiming Jesus as "King of the Jews", "the son of David", and "the Messiah" (a title bestowed traditionally upon the rightful king of Judah) have all been held by the Church to be metaphorical. Christ's real kingdom is in Heaven, the Church has always maintained - not in Israel. Pilate referred to Jesus as "King of the Jews" *mockingly*, they say. After all, how could he literally be king when he had no ancestors, no father, no brothers, no wife, and no heirs? Thus began a smear campaign and a genocidal persecution that has continued for approximately 2000 years.

The real reason why Mary Magdalene was "written out of the Bible", and otherwise maligned by the Church, was because her existence was evidence of the continuation of Jesus' royal line. Furthermore, *who she really was* indicated the true meaning of Jesus' mission. If the truth about Jesus' marriage to Mary were known, the entire edifice of Rome's doctrine may very well come tumbling down.

A Benjamite Queen

In *The Woman with the Alabaster Jar*, Margaret Starbird theorizes that little may be known of the marriage partially because it may have purposely been kept secret by Jesus and his closest followers. According to Starbird, this was a direct result of the *royal* nature of the union. It was, she says, a "dynastic alliance." She, like many others, believes that "Mary Magdalene" and "Mary of Bethany" were the same person, and writes:

"I have come to suspect that Jesus had a secret dynastic marriage with Mary of Bethany, and that she was a daughter of the tribe of Benjamin, whose ancestral heritage was the land surrounding the Holy City of David, the city Jerusalem. A dynastic marriage between Jesus and a royal daughter of the Benjamites would have been perceived as a source of healing to the people of Israel during their time of misery as an occupied nation."

Numerous researchers have connected Magdalene to the tribe of Benjamin, which provided Israel with its first king, Saul. Although Saul was soon deposed by David, a descendant of Judah (a tribe whom God himself had sanctioned to provide the kings of Israel), the tribes of Judah and Benjamin maintained a close relationship with the Benjamites, eventually becoming subsumed into the tribe of Judah. (More will be said on this subject later on.) As noted by Starbird, the city of Jerusalem itself was technically a Benjamite city, although the kings of Judah maintained it as their royal capitol. Benjamin (which means "son of the right hand" in Hebrew) was the youngest of the patriarch Jacob's twelve sons, so for this tribe to provide Israel's first king, as well as the Messiah's heir (through the Magdalene), would have been a great example of how, as Jesus himself states in the Gospels, "the last shall be the first, and the first shall be the last." But that is not all of the inheritance that a Benjamite princess like Magdalene might bring to the table. There are many other layers of meaning to her symbolic value.

When Jacob was lying on his deathbed, he handed out blessings and curses to each of his sons, as was the tradition at that time. And even though God himself had established the tradition that men should pass on the greatest portion of their inheritance to their firstborn son, with the Biblical patriarchs that rarely turned our to be the case, as the elder son was almost always disqualified for some reason or another. Thus, essentially skipping over his first three sons (who were cursed for actions they had taken earlier in life), Jacob placed the bulk of his blessing on his forth son Judah, to whom he said:

"Judah, thou art he whom thy brethren shall praise: thy hand shall be in the neck of thine enemies; thy father's children shall bow down before thee. Judah is a lion's whelp: from the prey, my son, thou art gone up: he stooped down, he couched as a lion, and as an old lion; who shall rouse him up? The scepter shall not depart from Judah, nor a lawgiver from between his feet, until Shiloh come; and unto him shall the gathering of the people be. Binding his foal unto the vine, and his ass's colt unto the choice vine; he washed his garments in wine, and his clothes in the blood of grapes: His eyes shall be red with wine, and his teeth white with milk." (Genesis 49:8-12.)

Meanwhile, to Benjamin, Jacob said the following:

"Benjamin shall ravin as a wolf: in the morning he shall devour the prey, and at night he shall divide the spoil." (Genesis 49:27.)

Author Olaf Hage, on his website "Hage Productions" (http://petragrail.tripod.com/mm.html) has written an article interpreting these words and what they say about Mary Magdalene. He sees Magdalene as a Benjamite princess, with an important dynastic inheritance stemming from her father, whom he identifies as Simon the Leper. Olaf Hage also equates Simon with another character from the Gospels: Nicodemus, one of the Sanhedrin council members, and the one who anointed (or prepared to anoint) Jesus' body for burial after his crucifixion, according to the Gospels. As Hage writes:

"The house of Benjamin was given the right to keep the written genealogies of the priests and kings, to decide which persons were entitled to inherit. The Torah says Benjamin will 'Divide the spoils' - that is, the inheritance of Israel... But the tribe of Benjamin could do more than keep written records that designated the Priest and King. It could anoint them."

This point addresses the scene in the Gospels which has earned Mary her association with her alabaster jar - her anointing of the head and feet of Jesus with spikenard. *Matthew 26:6-13* states:

"Now when Jesus was in Bethany, in the house of Simon the leper, There came unto him a woman having an alabaster box of very precious ointment, and poured it on his head, as he sat at meat. But when his disciples saw it, they had indignation, saying, To what purpose is this waste? For this ointment might have been sold for much, and given to the poor. When Jesus understood it, he said unto them, Why trouble ye the woman? for she hath wrought a good work upon me. For ye have the poor always with you; but me ye have not always. For in that she hath poured this ointment on my body, she did it for my burial. Verily I say unto you, Wheresoever this gospel shall be preached in the whole world, there shall also this, that this woman hath done, be told for a memorial of her."[1]

According to Olaf Hage:

"When Mary brought out the "genuine nard" and anointed Jesus, she was declaring Jesus the official king... This act of hers... is standard practice for an official royal anointing."

Margaret Starbird concurs, and adds:

"... in more ancient times, the anointing of the sacred king was the unique privilege of a royal bride. For millennia this same action has been part of an actual marriage rite, performed by a daughter of the royal house, and the marriage rite itself conferred kingship upon her consort."

Starbird echoes a theme that has been suggested by many authors before: that Jesus' church was, at the highest level, a Greco-Roman-Judaic mystery cult, in which Mary Magdalene performed the role of the Sacred Prostitute. She writes:

"The anointing performed by the woman at Bethany was similar to the familiar ritual practice of a sacred priestess or temple 'prostitute' in the Goddess cults of the Roman Empire. Even the term 'prostitute' is a misnomer. This term, chosen by modern translators, is applied to the hierodilae, or 'sacred woman' of the temple... At some periods of Jewish history, they were even a part of the ritual worship in the Temple of Jerusalem..."

The Alchemical Wedding

Seen in this light, the wedding of Jesus and Mary, which many people see as being represented in the Gospels by the story of the wedding at Cana, becomes nothing less than a Gnostic sex magic ritual, and Mary's anointing of Jesus was an integral part of it. Starbird continues:

"The anointing of the head had erotic significance, the head being symbolic of the phallus 'anointed' by the woman for penetration

during the physical consummation of marriage... Through this union with the priestess, the king/consort received royal status. He became known as the 'Anointed One' - in Hebrew, the 'Messiah.'"

Other writers concur that Mary Magdalene was a temple priestess or 'sacred prostitute' for Jesus' cult, and that she acted in this regard as Jesus' "Grail Maiden." Nicholas de Vere, in his book *The Dragon Legacy: The Secret History of an Ancient Bloodline*, states his opinion that the main sex magic ritual which was engaged in by this cult was the non-penetrative ritual of "Starfire", in which a mixture of menstrual blood and female ejaculate is consumed by the priest directly from the vagina of the priestess. It is consumed, says De Vere, because if the priestess is of the "Grail bloodline", these fluids will contain the "Philosopher's Stone" (a.k.a. "Ormus". "Occultum", or "white gold") - special secretions from the pineal gland found, he says, more concentratedly in the fluids of Grail bloodline members. If the priest is of the bloodline as well, as Jesus would have been, consuming these fluids would initiate a transcendental spiritual experience for the priest, and to a lesser extent, for any participating "guests" at the "wedding." This is the capacity in which Magdalene would have served as a "priestess" or "Grail maiden", and according to De Vere, she would have begun doing so at a very young age:

"She was twelve at the time and he was, according to the Bible, about thirty years old. The ritual employed was similar to that in which Lazarus partook, in that it involved symbolic death and resurrection. (See Luke 8: verse 41-56.) Following her initiation and during the period of her adolescence, as was common practice, Mary would have acted as Jesus' handmaiden or grail priestess."

De Vere claims that this was part of a family tradition for the member's of Jesus' inner cult, most of whom were biologically related to him. He believes Jesus' mother was a priestess as well:

"Both Jesus' mother Mary and his wife Mary Magdalene were called the 'crystal wombs from which shined forth the light of God', a description which suggests strongly the Tantric and Qabalistic concept of Starfire."

Something along these lines does seem to be indicated symbolically in the story of the wedding at Cana - Christ and Magdalene's wedding, according to some. The transformation of water into wine seems to point to an alchemical ritual, which sex magic certainly is, in which the water and wine could refer to female ejaculate and menstrual blood (respectively), particularly given the symbolism of Mary and her bloodline as "the choice vine." (More on this subject later.)

Indeed, such a symbolic connection appears to be made in *The Song of Solomon*, which is a coded document describing a royal sex magic ritual performed by the Judaic King Solomon (Jesus' ancestor and predecessor), with one of his many wives or concubines. Human body fluids like vaginal secretions, female ejaculate, semen, menstrual blood, and other things, such as sexual organs, are disguised as "spikenard", "wine", "myrrh", "living waters", "the Rose of Sharon", and "the Lily of the Valley." Quotes from the poem such as the following have, understandably, been interpreted as a sexual manner:

- *"Because of the savour of thy good ointments thy name is as ointment poured forth, therefore do the virgins love thee."*

- *"While the king sitteth at his table, my spikenard sendeth forth the smell thereof."*

- *"Thy lips, O my spouse, drop as the honeycomb: honey and milk are under thy tongue; and the smell of thy garments is like the smell of Lebanon."*

- *"Thy plants are an orchard of pomegranates, with pleasant fruits; camphire, with spikenard..."*

- *"I sleep, but my heart waketh: it is the voice of my beloved that knocketh, saying, Open to me, my sister, my love, my dove, my undefiled: for my head is filled with dew, and my locks with the drops of the night. I have put off my coat; how shall I put it on? I have washed my feet; how shall I defile them?"*

- *"I rose up to open to my beloved; and my hands dropped with myrrh, and my fingers with sweet smelling myrrh, upon the handles of the lock."*

- *"I would lead thee, and bring thee into my mother's house, who would instruct me: I would cause thee to drink of spiced wine of the juice of my pomegranate."*

Interestingly, the "bride" in this poem describes herself symbolically as "black", just as Mary Magdalene was represented in some European churches as the "Black Madonna." (We will get back to the symbolism of this in due course.) The poem states:

"Look not upon me, because I am black, because the sun hath looked upon me: my mother's children were angry with me; they made me the keeper of the vineyards; but mine own vineyard have I not kept."

Interestingly, Solomon refers to his bride as his "sister" in this poem. Sex magic rituals are, at root, a re-enactment of an ancient god (equivalent to the Egyptian Osiris) mating with his ancient consort (equivalent to the Egyptian Isis), and in many versions of this myth, including the Egyptian, these two are brother and sister. This would make sense if they were practicing royal sex magic, as Nicholas de Vere describes it, in which the participants are sharing sacred essences inherent in their divine blood. De Vere, like other writers before him, has chosen to analyze the hierogamy purportedly practiced by Jesus and Mary Magdalene in terms of the imagery of *The Song of Solomon*. He writes:

"...In this manner, Mary means 'spirit in the womb' or 'womb-fire.' It is in the latter instance that we have a direct reference to the Tantric Kaula ritual of enlivening or inflaming the chakra of the uterine region to produce the 'waters of life' or, as The Song of Solomon puts it, "The well of living waters."

Mary's symbol is the white lily of the valley,

the fleur-de-lys. As the 'Well of living waters", Mary's relationship to Jesus becomes clearer as the child handmaiden of the Messach, the Dragon God-King. 'Marie' is an ancient form of the word 'marry', meaning 'to join to unite with', as in alchemical marriage, divine enthea, hierogamy, the sacred marriage ritual of Solomon's Song..."

In the ancient traditions of hierogamy, or royal sex magic, the "wedding" takes place just prior to the sacrifice of the "sacred king" (symbolized by the high priest), and the sex ritual anointed him as king, just in time for his ritual death. This was the case in the ancient fertility cults, in which the death of the king ensured agricultural prosperity, and this was the case with Mary and Jesus. In Matthew's version of the anointing ceremony, which was part of the sacred marriage act, it was followed immediately by Judas' betrayal, which led to Jesus' sacrifice on the cross. Jesus even stated explicitly that she was anointing him "for his burial." This would make Mary a participant in the ritual slaying of Jesus. Nicholas de Vere sees this as being part of the symbolic ceremony, and apparently does not believe that Jesus was actually slain in the flesh. He writes:

"After Jesus' death, Magdalene went to the cell and found it open. Rather, I would argue that in accordance with the traditional ritual that accompanied her station, she was expected to stay in the cell and commune with the Ka of Jesus in the Underworld. Few people actually knew the real reason why she went...

That she went to heal him of his non-fatal wounds was a secret known only to an initiated few, among whom the apostles, it seems, were not counted."

Of the function of Grail maidens in general, De Vere has this to say:

"The girls, whose watery embrace is said to spell death, are the Shunnamites, the lilies or virgins who are portrayed in The Song of Solomon. In their connection with water, the nymphs are thus depicted as the embodiment of the wells of living waters. Their deathly embrace is but the death of

the ego, of the will, and of desire."

Others concur about the connection between sex and death in this sacred kingship ritual. Margaret Starbird writes that that sacred marriage "includes the torture and death of the anointed Bridegroom/King." Likewise, in an article on lost-civilizations.net, entitled "The Horse Sacrifice", the author writes about a ritual:

"... celebrated in Sumer and Babylon on the occasion of the New Year Festival (Akitu). In this ritual, the king would ritually mate with a sacred prostitute (hierodule) inside a shrine on top of the ziggurat. This building, a sort of stepped pyramid, represented the Cosmic Mountain, itself a replica of the Cosmos. Hence, the couple united inside the temple or the altar represented the Primordial Couple buried inside the Cosmic Mountain, in Paradise.

Very likely, the Heb Sed festival of the Egyptians, as well as the secret ceremonies celebrated inside the Egyptian temples and pyramids, were also ritual enactments of the Cosmogonic Hierogamy, the Sacred Marriage of the King and the Sacred Prostitute, the Hierodule of Bastit or of some other similar goddess, as we shall see further below.

In the ashvamedha, the wife of the officiating priest the mahishi simulated a ritual mating with the sacrificial horse. The mahishi (lit. 'the Great Cow') represented the Earth, much as the horse symbolized the Sun. Indeed, she also stood for the queen as the Primordial Whore, just as her husband (the mahisha) was an alias of the Horse, the Sun, the Primordial Male (or buffalo). The couple stood for Heaven and Earth and, more exactly, for Yama and Yami, the Primordial Couple of paradisial times."

It is looking more and more like Jesus' wedding was the most important aspect of his life, his ministry, and his political bid for the kingship of Israel - more so even than his death. In fact, his death looks more and more like it was symbolic, and that he did not really die, but rather was pretending to be sacrificed as part of an ancient ritual of marriage, death, and rebirth, the act of which turned him from a priest and a prophet into a god-king: the Messiah. Mary's association with the color black can be considered an extension of her embodiment of the archetype of Isis, the "black widow", who was symbolically veiled in darkness as she mourned for her dead husband, Osiris. The color black represents, in alchemy, the "nigrido", the prima materia from whence the Philosopher's Stone is made. This is also called the "death phase" in alchemy, and is further symbolized by a dead king (drowned or decapitated), or by a skull (like the one Mary Magdalen is almost always depicted with).

Although De Vere's theory may be correct, in that there was no penetrative intercourse, but only the consumption of body fluids, there may indeed have been intercourse as well, resulting in a child - a royal heir and son (or daughter) of God (at least symbolically). If there were such a child, it would be born after Jesus' symbolic death, and would be a "widow's son." This is the term used to identify Horus in the Rites of Isis, who was conceived when Isis mated with the dead body of Osiris. This she accomplished by putting together all of the pieces of Osiris' body (which his brother Set had chopped to bits), and providing a substitute for the one missing piece: his penis. This story is a disguised account of a sex magic ritual in which the priest is possessed by the spirit of Osiris, and acts as a "substitute penis" so that the dead god can impregnate the young priestess and breed a royal heir. The term "widow's son" has significance in the rites of Freemasonry, where it is applied to Hiram, the builder of Solomon's Temple, and all Freemasons refer to themselves metaphorically as "widow's sons." Also, in the Gospels, there is a story in which Jesus raises from the dead a man described as a "son of a widow." This tale clearly describes in metaphor yet another death and resurrection ritual performed by the cult of Christ. Jesus himself may have been conceived during one of these rituals, which may account for the purportedly divine nature of his conception.

From Jesus' own words, we glean that his entire ministry, and the "kingdom of heaven" itself, could be thought of as a "wedding", while the "church" which he was raising up was his "bride." This is how the Roman Catholic and Protestant Christian churches have chosen to interpret the numerous metaphorical references Jesus made to "the wedding", "the marriage", the "bride" and the "bridegroom."

In *Matthew 9:15*, we read:

"And Jesus said unto them, Can the children of the bridechamber mourn, as long as the bridegroom is with them? but the days will come, when the bridegroom shall be taken from them, and then shall they fast."

Later, in *Matthew, 25:1-13*, Jesus tells a fascinating parable indicating that only the chosen few will be able to participate as brides in this "wedding":

"Then shall the kingdom of heaven be likened unto ten virgins, which took their lamps, and went forth to meet the bridegroom. And five of them were wise, and five were foolish. They that were foolish took their lamps, and took no oil with them: But the wise took oil in their vessels with their lamps.

While the bridegroom tarried, they all slumbered and slept. And at midnight there was a cry made, Behold, the bridegroom cometh; go ye out to meet him. Then all those virgins arose, and trimmed their lamps. And the foolish said unto the wise, Give us of your oil; for our lamps are gone out. But the wise answered, saying, Not so; lest there be not enough for us and you: but go ye rather to them that sell, and buy for yourselves. And while they went to buy, the bridegroom came; and they that were ready went in with him to the marriage: and the door was shut. Afterward came also the other virgins, saying, Lord, Lord, open to us. But he answered and said, Verily I say unto you, I know you not. Watch therefore, for ye know neither the day nor the hour wherein the Son of man cometh."

And earlier in the same book, Jesus indicates that even the guest list at this "wedding" will be selective:

"The kingdom of heaven is like unto a certain king, which made a marriage for his son. And sent forth his servants to call them that were bidden to the wedding: and they would not come. Again, he sent forth other servants, saying, Tell them which are bidden, Behold, I have prepared my dinner: my oxen and my fatlings are killed, and all things are ready: come unto the marriage. But they made light of it, and went their ways, one to his farm, another to his merchandise: And the remnant took his servants, and entreated them spitefully, and slew them.

But when the king heard thereof, he was wroth: and he sent forth his armies, and destroyed those murderers, and burned up their city. Then saith he to his servants, The wedding is ready, but they which were bidden were not worthy. Go ye therefore into the highways, and as many as ye shall find, bid to the marriage.

So those servants went out into the highways, and gathered together all as many as they found, both bad and good: and the wedding was furnished with guests. And when the king came in to see the guests, he saw there a man which had not on a wedding garment: And he saith unto him, Friend, how camest thou in hither not having a wedding garment? And he was speechless.

Then said the king to the servants, Bind him hand and foot, and take him away, and cast him into outer darkness, there shall be weeping and gnashing of teeth. For many are called, but few are chosen."

In *Luke 12:36*, Jesus tells his disciples to be "like unto men that wait for their lord, when he will return from the wedding; that when he cometh and knocketh, they may open unto him immediately." And in *Luke 14:8* he warns them: "When thou art bidden of any [man] to a wedding, sit not down in the highest room; lest a more honourable man than thou be bidden of him..." In *John 3:39*, he tells his followers to be glad, even if they are not lucky enough to marry themselves, just to be able to witness the wedding:

"He that hath the bride is the bridegroom: but the friend of the bridegroom, which standeth and heareth him, rejoiceth greatly because of the bridegroom's voice: this my joy therefore is fulfilled."

In this light, the symbol of the Rose-Croix can be seen to represent the marriage of Christ (symbolized by the cross) and the Magdalene (symbolized by the rose, as she is to this very day). Though its roots are far more ancient than the time of Jesus (as it symbolized the primordial concept of the sexual union of god and goddess which Jesus and Mary were themselves trying to emulate), the Rosicrucians, who were initiates into the true mysteries of Christ, may have been directly referencing this particular alchemical wedding when they employed this symbol. This theory may bring us a new interpretation of the classic Rosicrucian text, *The Chymical Wedding of Christian Rosenkreutz*. In this story, the narrator is cordially invited (by an angel, no less) to a royal wedding with a very exclusive guest list. The path to get to the wedding is treacherous and difficult. Rosenkreutz is tested on wisdom and purity of heart several times at the gate to the castle, and again at the door, and must even purchase a special token to gain admittance. Once he is arrived, there are further tests, and several of the guests are eliminated. The goings-on of the wedding are very peculiar, mystical, and shrouded in metaphor - the typically impenetrable maze of alchemical allegory. The ceremony takes place over several days, and includes the death and rebirth of the king. It would be easy to see this text as an allegory for Jesus and Mary's ritual wedding. At one point during the narrator's stay at the castle, he stumbles upon the tomb of the "sleeping Lady Venus." As he describes it:

"The sepulcher was triangular, and had in the middle of it a kettle of polished copper... In the kettle stood an angel, who held in his arms an unknown tree, from which it continually dropped fruit into the kettle; and as oft as the fruit fell into the kettle, it turned into water, and ran out from thence into three small golden kettles standing by."

On the bed of the Lady Venus he finds a tablet upon which is written:

"When the fruit of my tree shall be quite melted down, then I shall awake and be the mother of a king."

In *The Dragon Legacy*, Nicholas de Vere analyzes several similar allegorical tales and legends involving trees that drop fruit into pools. About them, collectively, he has this to say:

"The well... [symbolizes] the womb and the vagina, below which is the vulva, the tree growing next to the well represents the lower and upper torso, the head and the arms of the virgin female. The twigs and branches of the tree symbolize the veins and arteries of rich, Holy Royal Blood, and the fruits of the tree represent the endocrinal glands that correspond to the chakras in Tantrism..."

The Curse of the Benjamites

So was Mary Magdalene a "sex goddess"? According to my research, she was. Moreover, her descent from the tribe of Benjamin may have made her particularly qualified for the role. This pertains to a peculiar story regarding this tribe that can be found at the end of *The Book of Judges*. In Chapter 19 of that book, we read:

"And it came to pass in those days, when there was no king in Israel, that there was a certain Levite sojourning on the side of mount Ephraim, who took to him a concubine out of Bethlehemjudah. And his concubine played the whore against him, and went away from him unto her father's house to Bethlehemjudah, and was there four whole months. And her husband arose, and went after her, to speak friendly unto her, and to bring her again, having his servant with him, and a couple of asses: and she brought him into her father's house: and when the father of the damsel saw him, he rejoiced to meet him." (Judges 19:1-3.)

The Levite and his "wife"/"concubine" spend several days at their father-in-law's house, and then begin their journey back to their home in Bethlehemjudah. On the way back it begins to get dark, so they decide to sojourn for the night in the Benjamite city of Gibeah. But no one there will take them into their house, so they sit down in the street, determined to sleep there. Then an old man who lives there comes over to them:

"And when he had lifted up his eyes, he saw a wayfaring man in the street of the city: and the old man said, Whither goest thou? and whence comest thou? And he said unto him, We are passing from Bethlehemjudah toward the side of mount Ephraim; from thence am I: and I went to Bethlehemjudah, but I am now going to the house of the LORD; and there is no man that receiveth me to house. Yet there is both straw and provender for our asses; and there is bread and wine also for me, and for thy handmaid, and for the young man which is with thy servants: there is no want of any thing. And the old man said, Peace be with thee; howsoever let all thy wants lie upon me; only lodge not in the street. So he brought him into his house, and gave provender unto the asses: and they washed their feet, and did eat and drink." (Judges 19:17-21.)

It is at this point that our story takes a turn for the stranger. The house is besieged by a group of Benjamites referred to as "sons of Belial", seeking to commit lewd acts of sodomy with the young Levite. As the text states:

"Now as they were making their hearts merry, behold, the men of the city, certain sons of Belial, beset the house round about, and beat at the door, and spake to the master of the house, the old man, saying, Bring forth the man that came into thine house, that we may know him.

And the man, the master of the house, went out unto them, and said unto them, Nay, my brethren, nay, I pray you, do not so wickedly; seeing that this man is come into mine house, do not this folly. Behold, here is my daughter a maiden, and his concubine; them I will bring out now, and humble ye them, and do with them what seemeth good unto you: but unto this man do not so vile a thing. But the men would not hearken to him: so the man took his concubine, and brought her forth unto them; and they knew her, and abused her all the night until the morning: and when the day began to spring, they let her go.

Then came the woman in the dawning of the day, and fell down at the door of the man's house where her lord was, till it was light. And her lord rose up in the morning, and opened the doors of the house, and went out to go his way: and, behold, the woman his concubine was fallen down at the door of the house, and her hands were upon the threshold. And he said unto her, Up, and let us be going. But none answered. Then the man took her up upon an ass, and the man rose up, and gat him unto his place." (Judges 19:22-28.)

You would think that the Levite had known, when the old man offered his concubine up to be raped by the sons of Belial, that something bad was going to happen to her, and thus he should not have been surprised to find her dead the next day. If he had any objection to this, one would think that he would have stopped the old man from offering her up. Yet he does not seem terribly upset, but nonetheless sets about to take revenge, by dividing his concubine's body into twelve parts, and sending one to each of the tribes of Israel! Presumably he did this as a way of informing them about the injustice that was done to him, to seek their help in avenging her death. The text reads:

"And when he was come into his house, he took a knife, and laid hold on his concubine, and divided her, together with her bones, into twelve pieces, and sent her into all the coasts of Israel. And it was so, that all that saw it said, There was no such deed done nor seen from the day that the children of Israel came up out of the land of Egypt unto this day: consider of it, take advice, and speak your minds." (Judges 19:29-30.)

Then, all eleven of the other tribes agree to wage war against the entire tribe of Benjamin, for allowing this injustice to take place in their territory:

"Then all the children of Israel went out, and the congregation was gathered together as one man, from Dan even to Beersheba, with the land of Gilead, unto the LORD in Mizpeh. And the chief of all the people, even of all the tribes of Israel, presented themselves in the assembly of the people of God, four hundred thousand footmen that drew

sword.

(Now the children of Benjamin heard that the children of Israel were gone up to Mizpeh.) Then said the children of Israel, Tell us, how was this wickedness? And the Levite, the husband of the woman that was slain, answered and said, I came into Gibeah that belongeth to Benjamin, I and my concubine, to lodge. And the men of Gibeah rose against me, and beset the house round about upon me by night, and thought to have slain me: and my concubine have they forced, that she is dead. And I took my concubine, and cut her in pieces, and sent her throughout all the country of the inheritance of Israel: for they have committed lewdness and folly in Israel. Behold, ye are all children of Israel; give here your advice and counsel.

And all the people arose as one man, saying, We will not any of us go to his tent, neither will we any of us turn into his house. But now this shall be the thing which we will do to Gibeah; we will go up by lot against it; And we will take ten men of an hundred throughout all the tribes of Israel, and an hundred of a thousand, and a thousand out of ten thousand, to fetch victual for the people, that they may do, when they come to Gibeah of Benjamin, according to all the folly that they have wrought in Israel.

So all the men of Israel were gathered against the city, knit together as one man. And the tribes of Israel sent men through all the tribe of Benjamin, saying, What wickedness is this that is done among you? Now therefore deliver us the men, the children of Belial, which are in Gibeah, that we may put them to death, and put away evil from Israel. But the children of Benjamin would not hearken to the voice of their brethren the children of Israel. But the children of Benjamin gathered themselves together out of the cities unto Gibeah, to go out to battle against the children of Israel." (Judges 20:1-14.)

The battle that followed was long and hard, and was almost lost, so well did this single tribe defend itself against the other eleven. Furthermore, the other tribes were guided by Jehovah himself, with the Levite priests interpreting the war commands he gave them through the oracular device known as the "Urim and Thummin." But in the end, the tribe of Benjamin was almost utterly destroyed - all but three hundred of the men were killed.

However, the victorious tribes had reason to lament. Now one of the tribes of Israel would surely become extinct! For during the war, the warriors from the eleven tribes had sworn an oath "before the Lord", in the city of Mizpeh (the same city where the only Benjamite king of Israel, Saul, was first presented to the people). All of the tribesmen had sworn that they would not allow their daughters to marry Benjamite men:

"Now the men of Israel had sworn in Mizpeh, saying, There shall not any of us give his daughter unto Benjamin to wife. And the people came to the house of God, and abode there till even before God, and lifted up their voices, and wept sore; And said, O LORD God of Israel, why is this come to pass in Israel, that there should be to day one tribe lacking in Israel? And it came to pass on the morrow, that the people rose early, and built there an altar, and offered burnt offerings and peace offerings. And the children of Israel said, Who is there among all the tribes of Israel that came not up with the congregation unto the LORD? For they had made a great oath concerning him that came not up to the LORD to Mizpeh, saying, He shall surely be put to death. And the children of Israel repented them for Benjamin their brother, and said, There is one tribe cut off from Israel this day. How shall we do for wives for them that remain, seeing we have sworn by the LORD that we will not give them of our daughters to wives?"

Yet there was one group among them, the "camp from Jabesh-gilead" (thought to be located in the territory of Gad), who had not taken the oath. So the rest of the Israelites went and killed every man and woman, except for four hundred virgins, that they found. These they captured and sent, for some reason, to the Canaanite city of Shiloh:

"And they said, What one is there of the tribes of Israel that came not up to Mizpeh to the LORD?

And, behold, there came none to the camp from Jabeshgilead to the assembly. For the people were numbered, and, behold, there were none of the inhabitants of Jabeshgilead there. And the congregation sent thither twelve thousand men of the valiantest, and commanded them, saying, Go and smite the inhabitants of Jabeshgilead with the edge of the sword, with the women and the children. And this is the thing that ye shall do, Ye shall utterly destroy every male, and every woman that hath lain by man. And they found among the inhabitants of Jabeshgilead four hundred young virgins, that had known no man by lying with any male: and they brought them unto the camp to Shiloh, which is in the land of Canaan. And the whole congregation sent some to speak to the children of Benjamin that were in the rock Rimmon, and to call peaceably unto them."

They then offer the 400 virgins to the Benjamites as wives. But strangely, even though there were 400 virgins, and only 300 Benjamite men, the virgins did not "suffice." As the text states:

"And Benjamin came again at that time; and they gave them wives which they had saved alive of the women of Jabeshgilead: and yet so they sufficed them not. And the people repented them for Benjamin, because that the LORD had made a breach in the tribes of Israel. Then the elders of the congregation said, How shall we do for wives for them that remain, seeing the women are destroyed out of Benjamin? And they said, There must be an inheritance for them that be escaped of Benjamin, that a tribe be not destroyed out of Israel. Howbeit we may not give them wives of our daughters: for the children of Israel have sworn, saying, Cursed be he that giveth a wife to Benjamin."

So they then offered the Benjamites "the daughters of Shiloh":

"Then they said, Behold, there is a feast of the LORD in Shiloh yearly in a place which is on the north side of Bethel, on the east side of the highway that goeth up from Bethel to Shechem, and on the south of Lebonah. Therefore they commanded the children of Benjamin, saying, Go and lie in wait in the vineyards; And see, and, behold, if the daughters of Shiloh come out to dance in dances, then come ye out of the vineyards, and catch you every man his wife of the daughters of Shiloh, and go to the land of Benjamin.

And it shall be, when their fathers or their brethren come unto us to complain, that we will say unto them, Be favourable unto them for our sakes: because we reserved not to each man his wife in the war: for ye did not give unto them at this time, that ye should be guilty. And the children of Benjamin did so, and took them wives, according to their number, of them that danced, whom they caught: and they went and returned unto their inheritance, and repaired the cities, and dwelt in them."

There is something somewhat confusing about this story. *The Book of Judges* is trying to convince us that the virgins from Jabesh-gilead "would not suffice", and so the Benjamites were forced to marry women from Shiloh. And yet the narrative had already revealed that the virgins from Jabesh-gilead had just been captured and sent to Shiloh! So in all likelihood, the girls from Jabesh-gilead that "did not suffice" were the same as the girls from Shiloh that they married. But for some reason, the text tries to convince us that these are two separate groups of girls. Furthermore, the fact that the girls of Jabesh-gilead were virgins, and that the "daughters of Shiloh" were dancing in the vineyards when the Benjamites were sent out to "catch" them, indicates an ancient fertility rite, much like ancient pagan Easter rituals, in which young virgins were captured and raped by young boys. So what is *The Book of Judges* trying to indicate? That the virgins were really from Jabesh-gilead, the only Israelite town that had not taken the oath against marrying their daughters to Benjamites; or that they were really Canaanite virgins from Shiloh? Either way, we are left understanding that all of the Benjamite generations that followed were descendants of these "virgins of the vineyards."

A Royal Race of Sex Gods

The story of the war with the Benjamites,

and the rape of the concubine that preceded it, appears to contain some significant elements in it. In substance, it is very similar to a story found in Genesis, in which Lot is visited by two angels (or "Watchers", in some translations). And just like the young Levite in the other story, there is something about the angels that the townspeople of Sodom (where Lot lived) found irresistible. They besieged the house of Lot and demanded that the angels come out to have sex with them. As the story goes:

"And there came two angels to Sodom at even; and Lot sat in the gate of Sodom: and Lot seeing them rose up to meet them; and he bowed himself with his face toward the ground;
And he said, Behold now, my lords, turn in, I pray you, into your servant's house, and tarry all night, and wash your feet, and ye shall rise up early, and go on your ways. And they said, Nay; but we will abide in the street all night. And he pressed upon them greatly; and they turned in unto him, and entered into his house; and he made them a feast, and did bake unleavened bread, and they did eat.

But before they lay down, the men of the city, even the men of Sodom, compassed the house round, both old and young, all the people from every quarter: And they called unto Lot, and said unto him, Where are the men which came in to thee this night? bring them out unto us, that we may know them. And Lot went out at the door unto them, and shut the door after him, And said, I pray you, brethren, do not so wickedly. Behold now, I have two daughters which have not known man; let me, I pray you, bring them out unto you, and do ye to them as is good in your eyes: only unto these men do nothing; for therefore came they under the shadow of my roof. And they said, Stand back. And they said again, This one fellow came in to sojourn, and he will needs be a judge: now will we deal worse with thee, than with them. And they pressed sore upon the man, even Lot, and came near to break the door. But the men put forth their hand, and pulled Lot into the house to them, and shut to the door. And they smote the men that were at the door of the house with blindness, both small and great: so that they wearied themselves to find the door."

Clearly, these two stories are connected on a symbolic level. So many of the details are the same, even the fact that angels (just like the Levite and his concubine in the other story) were going to sleep in the street until Lot (like the old man in the other story) took them in. The fact that the "angels" in the Lot story are called "Watchers" in apocryphal versions of the tale indicates that these beings were indeed of the same race described as "sons of God" elsewhere in *The Book of Genesis*.

We are speaking, of course, about *Genesis 6*, in which the "sons of God" (angels) are described as coming down from Heaven to impregnate human women. This incident is greatly elaborated on in *The Book of Enoch*, and other Judeo-Christian texts. The children born of these unions were considered abominations by God, and this is what caused him to bring about the Deluge, to wipe the Earth clean of the pestilence. Different permutations of this myth can be found everywhere, in Greek, Egyptian, Indian, and Babylonian myths.

Also, different versions of the Watcher myth, or references to it, can be found throughout the Bible and other Jewish legends. A Christian text called *The Book of the Cave of Treasures* describes how the "sons of Seth" were lured from the Mountain of Paradise by the "daughters of Cain", and enticed into having sex with them, against the expressed wishes of God, thus bringing damnation to the race spawned from this union, and bringing about the Flood as punishment. A Gnostic text called *The Origin of the World* describes how Eve was once raped by "the Prime Ruler [God] and his Angels" while in paradise, and thus gave birth to a cursed race implied to be that of Cain and his descendants.

In each of these accounts, there is something about these angels that makes them sexually desirous to humans, even to human males, and entices them to commit obscene acts. What was it about the Watchers that made them so irresistible to the Sodomites, and what was it about the Levite that made him so irresistible to the "sons of Belial" of the tribe of Benjamin?

In *The Book of Enoch*, the Watchers are described as being breathtakingly beautiful, with pure white skin and piercing, hypnotic eyes. It was these eyes after which they were named (in Hebrew they were called "ayin" - "those who watch, or see"), and the eyes themselves may have played the key role in causing these beings to seem so sexually attractive. The texts are very particular about describing how the Watchers "cast their eyes" upon the women they were about to seduce. [2] They also had enormous penises. *The Book of Enoch* says that they were consumed with lust upon the sight of human women, and as they descended from Heaven, "their parts of shame hung down like horses."

According to a website called "multiorgasmic.com", the Watchers were of a much higher level of sexual potency than human males, capable of having limitless orgasms without the "Male Refractory Period" (MRP) that prevents most human men from doing this. The website claims that the Watchers taught human females how to enjoy multiple orgasms as well. *The Book of Enoch* and other texts seem to back up this assertion. The Watchers were accused by God of teaching women to perform sexual abominations that they had never known of before, and of teaching them the use of make-up and jewelry, by which means these women then went about seducing other men. Thus was rampant promiscuity and fornication spread about the land. [3]

The race that was spawned by this miscegenation were described as monstrous, sinful, evil creatures, but the sins they were most prone to were sexual in nature. They were called "bastards", "souls addicted to lust", and "children of fornication." In the Bible, they are identified, among other words, by the term "Rephaim." Multiorgasmic.com claims that this term comes from the root word "Rapha", which they translate to mean "hard, potent, masculine, male, or virile." It also may be linked to the root of the word "rape." This links up with a Canaanite legend regarding a line of fallen kings known as "rp'um" - "Dispensers of Fertility." In addition, it may be connected to the legend of the Cainites (the descendants of Cain), who were said to have been so sexually insatiable that they kept two separate sets of wives: one for the purposes of procreation, and the other for the purposes of pleasure.

Multiorgasmic.com claims that the descendants of this race can be found today, and that they possess virility and sexual capacity beyond that of normal human males. In fact, they specifically believe that the Benjamites were among these descendants. On their website, they discuss hints that can be found in *Genesis* indicating that Benjamin, purportedly Jacob's second son by Rachel (and twelfth son in total), was actually the son of a Watcher. They point out that while the conception of each of Jacob's other children is specifically described in *Genesis*, Benjamin's is not. This happened even though Rachel's womb had been barren for decades before she bore her first son, Joseph, and then only by divine intervention - making the conception of a second son seem all the more worthy of mention. In addition, they point out that Jacob received a number of visitations from Watchers in the months preceding Benjamin's birth. On one night in particular, at a time which should have coincided with Benjamin's conception, Jacob made all of his wives and children sleep on the other side of the river while he famously wrestled with one of the angels - leaving Rachel alone and vulnerable to divine rape. When Rachel gave birth to Benjamin, the birth was so troublesome that she named him "Benoni" ("Child of Travail") just before she died of her pains. Benjamin was only renamed afterwards by his "father" Jacob. The people at multiorgasmic.com believe that "Benjamin" may mean "Son of the Min" - "Min" being an Egyptian term for a mythological race that appears to be equivalent to that of the Watchers. In any case, "Benjamin" is certainly similar to "Bene-ha-Elohim", the word translated as "sons of God" in *Genesis*. Benjamin also named his first son "Rapha", similar to "Rephaim", the Hebrew word for the human/Watcher hybrid race.

If the Benjamites were truly descendants of the Watcher, this may explain why they were considered worthy of the crown of Israel, and to be "God's anointed", even though Benjamin was the youngest of Jacob's children. Certain characteristics of the Benjamite King Saul may indicate such a parentage, namely that he was a head taller than all other Israelite men, and so beautiful that all women found him irresistible.

While the descendants of the Watchers were clearly regarded with awe by the rest of the human population, they were also clearly regarded with vehement hatred by God, who in all accounts would stop almost at nothing to destroy every remnant of their seed. This genocidal impulse demonstrates itself in *Genesis 6*, when God floods the Earth to rid it of the Rephaim. The Watchers only manage to salvage the bloodline of their descendants by saving a remnant of the population from destruction: in this case, Noah and his family.[4] Later on in *Genesis*, God destroys Sodom and Gomorrah, the inhabitants of whom, from their behavior, would appear to be Watcher descendants. This occurs immediately after the attempted rape of the Watchers by the Sodomites outside of Lot's house. Once again, the Watchers preserve a remnant of the population: Lot's family. In the apparently related tale of the Benjamites, the tribe is almost utterly destroyed after the rape of the Levite's concubine, and the attempted rape of the Levite himself. In this case, the remnant was preserved by mating them with the "daughters of Shiloh."

The Fate of the Benjamites

There are many theories about what happened to the Benjamites after the war. The general theory is that they were subsumed into the kingdom of Judah, their descendants primarily staying in the region around Jerusalem that had been allocated to their tribe. Thus many figures in the New Testament, including Mary Magdalene, and even the Apostle Paul (who, significantly, was originally named "Saul") were from the lineage of Benjamin. Indeed, some historians affirm that virtually everyone who lived in the region of Galilee, where Jesus lived, was of this lineage.

As multiorgasmic.com states:

"In fact, there is strong evidence that most if not all of Jesus' disciples were of the Tribe of Benjamin. This is due to the fact that the province known as 'Galilee' belonged to the Tribe of Benjamin. Thus to be a 'Galilean' was to be a Benjamite...

Additionally, the cities of Nazareth (town most identified with Jesus), Capernaum (where Jesus first announced his Messianic mission), Cana (where Jesus turned water into wine... *possibly at his own wedding), and Magdala (town most identified with Mary Magdalene) are all in Galilee and at that time populated predominantly by Benjamites. And of course there is the Sea of Galilee where so many other great miracles occurred.*

As it is well known, it was in Galilee that Jesus ostentatiously spent most of his ministry, being also identified often in scripture as 'Jesus of Galilee.'

It is further interesting to note that the very city of Jerusalem was originally a Benjamite city, given to the Tribe of Benjamin for their inheritance. It wasn't until the advent of King David that Jerusalem was claimed by him as his royal city and henceforth became a property of his own Tribe of Judah."

However, there is evidence that Benjamites ended up elsewhere also. As explained in *Holy Blood, Holy Grail*, by Baigent, et. al., the Priory of Sion's *Secret Dossiers* state that the Benjamites were exiled: "Their exile supposedly took them to Greece, to the central Pelopponesus - to Arcadia." The royal house of Arcadia later intermarried with the line that eventually resulted in the Merovingian kings of France. *Secret Dossiers* tells us that:

"One day the descendants of Benjamin left their country; certain remained; two thousand years later, Godfroi VI [de Bouillon] became King of Jerusalem and founded the Ordre de Sion."

Holy Blood, Holy Grail adds other details that appear to tie the Benjamites in with the Merovingian kings, and with Freemasonry:

"According to Robert Graves, for example, the day sacred to Benjamin was December 23 - Dagobert's feast day. Among the three clans that comprised the tribe of Benjamin there was the clan of Ahiram - which might in some obscure way pertain to Hiram, builder of the temple of Solomon and central figure in Masonic tradition. Hiram's most devoted disciple, moreover, was named Benoni, Benjamin's original name."

Indeed, there is a very good reason why Benjamin might have originally been named after

Hiram of Tyre, one of Phoenicia's greatest kings. According to Michael Bradley's *Holy Grail Across the Atlantic*, the Benjamites had significant ties to the Phoenicians:

"But it came to pass that most of the Benjamites left Palestine, and this was because of a civil war among the Israelites. The Tribe of Benjamin came into conflict with the other eleven Tribes because the Benjamites were apparently allied with the 'Sons of Belial' and would not attempt to impose Israelite laws and customs upon them. This war is covered in Judges 21 in the Bible. The result was that most of the Benjamites left Palestine, or were expelled by the victorious eleven Tribes. The 'Sons of Belial' with whom the Benjamites were allied, or against whom they refused to go to war...were none other than the Phoenicians of Tyre and Sidon..."

More than that, *Holy Blood, Holy Grail* seems to suggest that the Benjamites may have even considered the god known as "Belial" to literally be one of their ancestors:

"There is the legend of King Belus's son, one Danaus, who arrives in Greece, with his daughters, by ship. His daughters are said to have introduced the cult of the Mother Goddess, which became the established cult of the Arcadians. According to Robert Graves, the Danaus myth records the arrival in the Peloponnesus of 'colonists from Palestine.' Graves states that King Belus is in fact Baal, or Bel - or perhaps Belial [a form of the Mother Goddess often associated with images of a bull or calf] from the Old Testament. It is also worthy of note that one of the clans of the Tribe of Benjamin was the clan of Bela... Indeed, it is possible that the worship of the golden calf in Exodus... may have been a specifically Benjamite ritual."

The Holy Whores of Israel

It is clear from reading the Old Testament that in the eyes of the Hebrew Jehovah, the only thing worse than worshipping the gods of other, non-Israelite tribes was marrying the daughters of non-Israelite tribes. The Hebrews believed quite literally that the curses and blessings of Jehovah had the power to be passed on intergenerationally through patrilineal descent. They believed that a special covenant had been made between their ancestor, Abraham, and the Hebrew god which conferred an exalted status upon their people - a covenant that was confirmed later by Isaac and Jacob as well. This covenant had been sealed by the rite of circumcision, starting with Abraham, which Abraham's children, and all servants of Jehovah thereafter undertook. It was only by passing through this ordeal that a person not already of Abraham's bloodline could enter into the covenant, and then the blessings of Jehovah would be passed down through their bloodline as well. Thus could an unclean man be made clean.

But there was no such rite to bring unclean women into the covenant. Therefore, women born of uncircumcised men from non-Israelite tribes were considered unfit for marriage, because they were thought to carry within their very blood an allegiance to other gods. It is for this reason that only those born of Jewish women are themselves considered Jews. According to rabbinical tradition, this law is derived from *Deuteronomy 7:4*, forbidding the taking of non-Israelite wives, "For they will turn thy son away from following me, that they may serve other gods." Thus most marriages to foreign wives were considered illegitimate.

The children born of such marriages were thought to carry within their blood the curse of Jehovah. However, the belief in generational curses and blessings was not something unique to the Hebrews. Many elements of their early culture, including many aspects of their religion, were borrowed from the Canaanites, cousins of the Hebrew people. The Hebrews had taken part of Canaan (after many years of genocidal tribal wars) when Jehovah had directed them to seize this land. The concept that one could establish a family covenant with a deity, the blessings of which would be passed down to one's descendants, was among the elements that the Israelites picked up from their cousins.

The Bible describes the land of Canaan as being inhabited mostly by Rephaim, the offspring of the Watchers that the Bible refers to as "giants." If the Canaanites were giants, and they were also cousins of the Hebrews, that implies that the early

Hebrews were also giants, and of Watcher descent as well. Such a proposition is borne out by numerous Jewish legends (many already discussed in earlier *Dagobert's Revenge* articles) stating that all of the biblical patriarchs up to and including the twelve sons of Jacob were giants. It appears that the pantheon of deities that were worshipped by the Canaanites, and by other Middle Eastern tribes, in fact represented ancestral gods - the angels, or Watchers, who helped spawn their races in antediluvian times. And among this pantheon was Jehovah, who, before becoming the patron deity of the Israelites, was seen as being part of a family of gods. The goddess Astaroth (reviled in the Bible) was thought by some to be his consort.

But at some point, the Israelites became convinced that they had made a special covenant with Jehovah. He was their god, they were his children, and they were not to worship other gods or goddesses, or marry women from tribes outside of the covenant. Yet many did it anyway, even beloved, heroic biblical figures like David and Solomon. The entire royal line of Israel has been polluted numerous times by the marrying of "strange women." Inevitably, this always led to the tainted bridegrooms indulging in the worship of strange gods. Why might this be so? Why would they knowingly bring the curses of Jehovah upon themselves and their bloodline by marrying foreign women and worshipping strange gods?

The easy answer is that they thought that the foreign gods could offer them something that Jehovah could not. They thought that the blessings which could be obtained by allying themselves with the other gods outweighed the curses that Jehovah would inflict on them. Furthermore, if they understood these other gods to be ancestors of theirs, they may have felt they had a duty to serve them. There were undoubtedly dynastic and political advantages as well - rights and property gained through such marriages.

Issues such as these seem to be at the heart of the strange story of the Benjamites. We are led to believe from the narrative of the story that the other tribes declared war on the Benjamites because they failed to prevent the "sons of Belial" from raping the Levite's concubine, even though it was the old man who the Levite was staying with that offered her to them in the first place, and the Levite did not stop him. Closer examination reveals that behind this story lies an allegory for rape of a different sort.

According to *The Legends of the Jews*, by Louis Ginzberg, the real cause of the Benjamite war was spiritual. And we do see evidence of this in the text of *The Book of Judges*. For in the chapters preceding this story, *The Book of Judges* discusses a "man of Mount Ephraim" named Micah, the son of Samson and Delilah. Those familiar with this story know that Samson was a giant, who, like the Merovingian kings, purportedly had magical powers that were derived from his long hair. He was one of the judges of Israel (before they had kings), and his arch-enemies were the Philistines. Delilah was the Philistine wife he took, who is most famous for having sold the secret of Samson's magical strength (his hair) to the Philistines for a vast cache of silver, leading to Samson's capture and then death. She then gave some of this silver to her son Micah, who forged a number of pagan idols out of it, and then hired a young Levite to be a priest to those idols. *Judges* states: "Then said Micah, Now know I that the Lord will do me good, seeing I have a Levite to my priest." It is not explained why Micah would think that "the Lord" (presumably Jehovah) would appreciate him worshipping idols, but it is clear that Levites were considered well-equipped for the priesthood *no matter what gods* they ministered to (ironic since it was supposedly Jehovah, who ordained them as the priestly caste in the first place).

Anyway, Micah, his Levite, and their idols apparently became well-known to all throughout the land - perhaps partially because this unidentified Levite was, according to Louis Ginzberg, the grandson of Moses. At around this time, the members of the tribe of Dan were seeking out land to occupy, "for unto that day all their inheritance had not yet fallen unto them among the tribes of Israel." They decided to seize the land of Zorah, and, as per the usual Israelite custom, annihilate the local population. On their way to war, they stop by the house of Micah. Seeking spiritual aid in their conquest of Zorah, they stole Micah's idols, and his Levite, who went with them gleefully! As *Judges* tells us:

"And these went into Micah's house, and fetched the carved image, the ephod, and the teraphim, and the molten image. Then said the priest unto them, What do ye? And they said unto him, Hold thy peace, lay thine hand upon thy mouth, and go with us, and be to us a father and a priest: is it better for thee to be a priest unto the house of one man, or that thou be a priest unto a tribe and a family in Israel? And the priest's heart was glad, and he took the ephod, and the teraphim, and the graven image, and went in the midst of the people. So they turned and departed, and put the little ones and the cattle and the carriage before them.

And when they were a good way from the house of Micah, the men that were in the houses near to Micah's house were gathered together, and overtook the children of Dan. And they cried unto the children of Dan. And they turned their faces, and said unto Micah, What aileth thee, that thou comest with such a company? And he said, Ye have taken away my gods which I made, and the priest, and ye are gone away: and what have I more? and what is this that ye say unto me, What aileth thee?

And the children of Dan said unto him, Let not thy voice be heard among us, lest angry fellows run upon thee, and thou lose thy life, with the lives of thy household. And the children of Dan went their way: and when Micah saw that they were too strong for him, he turned and went back unto his house. And they took the things which Micah had made, and the priest which he had, and came unto Laish, unto a people that were at quiet and secure: and they smote them with the edge of the sword, and burnt the city with fire.

And there was no deliverer, because it was far from Zidon, and they had no business with any man; and it was in the valley that lieth by Bethrehob. And they built a city, and dwelt therein. And they called the name of the city Dan, after the name of Dan their father, who was born unto Israel: howbeit the name of the city was Laish at the first."

As *The Legends of the Jews* tells us, the worship of Micah's idols, which was widespread, enraged Yahweh, bringing repercussions upon the tribes of Israel for generations to come. Ginzberg writes:

"Especially the Benjamites distinguished themselves for their zeal in paying homage to [Micah's] idols. God therefore resolved to visit the sins of Israel and Benjamin upon them. The opportunity did not delay to come. It was not long before the Benjamites committed the outrage of Gibeah. Before the house of Bethac, a venerable old man, they imitated the disgraceful conduct of the Sodomites before the house of Lot."

The Book of Judges does not state explicitly that the young Levite who served Micah is the same Levite whose concubine was raped by the "sons of Belial." However, *The Legends of the Jews* certainly does. And it is this connection that brings the whole story into focus. Now we can understand what the story represents. The idol worship that was performed by Micah and his Levite was the same idol worship for which the Benjamite tribe had distinguished itself. Remember, *Holy Blood, Holy Grail* suggested that the worship of the golden calf was a "Benjamite ritual." It was probably a tradition they inherited from their friends (and most likely ancestors), the Canaanites. Now the Levites were the priestly tribe, and unlike the eleven other tribes of Israel, the Levites possessed no territory of their own. Rather, they were forbidden from owning any property at all. Instead, they were given special cities to live in throughout the territory of the other eleven tribes, and were obliged to earn their keep by performing priestly services, which members of all the other tribes were forbidden to do. Instead, each household paid 10% of its holdings to the Levites as a tithe, a tradition that goes back at least to the time of Abraham, who paid Melchizedek, the priest-king of Salem, 10% of his holdings.

It just so happens that Gibeah, in the territory of the Benjamites, was a Levite city. Given this, it is unlikely that the Levite was just passing through Gibeah, and happened to lodge there. He was more than likely performing priestly services for the old man, and his concubine may have played an integral role in those services. In short, the rites may have had a sexual component to them. Familiar with the nature of such rituals, the "sons of Belial" among the Benjamites may have had their passion stirred by the sight of the Levite, and came demanding that they be allowed to participate.

On an allegorical level, though, there is even more to this rape. For it seems as though the Levite may have learned to worship strange gods from the Benjamites. It is likely that the Benjamites taught the Levites who served them, and perhaps those of neighboring tribes as well, to perform these rites. The rape of the concubine represents, then, the perversion of Israel's priesthood, which has always been symbolized in Jewish scripture as Jehovah's "bride." The metaphor was probably literal, too, for the Benjamites likely married the Levites' daughters, and made their sons into idolaters, carrying in their bloodlines cursed covenants with strange gods.

Thus, when they declared war on the Benjamites, the other eleven tribes swore that they would not allow their daughters to marry Benjamite men. It is likely that this was the origin of the exclusively Benjamite tradition of matrilineal (as opposed to male, or "patrilineal") inheritance of land and titles. While only three hundred Benjamite men purportedly survived, there may have been many more widows who survived, who may not have been mentioned in the scriptural record (as most women were not). Adopting this tradition allowed the Benjamite women to pass on an inheritance, and allowed the tribe to perpetuate its heritage, although in a way that may not have been entirely recognized by the eleven other tribes. Perhaps that is why the belief was allowed to flourish that all of the Benjamites had either, if men, married out of the tribe (by taking foreign wives), or, if women, married into, and melded with, the tribe of Judah. Yet it is clear that even up to the time of Jesus and afterward, many Benjamites were well aware of their heritage and were perpetuating it. It is likely that this heritage was so well-preserved only because of the tradition of matrilineal inheritance.

But it is clear that the writers of the Hebrew scriptures, and later the Christian scriptures, wished to vilify, and to blot out from history, the tribe of Benjamin. And so their men were portrayed as rapists, and their women (like Magdalene) were portrayed as whores. For the word "rape", until recently, merely meant "unlawful sex." The notion that a woman should have any say in when and with whom she has sex is modern. In ancient times, to "rape" a girl was to have sex with, or even marry her, without the consent of her family. Likewise, a "whore" could indicate anything from a street harlot, to an adulteress, to a divorced woman, or a foreign woman, or even a rape victim. All such women were considered unclean and unfit for marriage.

Thus in a sense, the tribe of Benjamin itself became personified as womanly: because of its tradition of matrilineal inheritance; because of the emasculation that it suffered during the war with the other tribes; and undoubtedly, because it practiced the worship of a goddess, as well as multiple gods. And the tribe of Benjamite was personified as a "whore" because they were thought to have perverted Israel's priesthood with such forms of worship.

Indeed, there seems to be a distinct symbolic connection in Judaic literature between whoredom and worshipping strange gods. The Old Testament often describes profligate Israelites as having "gone a whoring after other gods." It is even worth noting that the profligate priesthood of St. John's *Revelation* is described as the "Whore of Babalon." As Margaret Starbird notes, there is "one underlying theme of the Hebrew scriptures - that God is the faithful Bridegroom and that his chosen symbolic "Bride", the community of the covenant, is unfaithful." Part of this connection undoubtedly stems from the fact that the Israelites blamed the influence of foreign women largely for the spiritual degradation of their people. Author Claudia V. Camp makes this point in her essay "Of Lineages and Levites, Sisters and Strangers: Constructing Priestly Identity in the Post-Exilic Period." In it she writes:

"In [The Book of Numbers], Israel 'yokes itself' to Baal of Peor by 'playing the harlot with Moabite women,' an episode whose telling itself inextricably combines language about wrong worship and wrong sex."

It is perhaps significant that just prior to being gang-raped by Benjamites at Gibeah, the

Levite's concubine had done some whoring of her own. *Judges 19:2* states: "And his concubine played the whore against him, and went away from him unto her father's house to Bethlehemjudah, and was there four whole months." Maybe this is why the Levite did not object when his host threw his concubine out to "the sons of Belial" to get raped in his stead.

Perhaps another reason why worshipping false gods was associated with "whoring" is that in Hebrew tradition, as in all ancient traditions, performing a priestly function was a paid job. Not only did the priests receive their tithes, but every action they performed on behalf of their clients was paid for, and there was a very important relationship between the money paid and the priestly function that was being paid for. The Hebrew scriptures stress this importance. It was not without significance that the silver which Micah used to make his idols was the same silver that had been paid to his mother Delilah (a foreign woman) for betraying her husband Samson. Delilah was an idol worshipper, and she sold the Lord's son, Samson, to an idolatrous nation, the Philistines. Symbolically, she prostituted herself. And there are even hints in *The Book of Judges* that she may have actually *been* a prostitute prior to her marriage to Samson. In Chapter 16, immediately before meeting Delilah "in the valley of Sorek", Samson visits a harlot in Gaza, and while he is with her the Philistines lie in wait to slay him. This seems to be yet another example of the Bible subtly implying that two seemingly separate characters are in fact the same character, by placing their stories next to one another in the narrative, and by revealing symbolic connections between the two. Both figuratively and, perhaps, literally, Delilah was a whore.

It was then, in a certain sense, the wages of prostitution (and of betrayal) that Micah used to make his idols of worship, and he and his Levite priest then sold indulgences from the idols to others. This is the true basis for the notion of tithing, and of providing "seed money" for a priesthood - a notion that is currently exploited by Christian evangelists. Originally, the idea was that the idols be made from the financial sacrifices of those who worshipped them. Even the golden calf fashioned by Aaron was made from the golden jewelry of the people who worshipped it. Thus it "contained", spiritually, their covenant with Belial, the deity it represented - a covenant bought with the price of that gold, which is why Moses had them drink the gold as a punishment - to internalize the curse which Jehovah had placed upon them for worshipping the calf. This is the same sort of ritual that the Benjamites and their Levites later enacted, including Moses' own grandson.

The Legends of the Jews makes it clear that the Levites were "prostituting" themselves to strange gods, but that doing so was considered an honorable way of living. Louis Ginzberg writes of the Levite, Moses' grandson, that:

"From his grandfather he had heard the rule that a man should do 'Abodah Zarah' for hire rather than be dependent upon his fellow-creatures. The meaning of 'Abodah Zarah' here naturally is 'strange', in the sense of 'unusual' work, but he took the term in its ordinary acceptation of 'service of strange gods.'"

Such rituals may have also been associated with prostitution because it did indeed involve "sacred prostitution" - i.e., sex rituals. It was *literally* prostitution, too, for the services that the priestesses of these rituals performed were paid for just like any other priestly service. It is likely that the "royal wedding" of Jesus and Mary, if it was indeed an alchemical sex magic ritual, as we suspect, gained donations for their priesthood as well. As I noted earlier, in *The Chymical Wedding of Christian Rosenkreutz*, the title character must pay a token in order to gain admission to the wedding. It is in this sense that some think Mary Magdalene may have actually been a prostitute - a sacred prostitute. Such is the opinion of Nicholas de Vere, who adds that, "It is very probable ... that the so-called Rites of Venus she ritually engaged in with the Messiah have been confused with other definitions of the word venal, which pertains not only to sex, but to payment for any service or goods."

It is of interest that the color red, and the term "scarlet woman" are associated with prostitution. De Vere associates this with the fact that Magdalene was "invariably portrayed with red hair in the Renaissance masterpieces." She is also often portrayed wearing red clothes. However, the association of red hair and garments with prostitution is quite older. We can trace it back to numerous sex goddesses worshipped in the sex rites of the ancient world, who were said to have "fire-red" hair. One such figure was the Greek Pyrrha, whose name comes from the word "Pyr" - "fire." Her name stems from the association with the temple rites of fire over which she officiated as a sacred prostitute. [5] The descendants of the Watchers, by the way, are believed by some to have had red hair.

The notion of sex magic and sacred prostitution would seem to have its roots in the original "sex crime" of the Watchers, mating with human women. The Israelites, and particularly the Benjamites, had many Watcher descendants among them, and it was their ancestral spirits who constituted the "strange gods" of idol worship. These people believed that the rites they performed helped them to form covenants with their gods, and in their sex magic rituals, they believed that they communed sexually with these gods, like their ancestors had done in the past.

As we know, the interbreeding between the Watchers and human women was condemned by Jehovah. Furthermore, the Watchers taught their wives all manner of sexual abominations that Jehovah did not deem appropriate for them to engage in. The entire episode between the Watchers and their wives can be categorized as a "sex crime", and thus can be alluded to symbolically with stories of "rape" and "prostitution." Perhaps this explains why, in addition to the sex rites already described, the same cults have often engaged in other abominations such as sodomy, as did the "sons of Belial." Such rites would have been considered an homage to the "ultimate sex crime" of the Watchers. For the profligate Israelites, flouting the rule of Jehovah, and thus his covenant, may have been part of the point as well.

The Forbidden Union

As a descendant of Benjamin (and possibly a Benjamite princess), Mary Magdalene embodied this symbolism by default, even though there was no injunction against marrying Benjamite *women*. But there may have been something else about her that earned her a reputation as a "whore", and made her unfit for marriage in the eyes of the rabbis. There is a belief among Catholics that she was an "adulteress" - specifically that she was the same adulteress whom Jesus saved from public stoning and absolved of her sins during an episode in the Gospels. However, "adulteress", like "whore", is a versatile word, and would have applied to a woman who had been divorced as well. In the book *The Legend of Thomas Didymus*, James Freeman Clarke suggests that Magdalene had once been one of Herod's wives, but had been divorced by him. In his version of the story, Magdalene was a high noble woman, and that was why Herod married her. But when he tired of her, he turned her out of his house, and married Herodias, the wife of his brother, making her his wife instead. According to James Freeman Clarke, it was on the grounds of Herod's previous marriage to Magdalene that John the Baptist objected to his new marriage to Herodias, and thus ended up getting beheaded. If Magdalene had been married previously, this alone would have made her a "forbidden woman", although, as we shall soon demonstrate, she was probably the perfect candidate in many other ways to be Jesus' bride priestess. [6] Jesus may have decided to go through with the marriage despite this, so as to intentionally commit a "sex crime" for ritual purposes - a sex crime that spawned a royal race, as that of the Watchers did.

However, if this were true, John the Baptist would have objected to the marriage of Jesus and Mary Magdalene, as he would have believed that the marriage would bring a curse upon Jesus' royal line of descendants. (This may explain why Jesus' relationship with John turned chilly towards the end, as the Gospels seem to indicate.) So too would most other priests and rabbis, which may be one of the reasons why this community disdained Jesus so much. Even some of Jesus' own disciples may have felt that he was bringing shame to their movement by marrying Magdalene. Thus they may have chosen not to acknowledge Jesus' marriage or progeny, and to malign the memory of the Magdalene in their writings. The Roman

Church followed suit later on for other reasons.

But at the same time, there were undoubtedly many advantages of Jesus and Magdalene getting together. As many authors have suggested, Mary might have been the chief royal heir of her tribe, and a descendant of the first King of Israel, Saul. Although Saul's line was usurped by that of David after his death, the Lord did make promises to Saul that, in Jesus' time, had yet to be fulfilled - the promise that his seed would also provide a second king to Israel - the last king! For Jesus, connecting himself to the line of Saul may have been integral to meeting the expectations of the prophesized Messiah.

God's Anointed:
The History of Kingship in Israel

When the Levite priesthood became corrupted with the worship of Micah's idols, even the high priesthood of the tabernacle, the sons of Eli, became corrupted. They were committing abominations in the tabernacle: eating the raw flesh of the sacrifices instead of following Jehovah's procedure, having sex with "the women that assembled at the door of the tabernacle" (priestesses?), and even, through negligence, allowing the Ark of the Covenant to be stolen by the Philistines. (It was soon restored, and Eli's sons were killed.) Jehovah enlisted the help of the prophet Samuel, who also became the high priest and the chief judge of the land, to bring the Israelites back into the fold of the covenant with Jehovah. In fact, according to *The Legends of the Jews*, Jehovah wanted to annihilate the inhabitants of the world, as he had during the Flood, because he was so angry at the Israelites at this time, and it was only at the pleading of Samuel that he backed down. But the people would not submit to his authority. As *I Samuel, 8:19-20* reads:

"Nevertheless the people refused to obey the voice of Samuel; and they said, Nay; but we will have a king over us; That we also may be like all the nations; and that our king may judge us, and go out before us, and fight our battles."

So God sent Samuel a Benjamite, a "mighty man of power", for him to anoint as king. It was only fitting, since the tribe of Benjamin had been held responsible for the corruption of the priesthood, and thus the nation, that a Benjamite king should be sent to help heal the wounds caused by that corruption. And there was no time to lose, since the Philistines were now at war with them, and they as yet had no leader to look up to. As *I Samuel 9:16-17* states:

"To morrow about this time I will send thee a man out of the land of Benjamin, and thou shalt anoint him to be captain over my people Israel, that he may save my people out of the hand of the Philistines: for I have looked upon my people, because their cry is come unto me. And when Samuel saw Saul, the LORD said unto him, Behold the man whom I spake to thee of! this same shall reign over my people."

Several extraordinary things about Saul made him an interesting choice as king. For one thing, as I have said, he bore the marks of Watcher descent. He was about a foot taller than other Israelite men, and *The Legends of the Jews* tells us his cousin Abner was "a giant of extraordinary size." He even successfully wrestled the giant Goliath one day, when the giant had attempted to steal the Tablets of the Law from within the Ark of the Covenant. He was also strikingly beautiful, and all women were uncontrollably attracted to him.

Another point worth noting is that many aspects of the story of Saul's anointing seem to reflect the symbolism of the Messiah. Recall that Jesus entered Jerusalem on the back of a donkey, to fulfill scriptural prophecies of the Messiah, and the manner in which he acquired this donkey was quite peculiar. As *Matthew 21:1-7* describes it:

"And when they drew nigh unto Jerusalem, and were come to Bethphage, unto the mount of Olives, then sent Jesus two disciples, Saying unto them, Go into the village over against you, and straightway ye shall find an ass tied, and a colt with her: loose them, and bring them unto me. And if any man say ought unto you, ye shall say, The Lord hath need of them; and straightway he will send them. All this was done, that it might be fulfilled which was spoken by the prophet, saying,

Tell ye the daughter of Sion, Behold, thy King cometh unto thee, meek, and sitting upon an ass, and a colt the foal of an ass. And the disciples went, and did as Jesus commanded them, And brought the ass, and the colt, and put on them their clothes, and they set him thereon."

The prophecy that Matthew was repeating was that of *Zechariah 9:9*:

"Rejoice greatly, O daughter of Zion; shout, O daughter of Jerusalem: behold, thy King cometh unto thee: he is just, and having salvation; lowly, and riding upon an ass, and upon a colt the foal of an ass."

Now in the case of Saul, it was fated by Jehovah that he should be anointed king by the prophet Samuel. And he met Samuel because he was looking for his donkeys, which he had lost three days earlier. He had heard that Samuel was a prophet, and sought his help. Like the story of Jesus and his disciples finding the asses, there is something about this scenario that seems as though it was set up ahead of time. *I Samuel 9:18-21* says:

"Then Saul drew near to Samuel in the gate, and said, Tell me, I pray thee, where the seer's house is. And Samuel answered Saul, and said, I am the seer: go up before me unto the high place; for ye shall eat with me to day, and to morrow I will let thee go, and will tell thee all that is in thine heart. And as for thine asses that were lost three days ago, set not thy mind on them; for they are found. And on whom is all the desire of Israel? Is it not on thee, and on all thy father's house?

And Saul answered and said, Am not I a Benjamite, of the smallest of the tribes of Israel? and my family the least of all the families of the tribe of Benjamin? wherefore then speakest thou so to me?"

Though Saul was almost too humble to accept the honor, shortly after eating a meal with Samuel, he was anointed king, in a ceremony reminiscent of Jesus' anointing by Mary Magdalene:

"Then Samuel took a vial of oil, and poured it upon his head, and kissed him, and said, Is it not because the LORD hath anointed thee to be captain over his inheritance?"

Afterwards, Samuel described to Saul the manner in which he would find his lost asses, and the description sounds somewhat similar to when Jesus told his disciples how they would find the asses upon which he would enter Jerusalem. Samuel even predicted that Saul would be met by prophets who would give him gifts (like the "wise men" who attended Jesus' birth), and that Saul would become a prophet himself. As the text states:

"When thou art departed from me to day, then thou shalt find two men by Rachel's sepulchre in the border of Benjamin at Zelzah; and they will say unto thee, The asses which thou wentest to seek are found: and, lo, thy father hath left the care of the asses, and sorroweth for you, saying, What shall I do for my son?

Then shalt thou go on forward from thence, and thou shalt come to the plain of Tabor, and there shall meet thee three men going up to God to Bethel, one carrying three kids, and another carrying three loaves of bread, and another carrying a bottle of wine:

And they will salute thee, and give thee two loaves of bread; which thou shalt receive of their hands. After that thou shalt come to the hill of God, where is the garrison of the Philistines: and it shall come to pass, when thou art come thither to the city, that thou shalt meet a company of prophets coming down from the high place with a psaltery, and a tabret, and a pipe, and a harp, before them; and they shall prophesy:

And the Spirit of the LORD will come upon thee, and thou shalt prophesy with them, and shalt be turned into another man. And let it be, when these signs are come unto thee, that thou do as occasion serve thee; for God is with thee."

When Samuel presented Saul to the people

at the Benjamite city of Mizpeh, he said, "See ye him whom the Lord hath chosen, that there is none like him among all the people?" The crowd responded by proclaiming "God save the king", which is now the title of the British national anthem. The only people to object to his kingship were the "children of Belial", who said, "How shall this man save us?"

Saul went on to become a beloved king, and is credited with having unified the Israelites like never before. The conflict with the Philistines that had caused the people of Israel to beg for a king was his main concern, and Saul organized the army like never before as well. Yet for all of the effort that Jehovah went to just to enthrone Saul, he quickly gave up on the king, and removed his blessing for what seemed like trivial reasons. Basically, there were a couple of incidents in which Jehovah commanded that certain enemies of the Israelites be slaughtered, but Saul took pity on them and allowed them to live. For this, Jehovah forsook him. He afflicted Saul with "an evil spirit", and instigated his downfall, in favor of a young servant of his named David.

David was the youngest son of Jesse, a descendant of Judah, and was renowned for his musical ability as a lyre player, singer and songwriter. When Saul first became afflicted with the evil spirit, and was feeling uneasy, he hired David to play the lyre in his royal palace, because it was soothing to his soul. David became a beloved friend of Saul's, whom he regarded as part of his family. David even married Saul's daughter, Michal, and became best friends with Saul's son Jonathan. But then the evil spirit caused Saul to become jealous of David. Jehovah enlisted Samuel in his plan to dethrone the line of Saul and anoint David the new king. Saul was aware of this, and the evil spirit caused Saul to want to kill David because of it.

But every time that the spirit seized him, and Saul tried to kill David, he would snap out of it just in time, and apologize for trying to kill him. Each time they would kiss and make up afterwards, and David would forgive him. But David was wary of him, and knew that he was a wanted man because he was fated to be the next king. Yet on one occasion in which Saul tried to have David killed, and David forgave him, Saul made a peculiar prophecy, and David made a peculiar promise. *I Samuel 24: 17-22 tells us:*

"And he said to David, Thou art more righteous than I: for thou hast rewarded me good, whereas I have rewarded thee evil. And thou hast shewed this day how that thou hast dealt well with me: forasmuch as when the LORD had delivered me into thine hand, thou killedst me not. For if a man find his enemy, will he let him go well away? wherefore the LORD reward thee good for that thou hast done unto me this day.

And now, behold, I know well that thou shalt surely be king, and that the kingdom of Israel shall be established in thine hand. Swear now therefore unto me by the LORD, that thou wilt not cut off my seed after me, and that thou wilt not destroy my name out of my father's house. And David sware unto Saul. And Saul went home; but David and his men gat them up unto the hold."

Thus the royal lines of Saul and David (of Benjamin and Judah) were inextricably linked forever, because of the promises that these two made to each other.

It was not long after Saul's final attempt to kill David that Saul perished during a battle with the Philistines. On that day, three of Saul's sons were killed, and Saul was so grief-stricken that he fell upon his own sword. When David was given news of this, he wept, and slew the messenger who had told him the news so gleefully, thinking David would be happy to hear it. David insisted that everyone honor Saul in his death, and mourn him.

Now this was not the end of the feud between the lines of Saul and David. The men of Judah took David as their king, while the Benjamites, along with the rest of the other Israelite tribes, took Saul's son Ishbosheth as their king. Battles raged between them for about six years, but David finally managed to capture Israel, and was anointed as their king, making Jerusalem the national capitol of the now united kingdom. He passed this kingdom on to his son Solomon.

But after Solomon's death, the kingdom split once again into the Southern kingdom of

Judah, ruled by Solomon's son Rehoboam, and the Northern Kingdom of Israel, ruled by Jeroboam, a descendant of the prophet Joseph, through the line of Joseph's twin son, Ephraim. The tribe of Judah made up the bulk of the kingdom of Judah, while Jeroboam's kingdom of Israel maintained the allegiance of most of the other tribes. These initially included the Levites, although Jeroboam later removed them from their priestly offices, and most of them then moved to Judahite territory. There still remained ten tribes in the kingdom of Israel, though, since the descendants of Joseph's two twin sons, Ephraim and Manasseh, each formed separate tribes. It was from these two tribes that all of the leadership positions in Israel were filled. But unlike after Saul's death, this time the Benjamites sided with the tribe of Judah, and were loyal to the house of David. *I Kings 12:21* tells us: "Rehoboam... assembled all of the house of Judah, with the tribe of Benjamin." It was as if the covenant between Saul and David was still affecting their descendants. This must have been the point at which the Benjamites became "subsumed" into the tribe of Judah, because from then on, they are no longer spoken of as being separate tribes.

So why did Jehovah allow the kingdom to split in this way? It was all part of his divine plan. Now although Jehovah had given up on his anointed king Saul apparently at the drop of a hat, he was not so fickle with David. Even though David's misdeeds and debauchery far exceeded that of Saul, and were only outdone by those of his son Solomon (misdeeds that included marrying foreign wives and worshipping false gods), Jehovah remained loyal to David and his bloodline. After all, he had promised David's ancestor Judah that "The scepter shall not depart from Judah, nor the lawgiver from between his feet... and unto him shall the gathering of the people be." And in *II Samuel 23*, David declared that Jehovah "hath made with me an everlasting covenant." When David was thinking of building a temple to Jehovah in Jerusalem, Jehovah spoke to his prophet Nathan:

"And it came to pass that night, that the word of the LORD came unto Nathan, saying, Go and tell my servant David, Thus saith the LORD, Shalt thou build me an house for me to dwell in? ... when thy days be fulfilled, and thou shalt sleep with thy fathers, I will set up thy seed after thee, which shall proceed out of thy bowels, and I will establish his kingdom. He shall build an house for my name, and I will stablish the throne of his kingdom for ever. I will be his father, and he shall be my son. If he commit iniquity, I will chasten him with the rod of men, and with the stripes of the children of men: But my mercy shall not depart away from him, as I took it from Saul, whom I put away before thee. And thine house and thy kingdom shall be established for ever before thee: thy throne shall be established for ever." (II Samuel 7: 4-5, 12-16)

So Jehovah had promised David's posterity a throne no matter what sins they committed, as part of his everlasting covenant. However, he did not promise David that he would rule over *all* of the tribes of Israel, but Judah only. Thus, when the other tribes seceded to create the Northern Kingdom of Israel, this was punishment for the sins of Solomon, and it was only because of Jehovah's covenant with David that is descendants were allowed to keep even this kingdom of Judah. In *I Kings 11:11-13*, we read:

"Wherefore the LORD said unto Solomon, Forasmuch as this is done of thee, and thou hast not kept my covenant and my statutes, which I have commanded thee, I will surely rend the kingdom from thee, and will give it to thy servant. Notwithstanding in thy days I will not do it for David thy father's sake: [but] I will rend it out of the hand of thy son. Howbeit I will not rend away all the kingdom; [but] will give one tribe to thy son for David my servant's sake, and for Jerusalem's sake which I have chosen."

Obviously, Benjamin and Judah were together considered that "one tribe."

Eventually, in 723 B.C., the Northern Kingdom of Israel fell to the Assyrians, and most of its inhabitants were exiled. This is how the "ten tribes of Israel" became famously "lost." Those whose families did eventually return for the most part had no recollection of their family or cultural history. But the Southern Kingdom was not immune to attack from outside forces. In 586 B.C., the Babylonian King Nebuchadnezzar captured Jerusalem, destroyed the temple, and took many, if not most, of the Jews into exile in Babylon. They were finally freed by Nebuchadnezzar's grandson Cyrus, but again, when they returned, they had lost much of their cultural heritage and history.

The Temple of Jerusalem was rebuilt in 520 B.C., but within 200 years the land had been captured again, this time by the Greeks, and their temple was once again desecrated. The Maccabean revolt and its aftermath lead to their independence once again, creating the "state of Judea" in 142 B.C. But 80 years later, they were again captured and subjugated, this time by the expanding Roman empire. In 20 B.C., the building of a third Temple of Jerusalem began, but this time it served a false, Hellenized priesthood backing the puppet regime of King Herod, who had been placed on the throne by the Roman Senate.

The Grafting of Vines

This is the world into which Jesus, a direct descendant of David, and rightful inheritor of his throne, was born into. It was a country not only of subjugated, enslaved people, but of a people confused by a lack of true history or heritage, and rendered impotent by having spent several generations struggling for control of their own destiny. None but the scribes among them knew anything about their history, or the details of their religion, and even among this caste there was little agreement, as evidenced by the wide range of sects and political movements that proliferated across Israel at that time. Only the Zealots - the anti-Roman militias - had any real plan of action for taking back control of the country. The rest of the Judeans, if they were not in league with the Roman authorities, just nursed a vague wish that some "Messiah", some scion from the house of David, would come along and save them. It had been so long since the house of David had truly ruled for any length of time, that it was a bit like modern-day Britons hoping for a new king to come from the bloodline of King Arthur. But nonetheless, the Jews hoped, and many believed he would come. He would stand up to the Goliath - Rome - the same way that small young shepherd boy, David, had

done, and with the flick of a wrist bring victory for Judea once again. Jesus saw himself as that Messiah.

But it was not merely the Judeans whom Jesus wished to lead to freedom. It was all of Israel, which was at that time split up into several different areas, including "Judea", "Samaria", and "Galilee." Many of the people who occupied these lands were descendants of the ten tribes of Israel that had seceded from Judah to form the Northern Kingdom of Israel. Samaria, home of the detested "Samaritans", was even named after the city of Samaria, which was once the capitol of the Northern Kingdom of Israel. These people would have had no interest in a Messiah from the house of David. Indeed, these people were awaiting a "Messiah-ben-Joseph" - a descendant of the kingly line of Ephraim, which had once ruled over the Northern Kingdom.

While there is plenty of evidence that Jesus was a descendant of David, there is no evidence that he was a descendant of the patriarch Joseph. However, it is interesting to note that his father's name was Joseph, and that, like Joseph, Jesus was a prophet. But perhaps, instead of trying to be both the "Messiah-ben-Joseph" *as well as* the "Messiah-ben-Judah", Jesus attempted to bypass the need for a Messiah ben-Joseph by embracing the kingly lineage that preceded both the kingdoms of David and of Jeroboam. This lineage, of course, was that of Saul.

Saul was the only king who these people had ever truly been united under. David never really commanded the respect of the other ten tribes the way Saul had. They were on the verge of seceding the entire time, and upon the death of Solomon, took the first opportunity they had. After Saul's death, the Israelites outside of Judah all wanted to follow Saul's son, and it was only after six years of bloody civil war that they submitted to David's rule.

When the Northern tribes broke off, the Benjamites stayed with the kingdom of Judah, and eventually blended in with the tribe of Judah. Why? Because the primacy of the royal bloodline of Saul was no longer being recognized by them. But despite the enmity that had existed between Saul and David, and the competition there had been between their bloodlines, they had always respected one another: partially because the royal lines had intermarried together, partially because both Saul and David had been "God's anointed", and mostly because the two men had made a covenant with each other that they would respect on another's descendants.

In addition, there had also always been a special relationship between the Benjamites and the tribes of Ephraim and Manasseh - the two tribes descended from Joseph. This was because he was the only full-blood brother of Joseph, being the only other son of Jacob's second wife, Rachel. (The rest of Jacob's sons were from his first wife, Leah.) Benjamin also had been the only one of the sons of Jacob who was not involved in the plot to sell Joseph into slavery. It was as compensation for the suffering Joseph endured at the hands of his brothers that the kingship of Israel was promised as a birthright to Joseph's son Ephraim. It is likely that a kingly promise was also passed on to Joseph's favorite brother.

This certainly seems to be what is eluded to in *Genesis 49*. When Jacob is giving out his blessings to his sons on his deathbed, Joseph's and Benjamin's are the last two given. To Joseph, he says:

"Joseph is a fruitful bough, even a fruitful bough by a well; whose branches run over the wall: The archers have sorely grieved him, and shot at him, and hated him: But his bow abode in strength, and the arms of his hands were made strong by the hands of the mighty God of Jacob; (from thence is the shepherd, the stone of Israel:) Even by the God of thy father, who shall help thee; and by the Almighty, who shall bless thee with blessings of heaven above, blessings of the deep that lieth under, blessings of the breasts, and of the womb: The blessings of thy father have prevailed above the blessings of my progenitors unto the utmost bound of the everlasting hills: they shall be on the head of Joseph, and on the crown of the head of him that was separate from his brethren."

This is followed by a very brief word given to Benjamin:

"Benjamin shall ravin as a wolf: in the morning he shall devour the prey, and at night he shall divide the spoil."

The reference to Joseph as a "fruitful bough" alludes to the royal bloodline of Ephraim that issued from him. As it turns out, "Ephraim" itself means "fruitful bough." The line, "The crown of the head of him that was separate from his brethren" could perhaps be a reference to the royal blessing of Benjamin, who, according to *The Legends of the Jews*, was chosen by Jehovah to be the ancestor of both the first and the last king of Israel.

The first half of Jehovah's promise for Benjamin was fulfilled by Saul. But the only way that the second half of the promise could be fulfilled would be if the last king was a result of a dynastic alliance between the royal lines of Saul and David, allowing him to reclaim the throne of Jerusalem *and* bring the old "kingdom of Israel" back into the fold. This is why a marriage between Jesus and Magdalene would have been perfect - the ideal blending of bloodlines - "the grafting of vines."

In the Priory of Sion's *Secret Dossiers*, which they published and deposited in the Bibliotheque Nationale in Paris, they described the Merovingian bloodline as being the result of "vine-grafting." On the surface, it looked like they were talking about viticulture, but really, they were referring to the fusing together of royal bloodlines. Grapevines had long been a symbol used in literature to denote royal bloodlines, and indeed, were used as such in the Judaic scriptures as well. In fact, there appear to be specific references in certain scriptures that allude to the royal line of Benjamin as being the "choice vine." You will recall that, when Jacob was handing out his sons' blessings, he said to Judah:

"The sceptre shall not depart from Judah, nor a lawgiver from between his feet, until Shiloh come; and unto him shall the gathering of the people be."

However, this blessing was followed by these peculiar words:

"Binding his foal unto the vine, and his ass's colt unto the choice vine; he washed his garments in wine, and his clothes in the blood of grapes: His

eyes shall be red with wine, and his teeth white with milk."

Recall the apparent connection between Saul's anointment as king, preceded by the odd loss, and then the discovery, of his asses, and the presentation of Jesus to Jerusalem, preceded by the mysterious discovery of "an ass" and "a colt the foal of an ass." Then compare these to the line in *Genesis* about a "foal" and an "ass's colt."

Finally, compare this to the prophecy of the Messiah found in *Zechariah 9:9*. Also, recall that this prophecy was repeated and referred to in *Matthew 21:5*, when Jesus sent his disciples looking for the two asses. Obviously, there is a continuity of symbolism here that is alluding to something very specific. And it also has something to do with royal bloodlines, owing to the fact that the line in the blessing of Judah referred to the "foal" and the "ass's colt" being bound to the "vine" and the "choice vine."

The consensus among biblical scholars links the symbols of the "foal" and the "ass's colt" to "a kingly estate." In other words, they represent royal thrones - the seat of power; the "driver's seat", as it were. Moreover, it seems to allude to the throne of a king, and the succeeding throne of his son (represented by the foal). And, it would seem, the throne of the son is even greater than that of the father. For while the father's throne is bound to the "vine", the son's throne is bound to the "choice vine." The only way in which the royal line could have become more "choice" would be by binding itself, through marriage, to another royal line of equal or greater significance. This then refers to the royal lines of Benjamin and Judah joining through Jesus and Mary Magdalene. The marriage would have made Jesus supremely qualified to be king over all of Israel, and their son would be even more so.

This then is the "grafting of vines" that lead to the bloodline, the Merovingian kings of France. This explains why Jesus' marriage to her would have been so important, and perhaps why the marriage, as well as the resulting offspring, were kept secret. It is perhaps worth noting that, according to Margaret Starbird, the word "Merovingian" means "vine of Mary."

Blessed and Cursed: The "Messianic Legacy"

I have, in the course of my investigation into the legends surrounding Mary Magdalene, we've surmised that the reason why her marriage to Jesus was excised from the Bible was because the editors of the scriptures wished to extinguish all awareness of the bloodline descending from Jesus. The Church promoted a religious view of Jesus as the "son of God" who "died for our sins", and this view did not include him being a political figure of any sort, let alone an anti-Roman militant with a claim to the throne rivaling that of the Roman puppet Herod. Furthermore, if they admitted that Jesus had descendants, they would have to admit the existence of a group that had a much more direct claim to the continuation of Jesus' movement. The Church made sure that knowledge of this would remain hidden by eliminating any overt reference to Jesus' ancestors, marriage or descendants, and by branding Mary Magdalene as a whore. Naturally, by labeling her as such, she would be the last person to be thought of as a possible mate for the Holy One himself.

Moreover, I have demonstrated that Mary Magdalene was most likely a royal heiress from the Benjamite line of Saul, possibly providing the perfect royal vine for Jesus to graft his Davidic inheritance onto. This would allow him to command the respect of descendants of all twelve Israelite tribes - to unite the kingdoms that had been separated for so long. As the child of both inheritances, their son would command even more respect. Thus, the prophecy of *Genesis 49:11* could be fulfilled, as well as God's promise that the tribe of Benjamin would provide both the first and the last kings of Israel. Also, marrying Magdalene may have given Jesus and his heirs specific rights over the city of Jerusalem and the surrounding area, which traditionally belonged to the tribe of Benjamin. I showed that Mary Magdalene would have been the possessor of this royal inheritance because of the Benjamite custom of matrilineal inheritance, which resulted from the curse that was placed on the Benjamites after the "outrage at Gibeah" described in *The Book of Judges*.

In addition, I explored occult traditions

which hold that Jesus and Mary Magdalene may have been the leaders of a royal sex magic cult, with Magdalene performing the role of a "temple priestess" or "sacred prostitute." Obviously, if this were true, then the belief system that Jesus represented was well outside of mainstream Judaism. Indeed, he and Magdalene were most likely followers of strange gods, the worship of whom involved sexual magic. The wedding at Cana may have been at once both a proper marriage ceremony and a sex magic ritual, the purpose of which was to (a) unite the King of the Jews with his royal dynastic bride; (b) anoint him ritually as the king, and; (c) to ritually conceive a royal heir. Thus, the metaphor of Jesus turning water into wine may have symbolized using sex magic to "graft the vines" of two powerful royal bloodlines. I showed that Mary Magdalene's status as a Benjamite princess may have made her especially qualified to act as a sacred prostitute, as the Benjamites were associated specifically with the performance of rituals for strange gods. In Hebrew culture, such practices were equated with harlotry, and the women involved in these practices were thought of as being responsible for corrupting their husbands. This is yet another reason why Magdalene may have been seen as a "whore." Such women were viewed as "foreigners", i.e., outside of the covenant with Jehovah, and so were their children. When Israelite men married such women, it was believed that they brought onto the bloodline of their descendants the generational curses of strange gods.

This may impart yet another purpose to the marriage between Jesus and Mary Magdalene. Jesus was the qualified king of the Jews, and his son would have been the qualified king of all Israelites. But perhaps he aspired to something more than that. Perhaps he wished for his descendants to be the kings of foreign lands as well. But in order to set himself up to be king of the Jews, while at the same time setting his son up for something larger, he may have needed to simultaneously fulfill Jehovah's messianic promises, and at the same time, break his family's covenant with Jehovah. The "new covenant" had to be created - a covenant which those of gentile races could join into. He needed to break the exclusive hold that Yahweh had on his bloodline, and open it up to the blessings of other gods. Taking Mary Magdalene to wife and breeding the royal heir with her may have fulfilled this purpose.

If Mary Magdalene was indeed Jesus' wife, and indeed was the mother to his messianic heir, then the blessings and curses, the rights and inheritances that she carried in her blood were just as important as his in defining the characteristics of the Merovingian bloodline of France that descended from them. This would have especially been the case if she was a Benjamite, from a tribe practicing matrilineal inheritance. This would explain why she was so revered by the mystery cults of Southern France. But it also explains why they represented her in the form of the Black Madonna. For in the eyes of the Jewish priests of Jesus' time, and in the eyes of the later Christian church. Magdalene's marriage to Jesus would have been seen as bringing a curse upon the bloodline that descended from them. It may have been for this reason that the Church insisted that the bloodline's very existence be kept secret. It may have also been for this reason that the initiates of the mystery cults of Southern France treasured these secrets like precious stones. The Grail has always been said to be both sacred and cursed, and in the case of the Merovingian bloodline, that appears to have been the case.

Endnotes:

[1] It is interesting that this anointing oil is considered symbolic of the anointments that would later be used by Nicodemus (Magdalene's father, according to Olaf Hage) to actually anoint Jesus' dead body.

[2] In the Watchers we may see the origin of notions like "the Evil Eye" and "the All-Seeing Eye."

[3] They taught the human women to use eye make-up in particular, undoubtedly to make them look more like the Watchers themselves.

[4] In non-biblical accounts, it is clear that it was the Watchers, and not Jehovah, who was responsible for saving Noah.

[5] It has been theorized that this same root word "pyr" is at the root of words like "priest" and "pharaoh."

[6] Being a pagan priestess or having any heathen ancestors would have disqualified her as well.

The Judas Goat: The "Substitution" Theory of the Crucifixion

By Tracy R. Twyman

One of the central tenets of the theory put forth in the book *Holy Blood, Holy Grail* by Michael Baigent, Richard Leigh and Henry Lincoln, is that Jesus did not really die on the cross, but that the crucifixion was a hoax perpetrated by Jesus and his closest disciples, in order to fulfill scriptures prophesizing the death of the Jewish Messiah. The hypothesis presented was that Jesus was crucified, but was given a toxin to make him appear dead, so that he could be taken down from the cross early. This was provided as an explanation for the sightings of Christ after his death (the so-called "Resurrection"). If this scenario had indeed occurred, it would have made it possible for Jesus to live on with his wife and his children (his royal heirs), and to participate personally in the establishment of the early Christian movement. A clue implying that this did in fact occur can be found in one of the Stations of the Cross at the Church of St. Mary Magdalene in Rennes-le-Chateau, France, in which Jesus is shown being carried into the tomb at night, contrary to scripture. According to the theory, this station actually depicts Jesus' still-living body being removed from the tomb by his fellow conspirators.

Mentioned in passing by the authors of *Holy Blood, Holy Grail* is another version of this theory, one long held by Muslims and heretical Christian sects throughout the centuries. This theory posits that it was not Jesus but a substitute that died on the Cross. Apocryphal scriptures bear witness to the adherence of this belief. In the *Second Treatise of the Great Seth*, one of the Nag Hammadi scrolls, it states:

"I did not succumb to them as they had planned... And I did not die in reality but in appearance, lest I be put to shame by them... For my death which they think happened [happened] to them in their error and blindness, since they nailed their man unto their death... It was another, their father, who drank the gall and the vinegar; it was not I. They struck me with the reed; it was another, Simon, who bore the cross on his shoulder. It was another upon whom they placed the crown of thorns... And I was laughing at their ignorance."

The Koran states something similar:

"...they did not slay him, neither crucified him, only a likeness of that was shown to them."

Also, according to *Holy Blood, Holy Grail*, other Muslim writers describe Jesus as "hiding in a niche in a wall and watching the crucifixion of a surrogate." The authors of *Holy Blood, Holy Grail* do not go on to speculate about who that substitute may have been, and seem to prefer the idea that Jesus, while crucified, was taken down from the cross alive, rather than that there was a surrogate. But Muslim and heretical Christian traditions whole-heartedly embrace the substitution story, and name the sacrificial victim as none other than Judas Iscariot, the most expendable, presumably, of all of Jesus' apostles. Some of the groups who have held this belief include the Manicheans and the Basilides. In addition, in the sixteenth century, something purporting itself as *The Gospel of Barnabas* was published. Most scholars summarily dismiss it as a "forgery." However, it does testify to the unusual beliefs that certain Muslim sects and Christian heretics held regarding the crucifixion. In this version of the story, after Judas had made the decision to betray Jesus, God sent angels to take Jesus "out of the world... in the third heaven." Meanwhile, he transformed Judas' appearance into a likeness of Jesus, just as the soldiers arrived to arrest him. It states:

"When the soldiers with Judas drew near to the place where Jesus was, Jesus heard the approach of many people, wherefore in fear he withdrew into the house. And the eleven were sleeping. Then God, seeing the danger of his servant, commanded Gabriel;, Michael;, Rafael;, and Uriel, his ministers, to take Jesus out of the world. The holy angels came and took Jesus out by the window that looks toward the South. They bare him and placed him in the third heaven in the company of angels blessing God for evermore.

Judas entered impetuously before all into the chamber whence Jesus had been taken up. And the disciples were sleeping. Whereupon the wonderful God acted wonderfully, insomuch that Judas was so changed in speech and in face to be like Jesus that we believed him to be Jesus. And he, having awakened us, was seeking where the Master was. Whereupon we marvelled, and answered: You, Lord, are our master; have you now forgotten us?

And he, smiling, said: Now are you foolish, that know not me to be Judas Iscariot! And as he was saying this the soldiery entered, and laid their hands upon Judas, because he was in every way like to Jesus. We having heard Judas' saying, and seeing the multitude of soldiers, fled as beside ourselves. And John, who was wrapped in a linen cloth, awoke and fled, and when a soldier seized him by the linen cloth he left the linen cloth and fled naked. For God heard the prayer of Jesus, and saved the eleven from evil."

Once everyone had been tricked into believing that Judas was Jesus, the substitute was made to suffer every pain and humiliation that has traditionally been attributed to Jesus. All the while Judas protested, and proclaimed his true identity, but he was thought to be mad, and that only increased the suffering inflicted upon him:

"The soldiers took Judas; and bound him, not without derision. For he truthfully denied that he was Jesus; and the soldiers, mocking him, said: Sir, fear not, for we are come to make you king of Israel, and we have bound you because we know that you do refuse the kingdom. Judas answered: Now have you lost your senses! You are come to take Jesus of Nazareth, with arms and lanterns as [against] a robber; and you have bound me that have guided you, to make me king!

Then the soldiers lost their patience, and with blows and kicks they began to flout Judas, and they led him with fury into Jerusalem. John and Peter followed the soldiers afar off; and they affirmed to him who writes that they saw all the examination that was made of Judas by the high priest, and by the council of the Pharisees, who were assembled to put Jesus to death. Whereupon Judas spoke many words of madness, insomuch that every one was filled with laughter, believing that he was really Jesus, and that for fear of death he was feigning madness. Whereupon the scribes bound his eyes with a bandage, and mocking him said: Jesus, prophet of the Nazarenes; (for so they called them who believed in Jesus), tell us, who was it that smote you? And they buffeted him and spat in his face.

When it was morning there assembled the great council of scribes and elders of the people; and the high priest with the Pharisees sought false witness against Judas, believing him to be Jesus: and they found not that which they sought. And why say I that the chief priests believed Judas to be Jesus? No all the disciples, with him who writes, believed it; and more, the poor Virgin mother of Jesus, with his kinsfolk and friends, believed it, insomuch that the sorrow of every one was incredible.

As God lives, he who writes forgot all that Jesus had said: how that he should be taken up from the world, and that he should suffer in a third person, and that he should not die until near the end of the world."

The Gospel of Barnabas seems to imply that the sacrifice of a substitute on behalf of Jesus was in fact the true fulfillment of scripture regarding the Messiah, as it states:

"Wherefore he went with the mother of Jesus and with John to the cross. The high priest caused Judas to be brought before him bound, and asked him of his disciples and his doctrine.

Whereupon Judas, as though beside himself, answered nothing to the point. The high priest then adjured him by the living God of Israel that he would tell him the truth.

Judas answered: 'I have told you that I am Judas Iscariot, who promised to give into your hands Jesus the Nazarene; and you, by what are I know not, are beside yourselves, for you will have it by every means that I am Jesus.' The high priest answered: 'O perverse seducer, you have deceived all Israel, beginning from Galilee even to Jerusalem here, with your doctrine and false miracles: and now think you to flee the merited punishment that befits you by feigning to be mad?

As God lives, 'you shall not escape it!' And having said this he commanded his servants to smite him with buffetings and kicks, so that his understanding might come back into his head. The derision which he then suffered at the hands of the high priest's servants is past belief. For they zealously devised new inventions to give pleasure to the council. So they attired him as a juggler, and so treated him with hands and feet that it would have moved the very Canaanites to compassion if they had beheld that sight. But the chief priests and Pharisees and elders of the people had their hearts so exasperated against Jesus that, believing Judas to be really Jesus, they took delight in seeing him so treated."

Later, it states that crucifixion had been specifically chosen by God as the proper method of death for Judas:

"God, who had decreed the issue, reserved Judas for the cross, in order that he might suffer that horrible death to which he had sold another. He did not suffer Judas to die under the scourges, notwithstanding that the soldiers scourged him so grievously that his body rained blood."

As Judas protested, he made it clear that he believed himself to be innocent of wrongdoing, and believed that it was Jesus who was an outlaw and a sinner. He told them that Jesus was a magician, and had transformed Judas into his own likeness by his demonic powers. Just before he died upon the cross, Judas cried out a plea that demonstrates his belief in his own innocence:

"So they led him to Mount Calvary, where they used to hang malefactors, and there they crucified him naked, for the greater ignominy. Judas truly did nothing else but cry out: God, why have you forsaken me, seeing the malefactor has escaped and I die unjustly? Truly I say that the voice, the face, and the person of Judas were so like to Jesus, that his disciples and believers entirely believed that he was Jesus; wherefore some departed from the doctrine of Jesus, believing that Jesus had been a false prophet, and that by the art of magic he had done the miracles which he did: for Jesus had said that he should not die till near the end of the world; for that at that time he should be taken away from the world."

So in this version of the story, the crucifixion did not accomplish the salvation of man from sin through the sacrifice of God's only son, but the substitution of that sacrifice. And instead of gaining believers for Jesus' cause, the crucifixion actually lead to an initial loss of faith amongst his followers – although, in the years to come, the notion of Christ's sacrifice on the cross would gain the Catholic Church nearly global hegemony. After his death, it was Judas' body, not Jesus', which was stolen away from the tomb by Christ's closest disciples. This is the scene depicted in the Station of the Cross in the church at Rennes-le-Chateau. *The Gospel of Barnabas* continues:

"But they that stood firm in the doctrine of Jesus were so encompassed with sorrow, seeing him die who was entirely like to Jesus, that they remembered not what Jesus had said. And so in company with the mother of Jesus they went to Mount Calvary, and were not only present at the death of Judas, weeping continually, but by means of Nicodemus and Joseph of Abarimathia; they obtained from the governor the body of Judas to bury it. Whereupon, they took him down from the cross with such weeping as assuredly no one would believe, and buried him in the new sepulchre of Joseph; having wrapped him up in an hundred pounds of precious ointments."

It is easy to see why this "Gospel" was

embraced by Islamic sects. In it Jesus is portrayed as a holy man, but as mortal, not the "Son of God", and the coming of the Prophet Muhammad is predicted:

"And though I have been innocent in the world, since men have called me God, and Son of God, God, in order that I be not mocked of the demons on the day of judgment, has willed that I be mocked of men in this world by the death of Judas; making all men to believe that I died upon the cross. And this mocking shall continue until the advent of Muhammad, the Messenger of God, who, when he shall come, shall reveal this deception to those who believe in God's Law."

One of the many criticisms made by Jewish scholars against the theology of Christianity is that the symbolism of Jesus' sacrifice on the cross is an apparent confusion of two totally separate Judaic rituals. As Jesus purportedly died on Passover, and as he repeatedly is referred to in the New Testament as the "Paschal Lamb", it is easy to associate Jesus' sacrifice with the symbolism of Passover. Yet according to Louis Ginzberg's *The Legends of the Jews*, the sacrifice of the Paschal Lamb represents the covenant made between God and the Israelites, in which they agreed to abandon the idol worship the Egyptians had taught them in favor of the sole worship of God. As Ginzberg writes:

"Unto this purpose He commanded them to sacrifice the paschal lamb. Thus they were to show that they had given up the idolatry of the Egyptians, consisting in the worship of the Ram."

The metaphor implied by this is quite different from that of the sin-offering on the day of atonement (Yom Kippur), with which Jesus is also repeatedly connected in the Bible. [1] More specifically, two goats are sacrificed on Yom Kippur for this purpose. The ritual is first described in *Leviticus 16*:

"And Aaron shall cast lots upon the two goats; one lot for the Lord, and the other for the scapegoat. And Aaron shall bring the goat upon which the Lord's lot fell, and offer him for a sin offering. But the goat, on which the lot fell to be the scapegoat, shall be presented alive before the Lord, to make atonement with him, and to let him go for a scapegoat into the wilderness... Then shall he kill the goat of the sin offering, that is for the people, and bring his blood within the veil... and sprinkle it upon the Mercy Seat...

...And Aaron shall lay both hands upon the head of the live goat, and confess over him all the iniquities of the children of Israel, and all their transgressions in all their sins, putting them upon the head of the goat, and shall send him away by the hand of a fit man into the wilderness. And the goat shall bear upon him all their iniquities unto a land not inhabited..."

It is clear that, while still identifying himself with the Paschal Lamb, Jesus was drawing a connection between his death and the Yom Kippur ritual as well. It is ambiguous, however, whether he identified himself more with the sin-offering, or with the scapegoat. According to some theologians, he was both. As Suzetta Tucker writes on her website, "The Bestiary":

"These goats were symbolic of the two aspects of Christ's crucifixion. The slain goat prefigured the death of Christ upon the cross to make atonement for sins. The scapegoat represented His taking the guilt of the sins of the world upon His own head and carrying it away from His people into the wilderness of Hades." [2]

So although there exists in the crucifixion story a blending of ancient Judaic symbolism, it is a blending of symbols that already bore many connections. One of the most obvious connections between the sacrifices of Yom Kippur and Passover can be found in the figure of Azazel, a demonic being to the Israelites (and a god to nearly every other Middle Eastern culture). Azazel is named in *The Book of Enoch* as being the leader of the rebellious Watchers, the "fallen angels" of Judeo-Christianity. After his fall from Heaven, Azazel apparently became, in Judeo-Christian lore, judge of dead sinners in Hell, and it was to him that the scapegoats were sacrificed. Alternate translations of *Leviticus 16:8* state that God told Aaron to "place lots upon the two goats, one marked for the Lord, and the other marked for Azazel." Thus Azazel is identified as both the recipient of the sacrificed scapegoat, and the scapegoat himself.

Indeed, Azazel was said to have been horned, and thus was identified with the goat. This deity is identical with that of Amon (or Ammon), the ram which was worshipped by the Egyptians, and which is symbolized by the Paschal Lamb. Amon, or Azazel, is also the "Goat of Mendes" upon which Baphomet, the idol worshipped by the Knights Templar, was based, as is the modern conception of Satan. In *The Satanic Bible*, Anton LaVey writes of "The Symbol of Baphomet" that:

"Through the Ages this symbol has been called by many different names. Among these are: The Goat of Mendes, The Goat of a Thousand Young, The Black Goat, The Judas Goat, and perhaps most appropriately, the Scapegoat."

It is noteworthy that the term "Judas Goat" refers to a technique used on livestock farms in which one animal is used as a decoy to lead all of the other animals to the slaughterhouse.

The scapegoat ritual is thought of as a uniquely Judaic ritual, and yet it is most likely that a similar ritual was practiced by the Israelites and neighboring tribes long before it was recorded in *Leviticus*. There is an interesting article which can be found on lost-civilizations.net, named "The Horse Sacrifice", which seems to link the scapegoat sacrifice to an even earlier ritual. This ritual was practiced in the ancient Indus Valley, and featured the dual sacrifice of a horse and a goat. According to the article, this ritual was a remnant of a rite originating in the lost continent of Atlantis, and it was performed when a king wished to declare himself the "Universal Monarch." Thus by performing the ritual, the king was declaring war on anyone who opposed his absolute rule. [3] The two sacrifices, according to the article, represented the two mythological brothers whose feud over universal kingship led to the war that, the article claims, caused the downfall of Atlantis - the origin of the Cain and Abel archetype. Further layers of meaning link these two sacrifices to the risen and fallen Sun, or Atlantis sunken and arisen. The article states that some traditions regarded the two brothers as twins. In a subchapter called "The Origin of the Cross", it states:

"Both sacrificial victims of the ashvamedha the horse and the goat were killed, impaled and roasted. Then the worshippers ate communally their roasted meat and the broth prepared from their remains. Before their sacrifice, the victims were tied to the sacrificial pole, called skambha or stambha or, yet, stavara.

The skambha (lit. 'prop', 'pillar') was considered the Pillar of Heaven, the axis or support of the skies. It was identified with Brahma and with Shiva, the two world-supporters, as well as with Purusha, the Primordial Sacrifice. The skambha had the shape of a cross or, also, of a Y, precisely that of the Cross or Rood. Like the Cross, it was equated both to the Pillar of Heaven and to the Tree of Life. Many authorities, such as F. Max Mueller, have pointed out the fact that the name of the Cross in the original Greek is stauros, and that this word derives from the Sanskrit stavara (pronounced 'stawara'), its Hindu archetype in the ashvamedha sacrifice.

Of course, all such coincidences are the result of diffusion, and we see how the Evangelic notion was derived from Hindu archetypes. This is further rendered plausible by the fact that, in the earliest iconographies, the crucified Christ had a horse's head..." [4]

This brings us to yet another interesting piece of heretical Christian thought that has been widely circulated amongst esoteric circles: the idea that Jesus had a twin. The notion appears in the work of Leonardo da Vinci, who placed a second Jesus figure amongst the apostles in his *Last Supper*. Although it is well-known by religious scholars that Jesus had both brothers and sisters, only one figure in the Bible is thought to have possibly been Jesus' own twin: the apostle Thomas.

One of the most obvious clues pointing to this possibility is that the name "Thomas" itself means "Twin." Furthermore, this apostle was referred to more than once as "Thomas Didymus", or "Thomas called 'Didymus.'" The word

"Didymus" also means "twin" in Greek.

Like many of the apostles, it is hard to get a clear picture of Thomas from reading the canonical gospels. But everything that is known of him is peculiar. The story of the raising of Lazarus has been thought by some scholars to be a veiled description of an initiation rite for a secret society. It appears that Jesus was the Grand Master of this secret society, and that the death and resurrection of Lazarus was part of his initiation into the cult. The tale told in *The Gospel of John* is more indicative of this then all the other accounts, and in this version, upon being told that Lazarus is dead, Thomas declares, strangely, "Let us also go, that we may die with him." Later on in the story, as Jesus prepares his apostles for his own (supposed) death, Thomas says to him, "Lord, we know not wither thou goest; and how can we know the way?" Jesus replies, "I am the way, the truth, and the life: no man cometh unto the Father but by me."

Thomas' final appearance in the Gospels occurs after the resurrection. For some reason, Thomas was not among them when Jesus made his first resurrected appearance to the apostles. When told about the Lord's appearance, Thomas does not believe it at first, until Jesus appears to him personally. It was this incident that earned this apostle the moniker "Doubting Thomas."

This is essentially all that the canonical gospels have to say about Thomas Didymus. But where the canonical story leaves off, the apocryphal story begins. These texts are very clear that indeed Thomas was Jesus' twin. In *The Acts of Thomas*, a young man's vision of Jesus is described:

"... he saw the Lord Jesus in the likeness of the Apostle Judas Thomas... the Lord said to him: I am not Judas who is also Thomas. I am his brother."

Elsewhere in the *Acts*, Thomas is described as, "Twin brother of Christ, apostle of the Most High, and fellow initiate into the hidden word of Christ, who dost receive his secret sayings..." This notion is reiterated once again in a Coptic text quoted in Baigent, et. al.'s *The Messianic Legacy* (sequel to *Holy Blood, Holy Grail*), where Jesus says, "Greetings Thomas [Twin], my second Messiah."

This idea of Thomas as a twin messiah appears to have been embraced by many of the early Christian groups. There was a Syrian sect called the "Christians of St. Thomas", and similar sects throughout the Middle and Far East. This is largely because Thomas is believed to have traveled throughout the East spreading the gospel after Jesus' death, and his supposed tomb can be found in India. Several of these sects believed that he was literally Jesus' twin brother. Many people were already receptive to this idea, because the archetype of twin gods or sons of God is one that can be found in the legends of many cultures throughout the world. In Edessa, Turkey, where *The Acts of Thomas* were written, the worship of the twin gods Momim and Aziz was replaced seamlessly by that of Thomas and Jesus.

In the *Dagobert's Revenge* article "Tammuz the Twin: The Beloved Disciple", author Thomas LaNeave picks up on the idea that Thomas, as Jesus' twin, acted as his *substitute* after his death. Noting that "Tammuz" means "twin-born", LaNeave relates the symbolism of St. Thomas the Twin to that of the Semitic sun-god Tammuz, whose tale of death and rebirth as the "twin-born son of the Sun" resembles in many ways the legend of Christ. LaNeave further notes that Passover, the date of Christ's Passion, takes place in the Jewish month of Tammuz. He comments upon the implication that in this case, "Passover" may have referred to the "passing over" of the royal messianic inheritance from Jesus to Thomas. He writes of the recurring theme of the "royal substitute" that can be found throughout the Bible, in which the divine royal inheritance is passed on to a substitute when the true heir cannot perform his royal function. The same "substitute" concept is employed when the death or sacrifice of one thing is substituted for the sacrifice of another, as in the scapegoat ritual, or as in the first Passover, when the blood of lambs was used as a substitute for the blood of the first-born of Israel, so that they would be "passed-over" when God's plague swept the land of Egypt.

So if Thomas was Jesus' royal substitute, one of the obvious questions that springs to mind is, "Could Thomas have been used as a substitute for Jesus on the cross"? The proposition becomes even more tantalizing when we learn from both *The Acts of Thomas* and the apocryphal *Gospel of*

Thomas that this disciple's full name was "Judas Thomas." Indeed, a person by the name of "Jude", "Judas", or "Jude the Twin" is repeatedly named in the canonical gospels as being one of Christ's biological brothers, and it seems pretty clear that he and Thomas are the same. It also seems hardly coincidental that another Judas, labeled "Iscariot", is named by *The Gospel of Barnabas* as having been crucified in Jesus' place, and as having an identical likeness as Jesus, like a twin.

The Gospel of Thomas is one of the most treasured of the so-called "Gnostic" texts. Purely an initiation document, every line of this gospel is written in code, concealing the spiritual secrets of alchemy, with an emphasis on "making the two become one." This is interesting if considered in the light of the notion that Jesus had a twin, but that only one of them was remembered. Something very specific seems to be hinted at in these lines:

"Jesus said to His disciples, Compare me to someone and tell Me whom I am like. Simon Peter said to Him, You are like a righteous angel. Matthew said to Him, You are like a wise philosopher. Thomas said to Him, Master, my mouth is wholly incapable of saying whom You are like."

Perhaps Thomas' reply to Jesus' question, "tell me whom I am like", is a hint that it was Thomas himself whom he was like, because they were twins.

But could Christ have made his own twin brother die in his place? There is no doubt that Jesus did not really want to die on the cross. And from what we know of him, it would seem that he had every reason to live. The picture of Jesus which is emerging from contemporary scholarship is that of a wealthy man with a legitimate claim to both the royal throne and the high priesthood of Israel, who was married to a woman with her own royal qualifications, most likely with a royal heir either already born or in utero by the time of his supposed death. He had a strong and powerful family, friends and supporters all over Israel, many of them fanatical devotees. All evidence indicates that he knew his movement was destined for greatness. The backlash from Rome, and from the elders of Jerusalem, undoubtedly boosted his morale, for he knew that he must have really been touching a nerve to be perceived as such a threat. He may have seen his arrest, trial, and execution as being inevitable, however, and may have foreseen the value of letting the opposition, as well as the fanatical public, believe that he had been executed. Thus he may have conceived of the "Passover Plot" written of in the best-selling book of the same title by Hugh Schonfield. Jesus would play the part of the dying and resurrected messiah – fulfilling Old Testament Judaic prophecies while appealing to the mystical sensibilities of Greeks, Romans, and Hellenistic Jews, by blending his messianic mythos with that of the pagan sun-gods. But in order to stage a death and resurrection (barring the miraculous, of course), Jesus would have to use his twin brother, Judas Thomas. Furthermore, they would have to make a choice. One brother would have to die, while the other lived on, perpetuating the throne, the priesthood, and the messianic fantasy.

In the canonical gospels, as Jesus nears the moment of his arrest, he continually prays to God that "this cup may pass away from me" – that he might be spared the cross. Thomas, on the other hand, declared in *The Gospel of John* his willingness to die with Lazarus. Might he not be even more excited about the idea of dying in the place of the Messiah – in fact fulfilling one of the main roles of the Messiah himself? Could this explain Jesus' declaration in *The Gospel of Thomas*, stating that Thomas had "become intoxicated with the bubbling spring which I have measured out"? If Thomas had been enlisted to die in his place willingly, he would have been forbidden to tell the other disciples. Perhaps this is what is hinted at in *The Gospel of Thomas* where it says:

"And He took him and withdrew and told him three things. When Thomas returned to his companions, they asked him, What did Jesus say to you? Thomas said to them, If I tell you one of the things which he told me, you will pick up stones and throw them at me; a fire will come out of the stones and burn you up."

Is it possible that Judas Thomas, the

messiah's supposed twin, is the same as Judas Iscariot, the man who supposedly died in his place? The story told in *The Gospel of Barnabas* is one of treachery and trickery, not of a willing human sacrifice dying for his cause. Perhaps Judas was under the impression that Jesus would be the one to die, and that it would be his job to play the resurrected Jesus after his death. Perhaps he believed that the death would be faked - that he would be revived again after his body had hung on the cross, and had been placed in the tomb for show. Or perhaps both Judas and Jesus were secretly plotting to betray one another, and it was Jesus whose trickery won the day over that of his brother. Certainly there are many reasons why Jesus and Judas, like many mythological twin gods before them, might have had a long-standing sibling rivalry. For any child, sharing with a brother or sister, especially a twin, has always been a bit annoying. But imagine what it must be like for twins to be born into a royal, priestly, or even divine inheritance. According to Jewish custom, the twin who emerges from the womb first is the first-born heir, entitled to all the rights and privileges thereof. There is more than one story in Jewish legend in which such a scenario is related. Invariably, one twin pokes his arm out of the womb, and the midwife ties a string around the infant's wrist to mark him as the firstborn. But then the arm gets sucked back up into the womb, and the other twin's body pops out in full, making him the first-born. The child grows up expecting to be the heir, but all along the twin brother knows that he has been cheated, and plots revenge.

Even if such an instance had not occurred in the birth of Jesus and Judas, it is easy to see how Judas, consumed with jealousy and resentment, could have imagined that it had. Either way, the knowledge that the order in which the twins had emerged from the birth canal was the only thing that barred him from the kingship of Israel must have eaten away at Judas Thomas. Perhaps Jesus sensed that Judas was plotting to betray him, and concocted a way to neutralize his enemy with maximum benefit to the cause. There would even be a secret symbolism of sacrifice known only to those who were in on the plot – one having to do with the dual goat sacrifice of Yom Kippur. The twin (Judas) who hung upon the cross could act as the atoning sin sacrifice, providing the salvation of man from the punishment of sin. The one who fled into hiding to secretly spread the ministry of Christ to the "wilderness" outside Israel would act as the scapegoat, taking the weight of the people's sins onto himself and away from them, just as Jesus declares himself to be doing in the gospels. This may explain the many sightings of Jesus both in and outside of Israel after the crucifixion, as well as the sightings of Thomas, since Jesus may have used his brother's name in certain instances.

Many people will not believe that Judas Iscariot and Judas Thomas could possibly have been the same person. The general consensus is that they are not, and in fact, many lines in the gospels go to great lengths to maintain this. In *Matthew*, both a "Thomas" and a "Judas Iscariot" are listed among the twelve apostles, as is the case in *Mark*. *Luke* lists both "Thomas" and "Judas, the brother of James", *as well as* "Judas Iscariot, which was also the traitor." [5] *John* does not definitively list the apostles, but he refers separately to "Thomas" and to "Judas Iscariot, the son of Simon." Also, during a discussion with his apostles in *John 14*, Thomas is quoted as saying, "Lord, we know not wither thou goest; and how can we know the way?" A few lines later in the chapter, it reads:

"Judas saith unto him, not Iscariot, Lord how is it that thou wilt manifest thyself unto us, and not unto the world?"

While it is possible that John wanted us to see this person as Judas Thomas, he was also quite clearly trying to distinguish him from Judas Iscariot.

But is this just a cover story? Biblical scholarship is full of disagreements about whether or not certain gospel characters described and/or named differently in separate instances are in fact the same. For instance, opinion is divided over whether or not Mary Magdalene and Mary of Bethany were the same. Such disagreements did not begin with modern scholarship, but are exhibited by the authors of the scriptures themselves. And if the scenario hypothesized in this article were in fact true, one would expect most if not all of these scriptures, both canonical and apocryphal, to be full of disinformation and carefully hidden clues regarding the subject (discernable only to the initiated). You would also expect opinions by even the first-hand witnesses of the crucifixion to be varied, as probably none but Jesus and Judas themselves knew the full story. It cannot be ruled out at all that Judas Thomas and Judas Iscariot were the same figure. Certainly Judas Iscariot seems to be one of the most misunderstood figures in the entire saga of Jesus.

Much of what we know of Judas comes from *The Gospel of John*, which is the only one to identify him as the treasurer for Christ's ministry, although it does not say what he did *before* he joined the ministry. And John's is the only gospel to identify Judas as the "son of Simon" – the only indication we have of who his family was. "Iscariot", according to many scholars, supposedly means "of Kerioth", a town in the land of Judah. But others claim that "Iscariot" is a corruption of "Sicarius", a word identifying him as a member of the radical Zealot movement, which pushed for Israelite independence from Rome. It is thought that Christ and his family were involved in this same movement. It has also been noted that almost every mention in the gospels of Judas Iscariot is accompanied by a reference to his betrayal. Both *Matthew*, *Mark*, and *Luke* call him "Judas Iscariot, who also betrayed him." Every description of Judas in the New Testament is so overwhelmingly negative that Judas seems to embody a sort of Antichrist archetype. Indeed, even Jesus himself identified Judas as an incarnation of Satan. In *John 6:70*, Jesus is quoted as saying to his apostles, "Have I not chosen you twelve, and one of you is a devil?" John continues: "He spake of Judas Iscariot, the son of Simon: for it was he that should betray him, being one of the twelve." The authors of *The Messianic Legacy* make further mention of this aspect of Judas Iscariot as Christ's antithesis:

"Symbolically speaking, Judas is the evil brother, the dark side of which Jesus is the light. In Judaeo-Christian tradition, the antithesis between them is another manifestation of the conflict dating back to Cain and Abel... If Jesus ... becomes synonymous with God, Judas – dragging the Jews in general with him – becomes the very embodiment of God's adversary."

But why did Judas betray Jesus? And if Judas hated Jesus so much from the very beginning, why did Jesus choose to keep him on as an apostle? The reason for Judas' betrayal becomes clear if we accept that he and Judas Thomas are the same, and that he is Jesus' twin brother – a true contender for the messiahship in his own right. In *Matthew*, *Mark*, and *John*, there is an incident that precedes (and in *Matthew* and *Mark*, immediately precedes) Judas' betrayal. It is the anointment of Jesus with spikenard by a woman with an alabaster jar – a woman identifiable with Mary Magdalene when all of the accounts are compared. This event has been long recognized by biblical scholars as a *royal* anointing of Christ as king and messiah, since spikenard was traditionally used for this purpose, and since Magdalene was not only the wife of Christ, but a scion of the tribe of Benjamin – a tribe assigned the task of anointing Israel's kings. If Judas believed that he was the rightful messiah, or at least the rightful co-messiah, this act would have enraged him, as it constituted a complete denial of his rights in favor of Jesus as the sole king. The gospels describe exactly this. *John 12: 4-6* says:

"Then one of his disciples, Judas Iscariot, he that was about to betray him, said: Why was not this ointment sold for three hundred pence, and given to the poor? Now he said this, not because he cared for the poor; but because he was a thief, and having the purse, carried the things that were put therein."

The other reason given for Judas' betrayal is more metaphysical. The gospels tell us that Judas was possessed by a demon! Moreover, they say that it was Jesus himself who infected Judas with that demon. This may be connected to a belief amongst Jesus' contemporaries that he and John the Baptist were both sorcerers, and that John had been in control of a demon, the control of which passed to Jesus upon John's death. He may have passed this demon on to Judas after programming it to have Judas "betray" him to the Sanhedrin. Jesus foretells his betrayal numerous times throughout the gospels, and finally, at the

Last Supper, he actually identifies his betrayer. In *John* we read:

> *"When Jesus had said these things, he was troubled in spirit; and he testified, and said: Amen, amen I say to you, one of you shall betray me... He it is to whom I shall reach bread dipped. And when he had dipped the bread, he gave it to Judas Iscariot, the son of Simon. And after the morsel, Satan entered into him. And Jesus said to him: That which thou dost, do quickly. Now no man at the table knew to what purpose he said this unto him. For some thought, because Judas had the purse, that Jesus said to him: Buy those things which we have need of for the festival day: or that he should give something to the poor."*

The fact that Jesus predicts Judas' betrayal, and that Judas does not seem surprised at the accusation, is telling. So too is the fact that Jesus makes no attempt to stop him from doing this, but instead tells him to hurry up and get it over with. And later that night, when Judas arrives with the Roman guards to arrest him, Jesus is fully aware of what is about to befall him. He allows Judas to come up and identify him to the Romans by kissing him on the cheek, saying "Hail Rabbi." Jesus plays his part accordingly, replying, "Judas, betrayest thou the son of Man with a kiss?" More than that, Jesus is shown as actually rushing out with his disciples to meet Judas and the Roman guards. In *Matthew*, he wakes his sleeping apostles just before Judas' arrival and says, "Rise, let us be going: behold, he is at hand that doth betray me." Thus, many scholars believe that the entire "betrayal" scenario was concocted, rehearsed, and enacted in collusion between Jesus and Judas. *The Messianic Legacy* states:

> *"It is not that Judas is actually betraying Jesus. On the contrary, he has been deliberately selected by Jesus, probably to his own chagrin, to discharge a distasteful duty so that the drama of the Passion may enact itself in accordance with Old Testament prophecy. When Jesus proffers the dipped morsel, he is in fact imposing a task upon Judas... In short, the whole business has been carefully planned, even though the other disciples seem not to have been privy to the arrangement. Judas alone seems to have enjoyed Jesus' confidence in the matter."*

Seen in this light, Judas appears as someone to be admired rather than demonized:

> *"Commentators on the New Testament have long recognized how vital, how indispensable, Judas is to the entire mission of Jesus. Without Judas, the drama of the Passion cannot be enacted. As a result, Judas must have been seen as something very different from the scurrilous villain of popular tradition. He emerges as precisely the opposite – a noble and tragic figure, reluctantly consenting to play an unpleasant, painful, and obligatory role in a carefully pre-arranged script. As Jesus says of him: 'I have watched over them and not one is lost except the one who chose to be lost, and this was to fulfill the scriptures.'"*

It is in this view that certain heretical Christian groups have seen Judas throughout the years. One such group, interestingly called "the Cainites", are said by chronicler St. Irenaeus to have possessed an apocryphal *Gospel of Judas*, extolling the betrayer's virtues as a critical player in the redemption of mankind. This "gospel", if it ever really existed, has been lost.

But the canonical gospels make it clear that Judas was not blessed, but cursed by Jesus for his actions – quite literally. *Matthew 26:24* states: "The son of Man goeth as it is written of him: but woe unto that man by whom the son of Man is betrayed! it had been good for that man if he had not been born." Almost identical lines can be found in *Mark* and *Luke*. In *John 13:11* it says, "For he knew who should betray him; therefore he said, Ye are not all clean." Later, in *John 19:11*, as the manner of Jesus' death is being decided, Jesus says to Pilate, "Thou couldest have no power against me, except it were given thee from above: therefore he that delivered me unto thee hath the greater sin." ` Clearly, even though Jesus may have seen Judas' betrayal coming, and may have concocted a master plan that included this betrayal as its lynch-pin, Jesus still hated Judas, and not only wished to see him dead, but to see him die in the worst way possible, and to be cursed because of it. For from the perspective of pre-Christian

Judaism, to die upon a cross brought no salvation or redemption, but only malediction. Crucifixion is an old practice, and while the Romans perfected the art by erecting crosses, it had been practiced in ancient times by simply nailing the afflicted to a tree. In fact, mythological figures in both Norse and Greek legends have been martyred in this way, prefiguring the story of Christ. But in Judaic mythology, such a death was not seen as martyrdom. *Deuteronomy 21:22-23* states:

> *"And if a man have committed a sin worthy of death, and he be to be put to death, and thou hang him on a tree; His body shall not remain all night up on the tree, but thou shalt in any wise bury him that day; (for he that is hanged is accursed by God;) that thy land be not defiled, which the Lord thy God giveth thee for an inheritance."*

Knowing the scriptures as he did, it is unlikely that Jesus would have chosen this cursed manner of death for himself, even if he had been seeking martyrdom. He may, however, have reserved this manner of death for his greatest enemy, the betrayer. If this were the case, there would have had to have been co-conspirators in on it as well. Nicodemus and Joseph of Arimathea, who both sat on the Sanhedrin, are two likely suspects. They could have arranged to have Judas arrested in secret just after Jesus' arrest, and done the switch at any point while they were incarcerated. Then Jesus would have been sent away, according to the arrangement, and Judas would die in his place.

The image of Judas Iscariot hanging from a tree has mutated into a peculiar icon familiar to all Western occultists. I am speaking of the tarot trump common to most decks called "The Hanged Man." It usually shows a court jester figure hanging upside-down by one foot. Although this figure has been connected to that of the Grail hero Parzival by some who study the tarot, the Hanged Man was originally depicted holding a money bag in his hand, connecting him to Judas Iscariot.

However, it seems that this image has an even more ancient origin. It can be traced back to the Jewish legend of the Watchers: angels who purportedly descended from Heaven and mated with human women to breed a race of giants. This race was seen as an abomination by God, who did not approve of the miscegenation between angels and men. He also did not approve of them teaching their human descendants certain secrets, including sciences and sorcery. God thus decided to flood the Earth, to rid it of this hybrid race. He also decided to punish the angels who had fathered this race by imprisoning them within the center of the Earth.

Now the legends state that these Watchers had been led to sin by two angels in particular: Shemhazai and Azazel. And while Shemhazai seems to have taken the lead by persuading his fellow Watchers to marry human women, Azazel seems to have taken the lead in teaching secrets to mankind. And apparently, this was the greater sin, for Azazel became the scapegoat of the Watchers, receiving the bulk of the damnation that God placed upon them. God is quoted in *The Book of Enoch* as saying:

"All the earth has been corrupted by the teaching of the work of Azazyel. To him therefore ascribe the whole crime."

So Azazel took the blame on behalf of the Watchers for the sins that they all had committed. However, he is not said to have been particularly repentant. Shemhazai, however, repented greatly. As Louis Ginzberg's *The Legends of the Jews* tells us:

"Shemhazai then did penance. He suspended himself between heaven and earth, and in this position of a penitent sinner he hangs to this day. But Azazel persisted obdurately in his sin of leading mankind astray by means of sensual allurements. For this reason two he-goats were sacrificed in the Temple on the Day of Atonement, the one for God, that He pardon the sins of Israel, the other for Azazel, that he bear the sins of Israel."

So it does indeed seem that Shemhazai, Azazel's partner in crime, can be equated specifically with the goat of atonement sacrificed on Yom Kippur, just as Azazel can be equated with the scapegoat. And Shemhazai has been depicted in religious iconography, just like the Hanged Man, as hanging upside-down by a rope, in this case one that is suspended from Heaven. [6] Thus the figure of Shemhazai and the goat of atonement can be connected to the image of Judas Iscariot.

Although it is a popular belief that Judas hanged himself after betraying Jesus, having been consumed with guilt, only one gospel, that of Matthew, specifically mentions this. *Mark* and *Luke* refer to the apostles as "the eleven" instead of "the twelve" after Jesus' execution, but that only indicates that Judas was no longer a member of their party, as one would expect. It does not necessarily mean that he was dead, much less that he had committed suicide. The only other scripture that verifies this story is found in the speech of St. Peter quoted in *Acts 1:16-20*:

"Men, brethren, the scripture must needs be fulfilled, which the Holy Ghost spoke before by the mouth of David concerning Judas, who was the leader of them that apprehended Jesus: who was numbered with us, and had obtained part of this ministry. And he indeed hath possessed a field of the reward of iniquity, and being hanged, burst asunder in the midst: and all his bowels gushed out. And it became known to all the inhabitants of Jerusalem: so that the same field was called in their tongue, Haceldama, that it to say, the field of blood. For it is written in the book of Psalms: Let their habitation become desolate, and let there be none to dwell therein. And his bishopric let another take."

This "field of blood" of which Peter speaks is discussed in *Matthew* as well, although the story varies significantly. But to understand this, we must first review the significance of the thirty pieces of silver. All of the gospels agree that Judas sought out and received payment from the Sanhedrin in exchange for his betrayal, but only *Matthew* specifies the amount paid: thirty pieces of silver. But after Jesus' trial, Judas regrets his deeds:

"Then Judas, who betrayed him, seeing that he was condemned, repenting himself, brought back the thirty pieces of silver to the chief priests and ancients, saying: I have sinned in betraying innocent blood. But they said: What is that to us? Look thou to it. And casting down the pieces of silver in the temple, he departed: and went and hanged himself with an halter."

In the story told by St. Peter, it is implied that Judas bought the field with the thirty pieces of silver, and it became known as the "field of blood" because he died upon it. But in *Matthew*, the field is bought by the priests, after Judas had given the money back to them and hanged himself. In *Matthew 27: 6-10*, we read:

"And the chief priests took the silver pieces and said, It is not lawful for to put them into the treasury, because it is the price of blood. And they took counsel, and bought with them the potter's field, to bury strangers in. Wherefore that field was called, The field of blood, unto this day. Then was fulfilled that which was spoken by Jeremy the prophet, saying, And they took the thirty pieces of silver, the price of him that was valued, whom they of the children of Israel did value; And gave them for the potter's field, as the Lord appointed me."

So in this version, it is called the "field of blood" because it was purchased with the money that was paid for Jesus' life. Thus the field and the silver are forever linked as part of the same symbol and metaphor. But what could this metaphor be pointing to?

All the portrayals of Judas and his thirty pieces of silver show them being carried in a small purse. Thus, when Judas is shown in films and plays casting the silver onto the floor of the temple, he is invariably shown throwing the entire bag to the ground. Judas' association with a purse full of money is an integral part of his image. As I have already stated, *The Gospel of John* asserts that Judas was the purse-bearer of the apostles. The consistent message about Judas' character is that of a greedy person obsessed more with money than with the kingdom of God.

With this in mind, new light can be shed on a mysterious bas relief that can be found at the back of the famous Church of Mary Magdalene at Rennes-le-Chateau, France. It depicts Jesus making his "Sermon on the Mount." But strangely, at the bottom of the hill he stands on is a little money bag, out of which an object, long presumed to be gold, protrudes. Nobody has ever satisfactorily explained the presence of this money bag on this bas relief. Most of those who have commented on it have claimed it to be a clue left by the church's abbot, Berenger Sauniere, regarding a buried treasure he supposedly found on the church grounds. But it would seem now that this must certainly be Judas' purse. And why is it placed in such a peculiar spot? Judas himself is not even depicted in the relief. But the church confessional is positioned directly under this mural, and a wooden crucifix is set on top, so that, when viewed from a few feet away, the crucifix and the money bag appear to stand right next to one another. Was Sauniere hinting at his belief that it was Judas, not Christ, who hung on the cross? If so, why is the purse shown at the bottom of a hill covered with flowers?

 A prevailing theory about the treasure Berenger Sauniere supposedly found in or near his church is that is somehow constituted "incontrovertible proof" that Jesus did not die on the cross, and many think that this proof consists of Jesus' own remains, entombed not in Jerusalem, but in Southern France. Yet if Judas had died in Jerusalem in the place of Jesus, where was he buried? The most obvious answer is what *Acts* and *The Gospel of Matthew* seem to be hinting at: the potter's field, the "field of blood." After all, it is specifically stated in *Matthew* that this field was used for the "burial of strangers." In other words, it is a field of unmarked graves. If the secret of the crucifixion of Judas were to be kept, Judas' grave would have to go unmarked. Perhaps the hill covered with flowers in Sauniere's bas relief represents Judas' grave. If so, then by showing Jesus preaching atop this hill, he is showing that Christ's ministry is built upon the sacrifice of Judas. By placing this directly above the confessional, Sauniere may have been *confessing* his knowledge of this secret.

 Yet in order to pull off the "Passover Plot" as I have envisioned it, the plotters would have to have first entombed Judas as though he were Jesus, in the tomb reserved for him by Joseph of Arimathea, who would have been in on the plot. Then they would have had to steal away the body in the middle of the night, and bury it in the potters field, thus hiding the evidence of their crime, while at the same time creating the illusion of the Resurrection. That this occurred is indicated by *The Gospel of Matthew 28:12-15*:

"And when they were assembled with the elders, and had taken counsel, they gave large money unto the soldiers, Saying, Say ye, His disciples came by night, and stole him away while we slept. And if this come to the governor's ears, we will persuade him, and secure you. So they took the money, and did as they were taught: and this saying is commonly reported among the Jews until this day."

The removal of Judas from the tomb may have been secretly depicted by Sauniere in one of his Stations of the Cross, as discussed earlier in this article.

 In addition to hinting at his belief in the heresy of Judas' crucifixion, Sauniere also demonstrated his belief in twin Christs. At the front of the church, on either side of the altar, are statues of Mary and Joseph, each holding an identical Christ child, although one appears to have slightly darker hair than the other. A recurring theme in the church involves the multiple depiction of two twin angels, identical in look to the aforementioned twin Christ children, both emerging out of a seashell. And one of Sauniere's unsolved clues that he embedded in his redesign of the church grounds involves the repeated use of the number 22. Could this be indicating "two-two", "double-double", or "twin-twin" – in other words, "Thomas Didymus"?

 If Sauniere believed this proposed idea that Judas Iscariot was Jesus' twin, and that Jesus had tricked his rival brother into dying on the cross in his place, it would have shattered his Christian faith, but it could have also turned him in the direction of Gnostic Christianity and other, even more damnable forms of occultism. Such beliefs would have been regarded by his clerical peers as the highest heresy. This would explain why, after making his deathbed confession, Sauniere was refused Final Unction by a fellow priest.

 So is the Christian cross really a "T" for "Thomas"? Certainly, the evidence presented in this essay provides sufficient grounds for speculating in that direction. It seems possible, if not probable, that heretical groups like the Cathars, Knights Templar, and the Priory of Sion may have embraced such ideas. Proving that these are the true historical facts is another matter, but considering that verifiable "facts" regarding the life of Jesus are pretty sparse, and that nothing about him has ever been proven, it hardly matters. But there is one more notable similarity between the characters of Thomas and Judas Iscariot as portrayed in the gospels: they are both described as having a weakness in the area of faith. Both are said to have "doubted" Jesus' messiah-hood, and in Thomas' case, as I have said, "Doubting" became part of him namesake. One scene in particular, recorded in *The Gospel of John*, has earned him this namesake. [7]

The incident, described briefly earlier in this essay, occurs in Chapter 20, after Jesus has been resurrected. For some unstated reason, Thomas was the only apostle (besides Judas, presumably), who was not present when the resurrected Jesus first appeared to them. When the other apostles tell him of what occurred, Thomas refuses to believe their story. As the text reads:

"But Thomas, one of the twelve, called Didymus, was not with them when Jesus came. The other disciples therefore said unto him, We have seen the LORD. But he said unto them, Except I shall see in his hands the print of the nails, and put my finger into the print of the nails, and thrust my hand into his side, I will not believe.

And after eight days again his disciples were within, and Thomas with them: then came Jesus, the doors being shut, and stood in the midst, and said, Peace be unto you. Then saith he to Thomas, Reach hither thy finger, and behold my hands; and reach hither thy hand, and thrust it into my side: and be not faithless, but believing. Thomas answered and said unto him, My LORD and my God. Jesus saith unto him, Thomas, because thou hast seen me, thou hast believed: blessed are they that have not seen, and yet have believed.

And many other signs truly did Jesus in the presence of his disciples, which are not written in this book: But these are written, that ye might believe that Jesus is the Christ, the Son of God; and that believing ye might have life through his name."

Something about this entire narrative seems altogether fishy. I have said how John's gospel in no way makes mention of Judas' death, and indeed the only gospel to speak of Judas' suicide is that of Matthew. Most would assume that this detail is excluded because it is not worthy of mention. But why is it that in this scene, when Judas should be dead, or at the very least, no longer among the apostles, Thomas is referred to as "one of the twelve", instead of "the eleven"? All of the other gospels make it clear that at this point in the story, there are only eleven apostles. Is the author of John's gospel erring deliberately to draw our attention to something?

Perhaps the author is hinting (in secret code known only to initiates) that we, like Thomas, should not believe in the Christ who died on the cross. For why does Thomas find it necessary to see Jesus' crucifixion wounds in order to believe in the Resurrection? Presumably, if God had the power to bring him to life after three days of death, surely He could handle healing a few wounds. But if my hypothesis is correct, the author may be making a totally different comment. The character of "Thomas" is expressing his disbelief that the person they have seen "resurrected" is the same person who hanged on the cross. Of course not. The person who hanged on the cross was dead, and it was not Jesus! Who would know that better than Judas Thomas himself? After all, it was his hands that bore the print of the nails, and his side that had been pierced. Even though the author of John's gospel knew this, he could not say it, so he used the character of Thomas (who, according to my hypothesis, would have already been dead) as a literary device to impart a hidden grain of truth to this fictional account of the Resurrection. *The Gospel of John* is often described as a "Gnostic gospel", for it is clearly an initiation document meant for members of Jesus' inner circle. The truth about Judas is just one of the many secrets hidden within.

Appendix:

"Jesus said, 'Two will rest on a couch; one will die, one will live.'"
- The Gospel of Thomas

The above essay was written during the week of Easter, 2004. Since then a great deal of information on this and related subjects has come to my attention. Two books in particular have become invaluable in my research. The first is *In Search of the Birth of Jesus* by Paul William Roberts, published in 1995. This is a log of the author's travels throughout Iraq, Iran, and Syria tracking local legends regarding the magi who supposedly attended the birth of Jesus. In the process he encountered a group[of Mandaeans: a Gnostic Johannite sect (that is, followers of John the Baptist). They told him that all Mandaeans believe that not only was Judas Thomas Jesus' twin, but that it was this Judas who was crucified in Jesus' place. Furthermore, they believe that Jesus afterwards took on the identity of his brother, calling himself Thomas, and that he was the true author of *The Gospel of Thomas*, as well as supposedly *The Gospel of John*. The travels throughout the East that have been attributed to Thomas were accomplished by Jesus as well. As Mr. Roberts writes:

"After Persia, he returned west, living near Damascus in Syria before finally being forced to travel beyond the reach of Roman forces. Nabatean priests and Magi had helped him, arranging safe passage along the trade routes. Jesus had resided in Basra and Palmyra briefly before crossing through Mesopotamia, spending some months in Susa, then moving from Magian stronghold to Magian stronghold - places where any Essene Jew apparently would have been always welcome - until he reached the Indus Valley. Here, Brahmans, who maintained close ties with the Western mystical orders, initiated him into their deepest mysteries before escorting him to the relative safety of India's southwestern coast - not the southeastern coast where others have speculated he ended up, near Madras."

Moreover, Roberts' Mandaean informants told him that both twins had been blessed by the magi at the nativity:

"Hearing about Jesus and a twin brother, I still had never stopped to think what this would do to the Nativity story... [According to the Mandaeans the] Magi's astrological skills had... allowed them to foresee the potential dangers ahead. They informed those Nazarean-Essenes with whom they were in regular contact, and then made sure that Mary and Joseph escaped to Egypt, where Jesus and Thomas were raised by Essene Magians while their parents returned to Israel... There had been two Magi, after all: one for each child."

The other invaluable source of information I have found is Hyam Maccoby's *Judas Iscariot and the Myth of Jewish Evil*. In it he discusses all symbolic elements of the image of Judas. He repeatedly returns to the idea of Judas as Jesus' dark half, or doppelganger: a Black Christ. As he writes:

"The Christian myth is about sacrifice. Jesus, the incarnate God, suffers death in order to redeem mankind, and to procure eternal life for those who accept him as their saviour. But this description of the myth is not quite accurate. There are really two sacrificial figures in the myth, one of whom loses his life, and the other his soul. These two figures, who may be called the White Christ and the Black Christ, are both essential to the Christian myth, as to many similar myths...

Judas is not merely fulfilling an individual decision. He is fulfilling a prophecy. Yet no credit or happiness is allotted to him for doing what is fated and necessary. His reward for his share in the salvation of mankind is accursedness and damnation. He himself is a kind of sacrifice; he is the Black Christ who, through his destructive and self-destructive action, brings delivery to his fellow human beings... [It is] a double sacrifice, since it requires both the death of Jesus and the damnation of Judas."

He also comments on the idea of sacrifice in the ancient world, indicating that the nature of sacrifice requires a scapegoat to take the blame for the sacrifice:

"... the community wants the sacrifice to occur, because otherwise there will be no salvation, but it shifts the responsibility to some evil figure. The death of the victim is mourned with every appearance of heartfelt grief, for the deeper the grief the more complete the dissociation of the community from the death which they desired. The means by which the death came about is disowned, either by banishing, ostracizing or humiliating the executioner, or even... holding a trial of the knife with which the sacrifice was performed."

Maccoby's analysis of Judas' ceremonial role leads him to a fascinating conclusion: that the role played by Judas is a symbolic continuation of the role played by Cain when he murdered his brother Abel:

"A disguised example of this is the biblical Cain, who killed his brother, yet received divine protection in his wanderings, and was the founder of a city and the ancestor of the founders of the arts (Genesis 4:17-22); what the Bible calls a murder, was, in the Kenite saga from which the Bible derives the story, a salvic sacrifice. The Jews too, despite the loathing inspired by their alleged cosmic crime, have also been regarded with a certain awe. Even at their lowest ebb of powerlessness, they have been viewed as the possessors of magical power. The legend of the Wandering Jew (which has sometimes coalesced with the legend of Judas Iscariot) expresses this Christian awe of the Sacred Executioner, condemned to suffer for the act that brought salvation to mankind. In the New Testament, Judas Iscariot does not, like Cain or the Wandering Jew, receive the dubious gift of prolonged life; he dies by suicide in one version, by heavenly destruction in another. But in some later versions of the story, his charisma is enhanced. He becomes a prince, and a formidable person, with an awesome destiny. However much the aim of the myth is to foster detestation, it can never be quite forgotten that he is after all the Black Christ, an agent of salvation."

It does make sense to seek parallels between Cain's murder of Abel and Judas' murder of Jesus, or, as I have hypothesized, Jesus' murder of Judas.

For one thing, there is the obvious parallel, in that in both instances, both the murderer and the victim are brothers. And if one considers the symbolism of the scapegoat ritual that seems to be present in the sacrifice of Judas and Jesus (in which one – Judas – is sacrificed to atone for sin, and the other – Jesus – must go into exile, to bear the sin), it is obvious that the same symbolism exists in the Cain and Abel story. Like the scapegoat, Cain was sent off in exile to "the land of Nod" to bear the weight of his sins. But his sin was the killing of Abel, which, like the slaying of the World Bull by Mithras, is seen by mythologists as representing a sacrifice that was necessary for the fertility of the land. At another point in the book, Maccoby continues this analysis, likening the death of Abel to the death of Judas described in *Acts*:

"The graphic picture of Judas' blood and entrails spilling on to the raw earth of an open field evokes the story of Cain and Abel; Abel's blood was also spilled in a "field" (Genesis 4:8). God said to Cain, 'Thy brother's blood crieth unto me from the ground. And now thou art cursed from the earth, which hath opened her mouth to receive thy brother's blood from thy hand." (Genesis 4:10-11). The Hebrew Bible's doctrine that the spilling of blood dries up the land is a late development in human history; behind it lies the opposite idea that precisely the spilling of blood in human sacrifice renders the land fertile. The image of the earth 'opening her mouth' to receive blood is very ancient; originally this was a hungry acceptance by the earth goddess of her due.

The story of Cain and Abel, as we find it in the Hebrew Bible, is one of simple murder; but more than one scholar has argued that it is a transfigured account of human sacrifice, in which the earth was not accursed, but blessed, by Abel's blood."

This symbolic connection between Cain and Judas is interesting considering that it was the Gnostic group known as the Cainites that, out of all the heretical sects, held Judas in the highest regard. Irenaeus wrote of this sect that:

"[They] declare that Cain derived his being from

the Power above, and acknowledge that Esau, Korah, the Sodomites, and all such persons, are related to themselves. On this account, they add, they have been assailed by the Creator, yet no one of them has suffered injury. For Sophia was in the habit of carrying off that which belonged to her from them to herself. They declare that Judas the traitor was thoroughly acquainted with these things, and that he alone, knowing the truth as no others did, accomplished the mystery of the betrayal; by him all things, both earthly and heavenly, were thus thrown into confusion. They bring forward a fictitious history along these lines, which they call the Gospel of Judas."

A further interesting fact to add is that Judas' name as given by the gospels may have in fact included the word "Canaanite." This was an ancient tribe that, I have argued in previous articles, may have ultimately descended from Cain, but by the time of Jesus it apparently indicated a member of the fanatical Zealot movement. As Hyam Maccoby explains:

"... the theory that Iscariot means Zealot appears in third- and fourth-century Coptic versions of the Gospel of John. Here the word 'not' is missing in the phrase 'not Iscariot', but instead of Iscariot we find the word Kananites. The complete designation of Jesus's interlocutor at this point in the Coptic versions is thus Judas the Canaanite. Now obviously neither Judas Iscariot nor any other disciple was a Canaanite, since this nation has ceased to exist many centuries before the time of Jesus. But easily confused with the name "Canaanite' is the Hebrew word qan'ai, which means Zealot. The tendency of the Gospel writers to confuse this word with Canaanite is shown elsewhere. So what the Coptic versions alone have preserved is that Jesus's interlocutor in John 14 was in fact Judas Iscariot (the 'not' being omitted), and that an alternative name for him was Judas the Canaanite, i.e., Judas the Zealot...."

Maccoby believes that Judas Iscariot is the same as "Jude, brother of James", who is sometimes listed among the twelve apostles, and who is the supposed author of *The Epistle of Jude*. He further believes that this "James" is the same as "James the brother of Jesus", and thus that Judas was in fact Jesus' brother. And since Jesus was the King of the Jews, Maccoby writes that this would have made Judas a prince, and a candidate for leadership in the Jerusalem Church - the "church" (comprised largely of relatives of Jesus) that continued his "ministry", especially the Zealot royalist movement associated with it, after his death. Maccoby presents evidence that Judas follow Symeon the son of Cleopas as the leader of this church:

"...what is particularly interesting, for our purposes, is that Symeon's successor as leader of the Jerusalem 'Church' was no other than 'Judas of James', according to Apostolic Constitutions 7:46. The common view of later commentators, such as Ephraem, was that he was Judas, the brother of Jesus, the author of the Epistle of Jude. If this is true, then Judas was actually the third 'Bishop' (or more correctly Vice-Regent) of the Jerusalem 'Church'. Such an appointment is only what one would expect, given the royalist position of the group. What better candidate for leadership, pending the return of King Jesus, than his brother, Prince Judas Iscariot?"

Maccoby has further argued, although with less enthusiasm, for the idea that Judas Iscariot and Judas Thomas were one in the same. Rather than seeing this as literally and historically true, he tends to regard it as having merely a symbolic significance, although one that accords with my hypothesis:

"It might be argued that the apostle Thomas, known in East Syrian circles as Judas Thomas or Didymus Judas Thomas, is the same person as the apostle Jude, and that therefore the considerable literature, mostly legendary, about Thomas is part of the Judas-saga. Indeed, there were some ancient traditions (the Book of Thomas and the Acts of Thomas) identifying Thomas with Jude, and some modern scholars have argued in favour of these traditions and associated the authorship of the Epistle of Jude with Thomas. In particular, the legends about Thomas call him not only the brother but the twin-brother of Jesus. It seems, however, that though Thomas's real name was indeed probably Judas, he was not,

historically, a brother of Jesus. His nickname 'Thomas' does mean 'twin' in Hebrew', but he was the twin of someone else, not Jesus, and he was known by this nickname for the specific purpose of distinguishing him from the other Judas, the apostle and brother of Jesus. In the lists of Jesus's brothers, Judas is either the youngest or second youngest of the four, and the Gospel narratives hardly leave room for the supposition that Jesus had a twin brother. On the other hand, from a mythological standpoint, it is interesting that the legend of Jesus's twin brother arose, and that it was associated with a disciple called Judas. In the East Syrian literature, the twin-motif appears somewhat lacking in depth, and may be a secondary development, serving a Gnostic purpose. There is substance in the suggestion... that the legend was originally influenced by a Greek myth, especially that of the Dioscuri, Castor and Pollux. If so, it is altogether possible that the twin-motif arose at some stage of the development of the Judas-the-Betrayer myth. For the Betrayal stories in mythology often involve a pair of twins, one of whom betrays or murders the other, for a salvific purpose. Examples are the story of Romulus and Remus, Jacob and Esau. The twin-brother relationship expresses the identity of victim and slayer, found in an even more ideal form in stories of divine self-immolation, such as the self-hanging of Odin. I would suggest, therefore, that the notion that Jesus had a twin-brother called Judas arose first in the context of the Judas-as-Betrayer myth, but was erased from this by the needs of the Mary-as-Perpetual-Virgin myth (demanding that Jesus should have no brothers at all). It lingered, however, in Gnostic circles, attaches to Judas Thomas (Judas the Twin), as a symbol of the spiritual identity of every true Gnostic with Jesus."

Indeed, Maccoby believes that all of the Judases mentioned in the Gospels are in fact the same character. He writes:

"...I suggest the best hypothesis is that there was originally only one Judas, namely Judas Iscariot, and that when he was chosen for the mythic role of traitor, the good traditions about the historical Judas were shifted to a second Judas, who was at first assigned some of the sobriquets of the original,

but was gradually differentiated from him by being given different designations."

One of the motivations for demonizing Judas, Maccoby believes, is anti-Semitism. The early church, as well as Gnostic Christian sects, regarded the Jews as a cursed race – the murderers of Jesus. The Gnostics had a further reason to hate the Jews: they were the chosen servants of Jehovah, the Demiurge, whom they regarded as evil, and (they believed) the Jews had killed Jesus because he intended to redeem mankind from "the curse of the Law" of Jehovah. The Church, as well as most Christian sects, agreed that Jesus had to create a "New Covenant", and to abolish, the old, Judaic covenant, including all of the Judaic laws. At the time of Jesus, the term "Jews" often referred to those occupying the area of "Judaea", exclusively, and did not include other areas of Israel, such as Galilee and Samaria. As Jesus and most of his followers were initially, they were not thought of as "Jews", although they may be considered so today. Thus the early Christians were able to conceptualize Jesus as being both the King of the Jews and at the same time not a Jew.

Judas, if by his name alone, embodies the archetype of the Jewish race. Thus he was cast in the role of the Betrayer. But ironically, by executing Jesus, both Judas and the Jews are enabling the sacrifice that will purportedly abolish their own covenant with Jehovah. Thus the role of both Judas and the Jews in the sacrifice of Jesus had to be obfuscated in the scriptures.

Maccoby successfully demonstrates that Judas has been identified with the Jews, and with the Jews' murder of Jesus, throughout the history of anti-Semitism in Europe. There is certainly one obvious correlation between the portrayal of Judas Iscariot and prevailing Jewish stereotypes: Judas is shown as being predominantly occupied with financial concerns. He objects to the use of spikenard to anoint Jesus because of the cost, revealing a penny-pinching nature. In fact the sum for which he betrays Jesus is relatively small, demonstrating his pettiness. Maccoby highlights other earmarks of the Judas/Jewish stereotype:

"An additional feature of Judas in the Passion Plays was his red hair. This was not part

of the general Jewish stereotype, but an identifying mark of Judas himself, which he shared with Herod... It may be that redness, as the colour of blood, was reserved for those taking the leading murderous parts - Judas for his acceptance of blood-money and his association with the Field of Blood, and Herod because of his massacre of the Innocents....

In addition to the features of the Jewish stereotype, Judas was given special characteristics of his own. Chief among these were his red hair and his yellow gown...Since [red] was also the colour of Satan's hair in the Passion Plays and in art, the triple identification, Judas/Jews/Devil, was reinforced by his coloration. The yellow gown, on the other hand, is cognate to the yellow badge which Jews were compelled to wear, and which was a regular feature of their portrayal in art...

Indeed, the tradition of a red-haired Betrayer goes back to prehistoric times. Set, the brother, betrayer and murderer of Osiris, had red hair..."

Overall, it seems to me that these radical ideas - the concept of Judas Thomas as Jesus' twin or "second Messiah"; the idea of Judas Iscariot being crucified in the place of Jesus; and the idea that both Judases are indeed the same person - these are less useful as factual interpretations of the story of Jesus than they are as explorations of the symbolism of his story. They are an extension of the Scapegoat and Passover symbolism implicit in Christ's sacrifice, and an extension of the imagery of Judas as the Black Christ. And if Judas is seen as a sympathetic figure, as some romantic writers have chosen to portray him, the idea of him actually being Jesus' twin is all the more poetic. But if Judas dies on the cross instead of Jesus, the romance might be destroyed, for then Judas would not be martyred by damning his own soul to Hell for the sake of God's plan, and Jesus would not be martyred on the cross, thus accomplishing the stoning sacrifice for the sins of mankind. Yet this begs the question: if they were twins, were they both the sons of God, and thus, would the sacrifice of either one have sufficed?

The popularity of this and other "crucifixion substitution" theories demonstrates our ongoing desire to do away with the most difficult aspect of the orthodox Christ story. The idea that Jesus "died for our sins" is distasteful to us. It seems inherently unfair that God would sacrifice his own son, and in such a cruel way, especially since he was such a reportedly good-hearted and blameless man. If God were forgiving enough to allow all repented sin to be atoned, why should he require the death of his won son as a "payment"? After all, there are numerous examples in the Old Testament, and Jesus told several people that they were forgiven of their sins long before he was sacrificed. Many of us would prefer to believe that Jesus was sent merely to teach and to guide us towards a salvation through God that already existed. Thus the idea that one who was truly guilty, and the one who would have sent Jesus to the cross, was actually himself crucified instead. This is a comforting thought, perhaps, but it destroys the image of Jesus as all-loving, all-forgiving and all-sacrificing. The Jesus we know from the canonized gospels gladly took on undeserved punishment for the sake of us all, and would never have allowed another man to die in his place, no matter how lowly his deeds.

However, the history of heresy is built on such alternate interpretations of scripture, wherein hidden meanings that seem to be in between the lines of these scriptures are taken to their utmost logical (or illogical) conclusions, creating a shadow mythos based on a body of such heretical traditions, passed down through the generations as they pass through many permutations. As time goes on each heresy or alternate viewpoint weaves its way into the fabric of underground legend, and into literature, with sometimes only an echo of the original heretical tradition actually remaining. Thus, while I feel sure that the "Judas Goat" hypothesis presented here was a notion once held by heretics, only bits and pieces of it can now be found scattered throughout various legends. However, as I demonstrated earlier in this article, I am increasingly convinced that this idea formed a part of Berenger Sauniere's heretical belief system, and thus, perhaps, that of the Priory of Sion. Further evidence in this regard was recently discovered in Andre Douzet's book, *Sauniere's Model and the Secret of Rennes-le-Chateau*. This book is about a three-dimensional relief map of Rennes-le-Chateau that Berenger Sauniere commissioned to be made just before his death. Unfortunately he died before he got a chance to pick it up form the mapmaker. Apparently this map was not discovered until the author purchased it at an auction and realized the significance of it. But what was really unusual about the map was that Sauniere had landmarks on the map labeled with names that apply to known sites in Jerusalem, not Rennes-le-Chateau, France.

It is believed that Sauniere had this map made because he intended to pass it on to someone else before he died , or to have it discovered by them afterwards. Obviously he was trying to communicate some secret that he knew about Rennes-le-Chateau. A simple explanation is that he was trying to say that Rennes-le-Chateau was a holy site containing a sacred tomb, and was, like Jerusalem, the "center of the world." But its possible that he was specifically trying to indicate his belief that the tomb of Christ (or perhaps of his supposed substitute Judas) was located there in Southern France? One of the landmarks he specifically named on the map was labeled "the Tomb of Christ." If Sauniere believed that he had discovered by some means that the Crucified One (be he Judas or Jesus) was buried at Rennes-le-Chateau, he may have been specifically recreating the landscape and imagery of Jerusalem to indicate the presence of a tomb traditionally thought to be in Jerusalem. The landmarks that Sauniere had labeled on his map were "Golgotha", the "Garden of Gethsemane", the "Tomb of Christ", and the "Tomb of Joseph of Arimathea" - all locations significant in the story of Christ's arrest, crucifixion and burial. So it follows that he was trying to communicate some secret regarding these events, and somehow likening the location in which they took place to Rennes-le-Chateau. Now we know that Jesus was not arrested or crucified at Rennes-le-Chateau, but it is persistently thought that he might be buried there. But Sauniere could not erect something right on top of the burial spot indicating what it was if he wanted it to remain inviolate but still communicate his message. He could, however, erect something on the grounds indicating where Golgotha and the Garden of Gethsemane would be in relation to the tomb of Christ if a map of Jerusalem were superimposed upon Rennes-le-Chateau. If a person were supplied with this map, they would then be able to find the clues on the ground representing Golgotha and Gethsemane, and thus would be able to locate the tomb.

As I was looking at this map again recently, I noticed something very interesting. In the gospels it was Joseph of Arimathea who offered his own tomb, which he had originally built with the intention of having himself buried in it, for the body of Jesus. Why then is there both a tomb of Joseph or Arimathea *and* a tomb of Christ on the map? Even if we were to suppose that Joseph of Arimathea was buried next to Jesus later on, why would Sauniere mark that on the map? Everything else on the map pertains to Jesus' arrest, crucifixion, and burial. This would seem to be extraneous, unless you consider that Sauniere may indicating the idea of twin Christs (a la the "Judas Goat" theory), and that both were eventually buried side by side, perhaps at Rennes-le-Chateau.

As I continued flipping through Douzet's book, I noticed that he had made a similar observation:

"As far as the Catholic faith and Christianity in general [is concerned], there never was a 'tomb of Jesus Christ.' The only tomb was that of Joseph of Arimathea, intended to be used only by himself, but in the end used to keep the body of the Saviour, from where it would rise.

But on the model there is a 'tomb of Joseph of Arimathea' and another tomb, that of Jesus! With that single act, this model has attained an altogether different aspect: heretical, iconoclastic, and difficult to understand."

Douzet does not go on to speculate what heresy Sauniere was advocating specifically. But I think with the "Judas Goat" theory we may be able to answer that question! Indeed, though this theory may not be what we ourselves wish to believe about Jesus, it may be a useful tool for understanding the heretical beliefs of many influential people throughout history, and for understanding some of the mysterious clues that they have left behind. Hopefully, then, the information presented in this essay will be valuable to scholars in the future.

Endnotes:

[1] In the *Gospel of John, 1:29*, John the Baptist points also at Jesus and declares, "Behold, the Lamb of God who takes away the sin of the world."

[2] http://ww2.netnitco.net/users/legend01/goat.htm

[3] This links up with similar words recorded by Sumeriologist L.A. Waddell regarding the ancient Indus Valley.

[4] This is true, and it may bring new meaning to the line in the coded parchment found at Rennes-le-Chateau, which reads: "by the cross and this horse of God…"

[5] James is yet another person identified in the gospels as one of Jesus' biological brothers, so this Judas probably would have been as well.

[6] There is a stone depiction of this image in Rosslyn Chapel in Scotland.

[7] It is interesting that the words "doubt" and "double" are related, as "doubt" essentially means to "second-guess."

Dagobert's Revenge

VOLUME 5 NUMBER 1

LIMITED AVAILABILITY

In this Issue:

Tracy Twyman interviews Henry Lincoln, author of *Holy Blood Holy Grail*, *Key to the Sacred Pattern*, and *The Templars' Secret Island*

Boyd Rice interviews Marilyn Manson band member Pogo.

Plus the articles:

The Flowering Tomb: A Massive Hidden Structure Beneath Rennes-le-Chateau?

The Occult Roots of Christianity

Daughter of God: The Real Story of Joan of Arc

"... Work With the Square and Compass...": The Hidden Mysteries of Chess and Playing Cards

The Divine Couple

Between the Swastika and the Cross of Lorraine: The Priory of Sion During WWII

Out of Chaldea: The Secret Legacy of the Architect-Priests

'Le Heiron du Val d'Or,' from Henri Lobineau's Secret Dossiers

Giants on the Earth

To Get Your Copy of *Dagobert's Revenge* Volume 5, Number 1 Visit:
www.DragonKeyPress.com

THE MEROVINGIAN MYTHOS
AND THE MYSTERY OF RENNES-LE-CHATEAU

by Tracy R. Twyman

From occult expert and historian, Tracy R. Twyman, comes the new book *The Merovingian Mythos and The Mystery of Rennes-le-Chateau*. Twyman, the former Editor of *Dagobert's Revenge Magazine*, has been investigating the enigma of the Holy Grail and Rennes-le-Chateau for years, and has written extensively about it in various publications. Now at last she has fully disclosed the shocking conclusions of her exhaustive research.

In the pages of this volume, Twyman reveals the answers to dozens of questions that have remained unanswered for decades, centuries, and even millennia. She deciphers nearly all of the many clues pertaining to this mystery that have been left by the Priory of Sion, Berenger Sauniere, the Knights Templar, and the Freemasons. But more than that, she has decoded a tangled web of clues found in history, world mythology, Judeo-Christian scriptures, and the traditions of the occult, resulting in a bold reinterpretation of the story of human civilization. And the outcome is not what you would expect. The villains and protagonists are not who you might presume them to be. For the Holy Grail is a treasure both cursed and sacred, bestowing knowledge both of Good and of Evil. - 256 pages.

After reading this book, you will never think of history, mythology, or the Bible the same way again.

TO ORDER:
MAIL A CHECK OR MONEY ORDER FOR $19.95USD (+$4.50 S&H US & CANADA/+$8.50 ALL OTHERS) TO:
DRAGON KEY PRESS - PO BOX 8533 - PORTLAND, OR 97207 - USA
OR VISIT WWW.DRAGONKEYPRESS.COM

NEW DAWN
MAGAZINE

WE QUESTION CONSENSUS REALITY

Holistic Health ● Conspiracies ● Media Lies
Ancient Civilizations ● CIA ● Mind Control ● AIDS
Islam ● Secret Societies ● Spirituality
New World Order ● Metaphysics ● Prophecy
Occultism ● Cover-ups ● Terrorism ● Iraq

Visit us online www.newdawnmagazine.com

"I read many magazines, from all over the political and religious spectrum, but New Dawn is the one periodical I most look forward to each issue. It never fails to deliver provoking political analysis, hard-to-find esoteric insights, and valuable pointers to health alternatives. Do I agree with everything it prints? Certainly not. But there is nothing quite so stimulating as well-written articles challenging one's unexamined assumptions about the world we live in. New Dawn is hard to put down – or pin down. In short, it's a great magazine."
– JAY KINNEY, Publisher of GNOSIS magazine (1985-1999)

Covering Conspiracies & Metaphysics Since 1991

UFOs, Planet X, The DaVinci Code, The Iraq War.

They're all connected. Not in some master plot, but because they all appear in the pages of PARANOIA, the world's most popular conspiracy journal. Subscribe now with this special offer!

☐ YES, I want PARANOIA delivered to my door at a reduced subscription rate! I've enclosed a check or money order payable to PARANOIA.

☐ **$15** - 3 issues (1 yr) - Save $3!
☐ **$28** - 6 issues (2 yrs) - Save $8!
☐ Canada: $24 US Funds - 3 issues (1 yr)
☐ Others: $36 US Funds - 3 issues (1 yr)

Name _____
Address _____
City _____ State ____ Zip _____

PARANOIA publishes 3 times a year, in April, August and Dec. Your subscription will begin with the issue published after we receive your order.

You may photocopy this form.

PARANOIA, Box 1041, Providence, RI 02901
www.paranoiamagazine.com

THE DRAGON LEGACY
The Secret History of an Ancient Bloodline
by Nicholas de Vere

Are the Dragon Kings of ancient times the gods of our mythologies? This book outlines in detail the ancient dragon bloodline - where it came from and what it really means. Were those who carried this bloodline blessed with great powers? What influence did they have on the ancient world? De Vere reveals the beginnings of the Grail bloodline in an antediluvian Civilization, with a super-human, red-haired race of Grail Kings that conquered and ruled over the primitive hordes of the ancient world. It was they who created all of the traditions, customs and institutions upon which civilization depends. De Vere's *The Dragon Legacy* takes the next step beyond his previous book *Genesis of the Grail Kings*. This extremely well-researched book unveils many mysteries of the past, including who the elves, fairies and vampires really were, why blood itself was so important to this bloodline, what kind of magic once existed, and how it was lost.

The Dragon Legacy is available in book stores throughout North America through Ingram, Baker & Taylor, and New Leaf distributors, and in Europe (including the UK) through Bertram's distribution. It is also available on amazon.com and barnesandnoble.com.

AVAILABLE NOW ON AMAZON.COM AND AMAZON.CO.UK

www.ingramcontent.com/pod-product-compliance
Lightning Source LLC
Chambersburg PA
CBHW051208290426
44109CB00021B/2386